Dark Satanic Mills?

Religion and Irreligion in Birmingham and the Black Country

A full listing of all titles in this series will be found at the close of this book

Series Preface

The Evangelical movement has been marked by its union of four emphases: on the Bible, on the cross of Christ, on conversion as the entry to the Christian life and on the responsibility of the believer to be active. The present series is designed to publish scholarly studies of any aspect of this movement in Britain or overseas. Its volumes include social analysis as well as exploration of Evangelical ideas. The books in the series consider aspects of the movement shaped by the Evangelical Revival of the eighteenth century, when the impetus to mission began to turn the popular Protestantism of the British Isles and North America into a global phenomenon. The series aims to reap some of the rich harvest of academic research about those who, over the centuries, have believed that they had a gospel to tell to the nations.

Series Editors

David Bebbington, Professor of History, University of Stirling, Stirling, Scotland, UK

John H.Y. Briggs, Senior Research Fellow in Ecclesiastical History and Director of the Centre for Baptist History and Heritage, Regent's Park College, Oxford, UK

Timothy Larsen, Professor of Theology, Wheaton College, Illinois, USA

Mark A. Noll, McManis Professor of Christian Thought, Wheaton College, Wheaton, Illinois, USA

Ian M. Randall, Deputy Principal and Lecturer in Church History and Spirituality, Spurgeon's College, London, UK, and a Senior Research Fellow, International Baptist Theological Seminary, Prague, Czech Republic

STUDIES IN EVANGELICAL HISTORY AND THOUGHT

Dark Satanic Mills?

Religion and Irreligion in
Birmingham and the Black Country

Geoff Robson

Foreword by
Hugh McLeod

Paternoster:
thinking faith

First published 2002 by Paternoster

Paternoster is an imprint of Authentic Media
9 Holdom Avenue, Bletchley, Milton Keynes, MK1 1QR, UK
and
P.O. Box 1047, Waynesboro, GA 30830–2047, USA

08 07 06 05 04 03 02   7 6 5 4 3 2 1

British Library Cataloguing in Publication Data
A record for this book is available from the British Library.

ISBN 978-1-84227-102-5

Typeset by Profile
Printed and bound in Great Britain
for Paternoster
by Nottingham Alpha Graphics

*Dedicated to the memory of my wife Frankie
who gave me the happiest years of my life
but did not live to see this thesis in print*

Contents

Chapter 1.   Introduction   Page

Chapter 2.   The Economic and Social Setting

Chapter 3.   The Political and Religious Background

**Chapter 4.   The 1851 Census of Religious Worship in
                Birmingham and the Black Country**

List of Tables

FOREWORD

It is now more than forty years since E.R. Wickham's pioneering history of *Church and People in an Industrial City*. The debate about the role and fate of organised Christianity in the era of industrialisation and urbanisation has gone through several phases, and historians have come to contradictory conclusions about many of the major issues. The 'pessimists' who in the 1960s and 1970s pronounced most aspects of the churches' work as failure, who emphasised the secularity of the Victorian city and, in particular, saw the working class as massively alienated from religious institutions, and even from religious belief, were succeeded in the 1980s and 1990s by 'revisionists', who painted a much brighter picture both of the churches and of working class religion. Among the many refreshing features of Geoff Robson's book is that he does not belong to either of the two warring camps. One reason for the longevity of this debate is that the evidence is complex and often ambiguous. Robson recognises this complexity. He tests the theories against the evidence, and refuses to be content with cut and dried conclusions. The emphasis on complexity arises partly from the fact that, whereas most historians of Victorian urban religion have concentrated on a single city, or even a district within a city, Robson's is a regional study. And the starting-point of Robson's book is that Birmingham was very different religiously from the neighbouring Black Country, and that within the Black Country the differences between one town or one village and another were even greater. There was no single pattern of urban religion even within this one small corner of England. Having established these points, mainly through detailed analysis of the Religious Census of 1851, he then moves on from statistics to personal experience. Evangelism, popular religion, and the religious impact of cholera epidemics are not only carefully analysed, but also described with empathy and a wealth of illustrative detail. The quality which gives Robson's book its unique flavour, and which distinguishes it from other important studies in the same field, is the author's closeness to his subject. We join the Methodist miners holding dinner-hour prayer-meetings in the coal-pits, and the old woman at her washtub in the courts of central Birmingham attempting to refute the arguments of a Calvinist missionary. This is first-class academic history, based on a deep knowledge of the primary sources and a critical appraisal of all the relevant secondary literature. But it is not academic history of the detached and narrowly cerebral kind: it is sparked by a passionate concern with what religion meant to the miners, nailers, button-makers, or small shopkeepers of the Victorian Midlands, and with how their religion (or sometimes their irreligion) interacted with every other aspect of their lives.

Hugh McLeod
Professor of Church History
University of Birmingham
March 2002

Diagramatic Map: Birmingham and the Black Country

Pelsall

Bloxwich

Wednesfield

Aldridge

<u>Wolverhampton</u>

Willenhall   <u>Walsall</u>

Bilston

Darlaston

Sedgley

Coseley

Wednesbury

Gornal

Tipton

<u>West Bromwich</u>

<u>Dudley</u>

Handsworth   Erdington

Netherton   Oldbury

Kingswinford

Aston

Smethwick

Brierley Hill

Cradley   Rowley
Heath   Regis

<u>Birmingham</u>

Harborne   Edgbaston

Cradley

Lye

Moseley

Halesowen

<u>Stourbridge</u>

Oldswinford

Kings
Norton

Clent

Note

Not to scale. Principal towns are underlined.
Only places mentioned in the text are shown.
County boundaries are not shown.

CHAPTER 1

Introduction

1.1 The purpose of this thesis

The place of religion in Victorian and Edwardian society, and particularly in the lives of working class men and women, continues to fascinate historians. Some of the most recent writing takes up the task pioneered by Hugh McLeod and examines in depth the beliefs and practices of the period after 1870[1], for which the quantity and quality of the evidence is particularly rich. In some cases the focus has been on the institutions; churches, chapels and mission halls with their activities and clientele.[2] Others have concentrated on the beliefs and attitudes of individuals, derived from autobiographical reminiscences, surveys and, most recently, tape recorded interviews.[3] A few have had a particular emphasis, for example on the relationship between religion and politics,[4] but all have focussed on a specific locality and attempted to give a rounded picture of its religious life. The number and range of these local studies has contributed to a marked sophistication in the many more general studies of British religion published in recent years, for example by Parsons, McLeod and Hempton.[5] Most of these have moved beyond a narrowly English frame of reference towards an acknowledgement that England is only one part of the larger cultural entity of the British Isles, which, themselves, are both part of Europe and also closely linked, in their cultural and religious developments, with the North American continent. Alongside this concentration on the influence of Christian beliefs and practices a smaller but growing number of studies has examined the place of other religious traditions, brought initially by immigrant groups, within the increasingly complex religious situation evident in late twentieth century Britain.[6]

One of the main reasons for this concentration of scholarly attention on the late nineteenth and early twentieth centuries is the influence of sociological theory on the study of religious institutions, particularly the concept of 'secularisation' and its prediction of the inevitable decline of religious influences in advanced industrial societies. Testing the validity of such a model of the decline of religion on British industrial society has led to a number of analyses of church membership and attendance statistics. These invariably seem to support the 'secularisation' thesis, though the present religious diversity of urban society raises some questions about the validity of any analysis of recent practice which is limited to Christian institutions.[7]

The one national census of religious worship, that of 1851, has tended to be used in relation to those partial censuses carried out toward the end of the nineteenth century as a sort of benchmark from which to plot the rise and decline of institutional religion in late Victorian and Edwardian society. It has only rarely been seen as the product of earlier developments, although some studies, such as those of James Obelkevich on rural Lincolnshire and Mark Smith on Oldham and Saddleworth, do treat it in this way.[8] The most detailed treatment of the census, by Keith Snell and Paul Ell, who subjected its data to a sophisticated series of computer-assisted correlations, came out three years after this thesis was completed and therefore can only be given a passing reference.[9] This thesis begins by outlining the local context of the 1851 census returns for Birmingham and the Black Country and then explores the possible reasons for the striking differences in church attendance between these two geographically adjacent and economically interdependent parts of an industrial conurbation. The influence of demographic, occupational and institutional factors will be considered, plus the psychological effects of fear induced by cholera epidemics. The thesis then addresses the ways in which Christian churches tried to recruit and retain adult worshippers in the growing industrial conurbation, to understand the appeal of the religious messages they proclaimed amongst the working class and why the responses to them were so varied. Finally it uses some of the surviving source material contained in the journals of missionaries to the poor in early Victorian Birmingham, together with other evidence, to address the nature of what has been called 'popular religion' as distinct from the official beliefs and practices authorised by mainstream Christian churches.

1.2 What counts as religion?

In their description of 'the Orthodox Model' of secularisation Wallis and Bruce reject what they call a 'functionalist' definition of religion in favour of a 'substantive' one, "Religion for us consists of actions, beliefs and institutions predicated upon the assumption of the existence of either supernatural entities with powers of agency, or impersonal powers or processes possessed of moral purpose, which have the capacity to set the conditions of, or to intervene in, human affairs".[10] In order to be able to understand the need for such a religion, however, some idea of its function in human life is necessary. My own attempt, some time ago, was 'Religion holds together in an imaginative unity an awareness of the mystery of life with faith in an ultimate explanation and combines this with a moral appeal' to which was added 'and it is reinforced by a regular pattern of worship or other forms of spiritual discipline'.[11] Rather than suggest that this is in any way comprehensive I prefer the definition of Clifford Geertz, arising from his anthropological study of Islam in Morocco and Indonesia, which gets nearer to the heart of the actual experience of having a religion.

"Without further ado, then, a religion is:
(1) a system of symbols which acts to (2) establish powerful, pervasive, and long lasting moods and motivations in men by (3) formulating conceptions of a general order of existence and (4) clothing these conceptions with such an aura of factuality that (5) the moods and motivations seem uniquely realistic."[12]

This definition makes any attempt to define 'irreligion' very difficult because it would require the subject's own reasoned rejection of such an experience. Hence my title is to some extent polemical, reflecting the opinions of those who, in the mid-nineteenth century, described the beliefs and practices of their fellows. For example, Disraeli in his portrait of Wodgate where, "No church there has yet raised its spire" and where people, if asked "the name of their religion, . . .they will laugh: who rules them on earth or who can save them in heaven, are alike mysteries to them".[13] To him, and others who commented on the census of religious worship, irreligion meant an absence of conventional Christian knowledge and piety[14]. Disraeli's model for Wodgate, Willenhall in the Black Country, which he only knew from the reports of the Children's Employment Commission, lends support to the title of this thesis, which explores the nature of the beliefs and practices current at the time in so far as there is evidence for them. What counts as religion will include some things which contemporaries condemned as superstition as well as a wide range of attitudes towards the official beliefs and practices of the main Christian churches. Some of these were 'irreligious' in so far as they expressed disbelief in particular Christian doctrines, but most were modifications of Christian traditions handed down from previous generations. Census data on attendance at Christian worship is the starting point for probing deeper into the experience Geertz describes.[15]

1.3 Primary sources

This thesis is based on a cross-section of primary sources. The most important manuscript sources are the original returns for the 1851 census of religious worship and the journals of the missionaries to the poor in Birmingham during the 1830s and 40s. Surviving correspondence of Wesleyan itinerants in the Methodist central archives, two Anglican clergy, William Leigh of Bilston (in the Staffordshire Record Office) and George Barrs' notes on Rowley Regis parish (in Sandwell Archives, Smethwick) are the only other significant personal material. In addition to the Report of the Royal Commission on Ecclesiastical Revenues local Anglican diocesan archives have been used. These are much fuller for Lichfield than for Worcester for the period covered by this thesis. A much smaller amount of material from the Roman Catholic Archdiocese of Birmingham has been drawn upon. It has been impossible to locate or study all the surviving church and chapel records for the conurbation during this period, though several which are accessible in local archive centres have been used. Much more has been preserved from Birmingham than for the rest of the conurbation and this is centrally accessible whereas at least seven record offices share the sources for the other places included in this thesis.[16] The breadth of the area covered has meant that detailed analysis of individual membership lists and baptism registers has not been attempted.

The most important published sources are the evidence of the various Parliamentary commissions investigating children's education, employment and the mining industry. They are generally more thorough than the glimpses into religious life and organisation contained in the local press and denominational periodicals, though these have been extensively used. Pamphlets, sermons and the biographies of both religious leaders and lesser figures throw light on contemporary perceptions of what was happening, despite their frequently pious phraseology. Missionary journals and Parliamentary commissions balance the literary sources by providing verbatim evidence from working class people who left no other record of their experiences. The difficulties of generalising from individual statements are occasionally eased by the survival of parallel sources but these are exceptional. All too often detailed evidence is limited to a single source.[17]

Another problem is the dominance of clerical views on the religious life of the area. Whilst clergy and ministers set the tone of congregational life their views were not necessarily those of their hearers. Autobiographies of laymen and women tend to be limited, not only to the better educated but also to the nonconformist denominations.[18] As Frances Knight discovered, finding authentic sources for the religious experiences of Anglican laity is extremely difficult.[19] Although this is slightly offset by the missionary journals, all by laymen and reflecting lay opinion in the conversations they record, only one of the missionaries was an Anglican and no parallel sources exist for the Black Country. Moreover the people they met tended not to be pious Anglicans but rather, if admitting any religious allegiance at all, either Roman Catholics or Methodists, many in both categories no longer regular worshippers. Despite their limitations they provide important evidence of the 'popular religion' which influenced the lives of many whom Horace Mann called 'unconscious Secularists'.[20]

1.4 Secondary sources

Mann's commentary on the 1851 census of religious worship set the agenda for much subsequent scholarship. The alienation of the urban industrial working class from institutional religion was accepted by Wickham, Inglis and Perkin before it was challenged by Gilbert, Smith, Brown and, for a later period, Cox, Bartlett and Green.[21] Mann's pessimistic analysis has been revised by examining socio-economic, organisational and theological factors within nineteenth century urban history. The sheer size of towns was taken by Perkin as an indicator of their level of religious observance, this was refined by Inglis who pointed to the dominance of industrial towns amongst those with the lowest 1851 attendances.[22] Callum Brown effectively challenged Perkin's simplistic association between size and non-attendance by using Scottish and Welsh statistics to supplement those from England. Gilbert examined the socio-economic origins of nonconformists to explain the concurrent rise of nonconformity and early industrialisation. Short distance migration from countryside to towns was pointed out by McLeod as a significant factor in the regional pattern of 1851 church attendance.[23] Koditschek used both ideas, though primarily the appeal of nonconformity to rising entrepreneurial capitalists, to explain the 1851 church attendance in Bradford.[24]

To both Koditschek and Gilbert denominational rivalry effectively established the urban religious pattern. This factor has been addressed at the organisational level by Robin Gill, using census and other statistics to account for overprovision by both Anglicans and nonconformists in town and countryside.[25] Mark Smith also pointed out the importance of pastoral efficiency and evangelism in sustaining impressive levels of church going in Oldham and Saddleworth.[26] Theological factors are part of Michael Watts' interpretation of the expansion of Evangelical Protestant Dissent in England and Wales up to 1859. Combining maps based on the 1851 census with a comprehensive range of original sources he explains the success of Methodism, the most rapidly expanding denominational group, by its appeal to popular superstitions and fear of hell, especially during cholera epidemics.[27] The broader Evangelical tradition, including the Churches of England and Scotland, has been the subject of several studies, most of them relating Evangelical activities to other social and cultural trends.[28] Finally the theological beliefs of ordinary people, particularly those not closely attached to specific churches, have been analysed by Obelkevich, Clark, Hempton, Parsons and Williams, some of them using Cox's idea of 'diffusive Christianity' to indicate an indirect and derivative relationship with what has been called 'official religion', as distinct from irreligious secularism.[29]

1.5 Issues to be addressed

The accuracy of the published 1851 census report on religious worship for the area needs to be checked against the original returns before the contrast it reveals between Birmingham and the Black Country can be accepted.[30] The possible effects of population growth and town size can then be related to attendances in each sub-district in the conurbation. Gill's thesis on the relationship between denominational provision for worship and actual attendances and Gilbert's on the significance of the occupational pattern in determining nonconformist success will be tested along with the possibility that immigration from the surrounding countryside was a more influential factor in both the levels of attendance and their denominational distribution. Smith's emphasis on the importance of evangelism and pastoral efficiency will be addressed by examining the range of methods employed by the churches and attempting to assess their relative success. Watts' argument that appeals to fear were the main factor in promoting adult conversions and that Methodism, in particular, also exploited popular superstitions will be related to the religious responses to the 1832 and 1849 cholera epidemics and accounts of Methodist influence in Black Country mining communities. Finally, an attempt will be made to compare the evidence for 'popular religion' during this period with that obtained for the late nineteenth and early twentieth centuries by Clark and Williams to see whether there are significant common features as well as differences peculiar to the conurbation during the 1830s and 40s.

Notes

1 H. McLeod, *Class and Religion in the Late Victorian City*, London 1974.

2 e.g.. Stephen Yeo, *Religion and Voluntary Organisations in Crisis*, London 1976, Jeff Cox, *The English Churches in a Secular Society*, Lambeth 1870-1930, New York 1982, Alan Bartlett, 'The Churches in Bermondsey 1880-1939' Ph.D. Birmingham 1987, S.J.D. Green, *Religion in the Age of Decline*, 1870-1920, Cambridge 1996.

3 e.g.. David Clark, *Between Pulpit and Pew: Folk Religion in a North Yorkshire Fishing Village*, Cambridge 1982, Elizabeth Roberts, *Working Class Barrow and Lancaster 1890-1930*, Lancaster 1976, Sarah Williams, 'Religious Belief and Popular Culture, Southwark 1880-1939' D.Phil. Oxford 1993.

4 e.g.. Robert Moore, *Pit-men, Preachers and Politics*, Cambridge 1974.

5 G. Parsons (Ed), *Religion in Victorian Britain*, 4 vols., Manchester 1988; H. McLeod, *Religion and Society in England 1850-1914*, London 1996; D. Hempton, *Religion and political culture in Britain and Ireland*, Cambridge 1996.

6 see survey by Kim Knott in T. Thomas (Ed), *The British, their Religious Beliefs and Practices 1800-1986*, London 1988, pp. 133-177.

7 For example, Hugh McLeod, relying on the Birmingham Daily News religious census of 1892, gave the socially mixed suburb of Handsworth an index of church attendance of 33.6% of the population. There were, at that time, some twelve churches for a population of over 32, 000, including not only the Church of England and all the largest nonconformist groups, Baptist, Congregationalist and Methodist, but also smaller bodies such as the Quakers, Brethren and Mormons. In the 1970s a survey, which did not extend to actual attendance, nevertheless noted over sixty religious organisations providing for a population of around 60, 000. These included the groups already represented in 1892 plus the Roman Catholics and the Salvation Army but also some eighteen Black-led churches, two mosques, the largest of the Hindu mandirs and Sikh gurdwaras in Birmingham and several other places of worship belonging to minority groups within the Hindu and Sikh religious traditions. It could well be that religious practice in Handsworth in the 1970s, in a now more racially though less socially mixed area, was at least as high as it was in the 1890s. H. McLeod, 'Class, Community and Region', in M. Hill (Ed), *A Sociological Yearbook of Religion in Britain 6*, 1973 p.51, G. K. Nelson, 'Religious Groups in a changing social environment', in A. Bryman (Ed), *Religion in the Birmingham Area, essays in the sociology of religion*, Birmingham University 1976, pp. 51-59.

8 J. Obelkevich, *Religion and Rural Society*, Oxford 1976; M. A. Smith, *Religion in Industrial Society*, Oxford, 1994.

9 K. D. M. Snell and P.S. Ell, *Rival Jerusalems*, Cambridge, 2000.

10 S. Bruce, *Religion and Modernisation*, Oxford 1992, pp. 9-11, 21-25. The further claim that their operation is not susceptible to refutation seems to me an unnecessary assertion of a particular philosophical position, akin to logical positivism, on which a great deal of work has been done. The best recent summary is John Hick's, *An Interpretation of Religion*, London 1989, where Hick defends the rationality of religious belief, see especially chapters 12 and 13.

11   G. Robson, 'Religion for Young Humanists' in *British Journal of Religious Education*, Vol. 4 No. 3, 1982, p.137, and Religious Education 5-16, H.M.I. Curriculum Matters Series, suppressed by Government 1988, for which see G. Robson, 'Religious education 1985-1995' in *British Journal of Religious Education*, Vol. 19 No. 1, 1996, pp.15-16.

12   C. Geertz, 'Religion as a cultural system' in M. Banton (Ed.), *Anthropological approaches to the Study of Religion*, London and New York, 1966, p.4.

13   B. Disraeli, Sybil, or The Two Nations, London 1845, Book III, chapter iv.

14   This idea was not new, cf. Patrick Collinson's discussion of the sixteenth and seventeenth century evidence in *The Religion of Protestants*, Oxford 1982, pp. 195-241.

15   Although the census returns included numbers at Sabbath worship in synagogues, Jewish beliefs and practices have not been included in this thesis as the number of people involved was very small. There were only three synagogues in Birmingham and the Black Country in 1851.

16   Dudley, Lichfield, Sandwell, Stafford, Walsall, Wolverhampton, Worcester.

17   For example, although several sources detail the impact of the 1832 cholera epidemic on Black Country religious life only one survives for the 1849 epidemic.

18   This is brought out very clearly in Davidoff and Hall's study of the commercial middle class in Birmingham and Colchester which relies heavily on Independent, Unitarian and Quaker sources. Two autobiographies of Birmingham Wesleyans show the danger of generalising from a single source. Both had poor working class origins. David Barr, son of a shoemaker, arrived from Coventry as a commercial traveller. A local preacher, he made judicious friendships, married into middle class Wesleyan society and, after a successful career in insurance, held office on the Board of Guardians, School Board and Liberal Party. Mrs. A. Collier's husband was confined to a lunatic asylum and she took in lodgers who cheated her, but she started cottage meetings in her court, distributed tracts and became a class leader, before being employed as a Bible woman in 1859. Taken together they show something of the social range of Wesleyan lay leadership during the 1850s. L. Davidoff and C. Hall *Family Fortunes*, London 1987, D. Barr *Climbing the Ladder*, London 1910, E. Nightingale (Ed.) *Autobiography of Mrs. A. Collier of Birmingham*, 2nd. Edition, London 1885.

19   F. Knight *The nineteenth century Church and English society*, Cambridge, 1995 pp. 22-23.

20   H. Mann *Report on the Census of Religious Worship*, Parliamentary Papers 1853, LXXXIX, p. clviii

21   E. R. Wickham *Church and People in an Industrial City*, London 1957, pp. 107-108, K. S. Inglis *Churches and the Working Classes in Victorian England*, London 1963 p.20 H. Perkin *The Origins of Modern English Society, 1780-1880*, London 1969, pp. 197-202, A. D. Gilbert *Religion and Society in Industrial England*, London 1976 pp. 61-68, Smith, *Indusrial Society*, pp. 124-133, C. G. Brown, 'Did urbanisation secularise Britain?' in *Urban History Yearbook* 1988 pp. 1-14, Cox *Secular* pp. 136-142, Bartlett 'Bermondsey' pp. 286-294, 401-3, Green *Decline* pp. 202-204.

22   K. S. Inglis, 'Patterns of Religious Worship in 1851' in *Journal of Ecclesiasti-*

cal History Vol. XI, 1960 p.8.

23 H. McLeod, 'Class, Community and Region' in M. Hill (Ed.) *A Sociological Yearbook of Religion in Britain 6*, London 1973, pp. 39-43.

24 T. Koditschek *Class Formation and Industrial Society, Bradford 1750-1850*, Cambridge 1990, pp. 252-92.

25 R. Gill *The Myth of the Empty Church*, London 1993, passim.

26 M. A. Smith *Industrial Society* p.253, "regular church attendance in Oldham and Saddleworth may have exceeded 50% of the eligible population during much of the second half of the nineteenth century".

27 M. R. Watts *The Dissenters Vol. II*, Oxford 1995, passim and especially pp. 49-80, 100-132.

28 cf. D. W. Bebbington *Evangelicalism in Modern Britain*, London 1989, G. A. Rawlyk and M. A. Noll *Amazing Grace*, Grand Rapids, Michigan 1993, M. A. Noll, D. W. Bebbington and G. A. Rawlyk (Eds.) *Evangelicalism, Comparative Studies of Popular Protestantism in North America, the British Isles and Beyond 1700-1900*, New York, Oxford 1994.

29 Obelkevich *Rural Society* pp. 260-307, Clark *Folk Religion* passim, Hempton in Thomas *British* pp. 181-210, Parsons *Victorian Britain* Vol. II, pp. 64-87, Williams 'Southwark' passim, also J. Wolffe *God and Greater Britain*, London 1994 pp. 75-97.

30 Mark Smith found serious discrepancies between the published figures and the actual situation in Oldham in 1851. M. A. Smith *Industrial Society* p.250.

CHAPTER 2

The Economic and Social Setting

2.1 The lie of the land

The conurbation comprising Birmingham and the Black Country occupies an area roughly twelve miles square. By the mid-nineteenth century it consisted of an interconnected urbanised network covering a part of the Midland Plateau. This is an upland region, around 400 feet above sea level, isolated between the valleys formed by the rivers Trent, Severn, Avon and their tributaries. It straddles the watershed so that, although most of the streams draining the area flow via the rivers Tame, Rea, and Cole into the Trent and eventually out to the North Sea, those on the western side flow via the Smestow Brook and the Stour into the Severn and so down to the Bristol Channel.[1]

A ridge of high ground forms the main watershed running south from Wolverhampton up to Sedgley Beacon (716 feet), then via Castle Hill, Dudley (730 feet) through Rowley Regis (820 feet) to the Clent Hills where it rises to over 1,000 feet.[2] To the east of the watershed lie most of the places featured in this thesis, including Walsall, Willenhall, Darlaston, Bilston, Wednesbury, Tipton, West Bromwich, Oldbury, Smethwick and Birmingham itself. On the ridge or to the west lie Wolverhampton, Sedgley, Dudley, Kingswinford, Brierley Hill, Cradley Heath, Rowley Regis, Halesowen and Stourbridge. Between Walsall to the north and Birmingham to the south another ridge of high ground rises to over 700 feet at Barr Beacon. Between these two ridges the upper valley of the river Tame provides rather more level ground only punctuated by the low hills which formed the sites of several early settlements and which are still crowned, in the cases of Walsall, Wednesbury and West Bromwich, with the towers and spires of (very much restored or rebuilt) medieval parish churches.

2.2 Mineral Resources

The poor soil and uncertain drainage of the area contributed to its slow development in comparison with surrounding settlements during the medieval period. In terms of size and economic significance Birmingham and the Black Country were quite eclipsed by Coventry, Lichfield and Worcester, which also became the centres of ecclesiastical administration. By the end of the fourteenth century Coventry appears to have become the fourth largest city in England after London, York and Bristol.[3]

Nevertheless beneath the inhospitable surface were rich deposits of coal and ironstone, these together with the limestone and fireclay which surrounded them began to be exploited during the medieval period and enabled the area to develop steadily as a centre of manufacturing industry from the sixteenth century. Although Birmingham itself does not lie on any significant mineral deposits its proximity to those of the Black Country bound its early industrial development closely to them.

With the exception of most of Wolverhampton in the north-west and of Birmingham in the south-east coal seams underlie virtually the whole area, outcropping at or near the surface with sufficient frequency to have been easily worked well before the earliest recorded evidence, from Sedgley in 1273.[4] The main seam was the thickest in the country, the Ten Yard or Thirty Foot Coal, and its accessibility, together with its richness, made it an obvious source of wealth for anyone able to exploit it. A seam of ironstone (Gubbins Ironstone) lies immediately beneath the thick coal and can usually be worked along with it. This seems to have occurred at Sedgley as early as 1291.[5]

A particular brand of fireclay, the Old Mine Clay, lay in beds about 45 feet below the thick coal, and was mined from the seventeenth century in the area around Stourbridge and Brierley Hill.[6] Another clay, Etruria Marl, outcropping from just south of Wednesbury to Halesowen, formed the basis of a significant industry, the manufacture of engineering and other bricks throughout the nineteenth century.[7] The stone of the region was also a valuable resource. The limestone was used in agriculture from the medieval period and, later, in iron smelting. There was sandstone which could be made into grindstones and furnace hearths. In the south there was also a dolerite, known locally as Rowley Rag and used to this day in paving roads. All these have been quarried extensively within the Black Country, though not within the immediate vicinity of Birmingham, from at least the seventeenth century[8].

2.3 Industrial Development

Although the wool trade was the staple industry of Wolverhampton well into the sixteenth century by then metalworking had begun to predominate over all other industries in such places as Walsall, West Bromwich and Birmingham.[9] During the first half of the seventeenth century Dud Dudley, illegitimate son of Edward, Lord Dudley, took over the management of his father's iron furnaces around Dudley and began smelting iron with pit coal instead of charcoal. The Civil War destroyed his work, for he was a Royalist in a predominantly Parliamentarian area. Nevertheless the impetus, once given, continued until Abraham Darby succeeded, first turning coal into coke before using it in his blast furnaces at Coalbrookdale in nearby Shropshire. This led, by the mid-eighteenth century, to the transformation of the iron industry and the rapid exploitation of the thick coal and ironstone of the Black Country by John Wilkinson and his successors. Wilkinson erected his first blast furnace at Bradley near Bilston about 1758 and a forge for producing wrought iron in 1782. Although in 1740 there were only four blast furnaces in the area by 1788 there were six, by 1796 fourteen and by 1830 their number had risen to 123.[10]

Before wrought iron could be used in the manufacture of nails it had to be cut into rods which could be worked in a forge. This slitting process was mechanised in the seventeenth century by the Foleys of Stourbridge where the river Stour provided the power for a number of slitting mills.[11] By the end of the eighteenth century steam power had been harnessed to several essential processes in the iron industry. John Wilkinson was one of the first to buy a steam engine from Boulton and Watt's Soho Works in 1776 to blow a blast furnace. Steam engines were also used to haul barrows of coke, ironstone and limestone up an inclined plane to charge the furnaces. Improved furnace construction and puddling techniques in the early nineteenth century increased productivity whilst, in the forges and rolling mills, steam driven rollers and hammers shaped the iron into plates, sheets, bars and rods.[12]

Steam power improved the yield of the coal workings to meet the increased demands of the furnaces. The first Newcomen engine was set up in 1712 near Dudley to drain water from the mines and similar atmospheric engines were used throughout the century to pump water and to raise coals to the surface. A Watt engine was installed at Tipton in 1776 for drainage and by 1850 the steam engine had almost universally replaced the horse gin as a means of raising and lowering coal skips from underground workings. Nevertheless mining methods in the Black Country lagged far behind those of other coalfields leading to a wasteful loss of mineral resources. No plans were kept of underground workings, even by the Earl of Dudley the major coal owner let alone by the many smaller operators. Hence water from old workings regularly flooded newer ones so that, by the early twentieth century, it was said 'to resemble nothing so much as a waterlogged rabbit warren'. [13] In the first half of the nineteenth century, however, the exhaustion of the coalfield was not seriously contemplated. When old workings around Wednesbury and Bilston were becoming uneconomic new pits were being sunk further south. Whereas in 1800 there were none in West Bromwich by 1832 there were 58. Similarly, following an enclosure act in 1821, Rowley Regis parish became a centre of coal mining with 13 collieries by 1854. [14]

Few technological developments affected the metal industries in the first half of the nineteenth century, though a new method of welding metal tubes was successfully pioneered by a Wednesbury man, Cornelius Whitehouse, in 1825. Instead the area exploited a growing demand for such things as tubes in gas and water supply, axles and rails for railways, stoves, pans and hollowware products, together with the older established edge tools and the components of the gun, lock, saddlery and harness trades. Each specialism tended to become located in a specific township, so that Wednesbury specialised in tubes, Willenhall in locks, Darlaston in nuts and bolts, Cradley Heath and Old Hill in chains, Walsall in saddlery and two different districts of Birmingham in guns and jewellery respectively. Even the hand-made nail trade became specialised in certain areas, though it was in steady decline throughout this period. This specialisation gave a very specific character to individual places within the conurbation, however lacking in variety they appeared to outside observers. [15]

Glass manufacture was well established in the area by the nineteenth century. Stourbridge and its adjacent townships of Amblecote, Wordsley and Brierley Hill all had glassworks, some dating back to the seventeenth century. In addition to bottles, sheet glass, flint glass and crystal glass were all produced, the latter being engraved to a high standard. Birmingham had a small glass manufacturing capacity, largely linked to the jewellery trade whilst a short distance away, at Smethwick, was the Birmingham Plate Glass Company and the Spon Lane Works of Chance Brothers. The latter firm expanded between 1815 and 1851 when it glazed the Crystal Palace for the Great Exhibition. [16]

The location of the glass industry in and around Stourbridge can be partly attributed to the local fireclay which was particularly suitable for retorts and bricks for lining glass furnaces. These continued to be produced in substantial quantities throughout the nineteenth century whilst a few mines and firebrick works were established elsewhere. [17] The production of bricks for housing and, particularly, civil engineering increased greatly between 1800 and 1851. Staffordshire blue bricks lined canal tunnels, bridges, railway tunnels and cuttings, with a resulting expansion in that industry particularly around Tipton.[18]

Brass was the metal most used in Birmingham so that some of the raw materials had to be imported from a distance even though the brasshouses producing the metal itself were within the town. Here it was used, along with a vast range of other materials, in the buckle, button and 'toy' trades as well as in brass screws, locks, candlesticks, cabinet fittings, bedsteads and the cocks, taps, tubes and fittings increasingly required in steam engines and in the supply of piped gas and water.[19] Few Birmingham trades were concentrated in factories though one of these, the manufacture of steel pens, particularly by Joseph Gillott from about 1830, became somewhat untypically a showpiece of Birmingham industry. Gillott was visited by royalty and his pen factory employed over 500 people by mid-century.[20] Large and small factories, however, could rely on cheap motive power from steam engines whilst a gas flame provided a reliable and versatile source of heat for the many specialist workshops.[21] Despite its different raw materials and finished products this aspect of Birmingham industry linked it closely to the pattern of industrial organisation across the rest of the conurbation.

2.4 Communications

Avoided by the Roman builders of the Fosse Way and Watling Street and some distance from navigable rivers it is understandable that the area lagged behind the rest of the Midlands in economic development throughout the medieval period. A road from Worcester to Lichfield and beyond was being used from the fourteenth century and this passed through Birmingham. By this time market rights had been granted to Birmingham, Dudley, Halesowen, Walsall and Wolverhampton and roads between these places were gradually improved, culminating in various turnpike acts in the eighteenth century. Until it was repaired by Telford, however, the London to Holyhead mail-coach road between Birmingham and Wolverhampton was tortuous and difficult. Telford, between 1815 and 1823, improved the surface with Rowley Rag and cut by-passes round Wednesbury and Bilston.[22]

By this date the regional canal network, which began in 1767 with Brindley's Staffordshire and Worcestershire Canal (linking Wolverhampton to Stourbridge and then to the river Severn at Stourport) was almost complete. By 1772 Wolverhampton and Birmingham were also linked by a canal which passed through the heart of the Black Country and brought its coal and iron to Birmingham at greatly reduced cost. Birmingham soon lay at the heart of a complex network of canals which linked it not only with other industrial centres in the Midlands but also with London, Bristol, Liverpool and Hull. The canal builders overcame enormous constructional problems in penetrating the plateau, particularly the tunnels which crossed the watershed at Dudley and Lapal near Halesowen. The latter, over two miles long, was completed in 1815. The various canals operated at three different contour levels, crossing over each other in some instances. They needed lengthy flights of locks which not only delayed traffic but also led to considerable problems in maintaining water levels. During the first half of the nineteenth century new canals, branches and tunnels were cut, culminating in the Netherton tunnel, near Dudley, in 1855.[23] "By 1800, factories had already begun to cluster on the canal banks, attracted by the ease of transport of raw materials, the low tolls often allowed on coal destined for canal side works and by the advantages of free water supply for steam engines."[24]

If Birmingham's situation on a well drained sandy ridge above the crossing of the river Rea, with a plentiful natural supply of water from springs and wells, partly explains its development as a centre of trade from the thirteenth century its position at the heart of the canal network consolidated its national importance as a manufacturing town. This was reflected in the ways in which the railway system developed from the 1830s. Intense competition between the Great Western and the Midland Railway companies for the lucrative goods and passenger trade of the conurbation led to rival lines linking Birmingham and Wolverhampton with London and the North West. The history of the local railways need not be detailed here but, in addition to Birmingham's early success in attracting a rail link with London in 1838, to add to its 1837 link with Liverpool, there was the impetus given to the area by the increasing demands of the new industry for rails, engines and rolling stock. The local promoters of early railways were primarily concerned with transporting goods, not passengers. By gaining a lead in rail links with other areas Birmingham tried to ensure its continued business success.[25]

2.5 Population Growth

The first comprehensive population statistics for the whole conurbation, as distinct from estimates for individual towns and villages contained in trade directories and ecclesiastical visitation returns, are those of the 1801 Census. They give the total population of Birmingham and the Black Country as 185, 571. A comparison of these figures with the 1851 Census shows that whereas the total population of Great Britain (ie excluding Ireland) roughly doubled during the first half of the nineteenth century that of the conurbation increased three and a half times to 635,077.[26] This increase was not uniform across the area. Some towns, notably West Bromwich and Tipton experienced very dramatic increases, others, such as Walsall and Stourbridge, though more than doubling their population, did so at a steadier rate.

Table 1 shows the comparative population figures for each place in 1801 and 1851 in rank order of their size. Table 2 gives the rank order of their percentage increase in population between these two dates. Although the overall increase in population was considerably greater than the national norm the rate varied within this period. Plotting the increase on a decennial basis gives a clearer indication of the pattern than the stark contrast between 1801 and 1851. This is shown in Table 3. Because of the variations between each sub-district during the half century no rank order is possible in this case and so the order used is virtually that of the published list of the census enumeration districts.[27]

Certain decades were more critical than others in the population growth of each location so that no overall pattern emerges. The steady growth rate of the old town of Birmingham must be linked with the more precipitate development of Edgbaston and Aston, particularly in the 1820s and 30s, as well as the increase in Kings Norton after 1831, for the true overall population increase to be apparent. The population of greater Birmingham, thus defined, increased from 78,420 in 1801 to 255, 374 in 1851, a growth of 326% compared with only 286% for the central area and much nearer the overall growth rate of 342.2% for the conurbation as a whole.

In the immediate vicinity the only industrial districts to grow more rapidly were the Potteries of North Staffordshire (361%) whilst both Coventry (230%) in Warwickshire and the Worcestershire carpet manufacturing town of Kidderminster (257%) lagged well behind. In national terms the conurbation's growth rate is comparable with other industrial areas such as Tyneside and Leeds (both 324%) though not as great as Oldham, Sheffield or greater Manchester all of which quadrupled their populations during this period. Nowhere in the conurbation could compare with Bradford, especially in the 1840s when a 300% increase helped to raise the population to six times its 1801 figure.

Apart from greater Birmingham and Harborne the critical decade for most places appears to have been the 1830s but even here there are exceptions in Tipton and Sedgley. Such rapid population growth posed problems for church accommodation, particularly for the

Church of England with its inheritance of large medieval parishes. In Birmingham, for example, the growth of the local population had long been a cause for concern. As far back as 1772 a private Act of Parliament had authorised building two new churches in the town on the ground that existing churches were "not capable of containing one sixth part of the inhabitants professing the doctrine of the Church of England, to the great reproach of civil society, and contempt of Holy Religion"[28]

As the growth of the conurbation's population was the result of economic expansion its occupational structure will be addressed before its political and ecclesiastical characteristics are considered.

2.6 Uniformity and Diversity

Local tradition has it that Queen Victoria pulled down the blinds of her carriage as the Royal Train passed between Birmingham and Wolverhampton, so painful to her was the view out of the window. Certainly the impression gained by outsiders was of an undistinguished and unpleasant industrial environment, totally inhospitable to human civilisation and given over to noise, smoke and dirt. Birmingham trade directories in the late eighteenth century noted that "Birmingham is not a place a gentleman would chuse to make a residence". Its "close population, the noxious effusion of various metallic trades and above all the continual smoke arising from the immense quantity of coals consumed" rendered it no fit place for a gentleman[29]. If such was the case with Birmingham the Black Country was several degrees worse. Thomas Tancred, introducing the first Report of the Midland Mining Commission in 1843 describes it as follows;

"The traveller appears never to get out of an interminable village, composed of cottages and very ordinary houses. In some directions he may travel for miles, and never be out of sight of numerous two-storied houses: so that the area covered by bricks and mortar must be immense. These houses, for the most part, are not arranged in continuous streets but are interspersed with blazing furnaces, heaps of burning coal in process of coking, piles of ironstone calcining, forges, pit banks and engine chimneys; the country being besides intersected with canals, crossing each other at different levels; and the small remaining patches of surface soil occupied with irregular fields of grass or corn, intermingled with heaps of the refuse of mines or of slag from the blast furnaces."[30]

This impression of depressing uniformity obscured a considerable, if subtle, variety between individual places, each with their own identity and strong local loyalties. Unfortunately no statistical breakdown of the occupational structure of individual places is possible from the published report of the 1851 census which only gives occupational information on a county basis. The 1841 Census Report, however, added to these figures those from the principal towns in each county. Thus it is possible to reconstruct the situation in 1841 and to compare specific places within the conurbation. This task is not easy, as W. A. Armstrong pointed out.[31] Before 1841, lists of occupations were drawn up on a variety of different principles. "From 1841, householders' schedules were in use, and at the census office an attempt was made to group the occupations 'under definite rules and on uniform lines'. Nevertheless, although there was a great deal of rendering down and amalgamation of the many thousands of occupations mentioned on the schedules, the published figures for England and Wales covered 877 occupations, presented in alphabetical order, with very little attempt at further arrangement."[32] Whatever principles underlay the national abstract, the county tables are not consistent. The towns within the conurbation lay within the counties of Staffordshire, Warwickshire and Worcestershire but all the occupations are not recorded across all three counties.

The towns or parishes for which separate occupational information is printed are: in Staffordshire; Bilston, Kingswinford, Sedgley, Tipton, Walsall (including Bloxwich), West Bromwich and Wolverhampton,[33] in Warwickshire; Birmingham (including part of Aston),[34] in Worcestershire; Dudley and Oldswinford (this included Stourbridge but not Amblecote).[35] Thus a total of ten of the principal places within the conurbation is available for analysis on the basis of the published report. This has been attempted according to the occupational groupings proposed by Armstrong, though with some modifications to take account of local circumstances. Armstrong published the detailed breakdown of the occupational census reports for England and Wales worked out by Charles Booth in the 1880s and deposited with the Statistical Society[36]. From these it is possible to work out national norms for each broad category of the population as well as for specific occupations. These can then be related to the findings for individual locations to enable them to be compared with each other and with the pattern for England and Wales as a whole.

Table 4 gives a breakdown of these statistics under the general categories into which specific trades and professions fall. These are very broad: agriculture (including fishing), mining (including quarrying), building, manufacture, transport, dealing, industrial service (including such different occupations as banking and unskilled labour), public and professional services (including the armed forces and local administration as well as lawyers, teachers, clergy and medical practitioners), domestic service and those property owners of independent means. The largest category is that of dependants, which includes children as well as most married women, older people and those in hospitals and institutional care. The first column indicates a norm derived from Booth's statistics for England and Wales.[37]

Not surprisingly the correlation coefficient between the overall percentage of dependants and the percentage of those under twenty who were not employed is significant at r = 0.85.[38] As can be seen, in eight out of the ten places the proportion of the population aged below twenty ranged from just under to well over 50%. This may be a significant factor in the amount of support given to Sunday schools in the area as revealed by the 1851 census of religious worship.

Grouping the occupational tables of the 1841 census under the Armstrong/Booth categories enables comparisons between a local pattern and national norms. The one major disadvantage lies within the manufacturing classification where the structure adopted, quite sensibly, by Booth obscures the links between groups of trades related to the same basic industry. For example Booth separated out trades connected with different raw materials such as iron and steel, copper, brass and tin, leather and hair, all of which are used in the manufacture of saddlery, whilst harness manufacture is grouped with carriage building in another category.[39] This is not important when comparing the numbers involved in manufacture with mining or unskilled labour, but it makes work on the occupational profile of individual places dependent on technical knowledge. In the case of Walsall, for example, combining those trades contributing to saddlery and harness production shows well over a third of the total manufacturing population directly involved in this one industry.

A rather more complex extrapolation is needed in the case of the jewellery and 'toy' manufacturing trades of Birmingham which used a vast range of metals from brass and steel to silver and gold plus other raw materials as diverse as glass, bone, shell and gemstones plus the skills of engraving, enamelling, and setting. An estimate, from over 28 entries, shows at least a tenth of the manufacturing population of 40, 000 engaged in this specialist area, most of them located, as they are to this day, around St Paul's one of the churches built following the Act of Parliament of 1772.

The other Birmingham church facilitated by the 1772 Act, St

Mary's, was surrounded by the workshops of another complex trade, gun manufacture. The fact that just over 2, 000 entries for gunsmiths and barrel makers appear in the census listing does not exhaust the number involved. Wood-turners would produce the stocks, some 276 are indicated, and other metal workers the locks and fittings. Over 300 locksmiths are noted, but not all manufactured gun-locks which were also produced in Darlaston.

This attempt to isolate the leading industries from the census data shows that only a general description can be arrived at, except in the case of trades such as nailing which were relatively easy to indicate. As nailing became notorious as a depressed industry in the nineteenth century and has been cited as a source of recruitment for revivalist religious groups, particularly Methodists, it will be useful to indicate the 1841 evidence.[40] Table 6 shows, in column 1, the percentage of the whole population of each place engaged in nailing, and, in columns 2 and 3, the percentage of the employed male and female population respectively. This reveals a very patchy situation. All localities, even Birmingham, had some nailers though Bilston, with only two, a man and a woman, hardly counts at all. Of the rest the trade was heavily concentrated on the western side of the conurbation. Dudley, Sedgley and Oldswinford had the largest proportion of nailers and, with the inclusion of Tipton, a high percentage of employment for women. The exclusion from the 1841 report of data from places such as Rowley Regis and Halesowen, where nailing certainly existed, means that the picture is incomplete. However, nailing only provided a living for a minority of the population even in places like Dudley, which were recognised centres of the trade.

The 1841 census gives the number of unskilled labourers in each place listed. This is a significant indicator of the general level of technical skill required to obtain employment. Table 7 gives, in rank order, the percentage of unskilled labourers in the employed male population (column 1) adding (column 2) their percentage in the population as a whole to enable comparisons with Table 4.

The chief disadvantage of this analysis of the 1841 census is that the places listed, though both important and typical, do not give a complete picture of the employment pattern of the conurbation as a whole. Several smaller places such as Wednesbury, Darlaston, Willenhall, Oldbury, Smethwick, Halesowen and Rowley Regis are absent. Although their combined 1841 population was less than a fifth of the total population of those listed, their absence necessarily distorts the picture. Their significance is not solely economic. They included some of the highest and some of the lowest church attendance figures within the conurbation in the 1851 census of religious worship, so that their occupational characteristics take on an added importance if, as scholars such as Alan Gilbert have suggested, these were a significant influence on the pattern of churchgoing.[41]

In order to give a more comprehensive, though necessarily incomplete, picture of the industrial composition of the different registration sub-districts Table 8 has been prepared from data contained in a number of sources.[42]

2.7 Industrial organisation

By the mid-nineteenth century, with the possible exception of Willenhall, there was no place in which the population was entirely dependent on a single industry. This did not mean that some or all did not suffer periods of recession or, in some cases, virtual extinction. This was a hazard particularly of those Birmingham trades which depended much more on taste and fashion than on practical necessity for their markets. The dominant buckle trade of the eighteenth century almost disappeared when the fashion changed during the Regency period. Petitions to the Prince Regent were of no avail and many firms faced bankruptcy.[43] By contrast the long decline of the hand wrought nail trade was the direct result of competition from machinery not changing fashion.

As James Boydell, managing partner of the Oak Farm Iron Company of Kingswinford told Thomas Tancred in 1842, "I fear great injury will be done to our nailing population by an invention which I saw only yesterday in London, by which nails of an excellent quality are made by pressure, and they are turned out of a machine like flour from a mill." To which he added, "It seems likely, at least, to reduce the cost of hand-made nails considerably."[44] He presumably meant their cost to the public rather than the cost of their production. The lower production costs of machine-made nails would depress even further the living of the nailers, if they could afford to compete with machine-made nails at all.

The fact that this statement was part of the evidence printed in the First Report of the Midland Mining Commission, points to one of the features which distinguished the Black Country economy from that of Birmingham. As Table 8 indicates the Birmingham trades were by no means so interdependent as those of the Black Country and a depression in one of them could take place alongside the expansion of another. This was not generally the case in the Black Country where the dominance of the iron industry had a marked effect on the economy as a whole. The Mining Commission was part of the Peel Government's response to a miners' strike in both North and South Staffordshire in the summer of 1842. The real concern of Government was the influence that Chartist orators had gained over the striking miners and their sympathisers. In investigating the causes of the strike, however, Tancred very quickly discounted the idea that it was part of a political conspiracy subversive of public order, even though some sporadic acts of violence had been committed, most notoriously in the Potteries following a rousing open-air 'sermon' by Thomas Cooper on the text, "Thou shalt do no murder".[45]

The Chartists had simply capitalised on a situation typical of the locality where a depression in the iron trade led to the shutting down of furnaces and a rapid reduction in the demand for coal, ironstone and limestone. The Oak Farm Company, for example, owned 12 mines as well as furnaces and rolling mills. The response of the mine owners was a concerted decision to reduce wages by 6d a day, from 4/- to 3/6d for the best paid miners, known locally as pike-men, who undercut the thick coal with picks or 'pikes', and a similar pro rata reduction for the other mine workers. They gave notice that this would take place throughout the northern part of the coalfield at the end of July, provoking a strike which was joined by miners in the southern section who feared that their wages were about to be similarly reduced. The strike lasted just over a month, the men eventually being driven back to work at the reduced rates by sheer necessity, but not before they had frightened a Government with no strong local police force to maintain order in such circumstances. The report gives an eye-witness account of the working conditions, with insights into the social and religious condition, of the mining population so vivid that Disraeli lifted a whole section, without acknowledgement, for his novel 'Sybil or The Two Nations' published in 1845.[46]

Disraeli's other unacknowledged source for his portrait of Wodgate, the depraved working class community in Sybil, was the Children's Employment Commission of 1842.[47] Unlike the Midland Mining Commission the Children's Employment Commission was not a response of Government to a political challenge. It was the result of protests by the textile manufacturers that their employment of children had been singled out unfairly for restrictive legislation in 1833 and for the Ten Hours agitation which had gained the support of Lord Ashley. He broadened the scope of Parliamentary activity beyond the operation of the Act for the Regulation of Mills and Factories by proposing a Royal Commission of Inquiry into Children's Employment in general.[48] Together these reports provide contemporary evidence of the impact of the industrial organisation of both Birmingham and the Black Country on the lives of some of their most vulnerable inhabitants and of the efforts of the Established Church to minister to them.

Undoubtedly mining was the most physically dangerous occupation in the area, as Tancred pointed out, using statistics from the registration of deaths during the previous five years.[49] This was largely the result of the actual methods used in working the thick coal, which was where fatal mining accidents were most frequent. The pikemen, working in a line, undermined a section of the coal face leaving only a very thin rib, called a spern, to support the roof. Once the undercutting had progressed upwards to a point, about seven feet above the base of the seam, they worked on scaffolding cutting a channel upwards about 4 feet more thus loosening a section of the roof. This was then brought down by means of long handled picks called 'prickers' which cut away the sperns on either side. The resulting fall of a mass of coal from the roof was both wasteful of coal, as much was broken and unusable, and very dangerous. The operation, known as 'throwing' the coal, was often performed at night when there was less danger to other men and less noise so that the movements of the roof could be heard and the danger of sudden falls reduced.[50] Nevertheless the number of accounts of fatal accidents in Black Country mines given a religious interpretation in the Methodist periodical press is testimony to the depressing regularity of such occurrences. The thin coal and ironstone mines were not so dangerous to work in, hence wages in them were customarily less than those in the thick coal pits. In all the mines naked lights, mainly candles, were employed for illumination thus increasing the risk of explosions from fire-damp, another constant danger. The inherent dangers of the mining operations were compounded by the way in which the vast majority were managed, that is by sub-contractors called butties who had little interest in the safety of the men, only in the short term profit to be gained from the mine.[51]

Next to the miners the iron workers were most in danger from accidents caused by the nature of the smelting, puddling and rolling processes. Burns, scalds and more serious injuries including deaths were all reported as having happened over the previous year in and around Bilston by a local chemist, Robert Bew, in his evidence to Robert Horne, the Children's Employment Commissioner, in 1842.[52] Many factory workers were more in danger from unfenced machinery and the ramshackle buildings in which they had to work than from the nature of the work itself. In places such as Wolverhampton, Wednesbury and Birmingham the Commissioners were horrified both by the conditions they witnessed and by the indifference of many factory owners to the hazards to which their workers, particularly the children, were exposed.[53] Although many small scale industrial processes typical of Birmingham and places like Walsall and Wolverhampton did not appear as hazardous as mining or foundry work they could be just as injurious to health. For example, inhaling the dust produced by grinding edge tools or optical glass, or the vapour given off in brass founding and by the various chemicals and metals used in jewellery making, gold and mercury being a particularly harmful mixture. All was not gloom, many factories and iron works inspected were praised, Horne even refused to name one Wednesbury firm whose owner had promised to amend its ways.[54]

Whilst religious appeals based on the brevity and uncertainty of human life will need to be related to these aspects of local industry other more prevalent features affected the lives of most workers and their families. Three in particular were common to both Birmingham and the Black Country, the generally small scale of industrial units, the employment of outworkers using either domestic premises or small hired workshops and the system of sub-contracting, which left the workers very much at the mercy of those middle-men who employed them, rather than the manufacturer or mine owner who benefited from the end product of their labours. All three features were clearly described by G. C. Allen in his account of the industrial development of Birmingham and the Black Country. For the 1860 situation Allen relied on 'Birmingham and the Midland Hardware District', a composite volume edited by Samuel Timmins for the British Association meeting in 1865, and the third report of the Children's Employment Commission of 1862. The following account is mainly derived from these sources.

The small scale of the industrial units could result from any one of three separate factors. The simplicity of the operation itself might mean that neither large capital nor a large workforce was needed. In addition to the domestic nailers of the Black Country, the chain makers of Cradley Heath, the locksmiths of Willenhall and the pearl button makers of Birmingham come into this category. Indeed it was said that anyone could set up as a pearl button maker for a few shillings. He could hire tools for four shillings a week, and after obtaining shell on credit could sell his product weekly to the warehousemen, called 'factors' in this branch of industry.[55]

More commonly a composite operation was broken down into its component parts, each small enough to be carried on separately at the speed of the individual worker rather than in factory units. In this period Birmingham gun manufacture provided a classic illustration, "The master gun maker – the entrepreneur – seldom possessed a factory or workshop . . .Usually he owned merely a warehouse in the gun quarter, and his function was to acquire semi-finished parts and to give these out to specialised craftsmen, who undertook the assembly and finishing of the gun. He purchased materials from the barrel-makers, lock-makers, ramrod-forgers, gun-furniture-makers and, if he were in the military branch, from bayonet forgers. All these were independent manufacturers executing the orders of several master gun-makers".[56] The harness and saddlery manufacture of Walsall and Bloxwich followed a similar model, most items being made in workshops employing less than six workers. Springs, fenders, awl blades, nuts and bolts were only a few of the products in the same category.

Finally, even larger unified operations, such as mining and iron founding, did not involve individual units on a particularly large scale. Unlike the deep pits of the North-East, which required expert geological knowledge, skilled engineers and considerable capital investment to operate successfully, the thick-coal mines of the Black Country could be sunk easily and employed only a modest number of men. The increasing quantities of coal and iron-stone required by the iron industry were obtained by simply increasing the number of small, shallow pits. A similar situation persisted in the iron industry. As puddling is a manual operation the large ironmaster differed from his smaller neighbour only in the number of furnaces he operated. Each furnace employed about twelve men per shift with a further ten to twenty involved in carrying materials. "The typical ironworks, with three blast furnaces, thus employed 100 to 130 persons".[57] They were comparable to the mines most of which employed a hundred or less. In 1842, for example, there were nineteen colliery enterprises operating 69 pits at Netherton, near Dudley, and employing 1, 932 men and boys, an average of only 28 persons a pit.[58]

Allied to the small scale of most industrial units was the prevalence of domestic outworking many years after it had ceased elsewhere. The disappearance of the skilled male artisan weaver and woolcomber living in an out-township and his replacement by the unskilled, usually female, urban factory worker in Bradford between 1830 and 1850 described by Theodore Koditschek,[59] or the eclipse of the handloom weavers of Oldham and Saddleworth by 1840 indicated by Mark Smith,[60] have no parallels in the conurbation during this period. Instead domestic outworking continued, not only in trades such as nailing, chain making and jewellery in which traditional craft techniques survived, in some cases well into the twentieth century, but also in industries in which mechanised processes were introduced and concentrated in factories. For example, linen buttons were made by machine in three Birmingham factories but they were sewn on to cards by domestic outworkers.

There were some industries, such as glass manufacture, in which domestic outworking played no part and several large factories for complex processes requiring expensive plant such as rolling mills, wire and tube manufacture, but these existed in close proximity to the small scale workshops of the lighter industries and so never displaced outworking as a means of gaining a livelihood.[61]

Wherever they worked the great majority of men, women and children were subject to the sub-contracting system which dominated industrial organisation. The most notorious was the 'butty' system in the mines, which was blamed for virtually all their grievances by the striking miners in 1842 and characterised the Staffordshire coalfield until the late nineteenth century.[62]

Tancred defined the system as one in which, "the workmen are servants not of the proprietor or lessee of the colliery, but of a contractor who engages . . . to deliver the coal or ironstone at so much a ton, himself hiring the labourers . . . using his own horses and supplying all the tools necessary for working the mines".[63] As James Boydell described it, the mine owners pay for the sinking of the shafts, the headgear and a steam engine to work it, "we find engineers, ropes, timber for main roads, skips and rings and winding. The butty supplies the horses, the candles, the powder, the picks, and sharpens them, and lays down the railways and finds timber for propping up the coal." The butty employed an underground supervisor called a 'doggie'. "Doggies are a sort of foremen to the butties and are paid by the butties at a regular price, 1/6d a day more than the men. Their duty is to set men to work, to measure off the coal undergone etc." Boydell defended the use of butties as an inevitable consequence of the mining method used, that of 'stall working'. "The reason why I think charter-masters could not be dispensed with, and the men allowed to get all the profit for themselves, is that the coal falls in such great masses that each man's work would be impossible to be kept separate, since sometimes as much as 20 to 40 tons will fall at once in our very thick seam. Thus you cannot keep each man's work separate . . .and the men would not agree to divide the sum amongst themselves . . . I have often thought over the subject, and wished to do away with butties, and to pay the men directly, but I don't see how it would be possible . . . unless we adopted paying by day work, and that would never do."[64]

There were, nevertheless, a few thick-coal pits which did not employ butties and paid the men on a weekly basis in cash. The mine Tancred himself descended, Heath Colliery in West Bromwich, was one such.[65] These pits, however, required a degree of managerial expertise not readily available in the coalfield. Most

mine owners and their agents, like James Boydell, had more experience of agriculture than of mining and never went underground
themselves. They saved themselves trouble by sub-contracting the
work to miners who had served some time as doggies, amassed a
little capital, and were prepared to undertake the delivery of coal to
the furnace or canal boat at a fixed rate per ton for each grade of coal
on a short term lease or 'charter'. Because the rate was fixed the
charter was necessarily short-term, only a month's notice being
given by either party to terminate the contract. Hence the butty had
a vested interest in getting out as much of the best quality coal as
possible in the quickest and easiest fashion. This led to wasteful
methods, leaving much good coal which it was more difficult to cut
underground, and to a neglect of safety. For example, providing
fewer pit props than was prudent and sending men into dangerous
situations to 'throw' a mass of coal. The Midland Mining Commission found damning evidence of these and other abuses. Pikemen
were not paid for clearing stone from the workings but only for the
length of coal they undercut. They had no control over their long
hours, often being given only half a day's pay after working from 6
am to 2 pm because carts or canal boats had failed to arrive. Most
frequent were complaints of wages being paid at public houses kept
by the butties, so that those who spent most in drink got most work,
and 'truck' payments with only a small percentage in cash, often
deferred to the monthly 'reckoning' when the butty was paid by the
mine owner for the coals or ironstone he had delivered.[66]

Similar practices prevailed in other industries. Domestic nailers
obtained their iron rod on credit from the warehousemen, called 'foggers', who subsequently bought back, at a substantial discount, the
finished products on which the whole family may well have worked
day and night.[67] James Boydell described a Sedgley fogger as,

" . . . a middleman of the worst description. He takes all the
trouble off the nail-master's hands, by taking the iron and giving
it out to the nailers, and collecting the nails when made, and pays
money for them for the nail-master. For this trouble he repays
himself by co-ercing those he employs to buy his goods. He sells
beer and all sorts of articles, clothing, bread, floor, meal &c. I only
point this out as an instance, because I happen constantly pass his
shop daily, and to know it well."[68]

Whilst truck payments were an abuse peculiar to the Black Country, particularly in the iron industry, the sub-contracting arrangements were more universal and not limited to domestic outworkers.
The iron foundries were run on this system.[69] Many other industries
were similarly organised, with an 'overhand' sub-contracting for

the work and paying those whom he employed to do it. The names of these middle-men varied from one trade to another. Butties in the mines, 'foggers' in the nail trade, 'forehands' or 'overhands' in the iron works, 'setters-up' in the gun trade, 'fitters' in the machine-made nail and washer factories and 'factors' more generally, for example in the button, lock, saddlery and harness trades. In Birmingham the word 'factor' denoted a middle-man catering for the home market as only those concerned with foreign trade were called 'merchants'.

Clearly the scope for exploitation was considerable and instances observed by the Children's Employment Commissioners make harrowing reading. One result of this method of labour organisation, however, was the persistence of pre-industrial patterns of work discipline in the factory as well as the domestic workshop. 'Saint Monday' and often 'Saint Tuesday' as well were accepted as regular holidays whilst during the rest of the week long hours were worked to make up the quota of products due to be presented for payment on Saturday. The chief sufferers were the many children who worked alongside the adults.[70] Such a work pattern clearly gave adults more freedom in how they spent their time than more closely regulated factory work, for example, in the textile districts. How, if at all, religious organisations grasped these opportunities must still be considered, but they were a significant part of the social environment in which religious activities took place.[71]

2.8 Comment

The ways in which religious organisations adapted to the enormous changes described in this chapter would be crucial to their success in obtaining regular worshippers. The provision of places of worship, the appointment and deployment of the clergy and the opportunities for recruitment by all denominations from this rising population are closely related to the nature of their work and the possibilities it afforded them for self-improvement. These factors also have a significant bearing on scholarly discussion of the varying patterns of attendance at worship revealed in 1851 and the reasons put forward to explain it. In chapter 5 these explanations are considered in detail in the light of the economic and social characteristics of the conurbation when it is compared with other urban industrial areas. Together with the political and religious background set out in the following chapter they also inform the discussions of evangelism and popular religion which conclude the thesis.

Notes

1   M. J. Wise (ed) *Birmingham and its Regional Setting*, Birmingham 1950, pp. 3-14

2   *VCH Staffordshire*, Vol. 1, London 1908 and 1968, pp.42-43

3   Wise, *Birmingham*, pp. 135-144

4   *VCH Staffordshire*, Vol. 2, London 1967, p.72

5   ibid. p. 108

6   Wise, *Birmingham*, p. 167

7   ibid. p. 232

8   ibid. p.168, *VCH Staffordshire*, Vol. 2, pp. 191-197, 203-204.

9   *VCH Staffordshire*, Vol. 1 p.284; Vol. 17, 1976, pp. 34, 145; VCH Warwickshire, Vol. 7, 1964, pp. 81ff.

10 Wise, *Birmingham*, pp. 193-201.

11 *VCH Staffordshire*, Vol. 2 pp. 114-120.

12 Wise, *Birmingham*, pp. 201-208.

13 *VCH Staffordshire*, Vol. 2 pp. 85-88.

14 Ibid. p.76.

15 See particularly G. C. Allen, *The Industrial Development of Birmingham and the Black Country*, London 1929, pp. 49-98 and the location table on p.98.

16 *VCH Staffordshire*, Vol. 2, pp 224-229, *VCH Warwickshire*, Vol. 7, pp. 105-106.

17 *VCH Staffordshire*, Vol. 2, pp. 269-270.

18 Ibid. pp. 255-256.

19 Allen, *Industrial*, pp. 49-53.

20 *VCH Warwickshire*, Vol. 7, p.98.

21 Ibid. pp. 122-124.

22 *VCH Staffordshire*, Vol. 1 p.283, Vol. 2 pp. 278, 281-2, *VCH Warwickshire*, Vol. 7 pp. 26-30, 76.

23 *VCH Staffordshire*, Vol. 2 pp. 288-298, *VCH Warwickshire*, Vol. 7 pp. 33-37.

24 Wise, *Birmingham*, p.186.

25 *VCH Staffordshire*, Vol. 2 pp. 305-307, 310-313, *VCH Warwickshire*, Vol. 7 pp. 37-40.

26 *Parliamentary Papers, 1852-3, LXXXV*, Population Tables Vol. 1 pp. 25-26. Subsequent calculations are based on these tables, excluding the three rural sub-districts of Tettenhall, Kinfare and Wombourn within the Wolverhampton registration district (no. 379), but including Erdington figures within Aston (no. 395) although Erdington lay outside the borough of Birmingham at that time. Erdington figures are not included in the later analysis of the 1851 Census of Religious Worship for Birmingham and the Black Country.

27 There is one alteration to enable a distinction to be made between Birmingham and the Black Country. This involves displacing Harborne which, though now a suburb of Birmingham, at that time included the much larger Black Country township of Smethwick within the boundaries of its ancient parish. Instead of following Edgbaston, as it does in the printed tables, it has been annexed to the Black Country sub-districts. In Table 3 a gap separates it from Kings Norton which, although not then a part of Birmingham, contained the growing districts of Balsall Heath and Moseley

which, along with other places still rural in the mid 19th century, were later to be included within the city. Two wards of the borough of Birmingham; Duddeston and Nechells and Deritend and Bordesley; lay within the Aston registration district so that Aston, as well as Kings Norton and Edgbaston, has been included alongside Birmingham itself to give the full picture.

28 An Act for building two new chapels in Birmingham, 12 George III, c.64 (cf. *VCH Warwickshire*, Vol. 7 p. 368)

29 Grafton and Reddell, *A brief history of Birmingham*, 1797, p.4, Ward's *Directory of Birmingham 1798*, p.4 cited in Wise, *Birmingham* p. 182

30 T.Tancred, *First Report of the Midland Mining Commission*, Parliamentary Papers, 1843 XXIII, p. iv.

31 W. A. Armstrong, 'The Use of Information about Occupation' in A. E. Wrigley (Ed), *Nineteenth Century Society*, Cambridge 1972, pp. 191-310.

32 ibid. p.193.

33 Occupation Abstract, 1841 Census, *Parliamentary Papers 1844 XXVII*, pp. 164-175.

34 Ibid. pp. 192-199.

35 Ibid. pp. 206-210.

36 Wrigley, *Nineteenth Century*, pp. 255-283.

37 Some slight discrepancies in the percentage totals for Birmingham and the Black Country townships can be accounted for by the presence of an 'unspecified' employment category in the original tables. This amounted to about 2% of the population nationally but, as Booth considered the category unhelpful, he dropped it from his classification, though it remains, of course, part of the original published data. The small size of the entries under this category for the conurbation makes virtually no difference to the overall picture presented in Table 4.

38 This is significant at 1% level with 8 degrees of freedom. (See the Note on page 256 for the meaning of these terms)

39 cf Armstrong in Wrigley, *Nineteenth Century*, pp. 286-7.

40 see A. D. Gilbert, *Religion and Society in Industrial England*, London 1976, p.64.

41 Gilbert *Industrial England*, passim, especially chapter 5.

42 It indicates which townships principally shared those industries which were characteristic of the conurbation as a whole and where they had a particular specialism which was significant in the mid-nineteenth century. The main industries are mining, quarrying, iron founding, nailing, glass manufacture and the making of bricks and tiles. Only wrought nails are included under nailing, machine produced cut nails have been separately indicated. Within the wrought nail industry secondary specialisms were located in different places, for example, Dudley concentrated on horse and mule nails, Sedgley produced spikes, rose nails and gate nails, whilst Halesowen, Rowley Regis and its constituent townships of Old Hill and Blackheath made rivets. (see Allen, *Industrial*, p.75)

43 *VCH Warwickshire*, Vol. 7 p.101.

44 Tancred, *First Report, Midland mining*, p.64.

45 J. Saville, *The Life of Thomas Cooper written by himself*, (London 1872) Leicester 1971, pp. 186 ff.

46 cf Tancred, *First Report, Midland mining*, pp. 92-94 (Mr Parson's Tommy-

shop) with B. Disraeli, *Sybil*, London 1845, Bk. 3 Ch. 3.

47 R. H. Horne, *Second Report of the Children's Employment Commission, Parliamentary Papers XIII*, London 1843, Section Q, especially pp. 38ff. cf S. M. Smith, 'Willenhall and Wodgate; Disraeli's use of the Blue Book evidence', in *Review of English Studies*, New Series 13, Oxford 1962, pp. 364-384.

48 G. F. A. Best, *Shaftesbury*, London 1964, pp. 80-93.

49 Tancred, *First Report, Midland mining*, pp. cxxxv-cxxxvi.

50 Tancred, *First Report, Midland mining*, pp. 25-26.

51 *VCH Staffordshire*, Vol. 2 p.94 and Tancred, *First Report, Midland mining*, passim

52 Horne, *Second Report, Children's Employment*, p.q 49.

53 Horne, *Second report, Children's Employment*, p.Q 8-9, 84-85; R. D. Grainger, *Second Report of the Children's Employment Commission, Parliamentary Papers XIV*, London 1843, pp. 119, 156ff.

54 Horne, *Second Report, Children's Employment*, p.Q 7, 82, 85; VCH Warwickshire, Vol. 7 p.112.

55 Allen, *Industrial*, p.122.

56 Allen, *Industrial*, p.116 quoting Timmins.

57 Ibid. p. 146 quoting the 1863 Children's Employment Commission.

58 Tancred, *First Report, Midland mining*, p. 56.

59 T. Koditschek, *Class Formation and Urban Industrial Society*, Bradford 1750-1850, Cambridge 1990, especially chapter 3, pp. 79-104.

60 M. A. Smith, *Religion in Industrial Society, Oldham and Saddleworth 1740-1865*, Oxford 1994, ch. 1.

61 Allen, *Industrial*, pp. 112-141.

62 *VCH Staffordshire*, Vol. 2, p.100.

63 Tancred, *First Report, Midland mining*, p. xxxiii.

64 Ibid. pp. 64-66.

65 Ibid. pp. 23-27.

66 Ibid. pp. xxx-lxii and passim.

67 Horne, *Second Report, Children's Employment*, p. Q 77.

68 Tancred, *First Report, Midland mining*, pp. 64-65.

69 "The upper part of the blast furnace was in charge of a sub-contractor called a 'bridge-stocker', who kept horses, employed a gang of men, women and boys (termed fillers) . . . to supply the furnaces with the necessary materials . . . . The 'stock-taker' was the sub-contractor in charge of the lower part of the furnace, and his men prepared the sand and looked after the casting . . . As in the blast furnaces . . . sub-contracting . . . was common in the finished iron works. The puddler usually employed one or two men or boys as assistants at the furnace; the shingler had an underhand to help him move the iron; and in the rolling mills the work was done on contract between the employers and the master rollers, who themselves hired and paid the hands they required." Allen, *Industrial*, pp. 146-148.

70 In Birmingham the practice continued to receive critical comment not only from the Children's Employment Commission of 1862 but even from the Reports of Inspectors of Factories in 1874.

71 cf. Chapter 8, note 108 for Monday somnolence at Brierley Hill and Methodist attempts exploit it.

CHAPTER 3

The Political and Religious Background

3.1 Parliamentary representation

The political geography of the conurbation during the first half of the nineteenth century reflected its marginal position during the medieval period. Any one of four counties could be named as the county of their birth by those born within its boundaries depending, very often, on insignificant changes of location. Most of the Black Country lay within the county of Stafford, but this included the parish of Clent, detached within the county of Worcestershire, with its dependent chapelry of Rowley Regis, separated from its parent by the Worcestershire parish of Halesowen. At the heart of the Black Country lay Dudley, a detached part of Worcestershire, surrounded on all sides by Staffordshire, whilst to the south lay Stourbridge, in Worcestershire, together with its Staffordshire suburb of Amblecote. To the east of Rowley Regis lay Oldbury which, together with its smaller township of Langley were part of Halesowen parish and therefore in Worcestershire, though almost completely cut off from their parent by Staffordshire. Within Oldbury was a district called Warley, some of which constituted a detached part of Shropshire, known as Warley Salop to distinguish it from Warley Wigorn.[1] To the east of Oldbury lay Smethwick, part of the parish of Harborne in Staffordshire, whilst to the east of Harborne is Birmingham which, along with Edgbaston and Aston, was in Warwickshire. Thus a ten mile journey from Stourbridge to Birmingham could well lead the traveller in and out of four different counties, depending on the route taken.

This complex pattern meant that no single county Member of Parliament could claim to represent local interests and, as no borough representation existed for the conurbation within the unreformed Parliament, its affairs were somewhat patchily dealt with. By the late eighteenth century the convention was well established that one of the Warwickshire MPs was expected to act as the virtual representative of Birmingham, whilst a similar function was to be

performed for the Black Country by those members for Staffordshire and Worcestershire with property interests and patronage in
the area. Nevertheless the number of county electors within the
divided conurbation was never sufficient to outweigh the voters in
the much larger, predominantly rural, parts of the counties concerned so that a county member need not feel in any way threatened were an election to take place. Moreover the further convention that county seats were divided between Whig and Tory members by a gentleman's agreement meant that contested elections
were relatively rare. Most members were returned unopposed and
represented not so much the commercial and manufacturing sections of the electorate as those aristocratic county families to which
most of them belonged.

The clash between land owning and commercial interests during
and immediately after the Napoleonic wars meant that such 'virtual representation' was no longer assured. In October 1812 a public
meeting, chaired by the banker Thomas Attwood, took place in
Birmingham to censure Sir Charles Morduant, MP for Warwickshire
1804-20, for his failure to present a petition to Parliament pleading
for a revocation of the Orders in Council, claiming that he had "rendered himself unworthy of his constituents".[2] Nevertheless,
although Attwood's banking partner Richard Spooner contested the
seat in the two successive elections of 1820 and 1822 he failed to win
either contest. The voters of Birmingham and Aston numbered only
about a sixth of the total for the county and the country districts
gave him little support. This result convinced an increasing number
of the Birmingham middle class that they needed separate Parliamentary representation, thus laying the foundations of the Birmingham Political Union so prominent in the 1830s.[3]

The 1832 Reform Act enfranchised Birmingham and Wolverhampton giving them two members of Parliament each, whilst
Dudley and Walsall became single seat constituencies. The number
of county seats also doubled so that both Worcestershire and
Staffordshire had two divisions each returning two MPs. East
Worcestershire and South Staffordshire now contained the remains
of the Black Country as well as an even greater proportion of rural
voters since those of Dudley, Walsall and Wolverhampton were now
withdrawn. Wolverhampton Parliamentary constituency comprised not only the town of Wolverhampton but also Bilston and
Sedgley, which together had a greater population than Wolverhampton itself.[4]

The agitation for Parliamentary reform and, subsequently, for
broader democracy, whether through the People's Charter or some
other pressure group such as Joseph Sturge's Complete Suffrage

Union, gained considerable popular support in the area and sustained it by mass rallies and public meetings. These set the tone for more local developments and their excitement so captured the imagination of the young Marian Evans in nearby North Warwickshire that it features in several of the novels she later wrote under her pen-name of George Eliot, particularly Felix Holt and Middlemarch.[5] Nevertheless, even after 1832 not all county elections were contested. The two important seats of South Staffordshire were divided between Whig and Tory once more in 1841 by the same sort of aristocratic gentleman's agreement which had prevailed between 1747 and 1832, thus avoiding an expensive electoral contest. This time, however, the agreement was committed to paper and only ratified by the peers concerned, Lord Hatherton and the Duke of Sutherland for the Whigs and Lord Ward (the future Earl of Dudley) and Lord Bradford (Lord of the Manor of Walsall) for the Tories, after the leading ironmasters had been consulted.[6]

Elsewhere Parliamentary elections were not so quiet. Although in Birmingham two members of the Political Union, Thomas Attwood and Joshua Scholefield, were returned unopposed,[7] riots occurred at the 1832 elections in all three of the new Black Country borough constituencies. In Wolverhampton, for example, a stone throwing crowd intimidated both Whig and Tory candidates and their supporters so that the Riot Act had to be read and the Scots Greys called in from nearby Tettenhall to disperse the mob. The poll was eventually completed and Richard Fryer, the popular radical banker, had to concede second place to the Whig candidate, William Whitmore, whilst another radical joined the Tory in defeat. In these conditions of public hustings and open voting the attitudes of leading members of religious bodies, both Churchmen and Dissenters, could not fail to become well known. The political complexion of the religious leadership, at both local and national level, must therefore be considered as a significant factor in the overall response of different classes and social groups towards organised religion. In this instance the perpetual curate of Bilston, William Leigh, appeared on the platform at the declaration of the poll to support Whitmore and silence the radical spokesman, Simkiss, who was haranguing him. Leigh stated that though he was a clergyman and a clerical magistrate he was not blind to abuses and wished to see them reformed. He did not approve of clerical magistrates.[8]

3.2 Local Government

Historians of the working class and historians of the church have united in singling out the prominence of Anglican clergy on the

magistrates' bench in the late eighteenth and early nineteenth centuries as a key factor in alienating the working class from the Established Church and, in many cases, from organised religion altogether. Their prominence on the bench was a result of two factors.
Following the many enclosure acts of the eighteenth century their
wealth increased as tithes were commuted for money payments or,
more frequently, for land which could then be leased for agriculture, industry or building. This brought many clergy into the category of landowners with incomes of £100 or more, which made
them eligible for nomination to the bench.[9] The need for such
recruits was evident from the increasing business resulting from
Parliamentary legislation and the rise in the number of offences
against persons and property produced by a growing population.
Such offences, if they did not carry a sentence of death or lengthy
transportation, were not tried at the Assizes by a circuit judge but
by the local magistrates. Hence magistrates were required who
were both resident and active in each locality. Magistrates were
responsible for law and order, only they had the authority to read
the Riot Act during public disturbances and call for military assistance to keep the peace. In Warwickshire in 1830 twenty-one of the
fifty-four active magistrates were clergy, most of them residing in
the Coventry area.[10]

For W. R. Ward the chief impact of this increase in clerical magistrates was in the countryside. "Never before or since has England
seen so much clerical government as in the half century before the
Reform Act. The clergy seemed to be profiting from the upheaval in
the countryside and to be the instruments of government in pau-
perising the labourers . . .. there is not much doubt that while com-
mutation of tithe greatly reduced the friction between clergy and
farmers, it helped to alienate them from small freeholders and
labourers". Hence the reduction in the number of clerical magistrates by Bishop Blomfield after 1832 as he "knew what damage had
been done to their pastoral character by their well meaning activities in local government".[11] A. D. Gilbert quotes Cobbett's Rural
Rides in the 1820s in support of this view.[12] Such alienated labourers, moving into the urban industrial areas in search of work, were
not likely, therefore, to be as loyal to the Church of England as the
local parish clergy might anticipate.

The most notorious act of a clerical magistrate in the early nine-
teenth century, however, was not in the countryside but in the town.
E. P. Thompson, in his monumental study of 'The Making of the
English Working Class', analyses in detail the events and conse-
quences of the reform rally in St Peter's Fields, Manchester on 16
August 1819, known thereafter as Peterloo.[13] After describing the

disciplined and peaceful gathering of between sixty and a hundred thousand men, women and children he says, "My opinion is a) that the Manchester authorities certainly intended to employ force, b) that Sidmouth (the Home Secretary) knew – and assented to – their intention to arrest Hunt in the midst of the assembly and to disperse the crowd, but that he was unprepared for the violence with which this was effected."[14] The mounted Yeomanry, supported by the Hussars, advanced into the crowd with drawn sabres cutting about them indiscriminately, killing eleven and injuring over five hundred. The magistrate responsible was an Anglican clergyman, the Rev. W. R. Hay, who "was rewarded with the £2, 000 living of Rochdale. Earl Fitzwilliam, for protesting against the massacre, was removed from his Lord Lieutenancy" (of Yorkshire).[15]

However justified such actions were in the eyes of a government committed to maintaining the existing constitution, of which the Established Church was held to be an integral part, they were seized on by radicals in the towns and used against the Church of England as well as Lord Liverpool and Lord Sidmouth. In Birmingham agitation for Parliamentary reform was organised by George Edmonds, son of the minister of Bond Street Baptist Church, founder of the Birmingham Hampden Club in 1816 and originator of the mass public meetings on Newhall Hill which began in 1817.[16] In the wake of Peterloo he not only organised a large meeting on Newhall Hill to demonstrate sympathy with the sufferers but marched three or four hundred of his followers to Christ Church, the only town centre church with sufficient free seats for the poor, to listen in silent hostility to an anti-reform sermon from the incumbent, J. H. Spry, on 'The Duty of Obedience to Established Government' based on 1 Peter 2 verse 13.[17] After being arrested Edmonds was prosecuted in 1820 for seditious conspiracy, only emerging from prison in 1823 to plunge back into radical politics and, in 1829, to lead his followers into joining Attwood's Birmingham Political Union.[18]

The crazy political geography of the Black Country was overcome by the Lords Lieutenant of Staffordshire and Worcestershire nominating the same men within the area as Justices of the Peace for both counties.[19] As magistrates, once appointed, served for life the results of appointing clergy to the bench would continue as long as they remained in the area. David Philips, in his study of the Black Country Magistracy between 1835 and 1860, tabulates the occupations of those appointed during the tenure of each successive Lord Lieutenant of Staffordshire. They show that twelve out of a total of 167 appointments were clergy but that, of these, only four remained amongst the hundred and four still active on the bench in 1859.[20]

This was not the result of neglect on the part of Lords Lieutenant but of a change of policy by the government which, particularly after 1835, was extremely reluctant to sanction such appointments, all of which needed the Home Secretary's approval. Earl Talbot, Lord Lieutenant from 1812 to 1849, strongly disapproved of manufacturers, particularly ironmasters, being appointed to the bench. As he explained to Lord John Russell in 1835, "The rule has been in this county not to place Gentlemen in the commission of the Peace who are in trade, or they might be called upon to adjudicate in cases where they have an interest".[21]

Talbot, however, had few alternative sources of magistrates for the Black Country whose impartiality would be more apparent than that of the ironmasters. In the absence of resident gentry the clergy were frequently his only resource. However, from 1835, the only occasions on which his nominees, or Lord Hatherton's 20 years later, were challenged or refused were when they nominated clergy. A few were allowed but every one had to be a special case. Supporting Isaac Clarkson, vicar of Wednesbury, in 1837 Talbot wrote, "I receive desperate application from this place and the iron and coal district connected with it for an increase in magistrates".[22] In fact many Black Country clerical magistrates strongly opposed the abuses suffered by the coal and iron workers and were often the only ones prepared to hear cases against their employers. Leigh, speaking at the conclusion of the poll in Wolverhampton in 1832, claimed that, although opposed to clerical magistrates, he had been placed on the bench, after three years as incumbent of Bilston, " at the desire of the inhabitants who appointed him".[23] His initiative led to a private member's bill outlawing truck payments being passed by Parliament, but, as he was the only magistrate prepared to hear cases against the ironmasters, the law was blatantly disregarded.[24] Clerical magistrates were neither prominent on the bench nor, necessarily, alienating Black Country workers from the Church of England.

Before 1835 only Walsall was governed by a charter inherited, in an amended form, from an ancient medieval borough. All other towns, even those which had had some elements of borough status before the sixteenth century like Dudley and Halesowen, were governed by the officers of the manorial courts, the high and low bailiffs and the parish vestries. The tradition in Birmingham, broken only briefly after the Priestley riots in 1791, was for the high bailiff to be a Churchman and the low bailiff a Dissenter. The high bailiff had the right to call a town meeting and Thomas Attwood, when he held this position from the early age of 28, used it to build up support for his particular reform proposals.[25] Several local Acts of Parliament were obtained in the eighteenth century to establish improvement commissions for paving and lighting the streets and removing 'nuisances' as well as controlling markets, tolls from which provided a significant source of income. The first was obtained by Birmingham in 1769, followed by Wolverhampton in 1777 and Dudley in 1784,[26] whilst Walsall and Stourbridge had to wait until 1824 and 1826 respectively before obtaining their local commissioners.[27]

The 1835 Municipal Corporations Act remodelled the Walsall borough charter, transferring to the new council the powers of the improvement commission. Only Birmingham amongst the other towns sought immediate incorporation under the Act, obtaining its charter in December 1838. Wolverhampton waited until 1848 and Dudley until 1865.[28] Whereas other aspects of local government, the poor rates and church rates, frequently proved divisive the cause of town improvement provided a platform on which members of all religious bodies, Churchmen, Dissenters and Roman Catholics, could work together. This goes some way toward explaining the simultaneous occurrence of both conflict and collaboration in local affairs sometimes involving the same people but more often different members of the same religious communities. As Richard Trainor's study of local government in West Bromwich, Dudley and Bilston has shown, social harmony as well as social conformity were values dear to the leadership of all churches in the area, despite the conflicts between them on such issues as church rates and education.[29]

3.3 Poor Relief

The responsibility of each parish to relieve its own poor by means of an annual rate levied on property and entrusted to the elected but unpaid Overseers of the Poor by the parish vestry obtained here as elsewhere in England and Wales. In addition most ancient parish churches had charitable endowments for the benefit of parishioners, including the relief of poverty and sickness. The incapacity of this system to meet the needs of a growing population subject to the vagaries not only of the weather but also of the trade cycle and its disruption through wars and fiscal changes is well illustrated in the case of Birmingham. Although divided into two for ecclesiastical purposes by the Act for the building of St Philip's church in 1708 the town continued to operate as a single parish for the relief of the poor. Building a workhouse in 1733 did not significantly diminish the need for outdoor relief. The overseer's accounts, called the Town Books of St Martin's and St Philip's, begin in 1723 and for the

first half of the eighteenth century the entries give details of payments indicating both a personal knowledge of the recipients of
relief and a generosity toward strangers. For example,
    "14th July 1744, A stranger found bad in the street – 6d:
    10th April 1747, Dovey Eliz. and child 1- 0d
    For mending spinning wheel for ditto 1- 0d
    20th April 1747, Publishing Banns 3/- Fees 5/-
    Maintenance 3 days and sending William Forbs
    to marry Phoebe Proctor 6/6d Total 14- 6d"[30]
Later account books do not give such circumstantial detail, so
overwhelmed were the overseers by the sheer scale of the poverty
to be relieved. Outdoor relief was given to 466 people a week in
1766 rising to between two and three thousand in the 1790s. It never
fell below two thousand a week in the first half of the nineteenth
century[31] Having received its own local Act in 1783, establishing a
Board of Guardians Birmingham continued to administer the poor
law as a separate unit throughout the nineteenth century,[32] spending
over three times more per head of population than the neighbouring Aston Poor Law Union.[33] The Black Country parishes were gathered into five poor law unions under the 1834 Poor Law Amendment Act and, although new workhouses were built, they continued with outdoor relief, especially to the aged and the sick.[34]

3.4 Ecclesiastical organisation

If the political geography of the conurbation was complex the
organisation of the Church of England matched and even outdid it
in some respects. At diocesan level the area was divided between
the dioceses of Lichfield and Worcester. Lichfield included most of
Staffordshire and Warwickshire, though Rowley Regis, in Staffordshire was a part of Worcester diocese. From 1837, however, on the
recommendations of the Ecclesiastical Commission, the archdeaconry of Coventry was transferred from Lichfield to Worcester. The
bishop of Worcester took over episcopal oversight of Birmingham
and Aston, along with Rowley Regis and the Worcestershire parts of
the Black Country. Lichfield diocese retained the rest of the Black
Country but this included the deanery of Wolverhampton, an extra-
episcopal peculiar in which the bishop had no rights of visitation.
    Wolverhampton had been founded as a royal chapel before the
Norman conquest. It had successfully resisted visitation by the
Archbishop of Canterbury in the thirteenth century and continued
to be a collegiate church, with a dean and canons, until 1848.[35] In
1470 the position of dean was annexed to the prestigious royal
deanery of Windsor, though the canons continued to be separate

appointments. Only one dean of Windsor and Wolverhampton ever resided within the Wolverhampton deanery, so that its affairs fell into the hands of the local sacrist. Many of the canons, like the dean, were non-resident. The deanery comprised not only the parish of Wolverhampton but also the chapelries of Bilston, Wednesfield and Willenhall in the Black Country, as well as Pelsall just beyond.

The results of this situation are evident in the patchy records remaining for the historian. For example, the archdeacon of Stafford, George Hodgson, appointed in 1829 by Bishop Ryder, conducted visitations of his archdeaconry on a regular basis in 1829, 1830, 1837 and 1841. However, although his notes on the responses to his queries survive, he could not visit within the Wolverhampton deanery. Nor could he enter the parishes of Tipton or Harborne which, like several others in the diocese, were 'peculiars' attached to the prebendal stalls of Lichfield cathedral.[36] His fellow evangelical, William Spooner, archdeacon of Coventry from 1827, is unlikely to have been less diligent but no visitation records from Coventry archdeaconry seem to have survived its transfer to the diocese of Worcester.

Two aspects of Anglican organisation need fuller investigation; the provision of church accommodation and the deployment of the clergy. For this purpose the most comprehensive baseline is the Report of the Royal Commission on Ecclesiastical Revenues of 1835. There are, however, some important omissions relating to the conurbation, in particular the parishes of Handsworth and Rowley Regis and the chapelry of Smethwick. To this Report further information can be added from the archdeacon of Stafford's visitation returns and the evidence given to the Midland Mining and Children's Employment Commissions of 1842.

The church accommodation situation in 1835 is easier to describe than the deployment of the clergy. Although the ecclesiastical boundaries were not necessarily those of the sub-districts used in the 1851 census, to enable subsequent comparisons to be made the evidence from the Royal Commission Report has been re-arranged to match the order followed in Table 3. This has meant detaching Oldbury from its parent parish of Halesowen and Rowley Regis from Clent. Most of the rural parishes within the Wolverhampton, Aston and Kings Norton districts have also been omitted in order to concentrate on the urbanised area. The diocese to which the parish belonged in 1835 has been indicated by a capital 'L' for Lichfield and 'W' for Worcester in Table 9, which begins with the Deanery of Wolverhampton. The Report included some of the increased accommodation resulting from the Parliamentary grants for building new churches of 1818 and 1824. All such churches are indicated by asterisks, one for the 1818 'million' grant and two for the half million of 1824. Details have been checked by reference to Port's work on the Church Building Commission.[38]

In Table 9 the figures in the column between the name of the church and the accommodation indicate the number of curates reported to the Ecclesiastical Revenues Commission.[39] The Report is not consistent, some dependent chapelries are listed separately from their parish, others are not. Table 9 uses underlining for those with a designated pastoral district, except in the Wolverhampton deanery.[40] There the dependent chapelries are underlined but not those in Wolverhampton which had separate pastoral districts. These are shown by the population statistics given alongside each church.

It will be seen that only in Moseley and Coseley could all the inhabitants be accommodated at any one time in the Church of England and neither of them is typical. In Moseley a sixteenth century chapel of ease of Kings Norton had not yet been overtaken by suburban development. In Coseley a new Commissioners' church in 1829 explains the adequacy of provision in that part of Sedgley parish. "By and large, the architects of the Commissioners' churches worried their heads with two problems only. Firstly how to get two thousand people into a presentable rectangular box, with galleries, at so much a sitting; and second, how to make a great show at the west end and still keep within the spending limit."[41]

Those parishes where over a third of the 1831 population could be accommodated fall into two categories. Most were ancient parishes with medieval churches on the fringe of the conurbation and with little industrial population; Aston, Kings Norton, Harborne and Handsworth. The rest benefited from more recent church building. Erdington opened a Commissioners' church in 1823, at Cradley a chapel of ease had been built in 1792,[42] while in Birmingham St Philip's still kept the modest parish carved out from St Martin's in 1708 whilst the town had expanded around it, creating less than ten per cent capacity in St Martin's parish despite the four additional churches built there since the opening of St Philip's.

Half of the eight parishes or districts which could accommodate over a fifth but less than a third of their inhabitants had also benefited from Commissioners' churches; Wolverhampton St George, Bilston, Netherton and Kingswinford. Wolverhampton St John was built in 1776 and the medieval parish church of St Giles Rowley Regis, described as partly ruinous in 1802,[43] was rebuilt and enlarged between 1840 and 1851 increasing accommodation threefold.[44] Walsall's additional church, St Paul's consecrated in 1826, was built by the governors of the grammar school.[45] Aldridge lay on the outskirts of the conurbation.

Even with the help of Commissioners' churches in Birmingham, Aston and West Bromwich hardly any of the industrial areas of the conurbation could accommodate a fifth of their population. In central Birmingham, Duddeston, Oldbury, Tipton, Halesowen and Willenhall less than a tenth would be able to find a sitting in an Anglican church even if no account were taken of appropriated pews. This element greatly concerned the Church Building Commission which only gave grants on condition that there were "as many free sittings as circumstances would permit", which usually meant about 60%.[46]

The deployment of the clergy is not so easy to tabulate because it is not at all clear from the Report which of those clergy holding livings in plurality were actually resident in the parish for which they are named as incumbent. A little light is thrown on some parishes by the archdeacon's visitations. For example, that the incumbent of Handsworth, though resident, was too ill to perform any of his duties (or even to indicate the value of the living!) and that the incumbent of West Bromwich parish church was resident for half the year.[47] In many cases such evidence is missing so some guesswork has been needed in the following account. Taking the total of the resident incumbents and their curates in each parish or district it is possible to calculate the proportion of clergy to inhabitants in each location. Out of the thirty-eight districts into which the information in Table 9 is divided just under half (seventeen or 44%)had a ratio of one clergyman to every 5, 000 or more inhabitants. This is based on the assumption that two of the pluralists, the rector of Kingswinford and the perpetual curate of Brierley Hill, were resident full time in their parishes. If they were not then the number of places where each clergyman had to minister to 5, 000 or more inhabitants increases to half the parishes in the conurbation, and in some it involves 10, 000 or more. This is shown in Table 10.

Only fifteen out of the fifty incumbents are listed as pluralists, but at least two had further undisclosed incomes from their employment as schoolmasters. The incumbent of St Paul's Walsall was the master of the grammar school, though this may simply have meant that the school income subsidised the church as the living was only worth £50. Rann Kennedy, perpetual curate of St Paul's Birmingham, was also for fifty years second master of King Edward's School, thus augmenting his net income of £170.[48] If these two are included the total rises to just over a third. Six of these were also prebends of either Lichfield or Wolverhampton, in one case both. Seven were parish priests. The remaining two were the Bishop of Rochester, who held the living of Kings Norton which, although only worth £212, was attached to his wealthier living of Broms-grove, and the Dean of Windsor who held St George, Wolverhamp-ton. This Commissioners' church was only worth £155 a year, all of which provided the curate's stipend, but as it served a district of 8, 000 people it raises questions about the pastoral strategy of the joint deanery. The absence of any strategy was exacerbated by the fact that the Dean added at least £640 a year from Wolverhampton to £19, 380 he shared with the canons of Windsor.[49]

Apart from the Bishop of Rochester and the Dean of Windsor the richest pluralists held livings on the western side of the Black Coun-try. The line runs south from Kingswinford through Brierley Hill to Oldswinford before turning east to Halesowen. Within this area three incumbents held livings which combined to give them net incomes, once curates' stipends had been deducted, of over £1, 000. These were the rectors of Kingswinford (£1, 704) and Oldswinford (£1, 131) and the vicar of Halesowen (£1, 305). Within these parish-es the incumbents of Brierley Hill and Lye were much more modest with net incomes of £159 and £400 respectively. The other two plu-ralities belonged to the incumbents of West Bromwich (£558) and Birmingham St Mary (£426), the latter held by a noted evangelical, Edward Burn.

In her study, based on detailed evidence from the diocese of Lin-coln, Frances Knight endorses the view that for clergy, "in the mid-Victorian period £300 marked the boundary between keeping up a respectable middle-class appearance and having to struggle". [50] She quotes Bishop Kaye of Lincoln's 1834 pastoral charge to the effect that £200 was the absolute minimum a clergyman required to dis-charge his parochial duties and even a living of £500 a year would leave little to spare once family and parish obligations were ful-filled.[51] The Ecclesiastical Revenues Commission Report indicated that in England as a whole 54% of livings were valued at £300 and under whilst 16% were only worth £100 or less[52].

Calculating a mean for the conurbation is complicated by the lack of information about the value of two livings, Handsworth and Birmingham St Philip, for reasons already indicated. The value of Smethwick chapel has been derived from other sources and appears to have been £250,[53] whilst that of Rowley Regis was £40.[54] With this proviso the picture in the conurbation is very similar to the rest of the country, 56.25% of the livings being valued at £300 or less and 17% at less than £100. The mean average is just under £360 but this calculation includes two livings worth over £1, 000 (Birmingham St Martin £1, 048, Aston £2, 075) and two just below (Aldridge £905, Kingswinford £961). Removing these four livings reduces the mean average for the rest to £279 which brings them below the level capable of maintaining a middle-class style of living and nearer to the 'absolute minimum' indicated by Bishop Kaye. For an urban industrial area, however, it is well above the mean average of £174 for the thirteen livings in Oldham and Saddleworth tabulated by Mark Smith and much nearer the east midland counties of Nottinghamshire (£293) and Lincolnshire (£285) given by Frances Knight.[55]

The exact financial position of curates is slightly concealed by the fact that in most cases where more than one curate was employed the division of the joint stipend listed in the report is not indicated. In these cases the total amount has been divided by the number concerned. The range of stipends lies between £20 (Wolverhampton St John) and £200 (Kingswinford) with a mean average of just over £96. Only four of the twenty-seven curates received £150 or more, leaving thirteen, or just under half, with between £100 and £150 and ten with less than £100 for their services.

Tables 9 and 10 assume that, unless informed to the contrary, all clergy who were resident would actually perform their duties. This was not always the case and in one instance the presence of a curate was not an indication of the incumbent's pastoral concern but of his incapacity.[56] Looking only at the statistics derived from the contemporary evidence it is clear that, despite the small number of chapels of ease built in the eighteenth century and the ten Commissioners' churches of the 1820s and early 1830s, there were still areas considerably short of an Anglican presence in 1835. If the parishes and districts in which less than a quarter of the population could be accommodated by the Church of England and those in which each clergyman had to minister to 5, 000 or more inhabitants are taken together then a clear picture of ecclesiastical deprivation emerges. Fifteen out of the thirty-eight listed in Tables 9 and 10 fall into this category. Although in administrative terms they account for just under two fifths, in terms of the 1831 population served they amount to two thirds of the total for the conurbation.

These areas of deprivation fall into three groups and include a large part of the industrial heart of the conurbation as well as the central districts of its two largest towns. Wolverhampton St Peter, starting with the most northerly, is separated from Bilston by two districts where newer churches had improved the Anglican accommodation. Once Bilston is reached an unbroken urbanised area includes nine other deprived districts; Bilston, Wednesbury, West Bromwich, Tipton, Oldbury, Dudley, Rowley Regis and Halesowen. This list assumes that the 1851 accommodation figure for Rowley Regis is actually three times the amount available in 1835. It also includes the Netherton district of Dudley for, although a large Commissioners' church had improved the accommodation there, the curate had still to minister to 6, 500 people on £40 a year. Between Halesowen and central Birmingham lie Harborne and Edgbaston but once in Birmingham another area of deprivation is reached with the three central Birmingham parishes of St Martin, St Thomas and St George together with those districts of Aston parish which became part of the municipal borough of Birmingham in 1838, Deritend and Duddeston.

Those districts where both the church accommodation and the proportion of clergy to inhabitants were somewhat better range themselves round the fringes of the conurbation, including Walsall in the north-east and Stourbridge in the south-west, although even here there were places where resources were inadequate, notably Sedgley where only 15% of the population could be accommodated and two clergy ministered to over eight and a half thousand people.

For any improvement of this situation several sustained initiatives would be necessary, given the steady rise in the urban population despite cholera and other serious epidemic diseases. Church building had already begun, assisted by Parliamentary grants and the work of the Church Building Commission, which stimulated the setting up of diocesan and local bodies. There was also a striking increase in the number of ordinations nationally, rising from an average of 270 a year between 1770 and 1810 to 530 a year in the 1820s until between 1834 and 1843 the average became 535 a year. Peter Virgin, who charts this rise,[57] recognised the pressure imposed by the increasing number of ordinands on the finite number of livings, many of them poor and over half, taking England as a whole, in the care of pluralists. Episcopal power in this area was limited, given the principle of the parson's freehold and the tendency of clergy to treat their livings as personal property. The lack of any pension arrangements meant that many, like the vicar of Handsworth, clung on to livings when they were too old or sick to carry out their duties. "As at the end of 1833, 10% of the beneficed clergy were over seventy, and 40% were in their fifties and sixties". [58] New vigour was injected into the episcopate in the 1830s, particularly by Blomfield of London and Phillpotts of Exeter. However, after an appreciative survey of efforts to improve stipends and discourage pluralism and non-residence, Virgin concludes, "What was needed was a determined assault on the system of private patronage, but this never came."[59]

The pattern of patronage revealed by the Report of the Ecclesiastical Revenues Commission illustrates the difficulties facing any bishop intent on improving the Church's presence in the urbanised areas. Of the fifty livings listed in Table 9 the patronage of thirty-four, or just over two thirds, was in the hands of laymen and in sixteen, just under a third, members of the clergy acted as patrons. Six of the laymen were aristocrats and at least two more were substantial landowners. In all these cases they acted as lords of the manor in which the living was situated, controlling fourteen livings altogether. Two livings were in the gift of the Crown, nine in the hands of Trustees, one belonged to a corporation, four to individual laymen, including Sir Robert Peel, and in four the incumbent was elected by the vote of the householders. The clerical patrons ranged from the Bishop of Lichfield, who had control of four livings in the conurbation, the deans of Worcester, Lichfield and Windsor each of whom had two, to parish clergy six of whom had one appointment each, in every case to a daughter church within their own parish. This is set out in Table 11.

In addition to those advowsons pertaining to ancient manors and inherited by their present lords, the right of benefactors and their heirs to present to livings which their family had founded more recently was enshrined in some arrangements. The chapel of ease at Lye, in Oldswinford parish, had been built and endowed by the patron, Thomas Hill, a local manufacturer, in 1813,[60] whilst that of Smethwick, founded by Dorothy Parkes in 1719, continued to be administered by the trustees of her estate.[61] The sale of advowsons, a potential source of abuse which persisted throughout the century, is also illustrated in Table 11. The Holte family, lords of the manor of Aston, one of the wealthiest livings in the area, had died out in the male line in 1782 but, although the manor was still held by their descendants in the female line until 1872, the advowson seems to have been purchased by one of the incumbents, George Peake, vicar from 1823-30. On his death the trustees retained the living for the family and another George Peake became vicar from 1852-79. Another wealthy living, Handsworth, was bought by Sir Robert Peel from the lord of the manor, Wyrley Birch some time between 1830 and 1834, from whom it passed to Sir Robert's brother John, Dean of Worcester. When the Handsworth tithes were commuted in 1839 they brought in £1, 391-6s-6d in annual revenue to the vicar.[62]

Lay patronage did not necessarily lead to nepotism. Although there are some examples in the conurbation, notably Lord Foley at Oldswinford, a living worth £781 kept in the family, it was much more prevalent in the surrounding countryside. At this point in the nineteenth century lay patronage was more likely to result, in the hands of a patron who took his religion seriously, in the appointment of an 'Evangelical' incumbent. The lead in this regard had long been held by the Legge family, Earls of Dartmouth, supporters in the previous century of the Countess of Huntingdon, and lords of the manor of West Bromwich. The most significant initiative by the

Evangelicals, however, involved the foundation of trusts to purchase or establish livings which could then be guaranteed an
incumbent whose theology and churchmanship were acceptable to
that party in the Church of England.

The beginnings of this can be seen in the St Martin's Trust in
Birmingham. From 1781 to 1829 the rector of St Martins, Charles
Curtis, had preferred to reside in his other valuable rectory of Solihull. After his death the appointment of an Evangelical, Thomas
Moseley, enabled significant developments in Anglican pastoral
strategy, including the formation of three new parishes out of St
Martin's for Christ Church, the Commissioners' churches of St
George and St Thomas and the establishment, completed in 1837, of
a trust to control the presentation to these and other livings within
the old parish.[63] The Evangelical group formed a close-knit network
involving many of the leading families in the Birmingham area
including the Calthorpes, lords of the manor of Edgbaston and the
Spooners, one of whom, William, held the family living of nearby
Elmdon and was appointed archdeacon of Coventry by Bishop
Ryder.[64]

The other form of patronage which deserves comment is the election of the minister by the householders of the district. Its origin lay
in the foundation of a daughter chapel in an urban settlement within a much larger parish. That of St John Deritend and the chapels of
St Lawrence Bilston and St Giles Willenhall dated back to the
medieval period, St Thomas Stourbridge was only built in 1726, but
in all cases the cost of maintaining the incumbent, called either the
chaplain or the perpetual curate, was devolved by the patron to the
townspeople who thereby claimed the right to elect their local clergyman. In the Wolverhampton deanery the collegiate church still
retained the right to collect fees and contributions towards the
repair of its own building, a considerable grievance to the inhabitants of Bilston and Willenhall.[65] In all four places the election of a
minister was a lively affair accompanied by all the paraphernalia of
addresses, placards and hustings.[66] The unseemly scenes which
ensued led to the abolition of the practice at Stourbridge and control of the appointment by the Ecclesiastical Commission by mid-
century,[67] but at Deritend it continued until 1890.[68] Whatever its
shortcomings in terms of decorum such a procedure lent a popular
sanction to the ministry of those elected. This was the basis of
William Leigh's claim that his nomination as a magistrate had been
"at the desire of the inhabitants who appointed him".

Birmingham had taken advantage of the translation of the energetic Evangelical Bishop Henry Ryder from Gloucester to Lichfield
in 1824. He it was who ensured the Evangelical hegemony in St

Martin's parish and its daughter churches and appointed like minded archdeacons to Coventry and Stafford, both of whom extended Evangelical influence across a much wider area. His death in 1836, brought on by overwork, was followed by the transfer of Birmingham and Aston to another diocese and a less vigourous episcopal succession in Lichfield. Samuel Butler was 62 when he exchanged the headmastership of Shrewsbury for Lichfield, he was succeeded in 1839 by James Bowstead, translated from Sodor and Man, who was disabled by illness and died in 1843. Not until Bishop Lonsdale arrived from Kings College, London, was episcopal leadership restored in anything like the quality necessary for the continuing demands of the diocese. There is no recent scholarly work on the diocese of Worcester during this period but the impression given by previous publications is not one of vigourous episcopal leadership.

3.5 Dissent

It is not the purpose of this section of the thesis to trace the history of every denomination represented in the conurbation but simply to provide sufficient background information to set the 1851 census of religious worship within its local context. By the close of the seventeenth century all the component elements of 'old dissent' had established themselves in the area but the Presbyterians, successors of those Puritan ministers ejected from the Church of England after the Act of Uniformity of 1662 and their followers, were by far the largest segment. During the eighteenth century their numbers declined and their theology drifted away from Calvinist orthodoxy towards Unitarianism, a doctrine outlawed as blasphemy until 1813. The Quakers, who also had a considerable following in the area in the seventeenth century, failed to expand, in fact their Staffordshire Quarterly Meeting was united to that of Cheshire in 1783.[69]

Several new Independent congregations were established during the eighteenth century as a result of the preaching of George Whitefield and others from the Countess of Huntingdon's Connexion, which had gained the benevolent support of the Earl of Dartmouth. They visited Birmingham, Wolverhampton, Wednesbury and Gornal; Ruiton Chapel, Upper Gornal, in particular owed its foundation to their labours.[70] Independency in Birmingham, however, which was soon to claim the leadership of that denomination in the area and beyond, was the result of a doctrinal schism in the Old Meeting, as the former Presbyterian Chapel was called, in the 1740s. The Calvinist minority, who opposed the trend towards Unitarianism, established themselves at Carrs Lane in 1748.[71]

Keeping track of the various Baptist congregations is not easy as their division between General and Particular, with some Strict and Particular in addition, meant that no one group had an interest in providing an overview so congregations could arise and disappear without record. William Stokes' 'History of the Midland Association of Baptist Churches' published in 1855, gives some indication of the problems. Commenting on Bethel Chapel, West Bromwich, he says that though "for many years sound in faith . . .it gradually sunk into hyper-Calvinism and varied its course only to reach the lower and darker depths of anti-nomianism. It is now extinct." It was, however, still in existence at the time of the 1851 census, though not amongst the best attended chapels. The twenty-two churches named in his book at places within the conurbation may fall well short of the total number in existence earlier in the century as the 1851 census records at least thirty-eight.

A. G. Cumberland records some nine Baptist, thirty-six Independent and four Unitarian chapels founded or rebuilt between 1790 and 1850, in addition to those surviving from an earlier period.[73] The much larger number of Independent congregations is partly explained by the division of former Presbyterian churches, along the lines taken in Birmingham, between Calvinist seceders and Unitarian possessors, a situation which led, in Wolverhampton, to a famous legal case resulting in the Dissenting Chapels Act of 1844.[74] Each of the older towns now had its Unitarian, Independent and Baptist chapels but only in Birmingham, Dudley and Stourbridge were there Quaker meetings, those at Wednesbury and Wolverhampton had both closed and none had survived in Walsall into the nineteenth century.

In West Bromwich the Independents had entirely taken over the former Presbyterian chapel and no alternative Unitarian cause had been established,[75] but elsewhere, in Coseley, Tipton, Oldbury, Cradley and Kingswood, beyond Kings Norton, as well as in the larger towns Unitarian congregations continued though varying very much in vigour. The Walsall Unitarian cause, which had a new chapel in 1827, does not appear in the 1851 census of religious worship and may have suffered a temporary eclipse at mid-century. [76] Certainly Unitarianism in the area suffered from the 'Church and King' or 'Priestley' riots in 1791 which not only destroyed Joseph Priestley's house and scientific equipment but also the Old and New Meetings in Birmingham and the chapel at Kingswood. The fact that these were all rebuilt testifies to its resilience. Unitarians continued to be an active element in Birmingham and parts of the Black Country, such as Stourbridge, throughout the nineteenth century, providing leadership in social and civic affairs.

This is brought out in R. W. Ram's thesis on the social evolution of the five oldest Dissenting communities in Birmingham in the eighteenth and nineteenth centuries. These consisted of the Old and New Meetings (Unitarian), the Bull Street Meeting of the Society of Friends, Carrs Lane Independent and Cannon Street Baptist churches. Ram analyses the social composition of their membership by relating it to the local trade directories and their political influence through membership of bodies such as the Poor Law Guardians and Street Commissioners and, after 1838, the Town Council. Despite having a static or declining membership before the mid-nineteenth century the Unitarians and Quakers overwhelmingly outdid the Baptists in both social position and civic activity.[77] The Independents came somewhere between but nearer the Baptists, without yet making the impact they did later in the century under the leadership of R. W. Dale, whose vision of the Civic Gospel has been so effectively portrayed by Asa Briggs and E. P. Hennock.[78]

Given the fact that about 27% of all families in Birmingham were represented in the trade directories at any one time the average for the New Meeting was 63% and for Cannon Street 20%. A similar contrast is found in civic affairs where the New Meeting contributed out of all proportion to its numbers in Street Commissioners and Town Councillors. "This strength of representation was only ever rivalled by the Bull Street Meeting and Old Meeting among the Dissenting chapels".[79] In terms of sheer numbers, however, Carrs Lane was by far the most successful Dissenting congregation in nineteenth century Birmingham. Whereas membership of Cannon Street Baptist Church, founded in 1737, rose to a peak of 742 in 1837 only to fall away after that, Carrs Lane's membership reached a thousand under the ministry of John Angell James and surpassed it under Dale, who succeeded him as sole pastor in 1859.[80]

3.6 Methodism

Michael Watts in the second volume of his history of the Dissenters, from 1791 to 1859, admits that many Wesleyans were reluctant to count themselves Dissenters in the first half of the nineteenth century, being much happier to associate with the Church of England, in which many of them were baptised, and to attend Anglican Sunday services as a normal activity.[81]

Nevertheless these qualifications do not prevent him from treating them throughout the bulk of the volume as Dissenters in all but name. The issue goes to the heart of the struggle for the definition as well as the control of the Methodist movement following the death of John Wesley in 1791. It was the experience of many contemporary Wesleyans that they could live with this ambiguity quite comfortably no matter how frustrating this is for later historians. Thomas Collins, for example, was born at Solihull near Birmingham in 1810 and baptised in the parish church, he became a Wesleyan itinerant preacher at the age of 21 and remained one for the rest of his life, serving in Dudley in 1841-42. His father, after retiring from the Redditch needle industry, became a town missionary in Leeds and his younger brother was ordained into the Church of England ministry in Liverpool, dying there prematurely in 1857. Collins himself died in 1864.[82]

Benjamin Gregory, on whom Watts relies for his account of the Wesleyan Conference debate on the subject in 1834 and who was President of the Wesleyan Conference in 1879, says, "I have myself been Superintendent of a City Circuit in which one of the two Circuit stewards was at the same time a leader and a local preacher, and churchwarden of the parish church."[83] This dual loyalty was a familiar feature of the countryside. In fact, as Frances Knight points out, the Bishop of Lincoln's insistence in the 1830s that clergy did 'double duty', that is provide two services each Sunday in the parish church, far from improving Anglican attendance simply halved many congregations, especially where Methodists had attended the parish church in the morning and the chapel in the afternoon or evening.[84] Even in the towns, where Methodists were first allowed services in 'Church hours' by the Wesleyan Conference, such ambiguities remained. Birmingham in the 1790s provides a good example.

Just after the 'Church and King' riots of 1791, William Fish, a Wesleyan wrote,

> "Dr Priestley's and the Old Presbyterian meeting are burnt down only ye base walls are remaining. Priestley's dwelling house, library, manuscripts, philosophical apparatus etc. are burnt, several large houses in the outskirts of the Town and Country have shared the same fate. One part of the mob were for destroying our chappells, but the other part opposed them and prevailed because we were Church People. The soldiers arrived on Sunday night and the mob being aware of them left the town; where they are now I am not certain."[85]

The perception of the mob was timely, for the issue of whether Methodists should receive the sacrament of holy communion from their own itinerant preachers and not only those, like Thomas Coke, who were also ordained Anglicans, was about to divide the Birmingham society as it did many others. The issue has been treated, particularly by Bernard Semmel, as symbolic of political differences between democratic and authoritarian elements within Methodism, the former wishing to move openly towards the position of Dissent and the latter clinging to its links with the Church of England.[86] However, as David Hempton has pointed out, the main concern of the majority of itinerant preachers was the continuance of Methodism as they had known it under Wesley rather than any politically derived theory of church order. "What emerges most clearly from the correspondence of the Methodist leaders in the years 1791-93 is that those who opposed the administration of the sacrament and those who advocated it, were forced to construct a higher view of the ministry and the power of Conference . . ..What separated them was disagreement over the policies on which preachers should unite."[87]

John Pawson wrote to Joseph Benson, who was stationed in Birmingham at the time of the riots, "I received another printed letter from Birmingham last Sat. wrote in a remarkable good spirit and signed Julius Hardy by which I learn that you are not all of the same mind respecting the Church, but that you are a divided people . . . The letter I think comes with an ill grace from the Birmingham people. You have three chapels in that town and do you not preach and read prayers in two of them in Church hours? But yet you are a very good Church people notwithstanding."[88]

Julius Hardy, to whose letter Pawson refers, was a successful button manufacturer, nearly 28 years old in 1791, and recently married. He was open minded on the subject of the future of Methodism but not a supporter of Church and King mobs. He repudiated the anti-Republican ideology promoted by the government during the Revolutionary Wars and supported Fox rather than Pitt in politics. He approved the delaying tactics of the 1792 Wesleyan Conference on the sacramental question, as, in Birmingham, it had led antagonistic groups to moderate their views.

"Thus much I am persuaded of, the Methodists of Birmingham, taking them in general, are much more inclined to moderation than at the period of last Conference. Nay, several who some time ago were quite averse to the celebration of that divine ordinance out of the Established Church, I learn are now quite otherwise minded and not only have no objection to it, but are desirous of it. Others I believe have become neutral who, but a little while ago, opposed its introduction with all their might . . . the consequence of which is, I believe, an acquisition of numbers, both ministers and people, to the liberal side."[89]

The Trustees, on whom the society relied to pay off the building debts of the Methodist chapels, were divided whilst the class leaders and most members sided with those preachers who wished to celebrate the sacrament in the chapels.[90] Nationally the issue became linked with that of the ultimate authority of the Wesleyan Conference over the decisions of local society and circuit meetings through the activities of Alexander Kilham whom W. R. Ward describes as, "a brash young man of doctrinaire views and unconcealed dissenting opinions".[91] The details of these views are well expounded by Hempton who sees them as a partially justified, if polemically expressed, plea for greater lay influence in Wesleyan affairs at the connexional as well as the local level. Their failure was as much a result of their timing as of their provocative presentation. They coincided with a national economic crisis exacerbated by the war with France and the Pitt Government's repressive measures against political radicalism.[92] The Conference decisions of 1795, to allow celebration of the sacrament where a majority of the leaders, stewards and trustees requested it, and of 1797, to expel Kilham, led to small secessions in Birmingham. Ten leaders, two local preachers and over a hundred left in 1793 "because of the sacrament being administered anywhere", though two leaders and several members soon returned.[93] Five leaders, three of them also local preachers, left in 1797 taking with them about sixty members. In the absence of the circuit preacher, Samuel Bradburn, "Kilham came and opened a new place (or a place fitted up) for them and began a society".[94]

Circuit membership fluctuated between 1, 600 in 1791 and 1, 345 in 1800, but the transfer of Coventry to head a separate circuit in 1792 means that thereafter the figures represent fewer societies. In any event the Wesleyans were not seriously concerned at a small loss of members so long as the remainder were good examples of piety and morals. Other factors apart from divisions over relations with the Established Church and lay influence on a ministerial Conference governed these fluctuations, notably trade depression and revivalism. These were recurrent themes throughout the first half of the nineteenth century, as were continued problems over internal democracy within Wesleyanism, but up to 1849 no serious divisions occurred in Birmingham Wesleyanism and the position adopted in the 1790s, somewhere between the Church of England and Dissent but nevertheless distinct from either, prevailed.

None of the other Methodist bodies, which began with Kilham's Methodist New Connexion in 1797 and included the Primitive Methodists, expelled from the Wesleyans in 1810, gained anything more than a toe-hold in Birmingham before 1849. In this lies the main contrast between Methodism in Birmingham and in the Black Country. Methodism was established in the Black Country before it took root in Birmingham. Wednesbury, the scene of notorious riots against John and Charles Wesley and their followers in 1743, was the head of the original circuit which included Birmingham.[95] In 1802 it became a separate circuit once more, alongside Dudley from which Wolverhampton was separated in 1805 and Stourbridge in 1829. West Bromwich was separated from Birmingham in 1814 and Walsall from Wolverhampton in 1836 when Birmingham itself was divided into East and West Wesleyan circuits. Total Wesleyan membership figures for the circuits in the conurbation during the first half of the nineteenth century rose from 1, 824 in 1801 to 12, 388 in 1850, an increase of 679%, double the percentage rise in population of 339.5%. The comparison, however, slightly flatters the Wesleyans, for some places, such as Coleshill and Sutton Coldfield in the Birmingham circuits, lay just outside the conurbation. Nevertheless they accounted for only a small proportion of the membership totals compared with those societies within it.[96]

The publication of annual membership returns by the different Methodist bodies means that charting the expansion of Methodism within the conurbation is relatively simple, though providing a convincing explanation is not so easy. Primitive Methodism began to penetrate from its relatively accessible base in Tunstall, establishing a society in Darlaston in 1819 which became head of a separate circuit in 1820.[97] From this beginning separate Birmingham, Dudley, Brierley Hill and West Bromwich circuits were progressively formed as membership grew from 1, 551 in 1823 to 5, 427 in 1850, the year in which the last two circuits were established. This represented an increase of 350%, over one and a half times the percentage increase in population over the same period of 227%. As with the Wesleyans, however, the Primitive circuit boundaries went slightly beyond the conurbation, for example, the Darlaston circuit extended beyond Walsall to Brownhills in 1832.[98]

The most dramatic increase belonged to the Methodist New Connexion whose membership leapt from an overall total of 607 in 1836 to 2, 245 the following year. This, however, was not the result of evangelistic activity but of the divisions within Wesleyanism in 1835 and their aftermath, particularly in the Dudley and Stourbridge areas. The details have been well set out in Roger Leese's thesis on Methodism in the Black Country and need only be briefly outlined here.[99] A complicated series of events leading to the expulsion of Dr. Samuel Warren by the Conference of 1835, ostensibly on the issue of whether a ministerial training institution should be established, drew together a series of grievances both personal, in the case of Warren and some of his supporters, and constitutional, including the exclusion of laymen from Conference.

The rhetoric of the time, convulsed as it was nationally with Parliamentary, municipal and ecclesiastical reform, easily became extreme, both on the side of Conference and its secretary, Jabez Bunting and of those who opposed its authority. The Wesleyan Methodist Association, which Warren set up, drew most support from Manchester, Liverpool and Rochdale but gained a vocal representative from Dudley in John Gordon. He was a former Wesleyan preacher who had returned to Dudley, his family home, after resigning in 1834 because of Wesleyan opposition to disestablishment, the issue on which Joseph Rayner Stephens had been expelled. In the Dudley area he led the agitation for lay representation in Conference on a democratic basis and for self-governing local societies, putting motions to the circuit quarterly meeting and gaining popular support to the extent of removing several societies from the control of the Conference and its ministers.[100]

The spirit of the times is shown in Elijah Morgan's letter to Jabez Bunting in 1836 requesting a move. After describing the agitation and listing the chapels in the Stourbridge circuit lost to the Warrenites he says, "My health has suffered, my spirits greatly sunk and my character blasted far and near; we are called, thieves, robbers, Conference-Devils and that which is worse than all others in the ears of the people Tories".[101] Wesleyan membership in the Dudley circuit fell by over a thousand and by over six-hundred in Stourbridge. Gordon, however, did not stay with the Wesleyan Methodist Association and soon the whole of his Black Country following joined the Methodist New Connexion. Its local membership, nevertheless, failed to increase in the manner of either the Wesleyans or the Primitives. Its leading circuit was Dudley and weaker ones were based on Birmingham, Wolverhampton and Stourbridge. Total membership was fairly static but, in 1850, rose to 3, 277, falling back to 2, 505 by 1852, not far above the level of 1837.

3.7 Roman Catholics

The first half of the nineteenth century was a significant period of transition for Roman Catholics, illuminatingly described by John Bossy.[102] For him three aspects of change characterised the period from 1770 to 1850; firstly the demise of gentry domination over an essentially rural Catholic constituency, secondly the rise of the middle class urban laity, demanding a say in the administration of a church which they were supporting financially and finally the victory of the restored episcopal hierarchy over both laity and clergy. All of these changes would have taken place without the additional factor of Irish immigration and none were dependent on it, though the Irish element did affect the character of urban Catholicism to a greater or lesser degree. The transition is symbolised locally in the changes in the residence of the bishop, who, before 1850, was vicar apostolic of the Midland District. From 1756 to 1804 the bishops lived at Longbirch, a farm on the Chillington estate, near Wolverhampton, belonging to the Giffard family, one of several landed gentry in the area who had a tradition of Catholic loyalty. In 1804 Bishop Milner moved to a house attached to the church in Wolverhampton, which remained the bishop's headquarters until 1841 when Bishop Thomas Walsh moved to Birmingham. Here the chapel of St Chad had just been rebuilt as a cathedral, the first for Catholic use since the Reformation, in the Gothic style by A. W. Pugin, who also designed Walsh's monument after the Bishop's death in 1849.[103]

Bossy's sequence of events, though convincing in outlining the changing power structure within the Catholic community, did not mean total discontinuity with what had gone before. The urban laity, for example, who wished to have Catholic churches and schools worthy of their social position, told the Bishop in 1824, "that the time was arrived, when the Catholics of Birmingham should take that station in the town, to which their increasing numbers, wealth and respectability entitled them."[104] But subsequent improvements in the priest's house, making it "one of the most eligible missionary residences in the Midland District", and the purchase of land for a burial ground involved the laity in considerable debts which were only liquidated by an appeal to the Earl of Shrewsbury, the leading local Catholic peer and patron of Pugin.[105]

Within this period it was also possible for Catholics to continue the sheltered way of life on the estates of Catholic gentry which had typified the previous century. For example, James Plunkett was born in Southampton in 1831, the younger son of a retired army captain from Waterford. His mother came from Stourbridge and when she was widowed they moved to Tixall in Staffordshire, an entirely Catholic village on the estates of the Clifford family. James' autobiographical reminiscences paint a delightful picture of unselfconscious devotion sustained by family and community and re-enforced at Sedgley Park School, to which he was sent in 1840. Here his love of church music, as much as any other factor, led him to consider becoming a priest and he entered Oscott College, another local institution, in 1846, eventually going to Australia to help establish Catholic schools there.[106] His experience is corroborated by contemporary evidence. In his reply to Archdeacon Hodgson's visitation enquiry in 1830 as to the existence of an Anglican Sunday school at Tixall the incumbent simply said, "None, the children being all Catholics".[107]

Nevertheless, despite these qualifications, the growth of the Roman Catholic Church in the area was very much an urban phenomenon, the result of migration from the Catholic countryside, both English and Irish, and conversions from Protestant or irreligious backgrounds. The latter process is well brought out in the account, given in the Catholic Magazine in 1834, of the establishment of Catholic churches in Walsall and West Bromwich. The Walsall church originated in Bloxwich, then a village on the outskirts of the parish, in which a Catholic landowner had left a sum of money to help support a priest to conduct worship in his house. This duty was performed once a month by one of the two priests living in Wolverhampton until a further bequest, in 1800, enabled the purchase of a small shop which was converted into a chapel and served by a succession of French emigre´ priests who built up a congregation numbering 50 communicants by 1807. Their successor, Francis Martyn, further increased the congregation, drawing many worshippers from Walsall, so that, by 1819, he decided to open a second place of worship there. After initially using hired premises, the Assembly Rooms in which he also gave Sunday evening lectures, a "beautiful Grecian chapel" was finally opened in 1827, with generous financial help from the Earl of Shrewsbury.[108]

Martyn, meanwhile, had turned his attentions to West Bromwich, visiting the family of a mixed marriage, "being permitted by the master of that family, though a Protestant, to instruct his children, Mr M attended at the house once a week; and, finding that Protestants were eager to attend and hear him, he commenced a regular series of instructions, the fruit of which was the gaining of many souls to the true faith".[109] The resulting "handsome chapel dedicated to St Michael and the Holy Angels" was opened in 1832, over a third of the cost being met by the first resident priest, the Hon. and Rev. George Spencer.[110] He was the youngest son of the second Earl Spencer, born in 1799, educated at Eton and Cambridge and ordained rector of a family living in Northants in 1825. He was then an Evangelical Anglican who had scruples about the damnatory clauses of the Athanasian Creed. His opinions began to change after correspondence about Catholicism with an anonymous Frenchwoman and friendship with a recent convert, Ambrose Philips. He became a Roman Catholic in 1830, attending the English College in Rome for two years before taking up his appointment in West Bromwich, where he, "entered upon his missionary career with alacrity and zeal."[111]

The first Catholic chapel in the conurbation, after the Revolution of 1688, was part of Giffard House, built on their Wolverhampton land and with money donated by the Giffard family in 1743. It was set back from the Stafford road and approached through a court, thus assisting the anonymity of the worshippers who "were obliged", related a Mr Green, "to steal our way in small parties, or rather singly and by different and circuitous routes, to avoid observation".[112] The various Catholic Relief Acts of 1778, 1791 and 1829 were followed by more open provision, including the enlargement of the Wolverhampton chapel, the opening of those at Bloxwich, Walsall and West Bromwich already mentioned, and others in Birmingham (1786, 1809, 1849), Sedgley and Stourbridge (1823), Bilston (1834), Dudley (1842) and Oscott, just north of Birmingham in Handsworth parish. A house at Oscott had been built in about 1752 as a residence for the bishop, though he never actually lived there. A chapel was added in 1788 and a college, initially a seminary for ordinands, commenced in 1794. Under the presidency of the future Cardinal Wiseman, from 1838 it became also a public school moving to grander premises partly designed by Pugin. The other Catholic residential school, intended for the sons of the commercial middle class and already mentioned, Sedgley Park on the outskirts of Wolverhampton, was founded in 1762.[113]

The impact of Irish immigration on the Roman Catholic Church in Birmingham during the first half of the nineteenth century has been investigated by Judith Champ.[114] Compared with the situation in Liverpool or Manchester, Irish Catholic immigrants to Birmingham never swamped the native English, arriving later and in smaller numbers than in those more northern towns. They found a Catholic Church already well established, sympathetic toward the Irish cause, especially in the person of its leading priest from 1824 (until his opposition to the Bishop's cathedral project led to his removal in 1842), Thomas McDonnell.[115] The new arrivals tended to favour only one of the two chapels existing in Birmingham before the foundation of the Oratory in 1849. The 'Irish' church in effect was the least socially favoured, initially this was the 'new' chapel of St Chad, but, when this was rebuilt as a prestigious Cathedral in 1841, Irish allegiance was transferred to St Peter's, the original chapel dating back to 1786. The total number of worshipping Catholics in the town rose dramatically in the first half of the century reaching around 15, 000 by 1851. Judith Champ reckons, on the basis of an analysis of surnames in the registers, that only about half of this Catholic population was of Irish origin. Nevertheless they included a high percentage of poor manual labourers, altering the social composition of the community which had previously matched that of the town as a whole. "Whatever the success of the Catholic revival in Birmingham (and it was considerable) it was powerless to prevent the average urban Catholic from being less affluent, less stable, in poorer health and housing conditions, and more divided from his fellow Catholics in 1850 than he was in 1800".[116]

Notes

1   *VCH Worcestershire*, Vol. 3, 1913 (1971) p.136, only in 1844 was the whole transferred to Worcestershire.
2   *VCH Warwickshire*, Vol. 7, p.290
3   ibid. p.291
4   Table 1 and V. I. Tunsiri, 'Party Politics of the Black Country 1832-67', Birmingham MA 1964.
5   cf. R. Ashton, *George Eliot a life*, London 1996 passim, especially pp. 12-16, 280-287, 296-328.
6   P. J. Doyle, 'The General Election of 1841; the representation of South Staffordshire', in *South Staffordshire Archaeological and Historical Society Transactions*, Vol. XII, 1971, pp. 57-61.
7   C. Gill, *History of Birmingham*, Vol. 1, Oxford 1952, p.212
8   G. P. Mander and N. W. Tildesley, *History of Wolverhampton*, Wolverhampton 1960, pp. 168-173.
9   W. R. Ward in, R. E. Davies, A. R. George and E.G. Rupp (Eds.), *A History of the Methodist Church in Great Britain*, Vol. 2, London 1978, pp. 21-27, Gilbert, *Industrial England*, pp.80-81.
10 M. R. Rowlands, *The West Midlands from AD1000*, London 1987, p. 211.
11 Ward in R. E. Davies et al, *Methodist Church*, Vol. 2, p. 25
12 Gilbert, *Industrial England*, p. 81
13 E. P. Thompson, *The Making of the English Working Class*, London 1963, Harmondsworth 1970, pp. 734-768.
14 ibid. p. 750.
15 ibid. p. 751.
16 see R. B. Rose, 'The Origins of Working Class Radicalism in Birmingham', in *Journal of Labour History iv*, November 1965, Canberra, pp. 6-14, especially 11-12.
17 *Aris's Birmingham Gazette*, 22 November 1819, *VCH Warwickshire*, Vol. 7, p.290
18 Rose, 'Radicalism', p.12.
19 D. Philips, 'The Black Country Magistracy 1835-60', in *Midland History*, Vol. 3, Birmingham 1976, p.164.
20 Philips, 'Magistracy', pp. 162-163.
21 quoted by Philips, 'Magistracy', pp. 168-169. These particularly involved the Master and Servant Act of 1823, the Truck Act of 1831 and the Mines Regulation Act of 1842. In 1837 he put the point more forcefully, such manufacturers, if appointed to the bench, "residing in a district in which the trade they follow is almost the exclusive trade of that neighbourhood, . . . will have to settle disputes in the very trade and manufacture in which they are engaged. I fear it will be difficult to persuade the people, that however respectable they may be, they have not had one Eye to their their own

Interest in forming these decisions"
22 ibid. p.172.
23 Mander and Tildesley, *Wolverhampton*, p.173.
24 Horne, *Second Report, Children's Employment*, p.Q68.
25 cf. D. J. Moss, *Thomas Attwood*, Montreal and London 1990, pp. 5, 34, 36-43 and passim.
26 Rowlands, *West Midlands*, pp.192-193.
27 *VCH Staffordshire*, vol. 17, (1976) p. 217, *VCH Worcestershire*, Vol. 3, London 1913 (1971) p.215.
28 C. Gill, *Birmingham*, p. 225, Rowlands, *West Midlands*, p. 285, VCH Staffordshire, Vol. 17 p. 217.
29 R. H. Trainor, *Black Country Elites*, Oxford 1993, pp. 182-183 and passim.
30 Town Book of St Martins and St Philips, Birmingham Reference Library (BRL) no. 380973
31 VCH *Warwickshire*, Vol. 7, p.323.
32 C. Gill, *Birmingham*, p. 149.
33 VCH *Warwickshire*, Vol. 7, p.323.
34 for details see G. J. Barnsby, 'Social conditions in the Black Country in the nineteenth century', Ph D Birmingham 1969, which has a chapter on poor relief, mostly devoted to workhouse conditions.
35 see *VCH Staffordshire*, Vol. 3, pp. 323-330.
36 see details in Staffordshire Record Office *Cumulative Hand List Part 1*, Lichfield Joint Record Office, Stafford County Council 1970, Appendix 2.
37 *Parliamentary Papers, House of Commons*, 1835, XXII.
38 M. H. Port, *Six Hundred New Churches*, London 1961, Appendix 1.
39 The population and church accommodation figures for Handsworth have been taken from the archdeacon's visitation of 1830; D. Robinson (Ed) 'Visitations of the Archdeaconry of Stafford 1829-1841', *Collections for a History of Staffordshire*, Fourth series, Vol. 10, Stafford 1980, pp. 12-13. Those of Rowley Regis and Smethwick come from the 1831 population census and the original returns for the 1851 census of religious worship. The Royal Commission Report stated simply that at Oldbury church accommodation was "sufficient", but the Midland Mining Commission said that it was only sufficient for 254 people before the rebuilding of the church in 1841, cf. Tancred, *First Report, Midland mining*, p.37.
40 The case of St James Ashsted in the Duddeston district of Aston parish is not clear. It is listed separately in the Commission Report but, although opened as a proprietary chapel in 1791, it did not receive a pastoral district until 1853 yet the Report appears to have assumed that it had some responsibility for the whole population of Duddeston, cf. *VCH Warwickshire*, Vol. 7, p.364
41 J. Summerson, *Architecture in Britain 1530-1830*, Harmondsworth 1953, p.318.
42 see M. Ransome, 'The State of the Bishopric of Worcester 1782-1810', *Worcestershire Historical Society, New Series*, vi, Worcester 1968, p. 40.
43 Ransome, *Worcester*, p.47.
44 The figure given for Rowley Regis in Table 9 is, therefore, unlikely to reflect the 1835 situation, cf. F. W. G. Barrs, *Four sermons by the late Rev George*

Barrs, 2nd Edition, Birmingham 1879, p. xviii

45 *VCH Staffordshire*, Vol. 17, p.236.

46 Port, *Six Hundred*, p.32, O. Chadwick, *The Victorian Church Part 1*, 3rd Edition, London 1971, p.330

47 D. Robinson, *Stafford*, pp. 13, 30.

48 *VCH Warwickshire*, Vol. 7, p.371.

49 Another questionable plurality was that of St Philip, Birmingham, an important town centre church even though it served a far smaller parish than St Martin's. This was attached to the Treasurership of Lichfield cathedral and no income is given. The entry for the canon residentiary of Lichfield, who was also treasurer and held a perpetual curacy in Shropshire, is virtually impossible to make sense of in financial terms but he is unlikely to have made much contribution to the church life of Birmingham. The two other prebends of Lichfield, the incumbents of Tipton and Harborne, gained between £300 and £400 a year from their Black Country parishes in addition to undisclosed prebendal income. The prebends of Wolverhampton likewise do not declare their additional income but the incumbents of St Peter's and St Paul's were each prebends as was the perpetual curate of Wednesfield. Perhaps because Wednesfield was only worth £63 he paid his curate £28 whilst holding prebendal stalls at Lichfield as well as Wolverhampton, two livings in Staffordshire, one in Shropshire and one in Cheshire. These gave him an income of at least £535 in addition to the value of his prebendal stalls.

50 F. Knight, *The nineteenth-century Church and English society*, Cambridge 1995, p. 131 referring to A. Haig, *The Victorian Clergy*, London and Sydney 1984, p.304.

51 Ibid. p. 132.

52 cf P. Virgin, *The Church in an Age of Negligence*, Cambridge 1989, p.277.

53 *VCH Staffordshire*, Vol. 17, p.124.

54 Ransome, *Worcester*, p.47.

55 M. A. Smith, *Industrial Society*, p.47. Knight, *Nineteenth Century*, p.131.

56 see G. Robson, 'Between Town and Countryside', in D. Baker (Ed.) *Studies in Church History*, Vol. 16, Oxford 1979, p. 404; N. W. Tildesley, 'William Moreton of Willenhall', in *Historical Collections, Staffordshire Fourth Series*, Vol. 6, Stafford 1970 pp. 171-185.

57 Virgin, *Negligence*, pp. 135-137, 202.

58 Ibid. pp. 161-163, 258.

59 Ibid. p.265.

60 see E. Hopkins, 'Religious Dissent in Black Country Industrial Villages in the First Half of the Nineteenth Century', in *Journal of Ecclesiastical History*, Vol. 34, no. 3 July 1983, p.414.

61 *VCH Staffordshire*, Vol. 17, p.123.

62 *VCH Warwickshire*, Vol. 7, pp. 60, 369, 375.

63 cf D. E. H. Mole, 'The Church of England and Society in Birmingham 1830-66', Ph.D. Cambridge 1961

64 see L. Davidoff and C. Hall, *Family Fortunes*, London 1987, pp. 84-85.

65 *VCH Staffordshire*, Vol. 3, pp. 328-329.

66 for Bilston and Willenhall see Robson, 'Town', pp. 411-413.

67   *VCH Worcestershire*, Vol. 3, p.221.
68   *VCH Warwickshire*, Vol. 7, p.364.
69   *VCH Staffordshire*, Vol. 3, p.123.
70   F. W. Hackwood, *Sedgley Researches*, Dudley 1898, pp. 74-75.
71   J. A. James, *History of Carrs Lane Church*, 1850, in ibid. *Autobiography*, London, 1864, p.25.
72   W. Stokes, *History of the Midland Association of Baptist Churches*, Birmingham 1855, q.v.
73   A. G. Cumberland, 'Protestant Nonconformity in the Black Country', Birmingham MA, 1951, p.61.
74   Ibid. chapter 3. *VCH Staffordshire*, Vol. 3, pp. 130-131.
75   *VCH Staffordshire*, Vol. 17, p.68.
76   Ibid. p. 249.
77   R. W. Ram, 'The Social Evolution of Five Dissenting Communities in Birmingham 1750-1870', PhD. Birmingham 1972, summarised in R. W. Ram, 'Influences on the patterns of belief and social action among Birmingham Dissenters between 1750 and 1870', in A. Bryman (Ed), *Religion in the Birmingham Area*, Birmingham University 1976, pp. 29-44.
78   A. Briggs, *Victorian Cities*, London 1963 (Harmondsworth 1968), pp. 184-240, E. P. Hennock, *Fit and Proper Persons*, London 1973, pp. 61-176.
79   Ram in Bryman, *Religion*, p.34.
80   *VCH Warwickshire*, Vol. 7, pp. 436, 449; A. W. W. Dale, *Life of R. W. Dale of Birmingham*, London 1898, (1902 Edition) pp. 72, 141-142.
81   M. R. Watts, *The Dissenters*, Vol. 2, Oxford 1995, pp. 175, 463.
82   S. Coley, *Life of Thomas Collins*, London 1868, passim but especially pp. 28, 146, 150, 412.
83   B. Gregory, *Sidelights on the Conflicts of Methodism 1827-1852*, London 1898, p.244.
84   Knight, *Nineteenth Century*, pp. 24-36, 75-86.
85   Methodist Central Archives (MCA) John Rylands University Library, Manchester, Manuscript correspondence of Methodist Preachers, William Fish to Walter Churchy, 1791. (underlining original)
86   B. Semmel, *The Methodist Revolution*, London 1974 particularly pp. 114-124.
87   D. Hempton, *Methodism and Politics in British Society 1750-1850*, London 1984, pp. 61-62.
88   MCA Manuscript correspondence, John Pawson to Joseph Benson, 4 July 1791.
89   A. M. Banks (Ed.) *The diary of Julius Hardy, Button-maker of Birmingham*, privately printed 1973, page 73,
90   MCA, Manuscript diary of James Rogers, 8 January, 16 March 1795. See also T. Jones to J. Benson,
91   W. R. Ward, *Religion and Society in England 1780-1850*, London 1972, p.34
92   Hempton, *Methodism*, pp. 65-73.
93   MCA, Manuscript correspondence, John Pawson to Charles Atmore, 9 October 1793.
94   MCA, Manuscript correspondence, Samuel Bradburn to Mr Wood, 3 January 1799.
95   Anonymous pamphlet, *Some Papers giving an account of the Rise and progress*

of Methodism at Wednesbury in Staffordshire and other Parishes adjacent: as likewise of the late Riot in those Parts, London 1744, passim (BRL 342989); H. D. Rack, *Reasonable Enthusiast*, London 1989, p.272.

96 Figures are taken from the annual returns published in the Minutes of the Wesleyan Conference.

97 J. S. Werner, *The Primitive Methodist Connexion*, Madison (Wisconsin) 1984, p.118.

98 Walsall Reference Library, Manuscripts, Primitive Methodist membership rolls, Darlaston circuit.

99 R. Leese, 'The impact of Methodism on Black Country society 1743-1860', Ph.D. Manchester 1973, pp. 150-197.

100 See also Ward, *Religion*, pp. 161-174 for a detailed account of the dispute.

101 MCA, Manuscript correspondence, Elijah Morgan to Jabez Bunting 18 July 1836. (underline original)

102 J. Bossy, *The English Catholic Community 1570-1850*, London 1975. esp, pp. 295-363.

103 *VCH Staffordshire*, Vol. 3, p. 110, *VCH Warwickshire*, Vol. 7, p. 407.

104 'Catholic chapels in Staffordshire', in *Catholic Magazine*, No. V, Birmingham, 1834, p. 315.

105 ibid. p.316.

106 Birmingham Archdiocesan Archives, Oscott College, Manuscript Autobiographical Reminiscences of James Plunkett, written 1893.

107 D. Robinson, *Stafford*, p.70.

108 *Catholic Magazine*, No. V, 1834, pp. 307-312. (see also *VCH Staffordshire*, Vol. 17, p.240.)

109 Ibid. p. 312. (see also Bossy, *Catholic*, pp. 317-318.)

110 *VCH Staffordshire*, Vol. 17, p.61.

111 Private manuscript journal and papers at Order of Passionists, St Joseph's House, Highgate, London. see also G. Spencer 'A short account of the conversion of the Hon. and Rev. Geo. Spencer to the Catholic Faith' in *Catholic Magazine* Vol. III, London 1839, pp. 227-236 and U. Young, *Life of Father Ignatius Spencer*, London 1933.

112 *Catholic Magazine*, No. V, 1834, p. 306.

113 Ibid pp. 305-320, 382-384. *VCH Warwickshire*, Vol. 7, pp. 399-400, Bossy *Catholic* pp. 275, 356.

114 J. F. Champ, 'Assimilation and separation: the Catholic Revival in Birmingham c.1650-1850', Ph D. Birmingham 1984, especially pp. 27-49.

115 Ibid. pp. 162-184 and J. F. Champ, 'Priesthood and Politics in the nineteenth century: the turbulent career of Thomas Mc Donnell', in *Recusant History*, 18 (1987) pp. 289-302.

116 J. F. Champ, 'The demographic impact of Irish immigration on Birmingham Catholicism 1800-1850', in W. J. Sheils and D. Wood (Eds.) *Studies in Church History*, Vol. 25, Oxford 1988, p.242.

CHAPTER 4

The 1851 Census of Religious Worship in Birmingham and the Black Country

4.1 Mann's Report on the 1851 Census

From the very beginning the author of the Report on the 1851 Census of Religious Worship had to defend it against criticisms. Most of these stemmed from the desire to use it for purposes to which it was inherently unsuited and for which it never purported to provide statistical evidence. This was particularly true of attempts by controversially inclined 'Free Churchmen' to use its findings as proof of the Church of England's failure to provide for the spiritual needs of the nation and as support for their call for its disestablishment.

As far back as 1834, at a time of petitions from Dissenters in favour of their right to conduct their own marriages, enter the ancient Universities and be relieved from having to pay church rates, the Congregational Union conducted a survey of the 'Hearers, Communicants and Scholars Belonging to Churchmen, Dissenters and Wesleyans in Two Hundred and Three Towns and Villages' with a view to proving that the Established Church did not have the support of the majority of the nation. The results of the survey were published in the Congregational Magazine and have more recently been used by Robin Gill to establish possible comparisons with the 1851 returns.[1] By 1851 Dissenting agitation for disestablishment had its own organisation and could be guaranteed to use the census material to point to Anglican weaknesses. The Liberation Society's pamphlet, 'Voluntaryism in England and Wales or, the Census of 1851', was just one of the attempts to manipulate the statistics for polemical purposes.[2]

Equally strong on the other side were those Anglicans who condemned it for failing to reveal the supposed allegiance of the majority of the English people, if not the Welsh and Scots, to the Church of England, even though they may not be regular attenders at its Sunday services, particularly those held on Sunday 30 March 1851. Bishop Samuel Wilberforce of Oxford was the most prominent critic of the census on these grounds and attempted to discredit it by claiming that Anglicans had under-represented their true situation whilst Dissenters and Roman Catholics had deliberately sent in exaggerated returns, concluding, "Thank God the great majority of the people of this country do still belong to the Established Church".[3]

Attempts to use the figures for attendances given in the report to compute the actual number of attenders were begun by Horace Mann himself, although on a formula which, he almost admitted, was more favourable to the Church of England than to nonconformity. He compared the position of the Church of England with that of other Christian denominations by adding together the whole recorded attendance at morning services, half of those attending in the afternoon and a third of the evening attendance in order to take account of those who might have attended more than one service on census Sunday. "For my own part I have seen no reason to abandon my conviction of the general fairness of this estimate, which undoubtedly is so far from being unfavourable to the Church of England, that some of the Dissenters – the Wesleyans, I believe – have attacked it as being unfair to them; as it is their most numerous service which has been diminished by two thirds, while the Church of England suffers that diminution to its least numerous service."[4]

No matter what formula is used it is not really possible to get more than an approximation of the actual number of attenders. David Thompson attempted an alternative formula in his work on Leicestershire, by comparing the attendance at churches and chapels open at the same time of day and removing the numbers of Sunday school scholars from the totals. This was particularly relevant for rural places of worship where three services on a Sunday were the exception. In those circumstances comparing the best attended services gave him grounds for "a comparison of religious affiliation".[5] Such comparisons depend on work on the original returns from which alone the deduction of Sunday school scholars can be made and the actual times of services determined. Even then there are difficulties in deciding which figures record actual attenders as distinct from an estimate. The rounded nature of many of the figures, particularly those given for the larger congregations, suggests the latter possibility.

These attempts to use the census for a purpose for which it was inherently unfitted have prejudiced many historians against it as a reliable source. For example, Owen Chadwick in his history of the Victorian Church and, more recently, Norman McCord for whom "its evidence is flawed."[6] Mann himself was at pains to counteract such prejudices at the time. He pointed out the limitations of the data available from the census but defended its reliability within those limitations.[7] The limitations, however, did not invalidate the contrasts which Mann pointed out between the levels of provision for and attendance at worship in different parts of the country, between different denominations, and between the villages and rural towns and the growing urban industrial centres.[8] This latter contrast was, for him, by far the most significant and produced, in his introduction to the Report on the Census, a memorable claim that it was the working classes who were absent from worship in these places because of a breakdown in social control.

"But our modern populous towns, erected more for business than for residence, mere aggregates of offices and workshops and overcrowded dwellings of the subordinate agents of industry, are inhabited by none whose means enable them to reside elsewhere. . . . The masses, therefore, of our large growing towns, connected by no sympathetic tie to those by fortune placed above them, form a world apart, a nation by themselves; divided almost as effectively from the rest as if they spoke another language or inhabited another land."[9]

This contrast between urban and rural churchgoing and, particularly, between industrial towns and other urban centres, has recently, through the use of electronic calculators, been given a statistical basis which Mann would have envied.

4.2 Inglis and the contrast between rural and urban church attendance

The first to use the new techniques to analyse the published data was K. S. Inglis in a pioneering article in which the attempt to compute actual attenders on census Sunday was sensibly abandoned. Instead the figures for morning, afternoon and evening attendances were used to produce an 'Index of Attendance' by dividing the total attendance on census Sunday by the population of the town or county as indicated by the 1851 Census of Population.[10] Inglis concentrated his attention on the urban areas, helped by the published Report which gave, in Table F, the totals for returns from all the larger towns, together with their 1851 population.

His figures seemed to confirm Mann's view that the larger the town the smaller the proportion of its population at Sunday worship. Inglis calculated the Index of Attendance for all places of worship in England and Wales as 61, for rural areas and small towns it was 71.4 whilst for towns with a population of over 10, 000 it was 49.7.[11] Only three large towns had an index exceeding that for rural

areas, Colchester, Ipswich and Bath. These were all in the south and
remote from the manufacturing districts. He discerned a similar
pattern in those towns with both the highest and the lowest figures
for church attendance concluding,

"These towns in which church-going was lowest included every
large town described in the general census report as a cotton
town, and the two greatest woollen towns, Leeds and Bradford.
The list contains every large coal town (except Wolverhampton),
the two great hardware towns Sheffield and Birmingham, and
every large town in Lancashire except Wigan and Rochdale.
Absence from religious worship, then, was most common where
the largest numbers of working class people lived – in London
and in many of the towns where the industrial revolution was
wrought."[12]

Within this conclusion, however, the case of Wolverhampton
stands out. Along with Bristol (56.7) it was the only town of over
100, 000 population and an Index of attendance (at 53.1) above that
for large towns (49.7). Its proximity to Birmingham, thirteen miles
away with an Index of 36.01, provides an even greater contrast and
raises doubts about the simple equation of industrialisation and
absence from public worship.

Inglis' further analysis of urban church-attendance in terms of its
denominational pattern pointed out the particular importance of
Methodism in sustaining what church, or rather chapel attendance
there was in most industrial towns.[13] This factor can be examined in
Birmingham and the Black Country by turning from the published
statistics to the original returns preserved in the Public Record
Office.[14]

The shortcomings of generalisations, like those of Inglis, based
only on the urban statistics in the published report, were revealed
by Hugh McLeod, who showed that, generally, high urban church
attendances occurred in regions of even higher rural attendance so
that a regional pattern, rather than a simple urban/rural contrast
emerged.[15] He explained the higher than average index of attendance recorded of Bristol (56.7), for example, by pointing to the
even higher figures of 69% for Somerset and 69.7% for Gloucestershire. This suggested that patterns of church attendance, established over many years in the countryside, were carried with them
by rural immigrants into the towns.[16] These patterns affected low as
well as high church attendance in industrial towns. The exceedingly low attendance at worship on Tyneside, for example, with indexes of attendance for Newcastle upon Tyne of 40% and Gateshead of
32.9%, were matched in rural Durham and Northumberland which

only reached 41%. In fact one of the lowest church attendances on census Sunday was 24.1% at Haltwhistle in Northumberland. Thus any analysis of the Returns for Birmingham and the Black Country must also take account of the rural hinterland from which these growing industrial towns drew most of their immigrant population.

The West Midlands appears to be the one area of the country which McLeod's hypothesis does not fit. He calculates the average index of attendance for rural areas as 64.8. In the West Midlands only Warwickshire exceeds this figure. My own calculations based on the published tables give an index of 67.09 for the rural parts of the county. Yet Birmingham has a very low index of 36.01. Elsewhere the picture is more bizarre. Staffordshire has a very low index of rural church attendance, 49.62. Wolverhampton, on the other hand, has an index of 53.08 according to the published tables. The case of Dudley is more complicated. Although a part of Worcestershire it is surrounded on all sides by Staffordshire. Nevertheless the index of attendance is higher even than Wolverhampton, at 55.32, whilst rural Worcestershire, though better at church attendance than Staffordshire, only has an index of 54.18. Only Evesham, in rural Worcestershire, with an index of 68.96 has a higher church attendance than McLeod's rural average, whilst the Dudley registration district as a whole exceeds all others in the county, apart from Evesham, with an index of 66.94.[17]

Thus the published statistics show an anomaly in the West Midlands. Church attendance in Birmingham is abnormally low compared with the surrounding rural area, but the Black Country towns are abnormally high, both in comparison with Birmingham and with their rural hinterland. The anomaly of Birmingham is partly reduced by noting that rural church attendance in Warwickshire varied from abnormally high near Rugby, which has an index of 84.15, to abnormally low near Coventry, where Meriden has an index of 30.75. Even supposing that rural immigrants to Birmingham came from the north western rather than the eastern and southern parts of Warwickshire the contrast between Birmingham and the Black Country is not removed. In the former case an urban area can drastically reduce the level of churchgoing, in the latter the urban areas actually improve on the rural indexes of attendance.

Table 12 shows the places of birth for each registration district and shows that the industrial areas of the West Midlands drew 80% of their immigrant population from the surrounding counties. Only in Wolverhampton, Walsall and Birmingham does a small proportion come from Ireland, no other significant immigrant group can be detected.[18]

McLeod also used the original census returns to analyse the patterns of attendance in the smaller registration sub-districts. These often represented distinctive working class neighbourhoods and middle class suburbs within the larger urban areas, frequently with contrasting church attendance, which could not be detected in the published figures for a whole Parliamentary Borough.[19] McLeod thus pioneered the methodology used in this thesis.

4.3 The reliability of the census returns for Birmingham and the Black Country

Before undertaking an analysis of the returns for the registration sub-districts, however, it is necessary to establish the general reliability of the census returns. Two different methods have recently been used to test their reliability. One, by Keith Snell, was to correlate the figures given for accommodation, generally recognised as more likely to be reliable than those for attendance, with the total recorded attendances for each of the major denominations.[20] The other, by Clive Field, was to compare the 'average' attendances given on the returns with those for the services on census Sunday.[21]

Before either can be attempted conjectural figures need to be substituted for those returns where neither actual nor average attendance was given. To credit such churches or chapels with no Sunday worshippers at all would distort the figures even more than an approximation based on other available data. Unfortunately such substitute figures can only be given for total attendance. They cannot be broken down into morning, afternoon and evening services nor can Sunday school scholars to be distinguished from the rest of the worshippers.

Snell in his work on the North Midlands interpolates missing figures based on the mean values for that denomination in that registration district.[22] He admits that this may not be as accurate a reflection of the real situation as the method used by John D. Gay. Gay uses a calculation based on the proportion of the total sittings for the denomination provided by that church or chapel within the registration district. The percentage which this represents is then used to increase the recorded attendance for that denomination by an equivalent amount.[23]

I have used Gay's approach but modified it to match the relationship between available accommodation and recorded attendance for that denomination within the registration sub-district rather than the registration district as a whole. In many cases the registration district contained a wide variety of townships and neighbourhoods. Where a return only gives an average attendance and not one recorded for census Sunday this average is used in all calculations.

Out of the total number of 476 returns from the 37 sub-districts, only ten (2.1%) gave no details of attendance and twenty-seven (5.7%) gave average attendance only, most in both categories belonging to the Church of England. In this they reflected the reservations shown by the Anglican hierarchy towards the Census of Religious Worship and, although relatively few gave their reasons for providing no information one who did, the curate of All Saints, West Bromwich, declared, "These figures not being required by the Census Act I beg to decline answering them unless required to do so by my diocesan". For some unknown reason census forms requiring only average and not actual attendances were issued in some registration districts, notably Wolverhampton, but also to the Church of England in Edgbaston.[24] This inevitably affected the number returning average attendance only.

This thesis includes the registration districts of Wolverhampton, Walsall, Dudley, West Bromwich and Stourbridge. These areas are normally recognised as being within the Black Country, although three sub-districts of Wolverhampton; Tettenhall, Kinfare and Womborne, with a total population of 13, 857 in 1851, were really a rural rather than an industrial part of the conurbation. To complete the Black Country statistics the Harborne sub-district of Kings Norton has been included. Although the ancient parish church and village of Harborne were parts of outer Birmingham the most populous part of the township was Smethwick, then in Staffordshire, now part of Sandwell and undoubtedly a Black Country industrial area. The rest of the Kings Norton district, which included Edgbaston, the most affluent suburb of Birmingham and the much poorer suburbs of Balsall Heath, Sparkbrook and Stirchley, has been added to the figures for Birmingham.

The Birmingham registration district, with its nine sub-districts, did not include the whole of the municipal borough of Birmingham in 1851. Since 1838 this had comprised, in addition, the parish of Edgbaston and two sub-districts of Aston; Deritend and Bordesley, and Duddeston and Nechells.[25] These, plus the Kings Norton sub-district, have been grouped together as providing the most complete coverage of church attendance in Birmingham.

In addition to the problem posed by missing attendance data on some returns, Field mentions two other defects which the Census presents to the historian, places of worship which were missed out altogether and clerical errors in handling those returns which were sent in.[26] Whereas well established churches and chapels were unlikely to be missed, the many small preaching rooms and domestic premises used by some groups, notably the Primitive

Methodists, Baptists, Independents and Unitarians, could have been overlooked, thus depressing the numbers returned for them.

In both Birmingham and the Black Country a reasonable proportion of temporary premises are included. The registration districts were in relatively compact urban areas and industrialised villages so returning officers could easily track down small groups of worshippers. Not all sub-districts returned worship in preaching rooms but just under half did so. The total of 22 comprised 10 preaching rooms, six houses, five schoolrooms and one hired hall. This latter was the Oddfellows Hall in Birmingham, hired by the Countess of Huntingdon's congregation as their chapel had been demolished to make way for the Midland Railway. Their total number of worshippers on census Sunday, four hundred and twenty-eight, was the largest in temporary premises, although an Anglican licensed room in Willenhall, with three Sunday services, returned an average of 490. Two Black Country locations gave no figures at all but the sum of those which did amounted to 2, 436, or 0.8% of the total overall attendance of 303, 634. Total attendance for the Black Country was 212, 290 and for Birmingham, including the added sub-districts from Aston and Kings Norton, 91, 344. These figures include Sunday school scholars and are taken from the original returns and not the published tables.

The denominational spread bears out Field's findings. Most houses or preaching rooms were used by Methodists, five by the Primitives, two by the Wesleyans and one each by Wesleyan Reformers and Methodist New Connexion. Four belonged to the Church of England, two were schoolrooms and two were rooms licensed for public worship until new churches were built. The Baptists had three, the Brethren two and, along with the Countess of Huntingdon's Connexion, the Independents, the Mormons and Christian Israelites each had one.

The second defect noted by Field is the prevalence of clerical errors in processing the returns. Three major errors in the published tables are the result of such mistakes. Doubling the numbers recorded for the Quakers in Stourbridge and Birmingham was the result of duplicate returns being made for the Friends Meetings in each place. The only other duplicate returns are for four Wesleyan chapels in Sedgley; Gospel End, Ladymoor, Can Lane and Lanesfield, where both chapel steward and circuit minister sent in a return. I have preferred the numbers recorded by circuit ministers, thus reducing the Wesleyan total by 2, 365. The most serious misreading of the census forms, however, occurred in Birmingham where the return for St Chad's Roman Catholic Cathedral stated that at each of three morning masses there were at least 1, 433 giving a total of 4, 300. On census Sunday there were also special evening services with a high total attendance of 1, 700 giving an overall figure of 6, 000. The published tables, however, give only 3, 383 morning and 1, 346 evening worshippers as a total for four Roman Catholic churches, thus underrepresenting the Roman Catholics by almost 4, 000. There were only three Roman Catholic churches in Birmingham in 1851, with total attendances of: St Peter's 890, St Chad's 6, 000, The Oratory 1, 830, making 8, 720 overall.[27]

These errors apart, some of the published tables are still misleading as Table 13 indicates. Moreover, the high attendance they give for Wolverhampton, and its subsequent status in the tables produced by Inglis,[28] needs to be put in context. The figures in the published table for urban areas are for the Parliamentary not the municipal borough.[29] This included not only the borough of Wolverhampton itself but the nearby town of Bilston and the parishes of Sedgley, Willenhall and Wednesfield. Bilston and Sedgley had between them a higher population than Wolverhampton[30] and a much higher Index of church attendance.

After correcting Sedgley figures by removing duplicate Wesleyan returns and interpolating estimates for missing Anglican returns for Wolverhampton the resulting Indexes of Attendance are; Wolverhampton 47.57, Bilston 58.69 and Sedgley 71.92. Hence a more detailed analysis of the sub-districts in the Wolverhampton Parliamentary Borough is needed to explain its remarkably high church attendance.

Two further checks upon the accuracy of the original returns can be made. One, following Snell, is to correlate available accommodation against recorded attendances. Clearly exaggerated attendances could not be accommodated in buildings whose seating capacity was specified. This can be done in two ways. The percentage of the population which could be accommodated in each sub-district could be correlated against the Index of Attendance. Secondly, the percentage of the population which could be accommodated by each major denomination can be correlated against that denomination's percentage of the total attendance. Such a correlation assumes a 'Protestant' pattern of worship, a single congregation for each service, rather than a Roman Catholic one of several masses in succession. Hence no Roman Catholic statistics have been used.

The results are as follows:

1. Twelve sub-districts of Wolverhampton and Walsall   r = 0.6241619
2. Twelve sub-districts of West Bromwich, Dudley and Stourbridge
   plus Harborne   r = 0.6968008
3. Nine sub-districts of Birmingham, two of Aston plus Edgbaston
   and Kings Norton   r = 0.8663087
4. Denominational correlations   *a) Black Country*   *b) Birmingham*
   Church of England   r = 0.72938   r = 0.87438
   Independent   r = 0.65964   r = 0.90194
   Baptist   r = 0.73224   r = 0.89012
   Wesleyan   r = 0.91394   r = 0.85061
   Methodist New Connexion   r = 0.9099   (insufficient numbers)
   Primitive Methodist   r = 0.89078   r = 0.60325

Snell does not give any comparable figures for the North Mid-lands but the above statistics are not highly significant, leaving the case for reliability unproven. The denominational correlations, however, are reasonably high, particularly so in the case of Methodism in the Black Country and the Baptists and Independents in Birmingham.[31] All of them are comparable with those Snell found "highly reassuring" giving him "considerable confidence" in the 1851 data.[32]

Field's additional test was to compare recorded attendances with the averages for the same places of worship to see how far they differed. "Such a comparison suggests that turn-out at the census did indeed tend to fall below the norm but not universally so nor always by a serious amount; in London Methodism, for example, the net discrepancy between the two sets of data was just 7%."[33] This test is possible in just over half of the churches of Birmingham and the Black Country, about the national average according to Field. Of the 476 returns, 10 (2.1%) gave no details at all, 27 (5.7%) gave average attendance only, 168 (35.4%) gave no average and in 19 (4%) the figures were either hard to compare or incomprehensible. Of the remaining 250 returns, 53 (11% of the total number) gave an average the same as the census Sunday attendance, in 57 (12%) the average was less and in 140 (29.9%) the average was greater than the census. Returns enabling a comparison between actual and average attendance accounted for 57.2% of the total attendance (173, 730 out of 303, 634) but the overall increase of average attendance over that on census Sunday was only 11, 354 or 6.5%, very much in line with Field's findings.[34]

There are significant differences between the Birmingham and Black Country figures for actual and average attendance, but with more doubtful figures in the Black Country returns. These are given in Table 14 below.

Table 14.

Differences between census Sunday and average attendance

	Number of returns	*Total census Sunday*	*Average attendance*	*Difference*
Black Country	194	118, 497	131, 262	+12, 765
Birmingham	56	55, 233	53, 822	-1, 411
Totals	250	173, 730	185, 084	+11, 354

A number of returns comment on the effects of Mid-Lent Sunday and other factors on attendances. Just over 10% stated that Mid-Lent Sunday had diminished their congregations; ten in Birmingham and forty in the Black Country. Ten others gave other reasons for diminished attendances, including bad weather (both in Aldridge), influenza (one Baptist church in Birmingham) and the effects of other services elsewhere, such as those which boosted Roman Catholic attendance at St Chad's Cathedral, Birmingham at the expense of St Peter's. The most intriguing comes from St James Church of England, Wednesbury where the curate states, "The parishioners consist almost exclusively of miners and colliers and labourers, too many of whom are compelled to Sunday labour". Six returns explain higher than average attendances, all due to special services.

Needless to say the differences between average and recorded attendance varied widely. In many cases they were very small, in a few they were difficult to credit, although all are included in the above calculation. A total of 102 returns, almost 55%, gave differences of less than 100 attendances. The others were as follows:

100 -199	44
200 -299	22
300 -399	9
400 -499	10
Over 500	10

Some of the high figures are explicable. In Birmingham the main Countess of Huntingdon's chapel had been demolished to make way for the Midland Railway. The congregation was meeting temporarily in the Oddfellows Hall but gave the average attendance of the former chapel. Mount Zion Baptist chapel in Birmingham attributed smaller congregations to the absence of a 'settled' minister whilst re-opening services at the Wesleyan Methodist Association chapel at Bath Street, Birmingham boosted their congregations by 679. The effects of recent disruptions in Methodism may be reflected in reduced attendances at the nearby Wesleyan chapel on Constitution Hill which recorded 527 less than their average.

On the other hand some Black Country figures, particularly amongst the Methodists, seem hard to credit. The Methodist New Connexion at Cradley Forge in Kingswinford, for example, had a chapel seating 500 and attendances at three services totalling 620, nevertheless they gave their average as 1, 020. The New Connexion particularly, but sometimes also the Wesleyans and Primitives, appear to have rounded figures up by fifties and hundreds when giving averages. The same seems to have occurred at several Anglican churches which claimed large average congregations. This is indicated in Table 15.

These eleven Anglican churches alone, each with a difference of three-hundred or more between census Sunday attendance and their average, account for over 44% of the excess of average over census Sunday attendance in the Black Country. Nevertheless the overall effect is less than 7% and so bears out Field's findings. It can, therefore, be fairly confidently stated that the attendance returns are a reliable guide to the actual situation obtaining in 1851 and so can be used to compare levels of churchgoing in Birmingham and the Black Country.

4.4 The pattern of churchgoing in Birmingham and the Black Country

Having established the general reliability of the original returns from the 1851 Census the next task is to produce an index of attendance from each registration sub-district. Gill, in his study of church provision and attendance, excludes Sunday school scholars from his calculations in order to make comparisons between the 1851 census and other surveys of worship in large towns made later in the century.[35] This can be done from the original returns which required Sunday scholars to be enumerated separately. Such an exclusion only affords an approximation of the number of adult worshippers as Sunday schools often had adult members and some churches, notably the Roman Catholics, had patterns of worship which children as well as adults were expected to attend. There is no need to assume that Sunday scholars were not also worshippers, though no other church in the conurbation was as careful as Mayers Green Independent chapel in West Bromwich which distinguished between the 192 scholars who attended worship and 70 others who did not. "The cause of separate services being the difficulty of teaching young children during a lengthened service in which they can take but little part". Nevertheless, this calculation has also been done. The results are set out in Table 16 in the order in which they appear in the Census.

The division of both Wolverhampton and West Bromwich into two registration sub-districts separated many churches and chapels from the residences of their congregations in a somewhat arbitrary way. Hence it makes sense to use a single consolidated Index for each town rather than imply that they could be divided down the middle into areas of high and low church attendance respectively.

The case of Birmingham is more complex. Not only would numerous residents of Edgbaston attend services in the many churches and chapels of the town centre but the division of the centre itself into registration sub-districts distorts the significance of indexes of attendance calculated on their resident population. The high figures for St Philip, for example, can be partly explained by the fact that this sub-district contained not only two well attended Anglican churches, St Philip's being particularly fashionable, but also the oldest Unitarian, Baptist and Wesleyan chapels plus the one Mormon congregation which returned a total attendance of 1, 865. The presence of St Chad's Roman Catholic Cathedral, drawing large congregations from well beyond its immediate vicinity, largely accounts for the high index of attendance in St Mary's sub-district, whilst St Peter's, the other central Birmingham sub-district with a high index, contained three Anglican churches, the strongest Independent church, Carrs Lane and the Unitarian New Meeting, once the pulpit of Joseph Priestley and still attracting over 500 to its morning worship. Thus a consolidated index for Birmingham as a whole, including the outer suburbs, seems a more reasonable indication of the overall church attendance, despite the fact that some predominantly working class sub-districts, Ladywood, St George, St Thomas, Duddeston and All Saints, fall below even this modest level.[36] Only Harborne, which is only partly in the Black Country, matches Birmingham for church attendance. Otherwise the contrast between Birmingham and the Black Country derived from the published figures is borne out by the original returns. It will be seen that in the Black Country only seven fall below 50% whilst only three in the Birmingham conurbation exceed that figure, for reasons already indicated.

Table 17 gives the rank order of Black Country sub-districts, excluding Tettenhall, Kinfare and Womborne which were outside the industrialised area. The order is then revised after the removal of Sunday scholars. Only Halesowen, Handsworth and Wolverhampton are significantly affected by this, other sub-districts remain at or very near their original position.

It could be argued that the initial Black Country indexes are inflated by the numbers of Sunday scholars, a feature less apparent in Birmingham. This is undoubtedly true when the two areas are taken as a whole. Out of a total attendance of 212, 290 in the Black Country, 53, 556, or 25.23%, were Sunday scholars. The equivalent figures for the Birmingham area are 16, 274, or 17.82%, out of a total attendance of 91, 344. Thus the removal of Sunday school scholars does reduce the difference between Birmingham and the Black Country by some 7%. But this does not mean that the wide range of attendances is only due to the proportion of Sunday scholars.

4.5 Gill and the pattern of denominational provision in 1851

In his book, 'The Myth of the Empty Church', Robin Gill uses census and other statistics to map the different patterns of provision by the Church of England and the Free Churches to meet the religious needs of the increasing urban and declining rural population between 1800 and 1990. He contrasts these with the very different pattern of Roman Catholic church building and attendance in the same period. His thesis is that denominational rivalry in rural areas and inter-denominational competition to establish new congregations in the towns led to over-provision of accommodation in both, leading, after 1851, to emptier churches even where the actual number attending worship amongst the population at large was increasing, as it did between 1851 and the end of the nineteenth century.[37] From 1821 to 1851 there was a considerable effort, particularly by the Church of England, to cater for the rising populations of the industrialised areas and other large towns. Within the Free Churches, Methodist expansion was not matched by the others, with some exceptions amongst the Baptists.[38]

The information provided by the 1851 Census enables the actual attendance to be related to the adequacy of church accommodation, not only at the time of the census, but during the preceding decades of the century. Hence it may be possible to decide whether the actual provision was too recent to have had much effect and to what extent churches had kept pace with rising population. There will inevitably be an element of inaccuracy as the 1851 returns give no information on churches which had closed in the preceding decades, although they do occasionally indicate some which had changed hands.[39]

Table 19 gives the percentage of the population which could be accommodated at any one time alongside the decennial percentage increase in population between 1801 and 1851.

Only the 'rural' sub-districts of Tettenhall, Kinfare and Wombourne did not have decennial population increases of over 20% during the first half of the nineteenth century. All others experienced population increases of over 25% in some decades and several had increases of over 50%, notably West Bromwich and Tipton. It is not surprising, therefore, that they struggled to keep church accommodation abreast of their rising populations. What is remarkable, considering that all except Birmingham started from a base provision of over 30%, is the number which by 1851 were providing for a higher proportion of their population than they were at the beginning of the century, despite the very large increases which had taken place. Even Birmingham had risen from less than 20% to just over 30%, Wolverhampton had almost kept its 41% whilst ten others (Willenhall, Darlaston, Bloxwich, Walsall, Wednesbury, Rowley Regis, Sedgley, Dudley, Stourbridge and Kingswinford) had increased the percentage of their populations for which church and chapel accommodation was provided. Not surprisingly West Bromwich and Tipton had failed to maintain their levels of provision of over 55%, but neither had fallen too far below, reaching 39.4% and 42.1% respectively.

Apart from the three 'rural' sub-districts there is no obvious relationship between the percentage of the population which could be accommodated in 1851 and the actual index of attendance. Nevertheless, a calculation, using Spearman's Rank Correlation Coefficient, comparing the rank order of accommodation with the 1851 index of attendance gives a figure of 0.72 which is highly significant, despite the evident differences between individual places.[40] Although the figures for both were high in Rowley Regis and Halesowen and almost as high in Sedgley where just under 50% of the population could be accommodated this was not true of Tipton (42.1%) or Bilston (36.6%) which also recorded high indexes of attendance. Even an analysis based on those sub-districts which increased their proportion of church accommodation within the decade before 1851 does not give unambiguous findings. For example, although it would clearly include Bilston and Rowley Regis amongst those with a high index it would also apply to Willenhall, Walsall and Aldridge where attendances were much more modest. Gill's thesis, that church accommodation as a percentage of population markedly improved in the two decades before 1851, is generally borne out by these findings but a more detailed analysis of the denominational pattern is required to substantiate Gill's claims regarding the Church of England and the Free Churches.

Table 20 gives the decennial proportion which could be accommodated by the Church of England and all the Free Churches (including the Wesleyans) combined, together with their Indexes of attendance. In all cases except Handsworth and Harborne the Free Church Index exceeded the percentage of the population which they could accommodate (with roughly equal proportions in both Edgbaston and Deritend). This would be in keeping with their normal pattern of building to accommodate existing congregations with some room for expansion.

The Church of England pattern, according to Gill, is almost the opposite, keeping open ancient churches with dwindling congregations whilst building extensively in developing areas regardless of whether new congregations were established. It is not surprising, therefore, that in half of the districts represented on the table the Church of England index of attendance is lower than the percentage of the population which it could accommodate. It is more remarkable that in so many, particularly some of those whose population had expanded very rapidly in the preceding half-century, the Church of England index was actually higher than the percentage which could be accommodated. In some areas on the fringe of the conurbation, where industrialisation was relatively recent, such as Handsworth, Aldridge and Harborne, the Church of England began from a position of obvious strength in having provision for over 50% (in the cases of Handsworth and Harborne) or nearly 40% (in Aldridge) of the 1801 population. On the other hand this was also the case in Halesowen where nonconformists had overtaken the Church of England by 1851 in both accommodation and attendance.

Where the Church of England started at a relative disadvantage, in Bilston, Oldbury, West Bromwich, Dudley and, to a lesser extent, Sedgley, the ground was never made up despite extensive church building in all these places. Two new Anglican churches in Bilston, two in Oldbury, four in West Bromwich, three in Dudley and five in Sedgley were all built after 1830. The low level of Church of England accommodation in proportion to population in Birmingham in 1801 was never really improved on despite strenuous efforts at founding new churches, particularly after 1820. This increasing urban population meant that the Church of England, with some difficulty, only just maintained its existing level of provision. Thirteen new Anglican churches were built in Birmingham and one in Edgbaston between 1820 and 1851, adding to the nine existing Anglican churches and increasing the available accommodation two and a half times. Nevertheless the fact that in the Birmingham urban area as a whole the Church of England index of attendance was higher, if only just, than the proportion of the population which it could accommodate speaks creditably for the pastoral effort which must have accompanied the increase in church building before 1851.[41]

The Free Churches as a group were not as successful in Birmingham in attracting attendances well beyond the proportion of the population which they could accommodate as they were in parts of the Black Country, particularly Willenhall, Bilston, West Bromwich, Rowley Regis, Tipton and Sedgley. This comparison, however, masks one significant difference, namely the much higher proportion of both accommodation and attendances ascribable to Methodism, in its various branches, in the Black Country when compared with Birmingham.

Table 21 gives the total attendances at Methodist services in relation to the total overall attendance. It will be seen that in no fewer than fourteen cases in the Black Country the removal of Methodism reduced the Index of attendance by over 20 percentage points whereas in the Birmingham area the equivalent operation led to reductions of less than seven percentage points. This high proportion of Methodist attendances in so many Black Country sub-districts covers a considerable range. It includes all of those sub-districts with high Indexes of attendance but also some of those where the overall index of attendance was low.

A fuller consideration of the impact of Methodism in the Black Country and its relative failure in Birmingham will be given in later chapters. For the moment it will suffice to note the significance of this factor in the difference between Birmingham and the Black Country in the 1851 census of religious worship.

There remains one other issue raised by Gill. Given the substantial church building efforts, particularly by the Church of England, immediately before the 1851 census how successful were these new buildings in attracting congregations in comparison with older established places of worship. Gill's comparisons between 1851 data and those obtained from newspaper surveys in the 1880s and 90s lead him to claim that, for the Church of England, "If the original churches in a large town are looked at separately, it transpires that they typically declined radically. It is the new churches that were most likely to have been full".[42] He illustrates this thesis from Newcastle upon Tyne and Birmingham where, in the latter case, Anglican churches were on average 50% full in 1851 but only 40% in 1892. On this basis, for example, he calculates that Anglican churches in Liverpool built before 1821 were less full in 1851 than those built more recently.[43]

Gill claims to calculate the relative fullness (or emptiness) of churches by dividing their amalgamated morning and evening attendances by the accommodation multiplied by one hundred.[44] Nevertheless this formula does not produce the sort of results he tabulates. Instead I have added together the combined morning and evening congregations, subtracted Sunday school scholars, divided the total by two and expressed the result as a percentage of the total available accommodation. This formula gives results comparable with those of Gill on the data available for Birmingham. Here there were twenty-two Anglican churches within the Borough boundary in 1851, nine built before and thirteen after 1821. In fact it was the nine older churches, most of them in the town centre, which were almost 60%(59.6) full on average whilst the thirteen newer ones had only 40% (39.9) of their seating occupied on census Sunday.[45]

A similar calculation can be made on certain Black Country sub-districts but not all had a large enough number of Anglican churches, new and old, for comparisons to be meaningful.[46] Wolverhampton had two churches built before 1821 and six afterwards. Three only sent in average attendances and two none at all so that only very tentative conclusions can be drawn, in particular Sunday scholars cannot be deducted from those which returned no attendances. With these qualifications, however, the two older churches were 36.7% full whilst the six newer ones were 58.6% full on average, clearly the newer churches had attracted the larger congregations in proportion to their seating capacity.

In West Bromwich the failure of the one ancient parish church to give any figures for attendance makes it impossible to compare it with the three new churches open in 1851. With one notable exception, in all the other cases where comparisons are possible the Birmingham pattern is repeated, older established Anglican churches being relatively more full than those built since 1821, though some of these were very new indeed. Table 22 gives the results of these calculations.

So far as the area covered by this research is concerned Gill's thesis only seems true of Wolverhampton and Bilston in 1851. In Birmingham and in most parts of the Black Country where comparisons are possible the older established Anglican churches still attracted relatively larger congregations. Newer churches had not yet established themselves to anything like the same degree, though in several cases their provision was very recent.[47]

My adaptation of Gill's formula can also be used to test whether sheer population size was a decisive factor in Birmingham's index of attendance when compared with the Black Country. If more people wished to worship in Birmingham than could be accommodated, existing churches and chapels ought to have been full. With the exception of the Roman Catholics, whose pattern of worship was very different, the percentage of accommodation actually used by the main Protestant denominations can be calculated. In most cases where a Sunday afternoon service is indicated the numbers involved match very closely those given for Sunday scholars. Hence, after deducting Sunday scholars, calculations based on only two services best approximate the adult occupancy. The results for the borough of Birmingham are: Church of England 55.5%, Baptist 53.8%, Independent 47.8%, Wesleyan 44.8%, Unitarian and Church of the Saviour 41.4%.[48] These figures indicate that Birmingham churches, though reasonably full, were not yet swamped by the number of worshippers demanding accommodation. If most people stayed away it was not for lack of available seats.

4.6 Provisional Conclusions

Study of the original returns for the 1851 Census of Religious Worship sustains the contrast between levels of attendance in Birmingham and the Black Country revealed by the published report but reduces the starkness of the contrast when the percentage of Sunday school scholars is taken into account. Analysis of the sub-district returns reveals considerable variation in Black Country church attendance, albeit still at levels higher than the Birmingham area as a whole. Church and chapel building generally kept pace with population growth but rarely provided for more than 50%. Methodist attendances are a significant factor only in the Black Country. Anglican churches built in the thirty years immediately before the census had attracted larger congregations, compared with the older Anglican churches, only in Wolverhampton and Bilston. Attendances in Birmingham were not necessarily inhibited by lack of seats as almost half the available accommodation was unoccupied.

An assessment of John McPhail's thesis on 'Religious attendance and provision in Birmingham, the Black Country and surrounding areas' is given in the Appendix.

Notes

1   *Congregational Magazine*, 1834, pp. 781ff. R. Gill, *The Myth of the Empty Church*, London 1993, pp. 108-109, 300. Unfortunately they do not include Birmingham or any places in the Black Country.

2   *Voluntaryism in England and Wales; or the Census of 1851*, London 1854, cf. D. M. Thompson, 'The Religious Census of 1851' in R. Lawton (Ed.) *The Census and Social Structure*, London 1978, pp. 241-286.

3   House of Lords, 11 July 1854: *Parliamentary Debates, 3rd series, Vol. CXXXV*, columns 23-33.

4   H. Mann, 'On the Statistical Position of Religious Bodies in England and Wales', in *Journal of the Statistical Society of London*, Vol. XVIII, London 1855, p. 147.

5   D. M. Thompson, 'The 1851 Census, problems and possibilities', in *Victorian Studies*, Vol. II, 1967, p.97.

6   O. Chadwick, *The Victorian Church*, Part I, London 1966, p.368: N. McCord, *British History 1815-1906*, Oxford 1991, p.242.

7   Most of his lecture to the London Statistical Society already quoted is taken
     up with defending the methodology employed and the checks made by
     registrars. Criticism of the voluntary nature of the census was answered by
     the claim that the registrars checked each return for accuracy and that
     those who filled them in knew that this procedure would be followed. So
     anxious was he to counter Anglican attacks that he felt it necessary to add,
     "Of the twenty or thirty clerks who dealt with the Returns at the central
     office only two were dissenters, and they were only occupied for a portion
     of the time." In letters to The Times in 1860 and 1870 he insisted on the lim-
     itations of the census, "The inquiry undertaken in 1851 related to the pro-
     vision for religious worship and the extent to which the means provided
     were made use of. It was not an enumeration of the professed adherents of
     the different sects." The Times, 22 July 1870.
8   Introduction to the Report on the Census of Religious Worship, *Parliamen-
     tary Papers 1853, Vol. LXXXIX*, pp. cxxx, clv, Table A, Table B, and Table C
     in *London Statistical Society*, Vol. XVIII, p. 157.
9   Ibid. p. cxxviii.
10   K. S. Inglis, 'Patterns of Religious Worship in 1851', in *Journal of Ecclesiasti-
     cal History*, Vol. XI, 1960.
11   Inglis, 'Patterns', p.80.
12   Ibid. p. 82.
13   Ibid. pp. 85-86.
14   Public Record Office, Kew, filed as H.O.129.
15   H. McLeod, 'Class, Community and Region, the Religious Geography of
     Nineteenth century England', in M. Hill (Ed.) *A Sociological Yearbook of Reli-
     gion in Britain*, Vol. 6, London 1973, pp. 29-72.
16   Ibid. pp. 35-43.
17   Mann, *Religious Worship*, pp. 73-78.
18   *Parliamentary Papers 1852-53, LXXXV*, Population Tables, Vol. 1, pp. 523-
     534.
19   McLeod, 'Religion', pp. 48-58.
20   K. D. M. Snell, *Church and Chapel in the North Midlands, Religious Observance
     in the Nineteenth Century*, Leicester 1991, pp. 10-11.
21   C. D. Field, 'Non-Recurrent Christian Data', in *Reviews of United Kingdom
     Statistical Sources, Vol. XX; Religion*, Royal Statistical Society and Economic
     and Social Research Council, London 1987, p. 289.
22   Snell, *North Midlands*, p. 66
23   J. D. Gay, *The Geography of Religion in England*, London 1971, pp. 50-52.
24   In Wolverhampton three Church of England, one Baptist, one Wesleyan,
     one Primitive Methodist and the Roman Catholic church returned 'average
     only' forms and in Edgbaston St George, Church of England.
25   see *VCH Warwickshire*, Vol. 7, p.42.
26   Field, 'Data', pp, 232-233.
27   The compilers included the return for the Warwickshire Roman Catholic
     chapel at Wooton Wawen.
28   Inglis, 'Patterns', p.81
29   *Parliamentary Papers 1853 Vol. LXXXIX*, p. cclxxii.
30   see Table 1

31   Correlations 1 and 2 are significant at 5% level with 10 degrees of freedom, correlation 3 at 1% with 11 degrees of freedom, all correlations under 4 are significant at 1% level with 20 and 11 degrees of freedom for the Black Country and Birmingham respectively. See the Note on statistical methods (p. 256) for the meaning of these terms.

32   Snell, *North Midlands*, pp. 12-14. Snell has confirmed the general accuracy of the census in his more recent comprehensive study. Snell and Ell, *Rival*, pp. 34-53, 425-437, 449-452 and passim.

33   Field, 'Data', p.289.

34   The concept of an average seems to have baffled some non-conformists, particularly in the Black Country, and some conjecture has been involved in evaluating their returns. For example, at Mount Zion Methodist New Connexion chapel in Woodside, Dudley the attendances at the three services on 30 March 1851 are given as 90, 200 and 320 but the average, in the morning column, was given as 190. It seems reasonable to suppose that the trustee who filled in the form divided the total attendance by three. In this, and several similar cases, I have assumed an average the same as the recorded attendance on census Sunday. Writing out an average across more than one column is a commonly confusing feature. At Tabernacle Methodist New Connexion chapel Oldbury, for example, an average of 500 adults and 250 Sunday school scholars is written across morning and afternoon columns whereas the return for census Sunday gives 210, 40 and 400 adults at three separate services with 200 in the morning Sunday school. The clearest example of misunderstanding the nature of an average comes from Ebenezer Methodist New Connexion chapel, Wallbrook, Sedgley. Here there was no morning service and congregations were recorded as 175 in the afternoon and 120 in the evening, but 'averages' of 8, 928 for afternoon and 5, 068 for the evening were given. This would appear to be a total number of attendances for twelve months arrived at by adding together the numbers present on 52 Sundays, rather than an average weekly attendance. Whatever their origin these figures have not been included in my calculations.

35   R. Gill, *Myth*, pp. 107, 125 plus Tables 2 and 3, pp. 298-299.

36   The Birmingham sub-district with the second lowest Index, St Paul's, is hard to classify socio-economically. It only had two well established places of worship. One of them, Zion Baptist chapel, was the pulpit of the popular Christian Chartist Arthur O'Neill who had preached special sermons in aid of the branch schools connected with the chapel and so boosted his congregation on census Sunday. The other, St Paul's, was originally built to be entirely dependent on rented pews and, in the previous century, had counted such leading industrialists as Matthew Boulton and James Watt amongst its seat holders. On the other hand the area was the centre of the jewellery trade which was carried on by independent small craftsmen rather than by factory labour. The population, living near the town centre, could, of course, have attended worship elsewhere. It remains a fact, nevertheless, that this sub-district returned a smaller number of worshippers as a percentage of its population than any other in central Birmingham.

37   Gill, *Myth*, pp. 72-123. Gill uses other statistics in addition to the 1851 cen-

sus in discussing developments in the first half of the nineteenth century. Unfortunately none of these, such as episcopal visitation returns giving attendance figures or the survey of several urban and rural areas carried out in 1835 by the Congregational Union cover the area which is being considered here.

38   "What emerges very clearly from the urban census data is that the Church of England expanded more slowly but for longer than the Free Churches. Yet it continued (often to the present day) with churches that had tiny congregations and, in some cases, little surrounding population. The Free Churches expanded very vigourously, competing with each other and spreading attendances more and more thinly. They then collapsed dramatically." He continues, "claims about the inevitable secularising features of urbanisation, or of rural migration to urban areas, may require serious modification. Between the 1820s and 1851 it would seem that the Church of England did increase its urban attendances, just as the Baptists and non-Wesleyan Methodists did in the large towns and perhaps the Methodists as a whole in the conurbations." Ibid. pp. 80, 105.

39   For example, the Catholic Apostolic Church in Birmingham took over the former Scotch Presbyterian church in Newhall Street whilst in Brierley Hill the Anglican Chapel at Harts Hill had been purchased from the Independents in 1838.

40   Significant at well above 1% level

41   see D. E. H. Mole, 'The Challenge to the Church', in H. J. Dyos and M. Wolff (Eds.) *The Victorian City*, London 1973, Vol. 2, pp. 815-835.

42   R. Gill, *Myth*, p. 85.

43   Ibid. pp. 319, Table 15; 304, Table 7.

44   Ibid. p. 91, note 21.

45   Ibid. p.321, Gill does not attempt the comparison made here between pre-1821 and post-1821 churches in Birmingham.

46   In particular; Darlaston, Bloxwich, Aldridge, Oldbury, Rowley Regis, Halesowen and Harborne.

47   In Wednesbury, for example, two of the three had been built in 1848 and one in 1850, whilst the three in Willenhall dated from 1846, 1847 and 1849.

48   The Primitive Methodists, with only three small chapels, had an occupancy of 61%. The number of buildings for the other denominations is: Church of England 22, Baptist 8, Independent 14, Unitarian 7, Wesleyan 12. Temporary school and preaching room accommodation is not included.

CHAPTER 5

Interpreting the 1851 Census of Religious Worship

5.1 The urban context: class and denomination

Since its publication in 1854 the results of the census have been used to support, if not actually to prove, a range of very different conclusions. The significance of the census statistics appears to depend very much on the context in which they are viewed by the interpreter.

For example, R. A. Soloway, in his study of the Anglican episcopate's response to the social challenges of the first half of the nineteenth century, reports that Bishop Blomfield of London, was "saddened to discover that in Bethnal Green, where he raised funds for ten churches in as many years, only 6, 024 persons out of a population of 90, 193 attended any service", although "there are no pew rents or appropriated sittings in the new churches". Soloway suggests that leading bishops such as Blomfield and Wilberforce accepted the view that, "The census of 1851 showed that if there was one thing that the Establishment did not need in the towns it was more churches. Many of them were already virtually empty, and formed what Mann described as 'too conspicuous a difference between accommodation and attendants . . .'[1] Blomfield's gloom at the apparent failure of his church extension programme was slightly premature. As Hugh McLeod has pointed out, the ten new churches of Bethnal Green were better attended than those of most other East End districts. Only Whitechapel had higher Anglican attendances whilst Clerkenwell, Poplar, Stepney and, particularly Shoreditch were all lower.[2]

This tendency to accept Mann's interpretation of his figures continued long after 1854, particularly the absence of the urban working class from Sunday worship. Soloway takes it as axiomatic that "The revived Church in the nineteenth century had not lost the working classes; it never had them." [3]In this he was following Inglis whose influential study of 'Churches and the Working Classes in Victorian England' begins at 1850 and says of the census, "The statistical analysis and Mann's general observations made it a remarkable essay in the social pathology of English religion. It showed that well tried approaches to the working classes were having little success. It helped church leaders to realise just how solid was resistance to their ministry, especially in large towns."[4]

The pioneering work on urban religion, E. R. Wickham's study of Sheffield, published in 1957, prints the 1851 church attendance statistics for Sheffield but, instead of analysing them himself, Wickham simply quotes Mann's comments as proof of the urban workers' alienation from religious worship and, by extension, from religious influences, by the mid-nineteenth century, reflecting their neglect by the churches for many years before.[5] Wickham fitted the census evidence into the context of his work as head of the Sheffield Industrial Mission, an attempt to do in Britain what others, like the worker-priests in the French Catholic Church, had attempted, forge direct links between religious and industrial organisations.[6]

The Marxist historian Eric Hobsbawm also placed it in the context of the religious adherence of the working class during the industrial revolution. In his perceptive article, 'Methodism and the threat of revolution in Britain', the census is used to assert the relative lack of religious commitment, particularly Methodist, of the population of the "industrial areas of England and Wales. The large cities and some, but by no means all, of the backward mining and iron areas were relatively un-religious (that is to say, less than 25 per cent of the total population attended divine service on census Sunday)."[7] Hobsbawm was one of the first to point to the variations in church attendance in the industrial areas revealed by the census but his general view was that where nonconformity had a large number of adherents the reasons were obscure. "We know too little about the life of the common people in Britain during the Industrial Revolution to say with any confidence how they regarded their nonconformity. All we know is that Methodism advanced when Radicalism advanced and not when it grew weaker, and also that the great 'religious revivals' normally did not occur when economic conditions were coming to their worst, . . ."[8] By linking the census not merely with the growth of industrial areas but also with the impact of particular denominations Hobsbawm broadened the context of its interpretation, but still with the emphasis on the working classes.

Harold Perkin combined urban and denominational statistics from the census into an explanatory framework explaining the emergence of class divisions within nineteenth century English society. Perkin drew attention to religion's function as 'the midwife of class'. In his view sectarian religion enabled men and women to "give expression to emancipation from the dependency system" which characterised the old order. "This is not to say that the nineteenth century middle class . . .were all Old Dissenters, or that the new working class . . . were all Methodists . . .Old Dissent was no more than the core of the middle class . . .and if one door led into it from the Church, another led out of it to sophisticated forms of unbelief; and Methodism was but one religion of the working class, and as often as not the gate through which large numbers of working men passed to secularism or indifference, the ultimate spiritual state of the majority in the great towns of the industrial age."[9]

To sustain such large claims Methodist history was recast to represent a "sequence of stepping stones from the Church to agnosticism" avoiding any evidence pointing in the reverse direction. Thomas Cooper, for example, whom Perkin includes amongst those who left Methodism in the 1840s because of its political conservatism, spent his last twenty years of active life as a Baptist lecturer on Christian apologetics.[10] In order to prove two apparently conflicting arguments, namely the increase in nonconformity and the secularism of the industrial towns, Perkin prints two tables giving the number of places of worship built by Anglicans and non-Anglicans and the estimated attendance of each in towns grouped according to their population's size. The first showed that, compared with 14, 077 Anglican places of worship in 1851, non-Anglicans had 20, 390. The second "shows two broad trends; first, the larger the town the smaller the proportion of the population attending any place of worship; and, secondly, the larger the town, with the exception of London, the smaller the proportion of Anglican to all attendances." He then repeats Mann's interpretation of the figures, backed up by Engels, concluding, "where dependency was weakened, Anglican Church-going declined; where it was dead, church-going of all kinds decayed. Emancipation from both paternal and religious discipline went hand in hand with urbanisation."[11]

Perkin made no link between size of town and accommodation for worship nor the relationship between the towns and their surrounding countryside which has subsequently been shown to explain variations in church attendance. His major conclusion, that urbanisation in itself adversely affected church attendance, has been seriously challenged by Callum Brown in an influential article. In it Brown uses the Scottish as well as English and Welsh data. These were subjected to regression analysis, in which urban church attendances were correlated against three different variables; population size in 1851, growth rate per annum 1841-51 and growth rate 1801-1851. Brown's conclusion is "In short, the English and Welsh religious census of 1851 showed no statistically significant relationship between churchgoing rate and population size or growth for

towns and cities." In Scotland, however, where the towns listed separately covered a much wider range of population, from 2, 364
(Dingwall) to 344, 986 (Glasgow), one factor did emerge. "Thus,
towns with higher population growth rates over the period 1801-
1851 tended to have lower rates of church attendance, but only one
quarter of the variation can be accounted for by this factor."[12]

It must be emphasised that Brown is talking of statistically significant relationships. There may be other significant relationships
not amenable to statistical formulae. In fact Brown, in his statistics,
has also treated population growth and town size in isolation from
church provision, which must surely count as a significant factor
alongside population growth. Hugh McLeod has pointed out the
dramatic consequences for church attendance in Berlin of the Pruss-
ian state's failure to provide for the Protestant Established Church
during a period of immense population growth in the nineteenth
century, along with the absence of significant Free Church and
Catholic alternatives.[13] Not only buildings but clergy and church
organisation also need to be considered before realistic comparisons
can be made. Callum Brown does show awareness of these factors
in his article, only the statistical material effectively ignores them.
This may be because he has another context into which to fit the patterns of religion in the industrial towns of Britain during the last
two centuries. He sees the most significant factor in the nineteenth
century as the development of both capitalism and denomination-
alism in the rural areas before immigrants left them for the cities.[14]
Before considering this issue, however, the bearing of the census
findings for Birmingham and the Black Country on Perkin's arguments must be examined.

Although the contrast in church attendance between the largest
town, Birmingham, and the rest of the conurbation has already been
established a glance at Tables 16 and 17 shows that mere population
size is not a very accurate indicator of attendance. Dudley and West
Bromwich, with similar populations of 37, 962 and 34, 591 respectively, are well above Walsall with its population of 21, 203 and
higher than Stourbridge with 20, 238. Admittedly all four lie within
the 20, 000 to 50, 000 range of population grouped together by
Perkin, but it is certainly not true of the conurbation in general that
the smaller the population size the higher the church attendance.
Brown's added factor of rate of population growth between 1801
and 1851 has been set out in Table 2. A correlation between this and
the index of attendance for each sub-district, but with consolidated
indexes for greater Birmingham, Wolverhampton and West
Bromwich, gives a coefficient of $r = -0.3071$, certainly negative but
nevertheless very weak. The fact that the two sub-districts with the

most spectacular population growth in the first half of the century, West Bromwich and Tipton, are amongst the top six in index of attendance raises doubts over the sole significance of this factor to explain variations in church-going.

Perkin's other point, that the larger the town the smaller the proportion of Anglican attendances, gains little support. The two largest towns, Birmingham and Wolverhampton, each had higher Anglican attendances compared with those of Protestant Nonconformity. This is only partly apparent from Table 20 as the Edgbaston, Aston and Birmingham figures need to be combined to give an index for the borough as a whole. When this is done the results are: Church of England 17%, Nonconformists 15.8%. Only when the Roman Catholic attendances are added to the Protestant Nonconformists does the position change, this raises the Non-Anglican percentage for Birmingham to 19.5%, but the same calculation for Wolverhampton results in; Anglicans 27.6%, Non-Anglicans 20%. In neither case have the Anglicans been eclipsed by the Nonconformists, as Perkin's statement implies. What needs to be explained is the success of the Church of England in the two largest towns of the conurbation. Elsewhere in the Black Country the Anglican position was far less positive. When all the rest of the Black Country sub-districts are combined the results are; Church of England 18.4%, Non-Anglicans 36.2% of which only 1.8% were Roman Catholics. Using actual indexes of attendance in this comparison provides a more realistic picture than giving the percentage share of the overall church attendances obtained by the different denominations. Such figures would disguise the differences in church attendance between Birmingham and the Black Country which the index of attendance maintains.

Perkin's interpretation of religion as the 'midwife of class' was given systematic treatment by Alan Gilbert. His doctoral thesis was subsequently expanded in his book on 'Religion and Society in Industrial England'. He uses some of Mann's tables to illustrate his view that the expansion of nonconformity up to 1840 was primarily the result of recruitment from "particular social groups (such as artisans, labourers, miners, small freeholders, tradesmen, merchants and manufacturers) in particular cultural contexts."[15] He pointed to the opportunity nonconformity offered to occupational groups which felt neglected by the establishment as symbolised by the Church of England. "As well as legitimating their emancipation from the 'dependency system', Non-conformity endorsed the socio-economic aspirations of the artisan, trading and manufacturing classes which constituted the bulk of its catchment area."[16] Gilbert produces figures derived from his analysis of a sample of non-

parochial registers up to 1837 to support his very broad list of occupational groups from which nonconformity derived most of its
membership.[17]

This thesis ought to be testable in the conurbation by correlating
church and chapel attendance against the proportion of the different occupational groups in each place. Unfortunately this can only
be done from the 1841 data. The population in all the places
itemised had grown, between 15% and 37%, during the succeeding
decade[18]. Table 23 has been compiled using the 1851 index of attendance and the occupational information set out in Tables 4, 6 and 7.

The wide range of Gilbert's categories means that virtually the
whole employed population of the conurbation is included within
them. As Table 4 shows, only in Birmingham were more than 1%
employed in public and professional services and nowhere had
more than 1% in the transport category in 1841. As Gilbert specifically mentions nailers in his book they have been listed separately,
although also included within the manufacturing category.
Methodist figures have been extracted out from the larger Nonconformist grouping, within which they also feature. The Index for
Roman Catholics has not been included, so the total Index of attendance for each place will usually be greater than the sum of those in
Table 23.

Not surprisingly none of the eighteen possible correlations gives
a statistically significant result. The average of all eighteen is that r
= 0.7406. All are degrees of r = 0.7, they simply indicate that all
denominations were recruiting from the same rather restricted
range of occupations.[19]

The fact that the highest Nonconformist attendances were in
Sedgley and Tipton, places with the highest percentage of unskilled
labour is not part of a general pattern. Wolverhampton, with the
highest Church of England index, also had the highest proportion
of domestic servants but a correlation between domestic service and
each denominational grouping in turn gives virtually identical
results. Bilston and West Bromwich had almost identical nonconformist attendances despite the virtual absence of nailers in Bilston
and its much greater percentage of miners. These variations within
the Black Country occupational structure may still be important,
though not statistically significant, for the balance they indicate
between the different industries within each locality.

The heart of Gilbert's thesis, however, is the organisation and
economic status of those occupations at the time of their early
industrialisation. "Artisans employed in domestic industry had
been over-represented in early Evangelical Nonconformity in relation to most occupational groups. The association between Non-

conformist religion and the textile trades, for example, had been primarily a reflection of the disproportionate number of handloom weavers in chapel communities; and in iron manufacturing areas like the Black Country, nail makers, chain makers and other outworkers in iron had shown an unusual propensity for Nonconformist associations during the era of optimum Evangelical Nonconformist growth . . ." For Gilbert this period had ceased by the beginning of the Victorian era "when the transition from capitalist outwork to factory production was rapidly reversing this industrial trend." Thus, "During the 1830s and 1840s important social groups within the Evangelical Nonconformist constituency were not merely becoming less receptive to Nonconformist recruitment, they were becoming extinct."[20]

Despite the gloomy predictions of James Boydell, however, neither the hand-wrought nail trade nor the hand-made chain industry died out before 1850. In fact they continued to maintain a separate existence, domestic nailing still employed 18, 000 people in 1860 and hand-made chain, although a much smaller industry, continued in Cradley Heath and Old Hill well into the 1960s.[21] This meant that they continued to be sources of recruitment for the churches, particularly the Methodists who often provided leaders for the short-lived trade union activity which characterised these industries. Strikes were regular in the nail trade between 1830 to 1860 when a union of horse-nail makers, which had succeeded in raising wages, eventually succumbed to the Dudley Nailmasters' Association. A union known as the Chain and Trace Makers Anti-Truck and Price Protection Society was formed in 1844 but failed to secure permanent agreements from the employers.[22] Methodist officials did not necessarily support the strikers. In 1852 the Brierley Hill Primitive Methodist local preachers meeting resolved, "That Brother Southall, Halesowen, have no appointments next quarter and that he be recommended to withdraw from the position he holds with the nailers."[23] This, of course, did not prevent a succession of Methodist contributions to local trade union leadership, for example from three generations of the Perrins family of Lye near Stourbridge.[24]

To single out the Black Country as an obvious area for nonconformist recruitment because of the predominance of domestic outworking within some of its major industries oversimplifies a complex situation and could be an example of an explanation being found to fit a known fact, the success of nonconformity compared with the Church of England in attracting a working class following in the first half of the nineteenth century. As chapter two demonstrated, outworking in domestic or hired workshops, together with extensive sub-contracting typified the whole pattern of industrial organisation, not only in the Black Country but also in Birmingham itself throughout most of the nineteenth century and, in many industries, well beyond. This raises more questions than it resolves. For example, if domestic outworking offered a natural recruiting ground for nonconformity why was the response so patchy? As Tables 20 and 21 indicate not only was the nonconformist Index below the Church of England in Birmingham and Wolverhampton, it was barely ahead in Walsall and Wednesbury. It was also below 30% in Bloxwich and Willenhall where domestic outworking was notorious, not to mention Stourbridge and Kingswinford where it also fell marginally below this figure. It could well be that other factors, apart from occupational structure, were as important in influencing church attendance, including each denomination's share within the conurbation.

The change from domestic outworking to factory labour was most marked in textile towns like Bradford. Theodore Koditschek, in his study, sees religion performing the role of 'midwife of class', particularly the entrepreneurial middle class industrial capitalists who supported the prosperous Congregational and Baptist chapels. Although he refers regularly to Gilbert's book his main conclusions seem to refute Gilbert's thesis. According to Gilbert, "Factory workers in cities were much more difficult to mobilise than craftsmen employed in domestic industry had been; and, equally important, they did not constitute a catchment area in which Nonconformity had any intrinsic advantage over the Established Church. Capitalist outworkers had been close enough, socially, to the old 'dependency system' for Anglicanism to have retained unwelcome associations with prescriptive social control; but for factory workers the emancipation was generally too complete for this factor to operate."[25] In Bradford not only the rapid rise of the factory population but also the Ten Hours campaign and opposition to the New Poor Law, given vocal support by the curate of Bierley, George Stringer Bull, in the 1830s, along with his initiative in holding cottage meetings, should have enabled the Church of England to overhaul nonconformity if Gilbert's thesis is to be trusted.[26] In Koditschek's judgement this did not happen. Anglican paternalism was no match for nonconformist voluntaryism in attracting Sunday worshippers. "The full extent of the Nonconformist triumph in Bradford was revealed by the 1851 census, which showed that only 23% of all morning worshippers on census Sunday chose to attend Bradford's established churches. By contrast, almost 60 per cent worshipped in forty-one different Nonconformist chapels."[27]

Koditschek, relying on the printed census tables, points out that morning worship, traditionally the best attended Anglican service, only attracted 4.6% of an urban population of 103, 778. He does not add that this figure included Sunday school scholars. "Less than half of Bradford's available church sittings were occupied, as 95 percent of the population simply stayed away." By contrast, "the Nonconformists, on census Sunday morning, outnumbered the Anglicans by a margin of three to one. Although this still left many people untouched by organised religion, in so far as there was a dominant form of worship in mid-century Bradford it was the voluntary Nonconformist and not the established Anglican form. Indeed, the census statistics reveal that, by 1851, Bradford had become the most intensely Nonconformist town in England."[28]

As morning services were better attended than the evening ones on census Sunday in Bradford this was a fair comparison.[29] It is certainly very different from the pattern in Birmingham, although Birmingham was more than twice the size of Bradford in 1851. Only the Roman Catholic percentage of attendances was comparable, their Index in Bradford was 3.9% and in Birmingham 3.7%. The overall Index for Bradford was 42.7%, somewhat higher than Birmingham's 36% according to the printed tables. My calculations give it the higher figure of 37.5.[30] The denominational Indexes are; Church of England: Bradford 9.8, Birmingham 17%, Nonconformists: Bradford 28.5, Birmingham 15.8

Thus the denominational position of Anglicans and nonconformists is almost completely reversed with a considerably greater preponderance of nonconformists in Bradford than the equivalent Anglican majority in Birmingham.

Koditschek explains the Bradford situation almost entirely in terms of social class. The Church of England he identifies with a Tory oligarchy, "a band of wealthy Anglican manufacturers and professionals who were coming to dominate every other public institution in the town."[31] They controlled the ineffective Watching and Lighting Commission between its establishment in 1803 and its abolition in 1847 to make way for the new Town Council which was dominated by their rivals, the Nonconformist Liberals. He admits that Anglican church building belatedly attempted to keep pace with population, but dismisses most of it as biased in favour of the middle classes.[32] The Anglican initiative in the 1840s, under the energetic vicar, William Scoresby, in founding nine Anglican day schools and model lodging houses for young millgirls is not related to church attendance but dealt with in a separate chapter.[33] Despite the work of Oastler and Bull on behalf of factory children the Church of England is not credited with any influence amongst the working class. Only the Town Mission, founded in 1850, brought Evangelical Anglicans, along with nonconformists, into indirect contact with the urban poor through the work of Town Missionaries.[34]

Koditschek emphasises that nonconformist dominance in Bradford was really confined to three denominations, Baptist, Congregational and Methodist, the Wesleyans being much the largest amongst the latter. Despite suffering much heavier losses to the Wesleyan Association and Wesleyan Reformers than Birmingham Wesleyans during the stormy times of 1835 and 1849 the Bradford Wesleyans still attracted the largest attendances of any denomination on census Sunday. When to the Wesleyan total of 9, 785 the total Primitive, New Connexion, Reformers and Association attendances are added the total Methodist figures reach 16, 637. These compare very favourably with the combined Baptist and Congregationalist total of 10, 885.[35]

Koditschek's explanation is that whereas the Baptist and Congregational chapels became bastions of the more affluent middle class those of the Methodists retained their working class links. Even the Wesleyans had a sizeable working class following, "Even during the crisis years of the 1840s, workers constituted just under half of the membership of Kirkgate Wesleyan Chapel, while their participation in other chapels and in at least two of the breakaway Methodist connexions was even greater."[36]

In his view the independent polity of Baptists and Congregationalists inhibited their expansion, whereas Methodism's flexible organisation was much more effective in this respect. Unfortunately his appreciative treatment of the Primitive Methodists contains a factual error. "With 1, 980 attenders on census Sunday morning and 952 members officially on the books, the Primitive Methodists were the largest of the breakaway connexions and were unique in attracting a membership that was uniformly working or lower middle class."[37] In fact it was the total number of sittings, not attendances, which amounted to 1, 980, a misreading of the census tables which attributes a greater strength to the Primitives than they actually obtained, particularly when it is realised that the circuit membership figure includes several societies which lay beyond the boundaries of the town. The strength of the Primitives in Bradford, as Koditschek illuminatingly points out, was not in the central urban area but in Great Horton, a township on the outskirts where the older forms of industrial and community life persisted. He contrasts the success of the Primitives in Great Horton with the failure of the Prospect Street Baptist cause in the "downtown factory districts" where members were expelled or withdrew for a range of moral and personal reasons.

The denominational pattern of Birmingham nonconformity bears only a partial resemblance to that of Bradford. In Birmingham the combined Congregational and Baptist numbers were well above the Methodist total, even though the Methodists remained the largest single group. The Congregationalists and Baptists each had Indexes of 4.1% whilst the overall Methodist Index was 5.3, of which two thirds belonged to the Wesleyans. This shows how dominant the Wesleyans were within Birmingham Methodism despite their serious membership losses after the 'Fly-sheets' agitation which divided Wesleyanism, reaching its climax in 1849. The combined membership of the East and West Birmingham Wesleyan circuits had reached a peak of 3, 665 in 1847 but then dropped to 2, 490 in 1852, over a thousand members being lost after 1849. As by no means all Wesleyan losses constituted gains for the dissident Wesleyan Reformers the Methodist position within Birmingham nonconformity must be under-represented by the 1851 census.

Although to Koditschek the Bradford census results are predominantly a reflection of social class he does recognise that more was needed than social status to attract newcomers in a rapidly expanding town. "On the one hand growth resulted from the arrival of immigrants who brought their Nonconformist identities with them. On the other hand, it also came from the conversion of godless or nominally Anglican individuals who were encountered within the town." In his opinion "the Baptists and Congregationalists increased primarily as a result of the former, whereas the Methodist denominations proved to be most adept at the task of evangelical conversion."[38] Thus, implicitly at least, he introduces another, specifically religious, motive for chapel attendance alongside the appeal of status and respectability. Koditschek does not go on to explore the evangelistic methods of the Bradford churches to support his thesis. If taken seriously this could be a significant factor in explaining not only the denominational pattern but also the general level of church and chapel-going in urban industrial areas. It will be addressed in chapter seven of this thesis. Meanwhile his other point, the link between rural and urban denominational allegiance, requires further examination.

5.2 The regional context, urban and rural links

The apparent contrast between high rural and low urban church attendance noted by Mann was taken over more or less uncritically by others, such as Perkin, who used it to support his theory of class development. "The migrating workers moved from the countryside, where the social pressures were in favour of going to Church . . . to a small town where the social pressures were in favour of going to chapel, or to a large one where they were against going at all."[39]

This simple contrast between a submissive rural workforce worshipping regularly in their parish church and an alienated urban
proletariat worshipping nowhere was initially challenged by Hugh
McLeod in his comparisons between the high and low church attendance areas, urban and rural, revealed by the census.[40] He has since
followed it up as have Snell and Watts, who have mapped the varying levels and denominational distribution of church attendance
obtainable from the census.[41]

In his mapping of nonconformist attendances in England and
Wales, for example, Watts points to the pockets of Baptist strength
in the Pennines, particularly in the Haslingden (Lancs) and neighbouring Todmorden (Yorks) registration districts.[42] The latter could
help explain Koditschek's claim that Baptist immigrants to Bradford brought their denominational identities with them. Watts
traces this pattern to late seventeenth century evangelism whilst a
more recent activity could have built up rural Independency on
which Bradford Congregationalism may have drawn. This was the
itinerant evangelism which took place between 1790 and 1815 from
the Independent Theological College in Idle, just outside Bradford,
modelled on that of the Calvinist Methodists at Trevecca. According
to Derek Lovegrove, however, these expeditions by college students
normally involved support for existing churches rather than breaking new ground, though they necessarily had to be within reasonable travelling distance of Bradford.[43]

Rural nonconformity was not limited to Baptists and Independents, though the ambiguous position of the Wesleyan Methodists
in relation to the Church of England in the first half of the nineteenth century, particularly in the countryside, needs to be borne in
mind when reading Watts. Undoubtedly Methodism was stronger
than either the Baptists or Independents in the countryside around
Bradford, but what was more significant was the explicit policy of
Yorkshire Methodism to welcome immigrants to the towns from
rural societies. Brian Greaves' thesis on Methodism in Yorkshire
analyses the Methodist pattern from the 1851 census and points out
that all the main Methodist groups, Wesleyans, New Connexion
and Primitives, were strong in the county, that Methodist attendances were over 50% of the total in the Otley and Keighley registration districts and over 40% in Hunslett, all three adjacent to Bradford. Moreover in Leeds the central Wesleyan 'Boggart House'
chapel had a policy of welcoming immigrants into the local society[44]. Such a policy in the more rapidly expanding town of Bradford
may, along with their evangelistic zeal, help explain Methodist
strength.

Watts traces much of the strength of Independents and Baptists in the nineteenth century to their situation during the civil wars of the seventeenth. For example, in "those parts of eastern England and the south Midlands which had lain safely behind the parliamentary lines for most of the Civil War and where Puritans had been able to afford the luxury of debates about church government."[45] These also happened to be areas where, according to Lovegrove and W. R. Ward, some of their most effective rural itinerant preaching took place in the early nineteenth century, particularly that of the Bedfordshire Union.[46]

On the other hand Watts uses the successes and failures of seventeenth century Anglican provision to account for the general level of church attendance as well as the pattern of nonconformity in the nineteenth.[47] After tabulating Anglican church provision before 1800 alongside overall 1851 attendances Watts concludes, "throughout much of central England and Wales in particular, Methodism and Dissent grew so rapidly in the late eighteenth and early nineteenth centuries not because the Church of England was failing to provide churches in which people could worship, but because the established church had in fact sown the seeds of the Evangelical revival . . ., leaving the Methodists and Dissenters to reap the harvest. There may be no correlation between adequate Anglican provision in the eighteenth century and Anglican attendance in 1851, but . . .in many counties there was a correlation between Anglican provision in the previous century and overall religious observance in 1851." Having cited Wales as an area in which Anglican educational agencies laid the foundations for the growth of nonconformity he compares the results with England where, "the failure of the Church of England to provide adequately for the people of London, Lancashire, Durham, Northumberland and the industrial regions of the West Riding even at the end of the seventeenth century was reflected in some of the lowest overall attendance figures in the country a century and a half later."[48]

For this comparison Watts uses county statistics but a subsequent tabulation based on registration districts is used to map the denominational and overall attendance pattern in 1851. Unfortunately this is not easy to compare with other work on the census as Watts uses his own formula to arrive at the figures which he derives from the printed tables. He takes the total for the best attended services for each denomination, adds a third of the total for the other services and then divides the result by the population of the registration district. Although he admits that "this may exaggerate the strength of Nonconformity as compared with the Church of England and the Church of Rome" he says that it will not be 'as great as using Inglis' index of attendance."[49]

Rather than recalculate these statistics from the published tables I have used Watts' figures to see whether the relationship between urban and rural denominational attendances apparent in the case of Bradford can help explain the very different pattern in Birmingham and the Black Country. Watts introduces a further factor, the 'level of illiteracy', which he derives from the percentage of all of those who, in that registration district in 1851, 'signed' the marriage register with a mark. This showed that "there was a significant correlation between districts with a high level of illiteracy and districts with a high level of Nonconformist support."[50]

Before considering this aspect of Watts' argument the relative positions of the different denominations in the rural areas surrounding the conurbation will be addressed. These lay across what McLeod recognises as a significant dividing line between northern and western regions with large parishes containing several townships and southern and eastern counties where most parishes included only one township and their area was smaller.[51] Table 24 sets these out.

Not all the places within these registration districts were rural villages. With an 1851 population of 18, 462, Kidderminster was a sizeable town, as were several smaller places such as Lichfield, Tamworth, Solihull, Bridgnorth, Bromsgrove and Droitwich. Nevertheless they contained many predominantly agricultural villages as well as industrial settlements like the needle manufacturing area around Redditch and the Cannock coalfield. None of these figures suggests that immigration from rural congregations can account for the Methodist dominance of the Black Country or the strength of the Independents and Baptists in Birmingham. What they do seem to indicate is steady Anglican support. All of these districts are above Watts' national norm for the Church of England of 20.19% and some, such as Solihull, Bridgnorth and Cleobury are particularly high. The addition of districts only slightly further away such as Atherstone, Warwick and Stratford upon Avon would add further high Anglican attendances of 32.4, 33.2 and 35.6 (Watts' figures) respectively.[52] This suggests that the good showing of the Church of England, compared with Protestant Nonconformity, in Birmingham and Wolverhampton was related to allegiances formed in the birthplaces of many of their immigrant population. The unknown factor then becomes the pattern of rural attendance at the parish church, on the regularity and motivation of which considerable differences of opinion persist.

For some time the variations in rural church-going have been related to landownership as much as the presence or absence of resident clergy. David Thompson in his work on Leicestershire and

James Obelkevich in a later study of Lincolnshire distinguish clearly between 'close' and 'open' parishes. Obelkevich identifies four types ranging from those in which one landlord owned more than half the land to those with several landlords and a number of smaller holdings. In between were two categories, one nearer the 'close' and one nearer the 'open' type. "If close parishes tended to be Anglican, an unco-operative squire could obstruct the designs of the parson, and if open parishes tended to be Methodist, their rough ways could also make them hostile to all forms of organised religion."[53] Looking at the 1851 census in the light of this classification his conclusions were not surprising, "the more open the parish, the lower the level of attendance."[54] In general Church of England attendance was not high in South Lindsey, despite the many Wesleyan Methodists for whom worshipping at the parish church was a regular habit. As David Thompson put it, "It is therefore a mistake to imagine that villages are necessarily places where church attendance is strong . . . A rural migrant to a growing town . . . might well have come from a place where it was not normal to go to church."[55] In fact David Hempton has recently pointed out that, "In Silas Marner . . . George Eliot creatively inverts the conventional pattern of a relatively religious countryside contrasted with irreligious towns which seemed to have been irrefutably demonstrated by the census of religious worship in 1851. What is hinted at through Silas, however, is that the religion of the countryside was a rather pale mixture of deference, dependency, custom and community solidarity, while popular urban religion was based more on voluntary commitment to religious associations."[56]

As George Eliot was writing from her own Evangelical Anglican experience of village life in North Warwickshire in the first half of the century her evidence is particularly relevant. Silas, of course, was a member of a small Baptist chapel before he left the industrial town for refuge in the countryside. His religious education is undertaken by a friendly neighbour, Mrs Winthrop the wheelwright's wife, in order to help him bring up the little orphan girl Eppie, whom he has decided to adopt. Hence he needs to fit in with village custom, within which rites of passage and certain Christian festivals were celebrated by all, but regular church attendance could be interpreted as unsociably presumptuous; "to go to church every Sunday in the calendar would have shown a greedy desire to stand well with Heaven, and get an undue advantage over their neighbours . . .that would have implied a reflection on those who had had godfathers and godmothers as well as themselves, and had an equal right to the burial service." Mrs Winthrop was one of those "who were held to be good livers" and who "went to church with greater,

though still with moderate frequency."[57] The nature of rural religion
in Silas Marner, therefore, is very much seen and interpreted
through the eyes of Dolly Winthrop. A slightly different and more
genuinely devout picture is painted in Adam Bede. He, along with
all the other principal characters, are regular attenders at the Sunday service, held in the afternoon at the parish church as the rector
is a pluralist, and although some are tenants of Squire Donnithorne,
others, including Adam himself and his evening-school teacher Bar-
tle Massey, are independent artisans and tradesmen. Only Alick, the
shepherd, "had a general impression that public worship and religious ceremonies, like other non-productive employments, were
intended for people who had leisure."[58] The point is not whether
Silas Marner or Adam Bede gives the more accurate portrayal of
rural attitudes to church-going in North Warwickshire, both villages could well have existed and indeed probably did. George
Eliot's initial readers were acutely aware of how accurate her memory of specific details tended to be.[59]

5.3 The institutional context, education and evangelism

What distinguished Adam Bede from later rural artisans' children
such as Flora Thompson was his need for an evening adult school
to gain basic literacy and numeracy. Flora's childhood education at
the village National School, for all its shortcomings, was evidence
of the Church of England's determination to retain its traditional
influence in 'open' as well as 'close' parishes.[60] The growth of
Anglican schools in towns in the second quarter of the nineteenth
century has been claimed as a significant factor in sustaining its
influence in industrial areas. Dennis Smith, in a study of Sheffield
and Birmingham, suggests that the relative strength of Anglicanism in Birmingham was the result of the increasing number of
church day schools, despite the prevalence of child labour which
prevented many children from attending. According to Smith the
1851 educational census showed that 62% of day scholars were in
Anglican schools and Church of England Sunday schools accounted for 58.4% of the total.[61] Whatever the justice of his comparison
with Sheffield, however, the 1851 census tables do not support
Smith's conclusions. In fact I cannot derive his Sunday school figures from the census report. Not only so but a comparison of the
take-up of educational provision between Birmingham and the
Black Country does not give the Anglicans any advantage in Birmingham. Only the Church of England percentage of Sunday school
scholars is slightly higher in Birmingham than in the Black Country, its day school percentages are lower in Birmingham than in

Dudley and Stourbridge.

Such a judgement, of course, gives no indication of the quality of the education provided, particularly its religious elements. Nevertheless the statistical position is set out in Table 25. On the assumption that the population aged below twenty was divided equally between those aged 0-5, 6-10, 11-15 and 16-20 then between a quarter and a half of them could be available for education on weekdays or Sundays or both. Hence Table 25 gives the population under 20 years old as well as the numbers attending day and Sunday schools, the percentage share of the Church of England's provision, plus a combined figure for nonconformist and 'British' schools and for nonconformist Sunday schools. The percentage share of the total number of day school pupils in private and endowed schools is added to fill out the picture. The endowed schools included ancient grammar schools such as Queen Mary's Walsall and King Edward's Birmingham. Roman Catholic schools have not been included.

The percentage of the under 20 population in denominational day and Sunday schools was higher in the Black Country than it was in Birmingham. Although the Anglican share of day school pupils was much higher than the nonconformist, except perhaps in West Bromwich, in the case of Sunday scholars their positions were reversed. Only in Birmingham did the Anglicans approach the nonconformists in the number of Sunday scholars and even here they were several points behind. It is equally clear that the percentage of the under 20 population in any form of education was not high. Only in Stourbridge were more than 20% in day schools (26%). In the other districts percentages were:

Wolverhampton and Aston: 16%, West Bromwich: 18.5%, Dudley, Kings Norton and Birmingham: 19%, Walsall: 20%

Perhaps surprisingly the Sunday school percentage of the age range was not much higher, lower in the Birmingham districts than the day school percentages and only significantly higher in the Black Country. There they varied by over ten percentage points between the lowest, Wolverhampton, and the highest, Dudley.

Where does this leave Watts' assertion that there is a clear relationship between degrees of illiteracy and nonconformist strength? His own calculations, based on the national statistics, produce a coefficient of r = 0.74 which he considers 'highly significant'.[63] It should be possible to make a correlation between the percentage of the under-twenty population in education and the 'literacy' level indicated by those signing the marriage register. These figures highlight a contrast between Birmingham and the Black Country and are given in Table 26 below.

Table 26

Percentage of population under 20 and literacy levels indicated by Registrar General 1851.

District:	W'ton	Walsall	W Brom	Dudley	St'rbr'ge	Kgs Ntn	Birm'gham	Aston
% in education	16.0	20.0	18.5	19.1	26.1	19.1	19.0	16.0
Literacy%	44.0	41.5	52.0	34.3	39.5	78.0	63.0	61.7

The correlation between these two sets of figures is r = 0.64, a positive but not a highly significant result,[64] particularly as the number of districts is relatively small. The disparity between the percentage involved in education and the literacy level as indicated by signing the marriage register within the Birmingham area is particularly marked, but it is paralleled at a much lower level in the Black Country and is open to a number of interpretations. The most obvious is that there is no relationship between the number of children in education in any one year and the literacy of those older people being married at the same time. However, they do raise a question over Watts' idea of a direct relationship between the appeal of nonconformity and an inability to write. After all, Adam Bede was not the only one to have to attend an adult evening class. George Stephenson, whose portrait, but not his signature, adorns the current Bank of England £5 note, only began to learn to read at eighteen and had great difficulty signing his name in the marriage register at Newburn parish church when he was twenty-one.[65] Intelligence and ability within the nineteenth century working class were not limited to those who, by the time they became young adults, could write as well as read.[66] Keith Snell points out that the most significant correlation, at a national level, is between 'illiteracy', as measured by 'signing' the marriage register with a mark, and the incidence of child labour, a factor also positively associated with the level of Sunday school attendance. This finding bears out my comment in the previous note and sets Watts' assertion in a more realistic context.[67]

Whatever their early educational opportunities both immigrants to the conurbation and those born within it needed some active encouragement on the part of churches and chapels to ensure that they formed regular links with a worshipping congregation. This sort of activity is impossible to quantify and so has suffered some neglect by interpreters of the 1851 census. Mark Smith, however, in his study of Oldham and Saddleworth, gives it the most prominent place amongst the various factors which influenced the religious situation in that area. Although there was no popular rejection of the supernatural, the churches there had to cope with "a mushrooming population, changing patterns of work . . . and increasing social tensions All the churches faced communities that were to some extent

alienated from regular weekly church attendance and had to compete for scarce working class leisure time with an alternative . . . culture based on the public house. In response, the churches launched
vigourous building programmes and strove to maintain high stan-
dards of pastoral and devotional activity . . . they also embarked on
a continuous and increasingly co-operative programme of aggres-
sive evangelism." This sustained pastoral and evangelistic activity,
more than any other factor, accounts for the increasing influence of
the churches in that area as the century progressed.[68]

It could well be that something similar took place in Birmingham
and the Black Country but before investigating such activities further another factor, absent from Oldham and Saddleworth but not
from other industrial areas such as South Wales, needs to be considered, namely the incidence of cholera epidemics and their possible effects on the church-going pattern revealed in 1851.

Notes

1   R. A. Soloway, *Prelates and People*, London 1969, pp. 441, 444.

2   H. McLeod, *Class and Religion in the Late Victorian City*, London 1974, pp. 104, 122.

3   Soloway, *Prelates*, p.445.

4   K. S. Inglis, *Churches and the Working Classes in Victorian England*, London 1963, p.20.

5   E. R. Wickham, *Church and People in an Industrial City*, London 1957, pp. 107-108.

6   cf. J. Morris, 'Church and People thirty three years on', in *Theology* 94, March/April 1991, pp.92-101. Wickham's general thesis, that provision for worship had never matched the population growth in the industrial towns, was not new. The failure of church provision and the system of pew rents and appropriated sittings in those churches and chapels which were avail-able had become a commonplace, part of the Church of England's apolo-getic armoury when faced by the criticism that it had ceased to be the church of the nation at large. For example, in 1951 the F. D. Maurice Com-memoration Lectures, given by J. V. L. Casserley, a former lecturer in soci-ology at Exeter University, and entitled '*The Retreat from Christianity in the Modern World*', contained a chapter on 'the sociology of the retreat' in which the sheer imbalance between population growth and Anglican church accommodation in the first half of the nineteenth century in Lan-cashire and Birmingham was set out in detail to support the assertion that, "The unwillingness of the working-class masses to attend public worship dates from the lengthy period in which it was impossible for them to do so, for the simple reason that most of them had no church to attend." Casser-ley, *Retreat*, p.112.

7   E. Hobsbawm, *Labouring Men*, London 1964, pp. 22-33, the quotation is from page 27.

8   Hobsbaum, *Labouring*, p.32. But see E. P. Thompson's challenge to the last point in *Making*, pp. 427-433.

9   H. Perkin, *The Origins of Modern English Society 1780-1880*, London 1969, p.196.

10   Perkin, *Origins*, pp. 205, 355. cf. J. Saville (Ed.) *The Life of Thomas Cooper*, Leicester 1971, pp. 344-400.

11   Perkin, *Origins*, pp. 197-202.

12   C. G. Brown, 'Did urbanisation secularise Britain', in *Urban History Yearbook*, 1988, p.7.

13   H. McLeod (Ed), *European Religion in the Age of the Great Cities 1830-1930*, London 1995, pp. 11-15.

14   C. G. Brown, 'The mechanism of religious growth in urban societies', in McLeod, ibid. pp. 239-262.

15   A. D. Gilbert, 'The growth and decline of Non-conformity in England and Wales with special reference to the period before 1850', D Phil. Oxford 1973, p.176.

16   Ibid. p.189.

17   A. D. Gilbert, *Religion and Society in Industrial England; Church, Chapel and Social Change 1740-1914*, London 1976, p.63, Table 3.1.

18   see Table 3.

19   All are significant at 5% level with 8 degrees of freedom.

20   Gilbert, *Industrial England*, p.146.

21   Allen, *Industrial*, p.126, *VCH Staffordshire*, Vol. 3, p.265.

22   Allen, *Industrial*, p.271, see also A. Willetts, *The Black Country Nailer's Riots of 1842*, Dudley 1995.

23   Dudley Archives and Local History Services, Coseley, Brierley Hill Circuit Quarterly Meeting Minutes, 27 September 1852.

24   see the autobiographical reminiscences of Wesley Perrins in *Bulletin for the Study of Labour History*, 1971 and *Bulletin of the West Midlands Branch of the Wesley Historical Society*, Vol. 3, nos. 3, 4, 5, 1979-80. Wesley Perrins worked in his father's nailshop, attached to his birthplace, until 1935.

25   Gilbert, *Industrial England*, p.146.

26   see J. C. Gill, *Parson Bull of Bierley*, London 1963, pp. 54-77.

27   Koditschek, *Class*, p.252. These conclusions are very similar to those of Allan Maclaren on Aberdeen where the entrepreneurial middle class virtually took over the Kirk from the established landed and professional classes resulting in the massive secession to the Free Church in 1843. Cf. A. A. McLaren *Religion and Social Class, The Disruption Years in Aberdeen*, London 1974, passim.

28   Ibid. p.255.

29   *Parliamentary Papers 1852-53, LXXXIX*, p. ccliii. Morning numbers were; Church of England 4, 719, Nonconformists 12, 721; Evening numbers: Church of England 1, 957, Nonconformists 11, 081.

30   see Table 16

31   Koditschek, *Class*, p.159.

32   Ibid. p.254.

33   Ibid. pp. 545-551.

34   Ibid. p.577.

35 see Table F in the census report, *Parliamentary Papers 1852-53, LXXXIX*, p. ccliii.

36 Koditschek, *Class*, p.282.

37 Ibid. pp. 284-286. The Primitive Methodist attendances are correctly quoted on page 260.

38 Ibid. p.256.

39 Perkin, *Origins*, p.202.

40 H. McLeod in *A Sociological Yearbook of Religion in Britain 6*, pp. 29-72

41 H. McLeod in J. Langton and K. J. Morris (Eds.), *Atlas of Industrialising Britain 1780-1914*, London 1986 pp. 212-217 and H. McLeod, *Religion and Society in England 1850-1914*, London 1996, pp. 11-70. Snell, *North Midlands* passim, Watts, *Dissenters*, pp. 22-29, 35-48, 671-870, Snell and Ell, *Rival*, passim.

42 Watts, *Dissenters*, p.40.

43 D. Lovegrove, *Established Church, Sectarian People*, Cambridge 1988, p.79-80.

44 B. Greaves, 'Methodism in Yorkshire 1740-1851', PhD. Liverpool 1968, pp. 45-47, 243-244.

45 Watts, *Dissenters*, p.39.

46 Lovegrove, *Sectarian*, pp. 50-51, W. R. Ward, *Religion and Society in England 1790-1850*, pp. 48-49.

47 In this he is following precedents set in the 1950s by French religious sociologists like Fernand Boulard and Emile Léonard, who were building on the work of Gabriel Le Bras. For them both Catholic and Protestant patterns of religious practice in the 1950s were closely linked to those of the seventeenth century, reflecting the political position after the Wars of Religion and subsequent missions by the Catholic religious orders. F. Boulard, *Introduction to Religious Sociology*, London 1960, pp. 33-43, E.G. Léonard, *Le Protestant Francais*, Paris 1955, pp. 12-26.

48 Watts, *Dissenters*, pp. 46-47.

49 Ibid. p.672.

50 Ibid. p.102. Watts does not relate this variable to others which, on the face of it, would also be relevant such as the take-up of such educational opportunities as were available and the rate of immigration from outside the districts in which the marriages were recorded. Unfortunately the Registrar General's annual reports do not enable 'illiteracy' figures for sub-districts to be compiled to match other available statistics.

51 H. D. McLeod in *Sociological Yearbook of Religion in Britain 6*, pp. 31-32.

52 Watts, *Dissenters*, pp. 28, 700-703.

53 J. Obelkevich, *Religion and Rural Society, South Lindsey 1825-1875*, Oxford 1976, pp. 12-13.

54 Ibid. p.155.

55 D. M. Thompson, 'Churches and Society in Nineteenth Century England, a rural perspective', in G. J. Cuming and D. Baker (Eds.) *Popular Belief and Practice, Studies in Church History 8*, Cambridge 1972, p.270.

56 D. Hempton, *Religion and political culture in Britain and Ireland*, Cambridge 1996, p.132.

57 G. Eliot, *Silas Marner*, London 1861, chapter X.

58 G. Eliot, *Adam Bede*, London 1859, chapter XVIII.

59   Ashton, *Eliot*, p.205.

60   F. Thompson, *Lark Rise to Candleford*, London 1939, Oxford edition 1945, pp. 167-195.

61   D. Smith, *Conflict and Compromise, class formation in English society*, London 1982, pp. 130-131.

62   Compiled from *Parliamentary Papers 1852-53 LXXXV*, Population Tables pp. 523-524 and *XC Education*, pp. 148-149, 152.

63   Watts, *Dissenters*, p.102.

64   Not significant at 5% level with 5 degrees of freedom.

65   see facsimile reproductions in W. O. Skeat, *George Stephenson, The Engineer and His Letters*, London 1973, pp. 23, 128, 154.

66   Unfortunately the only evidence of the relative numbers of those who could read, compared with those who could also write, is limited to such sources as the reports of the Children's Employment Commission and is incidental rather than systematic. In investigating children's employment the commissioners visited many factories, taking evidence from young people and frequently noting their ability to read and write. In 1841 two different commissioners covered Birmingham and the Black Country. R. D. Grainger visited fifty-five factories comprising a considerable range of Birmingham trades. He concentrated on interviewing manufacturers, foremen and overseers, including only sixty children, 47 boys and 13 girls, in his written evidence. He did attach, however, a detailed table of all the children employed at one factory, Palmer and Holt, pin makers, a total of thirty-three, aged between eight and twelve years, indicating their literacy, educational background, clothing, health and parents' employment. Whereas seven out of twenty-one boys and five out of twelve girls could read, albeit some of them not very well, only four boys and no girls could write. This was not surprising as only twelve boys and three girls had had any day school education, though ten boys and six girls went to Sunday schools. These would normally only teach reading, those who wished to learn to write would have to attend the additional evening classes which most Sunday schools provided during the working week. Reading, of course, was much easier to practice out of school hours than writing. The latter accomplishment needed not only more skilful teaching but the means, in the form of pens, ink and paper, to practice regularly before legibility and fluency were acquired. There were, of course some young people, like the apprentices at Boulton's Soho engineering works, who were very capable and well read, but the majority could only read "an easy book" by spelling out the letters. Many were like Caroline Ormer, aged 16, who worked for Mr Dawes, coffin furniture manufacturer, of whom Grainger noted: "Cannot read or write, went for some time to Sunday school, but not regularly, learnt to read a little but 'has forgotten it all'."(R. D. Grainger in *Children's Employment Commission, Parliamentary Papers 1843, vol. XIV*, pp. f127, 161-163.) In his survey of the Black Country R. H. Horne interviewed a total of 320 children, 112 in factories (72 boys and 40 girls) and 208 (155 boys and 53 girls) in day and Sunday schools. The largest number, a hundred, was in Wolverhampton, but others were interviewed in Willenhall, Darlaston, Bilston, Dudley, Sedgley, Walsall,

Wednesbury and Stourbridge. He was more systematic in his questioning than Grainger so that the resulting evidence shows that whereas 72% of the boys and 68% of the girls could read, even if it was only in "the thin books", a mere 28% of the boys and 12% of the girls could write. This included writing their names as Horne got his interviewees, wherever possible, to sign his statement of their evidence. Despite a low level of written literacy, therefore, the Black Country child in the 1840s was as likely as that of Birmingham to be capable of reading.(Horne, *Second Report, Children's Employment*, passim.)

67   Snell and Ell, *Rival*, pp. 293-95
68   M. A. Smith, *Industrial Society*, pp. 268-271.

CHAPTER 6

Cholera Epidemics and Churchgoing

6.1 The 1849 epidemic in Birmingham and the Black Country

Whatever the difficulties of interpreting the educational and denominational patterns of Birmingham and the Black Country in the second quarter of the nineteenth century there are few in the area of public health. Both the great cholera epidemics of the century struck the Black Country particularly hard but scarcely touched Birmingham. The 1849 outbreak will be considered first in case it provides an explanation for the 1851 contrasts in church attendance. Table 27 shows each registration district's 1849 cholera mortality and 1851 index of attendance.[1]

The total number of cholera deaths in the Black Country in 1849 was 2, 527 in contrast with 42 in the slightly less populous Birmingham districts. There were no cholera deaths in Harborne sub-district so no adjustment is needed for Smethwick. Almost half the Birmingham deaths occurred in the workhouse,[2] a location notorious for spreading the disease but its lack of virulence elsewhere points up the contrast with the Black Country. As a statistic Black Country mortality amounted to 0.66% of its 1851 population whilst the Birmingham area's was 0.01%.[3]

Fear of cholera need not have been co-terminous with the incidence of the disease. Hence there is no necessary connection between mortality from cholera and church attendance. Nevertheless the fact that fear of cholera encouraged church attendance amongst the indifferent or hostile is borne out by contemporary evidence. The Midland Mining Commission of 1850 reported impressive outbreaks of piety in 1849 amongst the miners.

"There is no lack of religious feeling among the colliers and miners of the district, and it has so far operated upon their lives as to subdue the more violent elements of character, and to render them kind, humane and free from the graver crimes. Their tendency is indeed rather towards religious enthusiasm, as shown at various times of excitement, and remarkably so during the recent prevalence of the cholera. Very numerous . . . were the instances of prayer meetings held by them, either before they went down the pits in the early morning, or in the pits before they began their work, or during their dinner hour . . . Occasionally, as was stated to me by gentlemen who were present at some of these meetings, as many as one or two hundred colliers, &c., would assemble, and in one instance as many as 700; and after singing a hymn, would remain on their knees for nearly an hour at a time, following the prayers of one of their local preachers (usually one of their own body), and lamenting aloud their own sinful lives, specifying their own particular failings, such as spending so much of their money in drink, and giving so little to their wives and families, and resolving to amend."[4]

Seeing the epidemic as a punishment for sin, or a warning sent by God, was not unique to the miners. This view had been extensively preached during the 1832 epidemic in the Black Country, within the lifetime of most of those affected in 1849. But resolutions taken at the height of the cholera epidemic proved short lived. The report continues, " But within a fortnight of the disappearance of the cholera these meetings began visibly to decline; and the information given me . . . about six weeks after, was that many had been abandoned. The magistrates informed me that they had remarked a considerable falling off in the ordinary cases brought before them during the cholera, and a sudden increase as soon as the danger had passed."[5]

There is a difference between attending an emergency pit-head prayer meeting and becoming a regular worshipper at church or chapel. Nevertheless the Primitive Methodist Brierley Hill Circuit, reporting a fall in membership in 1851, stated, "That the principal cause of the decrease is owing to persons withdrawing from us since the colara".[6] Some religious groups had clearly benefited as a result of the epidemic. Whether such increased attendances continued long enough to influence the 1851 Census of Religious Worship still needs investigation, though the Primitive Methodist evidence raises some doubts about their long term effects.

6.2 Leese and the impact of cholera on Methodism in the Black Country

In his doctoral thesis on Methodism in the Black Country Roger Leese pointed to the dramatic rise in Wesleyan membership during the 1832 and 1849 cholera epidemics. He proposed that cholera was the main explanation and in this he has been followed by Watts.[7] Even if there was a decline in membership when the epidemics were over they still left a net gain. Leese only used Wesleyan membership statistics from the Dudley circuit and Bilston. To test out the thesis it would be preferable to include Wesleyan statistics from other Black Country circuits, Primitive Methodist figures and, for 1849, the Methodist New Connexion.

Unfortunately these only survive in a partial fashion, but there are membership figures for whole circuits even if not for individual societies. Only Methodist quarterly membership statistics enable the impact of cholera epidemics to be measured as these can be related to the actual incidence of the disease. We have to rely on surviving memoirs or pamphlets to gauge the response of other religious groups. Before doing this variations in the impact of cholera and its incidence in 1849 and 1832 in the Black Country will be compared.

6.3 The impact of cholera on specific places in the Black Country

The Registrar General's Report on the 1849 epidemic gives specific figures for each registration sub-district, enabling comparisons to be made with the 1851 Index of Attendance. These are set out in Table 28.[8]

Despite the close relationship between the rank orders of Bilston, Tipton and Sedgley in both cholera mortality and church attendance there is no regular pattern, as the positions of Willenhall and Rowley Regis indicate. In fact the correlation coefficient overall is negative; r = -0.51976, whereas the rank order, according to Spearman's coefficient is; r = 0.1193, also not statistically significant.[9]

Unfortunately no such statistics exist for the 1832 epidemic which preceded the official registration of deaths begun in 1837. We have to rely on contemporary accounts, none of them designed to be statistically accurate. Charles Creighton, in his 'History of Epidemic Diseases in Great Britain' gives a table, which covers some places where cholera was prevalent in 1832, but without noting his source. [10]He refers to Charles Girdlestone, vicar of Sedgley, who, in an appendix to his 'Seven Sermons preached during the prevalence of the Cholera in the parish of Sedgley', provides another list.[11] This differs from Creighton, giving generally higher mortality figures as Table 29 shows.

The most obvious discrepancy, over Dudley, suggests a typographical error by Creighton, otherwise his figures are comparable with Girdlestone's, though somewhat lower, except in the case of Tipton. Here a large discrepancy exists without any means of deciding between the two. Girdlestone claimed the resident curate of Tipton as one of his informants.[12]

Support for Creighton's figure comes from the Wesleyan minister, Samuel Sugden, who gave the number of cholera deaths as 300 on 13 October 1832.[13] As the disease was reckoned to last about a month at its height and to linger on for a further six weeks[14] then Sugden's figure, which is clearly an estimate, must have been given toward the end of the epidemic in Tipton. The final death toll in Tipton, therefore, would seem to be about midway between Creighton and Girdlestone's figures, at around 350.

The figure Creighton gives for Bilston is not only lower than Girdlestone's but is contradicted by the principal local source, the curate, William Leigh's account which Creighton quotes.[15] This records 742 deaths, much nearer to Girdlestone's figure, so that on these grounds Girdlestone is to be preferred. He should also be credited with knowing the cholera mortality of his own parish. Two other places can be added. In 1849 the registrar for Stourbridge noted in December, "There have been . . . 76 (deaths) from cholera since the first case occurred on 27 August last. There were 29 deaths more than took place in the visitation of the disease in 1832".[16] This gives a figure of 47 deaths in Stourbridge in 1832. An entry for Rowley Regis is a deduction from the curate, George Barrs' journals. He records 52 deaths between July and September and a further three during the latter month, a total of 55.[17] Table 30 uses Girdlestone's figures for Dudley and Sedgley, an estimate for Tipton, Leigh's figure for Bilston, Creighton's figures for the remainder, plus Stourbridge and Rowley Regis. Mortality is based on the 1831 population.

The rank order looks a lot closer to the 1851 Index of attendance, although the correlation between 1832 mortality and 1851 attendance is also negative; r = -0.5609. The absence of Halesowen gives most other places a higher rank order for church attendance than they would otherwise obtain. The rank order according to Spearman's coefficient is, r = 0.5714. This is a great improvement on 1849, but with five fewer entries.[18]

6.4 Effects of the 1832 cholera epidemic on churchgoing

R. J. Morris has pointed out that the progress of the cholera epidemic across Russia and northern Europe in 1831 led the government to institute quarantine regulations to prevent it reaching British ports from the Baltic. Reports of its devastating effects raised public alarm but a combination of hostility towards the medical profession and divisions within their ranks, plus commercial pressure from shipowners, meant that the cholera bacillus entered the country, passing from its entry point of Sunderland to inland areas in an apparently random fashion.[19]

Because of its unpredictable suddenness and unprecedented virulence the 1832 cholera epidemic was seen, in Girdlestone's words, "as a chastisement at the hand of God"[20] and a national day of solemn fasting was appointed for March 21st. In their accounts of the disease in their parishes both Girdlestone and Leigh note its religious effects, as does George Barrs of Rowley Regis in his journal. From the Methodist side the Wesleyan Methodist Magazine published reports of Black Country circuits affected by the disease.

Those reporting the epidemic from a religious standpoint would hope for increased churchgoing as well as reduced drunkenness and gambling. The publication of such reports was intended to encourage fellow Christians, particularly within the denomination concerned, and elicit charitable contributions to relieve the suffering caused by the disease. Nevertheless, there was no unanimity about any positive effects of the epidemic.

The most optimistic are the Wesleyans of Tipton and Dudley, both of which had high cholera mortality. Writing at the end of August 1832 J. Robinson, employed in an iron foundry, states,

"The moral effect of this visitation in Tipton, the parish in which I reside, has been of a most salutary description. The chapels in this District have received immense accessions of serious, attentive, prayerful hearers. I have been a pleased witness of these gracious effects. Immediately before my own doors, at breakfast time, I have witnessed bull-baiters, dog-fighters, and such like, appropriating the hour allowed them for bodily refreshment to the duties of religion; and pressing to the private prayer meeting."[21]

Robinson's account combines the moral effects, such as abandoning bull-baiting, with religious practices like attendance at prayer meetings, but the striking moral effects convinced him that the religious changes would be permanent.

"In the works with which I am more immediately connected . . . most of the bull-dogs have disappeared; and . . . the fighting cocks have, to the pleasure and comfort of the wives and children of the men, been consigned to the cooks. To you, Sir, the giving up of a bull-dog or a fighting bird may appear a trifling proof of the impression which has been made; but to me, who am well acquainted with the habits of our working population, it appears a marvellous thing; and is a result which . . . would not have followed from the enactment of the severest human laws".

One and a half months later the resident Wesleyan minister, Samuel Sugden, wrote confirming this impression and illustrating it with vivid accounts of "two awful deaths; one or two remarkable conversions; and the triumphant death of a poor collier." Certainly the Wesleyans had geared themselves up to turn the opportunity afforded by the epidemic to their, and in their view, God's advantage.

"From the commencement of the disease we have had upwards of one thousand cases of cholera, and three hundred deaths. The zeal and exertions of the Local Preachers, Class-Leaders, and Prayer-Leaders, during the prevalence of this epidemic, were very remarkable. They regarded this season of affliction as a spiritual harvest-time, during which it would have been a shame to slumber. Crowds of people daily fled to the sanctuary, for whose salvation these excellent men earnestly pleaded with God; and, in regard to many, they did not plead in vain".[22]

Such letters, written for publication, with edifying instances of sin punished and sinners converted, were part of evangelical culture, not only in its Wesleyan form. Nevertheless the Wesleyan itinerant ministry had plenty experience of sudden revivals which, just as suddenly, died away and the more sober account of the Dudley situation by William France is all the more impressive for this reason,

"When I arrived at Dudley, just after the last Conference, I found the pestilence nearly extinct at Tipton, but alarmingly on the increase here, and at many other places in the Circuit, which caused the people to flock to our numerous chapels in crowds, both to hear preaching, and to attend the meetings for prayer, which were held in many of them every night, as well as in private houses at mid-day . . .. The congregations we had to preach to were deeply serious. We had none of the noises which have frequently as much injured as they have disgraced revivals of religion among us. The people were too deeply affected to shout and make confusion in the worship of God. An anxious concern for the salvation of their souls was strongly depicted on their countenances . . . and often tears and sighs, and sometimes sobs and groans, indicated the intensity of their feelings. The classes soon began to be crowded with persons who wished to unite themselves to our societies."

As a result he hoped that about a thousand new members would be added in the circuit. "We hear very favourable accounts of those on trial generally; and though the dread of death no longer operates upon their minds, as it did when they sought admittance to our classes, they still continue to attend the means of grace with great seriousness and fervour . . . the congregations are not now so overwhelming as they were some time ago; yet they are still very large and attentive." He goes on to add, "It is also worthy of observation, that we have had little or nothing of attempts to help forward the work by artificial excitement. Indeed the excitement produced by a most manifestly divine influence which rested, and I trust still continues to rest, upon the people at large, seemed, and still seems, to forbid the improper meddling of man with the work of God".

His own cautious optimism is a result of considerable experience elsewhere, "I think I am not naturally sanguine in my expectations; and if I were, upwards of thirty years experience, as an itinerant Minister, would have no small effect in correcting my temperament . . . I greatly rejoice at what I have seen since I came to this Circuit, and the prospects that are still opening before us; but I rejoice with trembling."[23]

The most optimistic of the Anglicans was Girdlestone. His 'Seven Sermons preached during the prevalence of the cholera in the parish of Sedgley' were edited by him and supplied with a preface, providing "a narrative of that visitation" in December of 1832. In it he indicates the dates on which the first and last cases of cholera were recorded making it possible to decide how close his remarks were to the height of the epidemic. The first case in Sedgley was notified on 10th August and the last on 24th September. He had announced a "day of solemn Fast and Humiliation" for 6th September, and publishes the sermon preached on that occasion. Two further sermons are dated, 20th and 27th September and the final sermon on 6th November, which he had announced as "a day of solemn thanksgiving to Almighty God". Three others, undated, could have been preached during October while the epidemic's impression was still fresh. Girdlestone's comments on the results, therefore, are given just less than three months after the last case of cholera in the parish.

Like the Methodists of Tipton he celebrates the positive effects on public morals, particularly "a considerable diminution in tippling and drunkenness", a reduction in bull-baiting "and the voluntary destruction of bull-dogs by their owners, under the influence of religious convictions". There was an increase Sunday observance, also "a large increase of attendance on public worship". "I am thankful to bear testimony that it continues up to the present date" his church being " better filled than ever". Many come twice who only came once, others come who never came before, "And this attendance is not only more full and frequent, but also more punctual and devout; the number being now less of those who interrupt the devotions of their brethren, by entering after the service has commenced, and those voices being more numerous which join in the responses, give assent with an audible Amen, and swell in vocal psalmody the songs of prayer and praise."[24]

The titles and texts of Girdlestone's sermons give a false impression of their actual tone, despite the prefix that, "During the prevalence of Cholera we are anxious to impress upon our Parishioners that Sickness is God's chastening for the Sin of Man." This is emphasised by Morris but he does not fairly represent Girdlestone's approach.[25] There is no hectoring of the congregation, no threats of hellfire for the impenitent, no glorying in the fear produced by the disease. Instead there is a real concern that those terrified into piety should understand the nature of the religion on which they rely, so they are not deluded into false spiritual security. While exhorting his hearers to care for the sick he says, "I know of no member of this congregation, I know of no inhabitant of this parish, who has either taken flight from the scene of painful duty, or refused to take his share in discharging it. I know of many who have laboured, far beyond their usual habits, nay, I may say, beyond their strength, in attending on the cases of the diseased, and in securing as far as possible, the health of the community".[26]

These sermons are a testimony to one Evangelical clergyman's attempt to use the epidemic and its psychological effects to encourage a sensible Christian response. The Evangelical formulae are there, but they do not crowd out other concerns, nor do they give the impression of being mere cant phrases. He had, in the six years before the epidemic, gradually increased the number of communion services from three to twelve during the year and he notes with particular satisfaction, "we counted, at the last communion administered, a larger number than we ever remember to have seen assembled on a like occasion here before."[27] After the serious call to self examination before taking communion in the sermon on this subject he cannot have thought the increase in communicants resulted from some superstitious belief in the virtue of the sacrament to ward off disease and death.

Girdlestone's optimism was not shared by Leigh of Bilston, where mortality had been greatest. Writing in May 1833, six and a half months after the last case, Leigh exclaims,

"Every Christian reader will be anxious to know the effects of this most awful visitation upon the survivors in my own parish, and in the surrounding district. Alas! I am constrained to confess, and with shame and sorrow I do confess, that I can see nothing like proof remaining of religious impressions, or religious improvement. Whilst the pestilence was raging in all its deadly violence, . . . and our fellow mortals were falling by our sides on the right hand and on the left, I willingly admit there were, in every class, a seriousness of demeanour, and correctness of conduct, befitting the awfulness of our situation . . . But when the pestilence had ceased, then the God who who sent it in "His Wrath, " and removed it in "His Mercy, " was no longer in all our thoughts. The same indifference to "Heavenly Things" as heretofore was soon visible amongst all ranks, the rich and the poor, and the message from Heaven seemed disregarded. It is painful to make this representation, but, . . . I cannot, and I dare not, withhold the truth."[28]

Leigh and his curate, Fletcher, had closed their churches on the 19th of August to prevent a large gathering of people, thinking that cholera was contagious, one of the two current medical theories on the nature of the disease which Leigh's account endeavoured to support.[29] He admits that as many as could escape the town did so. Both Leigh himself and his wife were ill, though not with cholera, the following Sunday so Fletcher officiated at St Leonard's in the morning and at his own church, St Mary's, in the evening. "My friends informed me that the Church had a most desolate appearance. The private pews, for the most part, were empty, either from the proprietors having left the town, or from the sickness of their respective families. Those persons who did attend seemed most deeply impressed with the awfulness of their situation, and were most devout in their petitions to the Throne of Grace." By the 9th of September things were returning to normal, the private pews were "better filled than on the preceding Sabbath . . . .I was also greatly comforted to observe the free sittings for the poor almost entirely occupied". The following Wednesday was declared as "a day of Humiliation, and Prayer, and Thanksgiving. When the day arrived, the shops were closed, business suspended, and the different places dedicated to God's Service crowded with worshippers."[30]

After such experiences no wonder Leigh's disappointment was so emphatically expressed. Meanwhile at Rowley Regis a similar result had been produced more speedily. Whilst, at Bilston Leigh had closed his church, with deep misgiving, George Barrs acted differently. He had buried fifteen people of cholera in four days and preached on the Sunday afternoon on what seemed a very appropriate text, "If I shall send pestilence among my people, and my people, who are called by my name, shall be humbled, and shall pray, and shall seek my face, and shall turn from their wicked ways; then I shall hear from heaven, and shall pardon their sin, and shall heal their land" (2 Chronicles 7:13-14). Not surprisingly, "The subject attracted great numbers of hearers, for I made it known in the morning, that I intended to speak of the pestilence now in the land,

and should make known the only certain and infallible remedy for the evil."

Instead of the sympathetic approach of Girdlestone the parishioners of Rowley Regis were treated to a very different facet of Evangelical theology, a denunciation of recent political developments (particularly Catholic emancipation and the repeal of the Test and Corporation Acts), as national sins, for which God had sent pestilence across the land, "now Socinianism and Popery are become national sins. The barriers are removed that kept these worse than idolators from any share in the government of the country . . . .Popery and Socinianism are now countenanced by the laws of the land, and are made part and parcel of the religion of the State. Thus we are become, so far as the ruling powers are concerned, identified with those who trample under foot the deity, despise the salvation of Jesus Christ, and have worshipped the beast and his image . . . .The time seems now to be come, when Jehovah will vindicate his own honour, and convince men that he is not to be insulted by the proud worms of earth, with everlasting impunity. The pestilence shall do what the warnings of his word, and his dealings with other rebellious nations have not done."[31] Needless to say the one infallible remedy is the sole mediation of Jesus Christ, understood in narrowly Protestant terms.

The following Sunday Barrs was convinced his own safety was due to divine protection, "In the midst of all this contagion, and all these deaths, it has not yet come nigh me. Surely this is because the hand of Heaven has been my shield and defence." But by the end of September, not only had the epidemic ceased but also any accompanying piety. "No sooner has the violence of the disease abated, than many who, under a state of alarm, appeared among the worshippers in the congregation, and heard the word preached, seem to have fallen into their old state of false peace and security; for they are seen no more in the house of prayer. May not such proceedings be justly said to be indicative of hypocrisy, and provocative of further judgements?"[32] Fortunately for Rowley Regis such 'judgements' did not come in 1849 in the way they did to Bilston, Willenhall and Wolverhampton.

6.5 The effects of cholera epidemics on Methodist membership

The cautious optimism of William France that the 1832 epidemic would lead to a thousand additional Wesleyan members in the Dudley circuit can be checked against the membership statistics. Leese's claim that, even where numbers fell away later they still left a net gain depends on how long a run is needed to decide on net gains and losses, particularly amongst the Wesleyans.[33] The 1832 cholera epidemic was quickly followed by the repercussions of the Warrenite controversy within Wesleyanism. As a result, the Methodist New Connexion carved out a sizeable empire for itself in the Black Country, at the expense, particularly, of the Dudley Wesleyans. The 1849 epidemic co-incided with the notorious 'Fly-Sheets' agitation which, once again, split Wesleyanism, reducing membership dramatically in many places. Even in areas like Cornwall, however, where active campaigns of denigration against Conference supporters were mounted, particularly by Samuel Dunn, cholera actively assisted prayer for revival by concentrating Wesleyan attentions on evangelism rather than Connexional politics.[34] On the other hand such events should not have affected the other Methodist denominations so that they, at least, ought to have profited peacefully from any gains from the cholera.

As Methodist circuits were neither co-terminous with the districts on which cholera mortality statistics are based, nor with each other, only general conclusions are possible from their membership statistics. In both periods Primitive Methodist numbers expanded sufficiently to warrant the establishment of new circuits by dividing an existing circuit into two. Dudley became a separate circuit by being separated from Darlaston in 1833. Brierley Hill circuit was separated from Dudley and West Bromwich from Darlaston, both in 1850. This is the reason for the rather erratic percentages for Primitive Methodism in Tables 31 and 32.

These give the percentage rise and fall in circuit membership of the various Methodist circuits for the two periods during which cholera epidemics took place. (The Dudley Methodist New Connexion circuit was only formed in 1832.)

The tables indicate the dramatic impact of cholera on Methodist membership, particularly in 1832. The Dudley Wesleyans almost added the thousand members hoped for in 1832-33, only to lose them again during the Warrenite controversy two years later. In all circuits rapid gains were made in 1832-33, followed, in most cases, by a tailing off later but, nevertheless, leaving all but Dudley Wesleyans stronger in numbers than before. The Primitives were sufficiently encouraged by their increase to divide the Darlaston circuit, and, though both Primitive circuits declined thereafter, the aggregate Primitive membership within the Black Country still increased on its pre-cholera level.

The pattern was almost repeated in 1849, though with less dramatic increases in membership. The Wesleyans showed an overall net loss, as a consequence of the 'Fly-Sheets', West Bromwich and Walsall being particularly affected. This time, once again, the Primitives were sufficiently confident to divide their circuits, and, although individually the new circuits immediately declined in membership, the Connexion as a whole benefited with even greater percentage gains than in 1832. The MNC, on the other hand, showed less spectacular gains than on the former occasion but, this time, they did not have the advantage of a large body of dissident Wesleyans as an additional source of recruitment.

A further comparison between the Black Country situation and the parallel position of Methodism in Birmingham and in England as a whole can be made. It must be pointed out, however, that the dominance of the Wesleyans in Birmingham and their particularly heavy losses there after the 1849 Conference distorts the picture considerably. Another significant difference is in the extent of the circuit boundaries represented in the figures for both the Primitives and the MNC. The Birmingham Primitive Methodist circuit stretched well into Worcestershire, with branches at Bromsgrove and Redditch. The MNC stretched back into Staffordshire with societies at Lichfield, Cheslyn Hay and Yoxall as well as Birmingham. Hence neither connexion can really compare with the Wesleyan figures which were much more closely related to Birmingham and its immediate neighbourhood.

The national statistics for England have been taken from Currie, Gilbert and Horsley's book on 'Churches and Churchgoers'. The aggregate total includes the Bible Christians, whose expansion tended to parallel in the south-west that of the Primitives in the midlands and the north-east and the Wesleyan Methodist Association, which had one chapel in Birmingham and none in the Black Country.[35] The Wesleyan Reformers, who did not have permanent premises in Birmingham until later in the 1850s, are not included in the local statistics. The resulting figures are given in Tables 33 and 34.

The spectacular rise and subsequent fall in Black Country Methodist membership in all three connexions during the time of the 1832 cholera epidemic was not paralleled either in Birmingham or in England as a whole. Nevertheless Birmingham Methodism also increased its membership steadily during this period, ahead of the national norm, and ended with a very similar overall net gain. This seems to indicate that, although the Black Country figures are undoubtedly striking, they may have been part of a wider trend in which the cholera was only one, though the best publicised, of several factors. The 1849 situation is less straightforward because the Birmingham percentages are so notably affected by the disruption of Wesleyanism, which also, of course, influences the national picture. Nevertheless the fact that Black Country Wesleyanism made a small percentage gain whilst Birmingham, in particular, suffered a catastrophic loss argues in favour of the epidemic directing attention away from connexional agitation in the Black Country. The Primitive figures in both parts of the conurbation are in contrast with national trends, much better in the Black Country and much worse in Birmingham, whilst the MNC made modest gains in both, nothing like their percentages in 1832 but still slightly better than the national trend. It is, of course, impossible to tell from the figures how much of the MNC increase in Birmingham consisted of dissident Wesleyans.

Taken overall Methodist membership in the Black Country increased during both cholera epidemics and, although it decreased thereafter, substantial additional numbers remained. How far this is attributable to recruitment during the epidemics still needs to be established by a closer look at those societies in places with high cholera mortality. Unfortunately this can only be done for the Wesleyans as no individual society membership records survive for either the Primitives or the MNC for this period. A hint that they could be parallel appeared in a report from the Darlaston circuit in the Primitive Methodist Magazine for 1835, "We have had to put about 300 out of society, the greater part of whom joined us during the cholera".[36]

The only circuit for which local Wesleyan statistics survive from 1832 is Dudley. These are given in Table 35 and reveal the relatively small membership of most societies before the cholera epidemic, fourteen of the eighteen had less than 100 members and six less than 50. Nevertheless, in nearly all cases these small societies almost doubled their membership immediately after the cholera. The exceptions, Rowley and Old Hill, were in the areas least seriously affected by the epidemic, although even here at least 55 cholera deaths occurred (see Table 30).

The majority of these new members, however, were not retained in the societies. By December 1834 membership of the main societies in Dudley and Tipton had settled back at, or below, its pre-cholera level of June 1832. Only Bloomfield society, in the Tipton area, made any substantial long term gains. The other Wesleyan society whose membership was successfully increased during this period was Oldbury, but there cholera mortality was lower even than Rowley Regis so no certain link can be made between the two events. Some of the smaller societies did increase their membership but from so low a numerical base that the percentage increase gives an unduly favourable impression. Most of these were in the Dudley and Sedgley areas where cholera can be accepted as a major contributory factor.[37] The surrounding circuits show similar ambiguities (see Table 31). Wednesbury had a higher cholera mortality than Oldbury and the circuit as a whole added over a thousand members in the period up to 1835. The Wednesbury circuit included Darlaston and part of Tipton, both of which suffered, along with Wednesbury itself, in the epidemic. West Bromwich, on the other hand, had an even lower cholera mortality than Oldbury but had almost doubled its membership by 1835. Unfortunately, in the Wolverhampton circuit, the membership figures for Bilston do not survive beyond March 1832 so there is no way of calculating the effect of the worst cholera mortality on local Wesleyan membership.

In 1849 the records allow comparisons between individual societies in the Dudley, Wolverhampton and Bilston areas with cholera mortality. These are given in Tables 36 and 37 and have been carried forward to March 1851 to show whether the cholera epidemic affected the Census of Religious Worship.[38]

Cholera made very little difference to Wesleyan strength in 1851. Admittedly some large short term gains accrued in such centres of the epidemic as Bilston where over a hundred members were gained and lost between June 1849 and September 1850. Willenhall, with cholera mortality second only to Bilston, showed no such spectacular rise and fall but a small net gain rather than the slight overall loss sustained by Bilston. None of the larger societies in either circuit made any significant gains, most recorded an overall loss. The societies with large percentage increases began from a much smaller numerical base. However, nearly all are close to areas of high cholera mortality. Woodside lies between Dudley and Kingswinford, Coseley between Wednesbury and Sedgley, Gornal Wood is between Sedgley and Kingswinford, Lanesfield between Sedgley and Bilston, Monmore Green between Wolverhampton and Bilston and Wednesfield between Wolverhampton and Willenhall. However, the sequence breaks down at Ettingshall, Can Lane and Bloomfield, which also lie in the area between Wednesbury, Bilston, Sedgley and Tipton. Proximity to a centre of cholera infection did not guarantee increased Wesleyan membership, in large or small societies.

6.6 Conclusions

There is no recent historiographical discussion of which I am aware of the effects of cholera on churchgoing in other areas of Britain badly affected by the disease, though it would be interesting to consider the evidence from Merthyr Tydfil. Merthyr recorded 1, 682 cholera deaths in 1849 and much higher than average church attendance in 1851 than other industrial towns of comparable size.[39] This is noted by Christopher Turner in his article on Welsh revivalism in the nineteenth century. He mentions the impact of cholera epidemics but makes no direct correlation between the two.[40] Nevertheless, despite the impression made on contemporaries by the religious fervour witnessed during the epidemics, both in 1832 and 1849, all the evidence from the Black Country points to relatively modest long term gains, if any, in terms of regular church attendance. Anglican evidence for 1849 is not available in the form which it took in 1832, but the 1832 evidence did not suggest that more than short term impressions had been made by the endeavours of the clergy involved in ministering to the victims of cholera.

This appears to parallel the findings of Richard Evans, whose comprehensive study of the 1892 cholera epidemic in Hamburg and its antecedents includes a chapter on public responses entitled 'fear and panic'.[41] In it he singles out three common responses, particularly within the Hamburg working class. This was by far the worst affected section of the population, despite the fact that in 1892 the cholera bacillus was transmitted generally throughout the city by means of an unfiltered domestic water supply, as it was on Tyneside in 1853.[42] Those middle class people not away on holiday in August 1892 attempted to secure their lives by mass flight from the city or by living in isolation from any contacts with the rest of the population. This left the remainder, who had no servants to screen them from danger, to fend for themselves. In such circumstances many resorted to drink, patent medicines and religion. The Lutheran church authorities reported special services 'extraordinarily well attended' and prayer meetings 'have also been attended by classes of the population which otherwise stand aloof from the church'.[43] Nevertheless the longer term effects were not substantial, though they were noticeable. The proportion of the Protestant population attending communion increased from 8.98% in 1880-84 to 10.02% in 1891-5, remaining at 9.58% in 1896 "but this proportion was still the lowest in Germany even after the epidemic."[44]

In Morris's view there were significant theological differences between public reactions to the major British cholera epidemics. Although in 1849, "It visited the same places and found the same state of unpreparedness", a contemporary medical journal stated that, "The vague but intense alarm which preceded the former visitation of the epidemic, has been exchanged for a calm and rational view of the real amount of danger."[45] By contrast with 1832, "the religious response was more muted. There was no official day of fasting, prayer and humiliation . . . God the Avenger was not dead but in retreat". In support he quotes the Bishop of London's sermon on the subject and the subsequent reasons given by Palmerston for rejecting a call for a national fast day in response to the 1854 outbreak. These both emphasised the importance of human actions in removing the poverty and insanitary conditions in which disease could spread rather than passively invoke Divine intervention to accomplish what human agency refused to attempt.[46] This muted official response is exemplified in the limited amount of evidence we have of the Church of England's role in the Black Country. Although the clergy were still prominent both in public life and in ministering to the victims of the disease they deferred readily to medical opinion and emphasised the sanitary rather than the theological lessons to be learnt from the epidemic.

Certainly the Wolverhampton Chronicle gives no impression of any fear or panic such as gripped Hamburg in 1892. In fact it gave much more prominence to a notorious London murder trial. On the 18th of July 1849 it reported the first local case of cholera at Tipton along with national figures from the General Board of Health. Throughout the summer factual reports continued, not only of outbreaks of cholera but of the efforts of local boards of health and Poor Law Guardians to remove filth in places like Bilston and Willenhall where mortality was highest. The chairman of the Wolverhampton Board of Guardians was the curate of St Mary's Bilston, J. B. Owen, one of an active group of local Evangelical clergy.[47] From the 26th of September a steady decrease in the number of cases was reported, an editorial on the 18th of October claiming upwards of 700 deaths in Bilston, over 300 in Willenhall and about 450 in Wolverhampton. At a meeting in St Mark's ward in early September the vicar, A. B. Gould, seconding a motion for medical inspection and the removal of nuisances, said, "He did not think it needed much argument to prove that the community was responsible for the adoption forthwith of such measures as might, under Divine Providence, check the progress of this fatal disease . . . and if the medical gentlemen would only be good enough to tell them what they could do all present would be happy to follow their instructions."[48]

Owen has left a brief account of the 1849 epidemic in Bilston, where cholera mortality, as in 1832, was at its highest. It appears to have been written soon after the epidemic and gives a more vivid picture of its impact than anything in the local press. "Many of the leading tradesmen, some of whom were suffering under diarrhoea, fled from the town", leaving notices on their shuttered shops, 'closed during the cholera', and that "to obviate the panic which was multiplying the havoc, and almost eclipsing the legitimate ravages of the disease, " many victims were buried by night.[49] Despite a later characterisation of the Bilston miner as prone to excessive tippling he does not mention any heavy recourse to drink during the epidemic, or to the patent medicines which were prominently advertised in the Wolverhampton Chronicle at the time.[50] He only incidentally refers to a religious response and couples it with the positive effects of the epidemic on attitudes to public health. The facts of high mortality "have already effected the adoption of extensive proposals of sanatory reform; they have created a large amount of serious, and I trust religious, impression, which I heartily pray may be solid, scriptural and abiding".[51]

More notable to Owen than any religious response was the awful hopelessness which accompanied the disease. "Many on being attacked, sank at once into a kind of apathetic fatalism, that seemed to fascinate them into the arms of death by the very terror of his presence . . . Such patients in a kind of sullen horror would not choose but die; – religion, friendship, science, affection, authority, example, reason, duty, animal instinct, all alike pled in vain- they would die, and die they did."[52] His one reference to any element of Divine judgement is part of a plea for charitable donations to support widows and children and is extremely cautious. "The very mystery that constitutes the essential awe attending the cholera, is a pro tanto demonstration of an agency more intrinsically Divine, and as such, God appeals to us alike in the judgement, and in the charity it has rendered necessary;"[53]

Whereas in Hamburg in 1892 the Church Council issued 30, 000 copies of a special address by the senior pastor and printed 70, 000 copies of a sermon in which 'the people were warned that the epidemic was God's punishment for their sins',[54] no such official interpretation of the 1849 cholera epidemic seems to have occurred in the Black Country. In the only editorial it devoted to the subject at the height of the epidemic the Wolverhampton Chronicle stated "'Temperance' is the very best protection against the assaults of disease".[55] Such medical advice as was offered through the press would not encourage people to repent earnestly of their sins, quite the opposite. With its first mention of the epidemic the Wolverhampton Chronicle included a lengthy letter by a local doctor who, rightly warning that there was no known cure for the disease, detailed the best preventive measures, regular habits and avoiding fear and anxiety; "mental cheerfulness should be promoted in every possible way".[56] This was not a new idea, Evans points out that similar views were expressed by medical officials in Germany in 1832 and repeated throughout the rest of the century, but promoting mental cheerfulness was hardly the object of sermons depicting the cholera as God's warning to sinners.[57]

Unfortunately, we have no accounts of local Anglican sermons on the subject from 1849. J. B. Owen preached at St James' Ashted on the Sunday set aside for thanksgiving for the exemption of Birmingham from cholera, but although noting that a £10 collection was donated to the relief of suffering in Bilston the press gives no indication of what Owen actually said.[58] Two other possible sources are equally uninformative. Owen was secretary of the Lloyd Clerical Meeting, a monthly meeting of local Evangelical clergy at the home of their most prominent member, William Dalton, 'to discuss the interpretation of Scripture and the doctrines of the Reformed Church'. The minutes for the period 1849-59 survive. They are limited to detailed verse by verse comments on passages from the New Testament including the book of Revelation, but no dates are given for any of the entries.[59]

Dalton himself has left twelve manuscript volumes of sermons preached at St Paul's Wolverhampton between 1839 and 1854. One sermon, preached on the Sunday after the first cholera cases were reported, 22 July 1849, could have afforded a homiletic use of the epidemic. The subject, from John 10 verses 1-5, led him to describe how Christians 'know their Shepherd's voice', concluding, "follow the Lord fully and then you have blessedness and safety united. You are kept from danger and you are kept in peace". He turns, finally, to address "one word to those that are still wandering far from Him . . . that are living for self, living for sin, living for this passing empty world . . . For them there is no peace or safety in a dangerous road, they may have sheep's clothing but they have not the sheep's nature or privileges." These wandering sheep are warned urgently, but in entirely general terms, to "cast away all your sins, repent, believe and turn to your God". This appeal may, on the day, have been fitted to the occasion but the manuscript sticks to pious generalities.[60]

The Methodists, however, had not abandoned the idea that the pestilence was a judgement on human sin as well as on human negligence and their view was still widely shared. The Wesleyan Conference appointed a fast day for all its members which was well supported. An eyewitness of the Cornish revival writes, "The dread name of cholera seemed to awake the people like the trumpet of doom. Anxiety became deep and general . . . The day appointed by Connexional authority for special fasting, humiliation and prayer was memorable. Though market day at Redruth, yet one thousand people bent their knees at every meeting; while at night not less than two thousand crowded in to hear the word".[61] In 1850 the Primitive Methodist Magazine's editor wrote, "Cholera, like a destroying angel, has marked the past year as one to be long remembered . . . Who . . . can deny that God has been using his paternal rod in severity, to teach his wayward family lessons of righteousness? In some cases facts show that his chastisement has been salutary; for stubborn hearts have yielded to Him . . . and the church has rushed to the salvation of man." Readers were encouraged to care for new converts so that "future years will testify that 1849 was among the princes of the years for its favours to man."[62]

The Methodist interpretation of the epidemic gained a response from large numbers of working class men, particularly miners, which contrasts sharply with that experienced by those who offered a religious message to cholera victims in Hamburg in 1892. Evans quotes the impressive record of Pastor Werner, who ministered to the sufferers in a working class parish. Whereas in many cases the wives of working men evinced a positive Christian belief in the face of death their husbands were at pains to deny any such convictions and angrily rejected the pastor's attempts to offer religious consolation[63]. Such rejection of the ministrations of the clergy contrasts with the experience of Owen, who, in addition to between twenty and thirty funerals a day, found "mothers, wives, children, husbands, brothers and sisters besieging my house with entreaties that I would come and pray with their suffering and dying relatives".[64] According to his son's memoir Owen was a welcome visitor in the homes of working men, holding cottage meetings at 7 am. four mornings a week 'for the benefit of working families', but his experience was by no means untypical.[65]

Each of the Methodist denominations increased its membership during the periods covered by the epidemics but only the Primitives kept any substantial number into succeeding years and even they recorded considerable losses once the fear of disease had subsided. Analysis of individual Wesleyan society membership, where that is possible, reveals that there is no necessary association between areas of high cholera mortality and increased membership. In some cases such increases did occur but in others, where there appeared to be an equally strong motive, they did not. Moreover some circuits and societies outside the immediate centres of the disease also increased their membership at the same time. This lends force to the possibility that other factors, besides fear of disease, were more instrumental in recruiting new Methodist members. Although there may have been some relationship between the 1849 cholera epidemic and the 1851 Index of church attendance, it is not a sufficient explanation of the difference between the Black Country and the Birmingham area in this respect.

Notes

1   Cholera mortality figures are taken from the Registrar General's report, G. Graham, *Report on the Mortality of Cholera in England 1848-49*, London 1852.

2   Ibid. p.269.

3   The Registrar General's Report, from which these figures are taken, gave the 1841 population which was the only baseline available at the time. A calculation based on that figure naturally gives slightly higher mortality rates but does not remove the contrast The results are: Wolverhampton 1.7%, Walsall 0.5%, West Bromwich 0.5%, Dudley 0.5%, Stourbridge 0.6%, Kings Norton 0.03%, Birmingham 0.02%, Aston 0.01%.

4   H. S. Tremenheere, *Second Report of the Midland Mining Commission, Parliamentary Papers 1850, XXIII*, pp. 23-24.

5   Ibid. p.24.

6   Dudley Libraries, Archives and Local History Service, Stourbridge Methodist Church manuscripts, Brierley Hill Primitive Methodist Quarterly Meeting Minutes, 24 March 1851 (spelling original).

7   Leese, 'Methodism', pp. 94-97, Watts, *Dissenters*, pp. 76-78.

8   Graham, *Cholera*, pp. 263-269. Local sources give much higher figures for Willenhall, 362 according to the cholera memorial in the town. cf. N. W. Tildesley *History of Willenhall*, Willenhall 1951, p.124. I have kept to the registrar general's figures throughout.

9   Spearman's rank order coefficient is not significant at 5% level.

10   C. Creighton, *A History of Epidemic Diseases in Great Britain*, Cambridge 1894, Second Edition London 1965, Vol. 2, p.825.

11   C. Girdlestone, *Seven Sermons preached during the prevalence of the Cholera in the parish of Sedgley, with a narrative of that visitation*, London 1833, Appendix. Creighton initially quotes Girdlestone's figure for Sedgley and then reduces it when printing his table.

12   Ibid. p. xiii.

13   *Wesleyan Methodist Magazine*, London 1832, p.819.

14   Girdlestone, *Seven Sermons*, p. xi.

15   W. Leigh, *An authentic narrative of the awful visitation of Bilston by Cholera in Aug-Sept 1832*, Wolverhampton 1832, Appendix.

16   Office for National Statistics, London, Registrar's Ms. notes, Stourbridge, 31 December 1849.

17   Barrs, *Four Sermons*, pp. 211-212.

18   Spearman's rank order correlation coefficient is significant at 5% level.

19   R. J. Morris, *Cholera 1832*, London 1976, pp. 21-77.

20   Girdlestone, *Seven Sermons*, p. ix.

21   *Wesleyan Methodist Magazine*, London 1832, p.748. He implies rather than argues for a direct link between this change in moral attitude and religious conviction by going on to describe a thanksgiving service promoted by another iron manufacturer for his workers under Methodist auspices. "The workmen in an adjoining establishment have been mercifully spared; and, in consequence, the proprietors of those works set apart Monday last as a day of thanksgiving; when our chapel at Great Bridge was thronged with the men, and attended by their master; and an appropriate and affecting discourse was delivered by our respected Superintendent, Mr. Walmsley."

22   Ibid. p.819.

23   Ibid. p.890.

24   Girdlestone, *Seven Sermons*, pp. xv-xvii.

25   Morris, *Cholera*, pp. 140-141.
26   Girdlestone, *Seven Sermons*, p.14.
27   Ibid. p. xix.
28   Leigh, *Bilston*, 64-66.
29   cf. Morris, *Cholera*, especially pp. 176-192.
30   Leigh, *Bilston*, pp. 46, 56.
31   Barrs, *Four Sermons*, pp. 209-210.
32   Ibid. p.212.
33   Leese, 'Methodism', pp. 97, 221.
34   cf Coley, *Collins*, pp. 306-314, Morris, *Cholera*, p.203.
35   R. Currie, A. Gilbert and L. Horsley, *Churches and Churchgoers*, Oxford 1977,
     Table A3. For Bath Street WMA chapel, Birmingham see VCH *Warwickshire*,
     Vol. 7, p. 461.
36   *Primitive Methodist Magazine*, Bemersley 1835, p.264.
37   Dudley Libraries, Archives and Local History Services, Coseley, Dudley
     Circuit Book.
38   Dudley Circuit Book; Wolverhampton Library, Darlington Street Methodist
     deposit, Wolverhampton Circuit Book; Willenhall membership taken
     from notes at the front of the register of collections kept at Willenhall
     Methodist chapel. Separate records for Walsall circuit have not survived
     for this period.
39   Creighton, *Epidemic*, p.845; Callum Brown in McLeod (Ed) *European Reli-
     gion in the Age of Great Cities*, p. 252, the Index of attendance for Merthyr
     was 88.5% and 1849 cholera mortality was 2.67%
40   C. B. Turner, 'Revivalism and Welsh society in the nineteenth century', in J.
     Obelkevich, L. Roper and R. Samuel, *Disciplines of Faith*, London 1987, pp.
     311-323. Turner points out that Merthyr could accommodate 66% of its
     1851 population in churches and chapels. This extremely high level was the
     product of sustained revivalism, reaching the industrial town from its rural
     heartlands, from which many of Merthyr's immigrant population came
     and with which they retained connections. Any religious response to
     cholera was therefore building on a well established revivalist tradition
     and not something sudden and inexplicable. See also E. T. Davies, *Religion
     in the Industrial Revolution in South Wales*, Cardiff 1965, pp. 55-57.
41   R. J. Evans, *Death in Hamburg, society and politics in the cholera years 1830-
     1910*, Oxford 1987, pp. 346-372 (Penguin Edition).
42   *Report of the Cholera Inquiry Commissioners, Newcastle upon Tyne*. Parliamen-
     tary Papers 1854 XXXV, pp. xxv-xxvii.
43   Evans, *Hamburg*, p.357.
44   Ibid. p. 362.
45   Morris, *Cholera*, p.200.
46   Ibid. pp. 200-214.
47   cf. J. D. Walters, 'The impact of Anglican Evangelicalism on the religious
     life of Wolverhampton and its locality in the period 1830-1870'. MA disser-
     tation CNAA, 1983, pp. 16-17. *Wolverhampton Chronicle*, 22 August, 5 and
     12 September 1849.
48   *Wolverhampton Chronicle*, 5 September 1849.
49   J. B. Owen, 'Sketches and incidents of the cholera at Bilston 1849' in A. E.

Owen, *Lectures and Sermons by J. B. Owen with a memoir*, London 1873, pp. 349, 354.

50   J. B. Owen, *The Wolverhampton Almanac and stranger's guide to South Stafford-shire*, Wolverhampton 1855, p.6.

51   A. E. Owen, *J. B. Owen*, p. 350.

52   Ibid. pp. 357-358.

53   Ibid. p.352.

54   Evans, *Hamburg*, p.358

55   *Wolverhampton Chronicle*, 12 September 1849.

56   *Wolverhampton Chronicle*, 18 July 1849.

57   Evans, *Hamburg*, pp. 234-5, 248-9.

58   *Wolverhampton Chronicle*, 26 September 1849.

59   A. E. Owen, *J. B. Owen*, p.30, J. D. Walters, 'Anglican', p.15, wrongly says that the meetings were fortnightly.

60   Wolverhampton Archives and Local Studies, Manuscript Sermons of William Dalton, Volume 11, pp. 59-60. Neither of the other sermons in the volume for these months, both preached in October on the sacrament of Holy Communion, makes any mention of the cholera.

61   Coley, *Collins*, pp. 306-307.

62   *Primitive Methodist Magazine*, 1850, p.2.

63   Evans, *Hamburg*, p.361.

64   A. E. Owen, *J. B. Owen*, p. 353.

65   Ibid. p.22.

CHAPTER 7

The Methods and Messages of Evangelism

7.1 The climate of controversy

Historians attempting to explain the relationship between the events of the 1830s and 40s and the forces at work within and alongside them have frequently needed the language of paradox. As G. M. Young put it, "From 1832 to 1847 the student of Victorian history finds himself the bewildered spectator of a warfare between Radicals who upheld Factories and Workhouses, Tories and Chartists who abhorred both, infidel Benthamites leagued with Conservative Anglicans against dissenting manufacturers, landowners denouncing the oppressions of Lancashire, and cotton masters yearning over the sorrows of Dorset." All were "mixed in an inextricable confusion of agitation".[1] This confusion involves religion even more than politics for, as Kitson Clark has pointed out, "by the second quarter of the nineteenth century religion had received so political a shape, or politics so religious a shape, that it was for many people almost impossible to separate the two."[2] This was certainly true of both Birmingham and the Black Country with the occasional added complexity not usually met with elsewhere.

For example, the following extracts come from two of the many placarded appeals addressed to the electors of Willenhall:

"Gentlemen, A report is in circulation that certain parties are about to solicit your Votes by the mean and infamous temptation of open and undisguised BRIBERY. It would hardly be believed (were it not avowedly declared by the parties themselves,) that men who have hitherto ranked in the world as Christians, should dare to come amongst you with such an insulting proposition. BRIBERY indeed! What—the ELECTORS OF WILLENHALL sell their souls for *Money!!! . . .*"

"Brother electors, A report which I believe to be true is now in circulation the substance of which is as follows:— It is asserted that the Committee of Mr Howells having calculated their chances of success, made an offer to Mr White's Committee of the votes they had obtained, but that this offer was refused by Mr

White's friends *on account of a disagreement as to terms*. Gentlemen, if this be so, is it not a deliberate attempt to control, or rather *to sell* your votes in a manner which calls for your firmest resistance? Iron and Ironfoundry Goods are so sold but I am sure that your independent principles will not allow your votes to be so disposed of."[3]

Their political tone contrasts with this account of a Birmingham organisation:

"The effect of the word has indeed been powerful, . . . The drunkard now delights in the refined joys of an enlightened religion, the man of violence feels a certain strength and confident faith in the power of truth, – the infidel is a humble admirer and hopeful partaker of the glorious Gospel of Jesus, wondering that the pride of ignorance should so long have blinded him to beauties infinitely transcending the mock philosophic babblings of a heartless and hopeless materialism."[4]

In fact both refer to activities in which politics and religion were inextricably entwined. The electors of Willenhall were voting, in August 1834, for a successor to the drunken William Moreton, for forty-five years perpetual curate of St Giles, their parish church. The living attracted six candidates. All presented testimonials to the churchwardens[5] and canvassed support before the open vote of the householders, a right few of them possessed in Parliamentary elections. The second extract describes the Birmingham Christian Chartist Church in 1841 whose leader, Arthur O'Neill, soon served a term of imprisonment for his part in the 1842 miners' strike in South Staffordshire.

Such an association of popular democracy with the Church of England and Chartism with a Christian Church were untypical, though they illustrate two extremes of the range of relationships between religion and politics possible at the time. Not all were considered generally acceptable. The Wesleyan superintendent of West Bromwich, Barnard Slater, accused O'Neill, unfairly, of using Christianity as a subterfuge to attract support for the Charter from the striking miners saying, "There were very few political chartists here; but *Christian* chartist was a name that took. It is almost blasphemy to prostitute the name of Christian to such purposes".[6] The more normal stance of the Church of England is revealed by William Leigh, elected curate of Bilston at a lively contested election in 1813.[7] He was a Liberal and acted as election agent for Lord Hatherton. Writing to Hatherton in 1835 he sent him a list of members of the new Conservative Association with the comment, "also observe that there are eleven clergymen putting themselves forward and yet if I only raise my voice when called upon, even on the dissolution of Parliament, I am instantly attacked for interfering in politics. Can anything be more unfair and unreasonable than this? In fact a Tory parson may do anything with impunity and a clergyman of liberal opinions must, to satisfy the Conservatives, be hanged, drawn and quartered at their pleasure".[8]

7.2 Church Rates

The one issue which regularly combined religion and politics was church rates. The annual election of churchwardens gave radicals an opportunity to harangue a vestry meeting and put those who believed parishioners should contribute to the upkeep of their church through a legal rate on the defensive. Politically motivated opponents could pillory them as supporters of an oligarchic establishment. The vestry also gave Conservatives an opportunity to reassert their claim to be upholders of the constitution in Church and State gaining, if they won, a symbolic victory over those whom they demonised as infidels and republicans. W. R. Ward has given a vivid account of the church-rate controversies in Manchester and Rochdale during the 1830s and 40s.[9] Nothing as dramatic occurred in Birmingham or the Black Country but the same forces were at work. Here they were more political than religious, not limited to Dissenting attempts practically to disestablish the Church of England in the manner indicated by Ward and endorsed by Gilbert.[10]

The earliest political opposition to church rates occurred in Dudley. Here the radical Samuel Cook opened his draper's shop in the High Street in May 1819. Its window displayed not only drapery but political posters, which earned him fines and prosecution for seditious libel. One of the most prominent local magistrates, who sent accounts of Cook's activities to the Home Secretary, was Luke Booker, vicar of Dudley from 1789 to 1835, whose sermons against 'sedition' in 1819 and 1831 were classic expressions of Tory ideology. Cook was prosecuted for non-payment of church rates and had his goods seized in 1827 and 1837. In 1844 he once again led opposition to the rate. He was not successful. After a confused vestry meeting a poll produced a majority of 271 in favour of the rate, a victory which was duly celebrated.[11] From April 1832 Cook was leader of the Dudley Political Union and when it merged into Chartism in 1838 he became its most vocal activist, being arrested in 1839 after the Birmingham Bull Ring riots and again in 1842, the first to suffer during the miners' strike. Opposition to church rates was only a small part of his programme. In 1834 he published 'Some principles of Dudley Radicalism' consisting of twenty-five points beginning, "No Easter Offerings, No Church Rates, No Tithes", ending with, "Moderate Labour: Good Wages: Sobriety of Conduct" and including "Universal Education, Universal Suffrage, Vote by Ballot" with other proposals soon to become part of the People's Charter.[12]

Similar politically inspired battles took place in Birmingham. The Duddeston-cum-Nechells Radical Reform Society was a Chartist association of small employers and artisans meeting monthly in the Black Horse tavern, Prospect Row. The minutes of their meetings from 1839 to 1846 show them to be well organised, canvassing at local and national elections, proposing their own list for offices such as overseers of the poor, opposing church rates and securing the election of an anti-rate churchwarden for Aston parish in 1843, but only after re-purchasing the goods of 12 people, distrained for non-payment the previous year.[13]

For church rate purposes St Martin's parish covered the whole of Birmingham. Church rates were regularly voted and collected during the 1820s but after 1831 things changed. The rector, Thomas Moseley, did not endear himself to the Birmingham Political Union by trying, unsuccessfully, to prevent them ringing St Martin's church bells to celebrate the election of 'Reform' candidates.[14] They responded by turning the annual vestry meeting into a forum to demand their political 'rights', knowing the speeches would be reported in the local press. The lead was taken by the radical veteran George Edmonds and T. M. McDonnell the Roman Catholic priest, both members of the Political Union. The result was a series of frequently rowdy and regularly adjourned encounters, in the church or, from 1834, in the newly erected Town Hall. On this occasion even Edmonds pleaded for a hearing for those in favour of a rate, but this did not stop McDonnell haranguing the meeting for two hours. These tactics so wore down the rector that in 1838 the Tory candidate withdrew, the rector stood down and McDonnell was called to the chair.[15] McDonnell continued his influence in 1841, when the meeting was addressed by a Chartist delegate as it was again in 1842, after McDonnell himself had been re-directed by his bishop to Torquay. On both occasions the rector was absent through illness and, in 1842, did not even nominate his own warden since the poll the previous year had produced a majority of 6, 555 against a rate.[16] Both sides knew that, even had a rate been passed, it could not be enforced, so the proceedings became theatrical performances rather than serious attempts to grapple with problems of church provision in the growing town. The contest so affected Thomas Moseley that he retired in 1846 on grounds of ill health. His successor, J. C. Miller, ended the entertainment by refusing to try levying a rate.[17]

In the Black Country church rates continued to be levied and vestry meetings were less likely to be transformed into political confrontations, though the results could still be exploited by those wishing to portray the church as an oppressor of the poor. William Lewis, Girdlestone's successor at Sedgley, regularly prosecuted his parishioners for non-payment of church rates and also enforced the collection of Easter dues, something Girdlestone refused to do. In 1845 four chairs were taken from the house of William Smith of Coseley "to satisfy the demand for a church rate of 7d. Another man whose bed was seized last year now has to sleep by his fireside".[18] Four Rowley Regis parishioners were summoned before Dudley magistrates for non-payment of church rates. "Two of the men appeared to be in very distressed circumstances, notwithstanding an order was made for payment of the rates".[19] At Rowley, however, the church party were themselves divided when a new district church, St Luke, Reddal Hill, was opened in 1849. The minister and churchwardens of St Luke's opposed a rate on the whole parish, placarding the doors of St Giles' during worship with an appeal for resistance and calling for a vote on the issue for the first time.[20]

The situation common elsewhere in which dissenters took up the issue on grounds of conscience was reflected to some extent. The Unitarian pastor of Coseley Old Meeting led opposition to Sedgley church rates. Proposing an adjournment while the vicar took a poll, he then "got on the table, put his own amendment, declared it carried by a show of hands and walked out with his party to partake of a good dinner which awaited them at the Lion." The tactic backfired for the remaining parishioners carried a two-pence halfpenny rate by 25 votes to 6 and Girdlestone closed the meeting to avoid taking a poll.[21] In Willenhall things did not go so smoothly. George Fisher, eventual winner of the 1834 clergy election, proposed a rate of 2d. in the pound in 1843 on the ground that the Church of England was the religion of the nation and deserved support for removing ignorance and combating Popery. His opponents appealed to the voluntary principle and an anti-church-rate amendment was passed almost unanimously. A peaceful, good tempered meeting perhaps reflected the harmonious relationship between church and dissent which clergy needed to maintain in a parish where they were elected by popular vote.[22]

7.3 Denominational conflict

The politicising of religion appears most clearly in the disestablishment movement which Ward and Gilbert trace to the Tories' use of

the church rate issue to avenge themselves on Radicals, particularly in Leicester where Edward Miall, its eventual director, was a
leading Independent pastor.[23] Gilbert spells out the links between
Miall's Anti-State Church Association and the Anti-Corn Law
League, which used the denominational organisation of dissent to
gain support. It was certainly a coup to get John Angell James to
denounce the Corn Laws from the Carrs Lane pulpit as a cause of
distress among the people,[24] but this was during one of the worst
periods of depression in living memory. It was not something he
normally did for single-issue causes, even when he supported them
at public meetings.[25]

James could be accused of wanting to have it both ways. Well
before his initiative in forming the Evangelical Alliance he was
active in public alongside members of all denominations in support
of philanthropic and evangelistic causes. In this he was only one of
many in Birmingham who carried forward in the nineteenth century that collaboration between dissenters and churchmen which had
typified the period before the Priestley Riots. Even at the height of
political and religious controversy, in the 1830s and 40s, the tradition was maintained. The Board of Health, Temperance Society,
Anti-Slavery Society, Bible Society, Town Mission, committees to
establish public baths and parks and the annual Relief Committees
all included a wide range of religious allegiances, the Roman
Catholic priest being a member of the latter as he was of the
Mechanics' Institute.[26] Gilbert, in his treatment of the rivalry
between church and chapel, fails to take account of this element of
ecumenical co-operation, which, in the case of James, was recipro-
cated in the posthumous tribute paid to him by J. C. Miller, the rector of St Martins. "Most of those who had grown up under Mr
James's influence regarded Edward Miall and the activity of the
Anti-State Church Society with suspicion and dislike" recalled the
son of his successor.[27]

Gilbert recognises, in his quotations from James, the other pressures underlying the increasing denominational rivalry for popular
support for institutional religion.[28] Not only was a resurgent Church
of England building new churches throughout the urban areas,
often, as James remarked, in the immediate vicinity of established
nonconformist chapels, but other groups with differing beliefs but
similar methods were competing for the ear of the artisan. The
growing industrial towns which, to Anglicans used to the hegemony of the parson in the rural parish appeared increasingly out of
control, to others offered hitherto undreamed of opportunities for
recruitment which they were eager to exploit. "In manufacturing
districts there is found a greater spirit of enquiry, and a greater free-

dom of thought and expression, than in less populous parts of the country, and, consequently, the pastor who avails himself of this opportunity, is sure to find his zeal rewarded, with many conversions, and an abundant harvest of souls". This comment in the Catholic Magazine, edited by McDonnell, referred to Walsall, which, in the possibilities it opened up to Catholic priests, contrasted sharply with their experience as chaplains to the landed gentry. "The Sunday evening lectures, at Walsall, were numerously attended, and eagerly listened to . . . The Assembly room was, therefore, soon found to be too small for the increasing congregation."[29]

Public lectures were only one of the most frequently exploited means of attracting recruits and were not, of course, limited to representatives of the churches. Owenite Socialists, Chartists, Teetotallers and Mormons were all active throughout the conurbation during this period. The sheer range of contestants competing for the ear of the public strikes a modern reader of the contemporary local press. Such variety gave rise to regular confrontations. The Chartists were expert at taking over not only vestry meetings but those of the Anti-Corn Law League and religious bodies like the Town Mission.[30] Defenders of traditional religion could also make a career out of public disputation with advocates of other doctrines. In May 1841 three thousand people heard debates on 'Socialism' on three successive nights in Birmingham.[31] This was understandable as William Pare, the Owenite superintendent registrar, had been removed from office by a campaign of denigration. Bishop Phillpotts had presented a petition, allegedly signed by 4, 000 inhabitants of Birmingham, to the House of Lords in January 1840 complaining of the spread of Socialism and asking for it to be made illegal.[32] This was followed up by a series of lectures by the self-appointed champion of orthodoxy, the Anglican Dr. John Brindley of Oldswinford Hospital in Stourbridge. He disputed with Owen himself in 1841, provoking a riot at Bristol, and in 1839 held a public disputation in Wolverhampton with Alexander Campbell the Owenite lecturer who had toured the Black Country.[33]

Defensive disdain toward all challenges to Anglican superiority was expressed in a sermon entitled 'The Marriage Vow' preached, on the occasion of Queen Victoria's marriage, at St Paul's, Birmingham. "Nor can I, while on this subject, suppress my indignant astonishment that any who profess and call themselves Christians . . . would rather derive a legality for their unions from the presence of a secular layman, no matter how base his character and creed may be, than conform to the ritual of the Established religion of their country."[34]

If Owenites were subject to regular misrepresentation this was easily outdone by the sustained attack on Roman Catholicism mounted by Anglican Evangelicals. The Wolverhampton area, always a regional centre for Catholicism and, until 1841, the bishop's residence, seems to have been given special attention. William Dalton, the leading Evangelical Anglican had been born in Ireland, graduated from Trinity College, Dublin and served curacies at Kilcoo, County Down and Liverpool before gaining a following in Wolverhampton by sermons on the threat of Popery after Catholic Emancipation in 1829.[35] The dominance of Evangelicals amongst the Anglican clergy in the conurbation during this period meant that anti-Catholic polemic was regularly produced in sermons, lectures and pamphlets. George Barrs of Rowley Regis, for example, preached on the second Sunday of every month against the Pope as Anti-Christ, reflecting the strain of millenarianism prevalent in Evangelical Anglican circles at the time.[36] This polemic reached a climax in 1850 with the restoration of the Roman Catholic hierarchy but, by then, the Catholic church was sufficiently well established for public meetings attacking 'Papal aggression' to be less amenable to scaremongering oratory. In contrast with their treatment at Stoke on Trent, the Catholic speakers in Wolverhampton and Bilston were given a respectful hearing. In Birmingham Town Hall the mayor called for religious toleration and, after a meeting lasting six hours, declared both Joseph Sturge's amendment in favour of religious liberty and the original anti-Papal motion 'not carried' on a show of hands, to the successive jubilation of each side.[37]

This chapter has merely set the scene for an account of the methods used by the major Christian churches in their attempts to capture the allegiance of the working class. Any description of these activities must include the atmosphere of conflict and controversy within which they were pursued and which inevitably coloured the presentation of their message. In addition to inter-denominational rivalry there were internal conflicts, particularly within the Wesleyans and the Church of England, which gained wide publicity and could have influenced the popular response.

The main question to be addressed is whether the difference in church attendance between Birmingham and the Black Country can be explained by variations in the approach to evangelism and its intensity. Whereas original sources for evangelistic activity are unusually good for Birmingham during this period, unfortunately those for the Black Country are much more patchy and incomplete. This means that few firm generalisations can be made which will cover that area as a whole. Wherever possible, however, attention will be given to those Black Country townships which had either particularly high or particularly low indexes of attendance to try to identify any significant features.

7.4 Old methods adapted to new situations

John Wolffe in his wide ranging interpretation of the relationship between religion and national life in the British Isles between the 1840s and the end of the second World War suggests that only after the 1851 census did the churches realise that provision did not automatically produce a response.[38] This conclusion was arrived at well before 1850 in both Birmingham and the Black Country. The contrary impression is largely derived from the appeals for government support by the Church of England and by Anglicans and nonconformists for contributions towards church building projects, couched almost entirely in statistical terms, that a growing population required more adequate accommodation. This is the emphasis in David Mole's study of the Church of England in Birmingham, where a special fund was commenced in 1838 aimed at building ten new churches in five years, but in fact only providing five churches in ten years even though these were on a much smaller scale than the Commissioners' churches of the two previous decades.[39]

The Midland Mining Commission's evidence shows that by the early 1840s the Anglican clergy were well aware of the shortcomings of large new churches in urban areas and the expectation that by their unaided efforts they could make an impact on the surrounding population. The Commission took evidence from twelve Anglican clergy, two from Birmingham, two from Tipton and one each from Wolverhampton, Bilston, Wednesbury, Sedgley, Oldbury, Dudley, West Bromwich and Kingswinford. The death of George Barrs, in August 1840,[40] left Tancred without information about Rowley Regis and, as the enquiry concerned the miners' strike rather than mining conditions generally, it did not extend to Halesowen or Stourbridge. It still gives a reasonably comprehensive picture of Anglican opinion, tinged with the hope that the government would respond to the views expressed with support for the hard pressed Established Church.

E. H. L. Noot, recently curate for the non-resident incumbent of Tipton, said of St Paul's, a Commissioners' church at Tipton Green, seating 1, 300 and opened in 1839, "It is a great mistake building such large churches, which a clergyman cannot fill with his voice nor the population the seats". The population of the district was actually nearly 10, 000 but Noot was right to feel that they would not flock to fill St Paul's simply because the building had been provided and just under half the seats were free. The current curate of St Paul's, A. Hawkes, suggested a plausible reason for further government support. "A clergyman who labours among the people, and enters their houses and sees the squalid poverty in which they live, . . . can see that nothing but the church can instil into their minds habits of order and of respectability. There would be a check on them through the visits of the clergy."[41]

Such an ideal, however, had already proved beyond the physical powers of the more experienced clergy of the Black Country. All explained that the normal demands of their extensive parishes could not be adequately met, let alone pastoral visitation which both they and many of their parishioners expected. As William Lewis of Sedgley put it, " This neighbourhood kills the clergy". He ascribed the premature death of his first two curates to over-exertion and "the present one is now in a declining state of health, entirely from the immorality of the population and the great labour undergone by him; he has been obliged to go away for his health". The recently appointed incumbent of Coseley is now ill and worn out, "and for several Sundays has been obliged to depend on chance for assistance. The church was obliged to be closed one Sunday entirely". Lewis described his round of Sunday and weekday duties, saying "the late vicar's health failed him before he left Sedgley, and he could not do so much." Pastoral visiting was, according to him, very much a priority, "I look upon a clergyman in many cases as of more importance than the church itself; the people must be visited at their own houses, and reminded of their duties, when sick they ought to be visited and consoled . . . If I can devote two hours a day to visiting, which is impossible, by the time I have got to one extremity of my district, others are wanting me at the others, miles off."[42]

Neither in Birmingham nor the Black Country were the clergy in favour of the creation of large numbers of new parishes. W. H. Cartwright of Dudley claimed that his solution to the increasing population worked well. The large parish remained intact but was divided into five districts, "one of them attached to the parish church and four of them having each a chapel of ease endowed with fees and pew-rents, which I make up to £120 a year to each incumbent". Three of these districts had Commissioners' churches built during the previous twelve years.[43] The incumbents of the district chapelries, being appointed by the vicar, would act in harmony as a team and not divide up the parish by different styles of churchmanship, but they would still have real pastoral responsibility and not have their appointments terminated on the death of the vicar.[44] Similarly John Garbett, rector of St George's, Birmingham and rural dean stated, "I was at one time much taken with Dr Chalmers' views of multiplying small parishes, but I now think there is a medium which is best". He favoured further division in Birmingham because "a minister should be known to all his parishioners. Curates cannot altogether replace the permanent minister. They do not, and cannot, feel towards the people as the incumbent does, nor do the people like them so well." Garbett, however, had the advantage of a lay worker at St. George's who relieved both him and his curate of some of the pressure sustained by most of his Black Country colleagues.[45]

To Anglicans within the parochial system pastoral visitation did not distinguish, in principle, between members of their own congregations and others, whether they belonged to another denomination or none at all. One way to operate this ideal in the urban situation was to divide the parish into districts and organise teams of lay visitors to work them in the manner pioneered by Chalmers, albeit with the advantage of the office of deacon within the Church of Scotland.[46] Several Black Country clergy hankered after some similar means of assistance, Lewis of Sedgley, Cartwright of Dudley, Fletcher of Bilston, Spry of West Bromwich and Clarkson of Wednesbury, all suggested that, "we want a regular order of deacons to visit the people, to read to them and to exhort them to attend church".[47] In the absence of an order of deacons the Church of England tried two other options, increasing the number of curates and, particularly from the late 1820s, establishing district visiting by lay volunteers from the more socially respectable members of their congregations. Neither initiative appears to have succeeded as well in the Black Country as it did in Birmingham.

Table 38 gives the numbers of Anglican churches and clergy in each registration district in 1835, 1845 and 1850 together with the Anglican index of attendance from the 1851 census. The Black Country and Birmingham totals are then given with the overall Anglican and (in italics) non-Anglican indexes.[48] The Birmingham group includes, in Edgbaston and Kings Norton sub-districts, some rural churches which, for census purposes, were within these districts without being part of the Anglican provision for greater Birmingham. They numbered five altogether in 1850. The dramatic rise in the number of clergy in Wolverhampton between 1845 and 1850 reflects the abolition, in 1848, of the Deanery and the redistribution of its revenues to support parochial clergy in the town rather than augmenting those of the Dean of Windsor.[49] In other places the increase was often the result of grants from the Church Pastoral Aid Society, the Evangelical organisation founded in 1836, which supported both ordained and lay workers of that theological persuasion.[50]

In 1835 both Birmingham and the Black Country had an average of 1.4 clergy per church but whereas this proportion did not improve in the Black Country in Birmingham it was almost 1.6 in 1845 and well over that figure by 1850. Although such statistics do not indicate any dramatic difference in Anglican manpower between the two areas, removing the rural churches from the Birmingham group would show that Birmingham had a clear advantage, averaging 1.7 clergy per church in 1845 and 1.8 in 1850. As the 1851 census was based on attendance at public worship this is a fairer as well as a more realistic way of measuring pastoral efficiency than simply dividing the total number of clergy into the population. A comparison made on this basis gives the Black Country a better ratio than Birmingham because its greater population was spread over a wider area whilst Birmingham's was concentrated in fewer parishes.

The result is; Black Country one clergyman to 3, 597 people, Birmingham one to 5, 290.

One of the earliest local attempts at organised district visiting on the lines advocated by Chalmers was in Sedgley where, in 1826, Charles Girdlestone had become the first resident vicar for almost fifty years.[51] By the end of December 1831 he had established the Sedgley Benevolent Visiting Society whose object was "to promote the welfare of the poor by the personal attention of those who are in better circumstances". For this purpose the parish was divided into districts each with two male visitors who were to visit each poorer family at least once a quarter "and report their condition to a quarterly meeting to be held in each village". The parish actually consisted of at least seven separate, though adjacent, townships, called villages in Girdlestone's scheme, which produced some eighteen districts, though only the central area of Sedgley itself, including Gospel End and Woodsetton, along with Upper Gornal were allocated specific districts in the original minutes, others such as Lower Gornal, Coseley, Ettingshall and Brierley were initially left as single units, though they would almost certainly require subsequent subdivision. Visitors were given instructions to avoid appearing to pry or patronise the poor, but nevertheless "to explain to them how to improve their condition by means of industry, frugality, cleanliness and sobriety", whilst giving preference to the poor in their own districts in "whatever clothing, food or medicine you are in the habit of giving away". Finally they were to "enquire into all cases of parochial relief . . . seconding such applications as most deserve attention and discouraging such as you find unworthy of it".[52]

The initial entries in the ledger are very thorough, listing the age and condition of each poor person, their family situation, trade, membership of any benefit clubs, landlords and religious persuasion. Later comments such as 'blind' or 'died of cholera 1832' indicate a continuing contact though they are not dated. The list of communicants and those to be confirmed for 1833 suggests that the scheme survived the cholera epidemic and may even have continued until Girdlestone left the parish in 1837. Lewis, his successor, maintained that, "We cannot adopt the plan of district visitors, as there are not the people to do it, nobody sufficiently unconnected with the people." Without acknowledging the work of Girdlestone he said that he "did try the thing at one time, and was obliged to give it up; some whom we employed I knew were screwing down the people they ought to visit".[53] How far his comments reflect a genuine failure to recruit suitable visitors rather than an excuse to abandon a scheme to which he had not the same level of commitment as Girdlestone it is impossible to determine. Fletcher of Bilston mentioned having had "a short time ago a District Visiting Society consisting of from 14 to 20 ladies", the implication being that it had ceased to function by 1842. Clarkson of Wednesbury briefly stated, "we have a District Visiting Society of ladies and women, but they cannot affect what is wanted", whilst Cartwright of Dudley frankly acknowledged the difficulty of recruiting visitors from tradesmen. "You can get very good people, but they have neither the requisite knowledge, nor the influence over the people, which persons in a little higher rank would have".[54]

Fortunately for Birmingham there appear to have been sufficient numbers of both men and women willing to become Anglican district visitors. In November 1829 the clergy divided up the town, most of which at that time lay within St Martin's parish, for purposes of pastoral oversight. District visiting was to be organised but, unfortunately, the local press contains no further information.[55] However, in 1842 John Garbett at St George's, a Commissioners' church opened in 1822 to which a separate parish had been assigned out of St Martin's in 1830, had a group of female district visitors.[56] At Bishop Ryder's church, built in a poorer part of the town and opened in 1838, M. A. Collisson claimed to have divided his pastoral district into 93 sections of 20 houses each for the purpose of district visiting, of which 80 sections, consisting of about 1, 200 houses, were visited every fortnight.[57] Collisson did not specify the gender of his visitors but the surviving report of the St Peter's District Visiting Society, from 1844, indicates that eight men and thirteen women formed the team of visitors for a pastoral district in an equally impoverished area. St Peter's had been consecrated in 1827 only to be burnt down in 1831 and finally re-opened in 1837. It did not receive a separate parish until 1847 so that before that it operated as a chapel of ease of St Philip's covering Dale End, one of the most deprived parts of the town centre.

By 1844 visiting had a wider scope than Girdlestone's scheme, including these objectives, "to impress upon those visited the duty of attending public worship, to encourage parents to send their children to the National and Sunday schools of the parish; to see that every family be provided with a Bible and Prayer Book . . . to administer temporal relief . . . to distribute tracts, to give notice of any person sick, or otherwise requiring spiritual aid".[58] St Peter's visitors were following in the footsteps of other Tract Societies and Town Missions which, from at least 1837, had conducted a vigourous, if unco-ordinated, assault on Dale End and other poverty-stricken parts of the town. It could be the activities of the other denominations as much as the area's destitution which stimulated Anglican efforts. Whatever their motivation, at least in Birmingham the Church of England was not falling behind in attempts to evangelise the working class. As Garbett put it, "I look upon myself more in the light of a missionary than of a parochial clergyman. What can I do amongst a population of such magnitude?".[59]

Publishing tracts was not, as such, a response to the increased urban population but its rising literacy provided them with a much larger market. Some Anglicans grasped these opportunities. Girdlestone produced a series of twenty-eight Sedgley Church Tracts between 1831 and 1836, whose subjects included the life of Christ, Christian missions and saying Grace, two volumes of 'Devotions for Family Use' and several published sermons.[60] By far the most successful, however, was the Independent, John Angell James, whose booklet 'The Anxious Inquirer after Salvation directed and encouraged', published in 1834 by the Religious Tract Society, had, by 1839, reached 200, 000 copies, plus an American edition and European and non-European translations.[61] The Wesleyans had their own central publishing house which distributed tracts and official publications via the travelling preachers joined, from the 1820s, by those Hugh Bourne produced for the Primitive Methodists.[62] Added to these were sermons in pamphlet form, frequently addressing local situations, like 'The Marriage Vow' already quoted. Their quantity and range afford insights into contemporary religious ideals and attitudes despite their verbose and ponderous style. As G. M. Young remarked, "the circulation of some Victorian sermons is a thing to fill a modern writer with despair".[63]

Preaching itself was undergoing adaptation in the growing industrial towns. For many years eloquent preachers had drawn large congregations in London and fashionable provincial towns. Now these were being joined by the centres of industrial conurbations like Liverpool, Manchester, Leeds and Birmingham. During the 1840s Birmingham gathered an increasing number of pulpit orators from across the denominational spectrum to add to those, like James, already well established in the town. In 1840 G. S. Bull, the 'Ten Hours Parson', moved from Bradford to St Matthew Duddeston, becoming vicar of St Thomas's in 1847.[64] By that time J. C. Miller, another able preacher, was rector of St Martin's. On census Sunday he filled St Martin's as Bull filled St Thomas's. Nevertheless, as David Mole acknowledges, the Anglicans had few preachers capable of matching the non-conformists.[65] In September 1849 a student at Spring Hill College, R. W. Dale, was asked by James to preach at Carrs Lane, an association which led him to become James' eventual successor.[66] By this time George Dawson, whom Dale very much admired, had given up the pastorate of Mount Zion Baptist Church, held since 1844, to found his own Church of the Saviour in 1847. He was followed at Mount Zion by Charles Vince and joined by Arthur O'Neill who, in 1846, led many of his Christian Chartist Church into the Baptist fold, becoming pastor of Zion Chapel, Newhall Street.[67] To complete the picture John Henry Newman came to Birmingham in 1849, following his reception into the Roman Catholic Church, there to spend the rest of his life as a member of the Oratory.[68] The Black Country could not compare with this array of pulpit orators, all of whom had a special concern for the urban industrial situation, though some acceptable Anglican and nonconformist preachers were found there.

7.5 New methods in urban contexts

Pulpit oratory was very much an art form addressed to an indoor audience, a congregation which had chosen to attend a place of worship.[69] The previous century had seen in the Methodist movement open-air preaching addressed directly to a non-worshipping and often hostile audience, initially by clergy of the Churches of England or Wales. They were joined by some of their more eloquent converts who became, particularly within the Wesleyan system, authorised preachers.[70] By the 1790s Independents and Baptists had adopted open-air preaching, but almost entirely in rural areas, a strategy repeated in the later nineteenth century.[71] By the early 1820s both Primitive Methodists and Bible Christians were also involved in open-air evangelism, albeit in different parts of the country. Although the Primitives began on the fringes of an urban area their initial impact was rural, in the Staffordshire moorlands and southern Derbyshire, where they acquired the nickname 'Ranters', before moving down the Trent valley into Nottinghamshire and Lincolnshire. At first the Black Country was the only urbanised industrial area where they had any lasting success.[72] The rural pattern, immortalised in Adam Bede by George Eliot, whose aunt was a Wesleyan preacher,[73] required only a friendly family in the village and an announcement, usually by word of mouth, where the preacher would be and at what time for a crowd to assemble. There was usually no competition, unless the parson or sexton rang the church bells to drown the preacher's voice. The town situation was very different.

"Preached in the open air, the company not so large as at other times. The causes of this may easily be told. Some fifty yards off a man of eccentric appearance was holding forth. He was surrounded by a hundred or more. A little way off a Ranter raved most vehemently . . . He also had his hearers. Although I had not so numerous an assembly I could not but rejoice at seeing the different efforts that were being made for the same end". So wrote Edwin Derrington, a Town Missionary employed by Carrs Lane, on Sunday 2 August 1840.[74] The prospect was no better on a Monday. Thomas Augustine Finegan was an Irish episcopalian employed by the Birmingham Town Mission in Dale End. On Monday 2 October 1837 his journal reports,

"Made another effort in Thomas St., was better received than on former occasions . . . in about 16 visits I made only one family refused to listen to me at all. The general observation was that so many men, women and boys come about their doors thrusting tracts and preaching on Teetotalism in the street, that it becomes to them as the common drug of a quack doctor – four persons have been seen at one time preaching in one street and each one recommending different places to go to. I saw nothing in the appearance of the preachers, or their tone of delivery, to attract the respect or attention of the people – I now begin to see the cause of the dislike of the Thomas St. people, for, said a sensible man to me, Sir, Ten or twelve times a day we have religion cram'd down our throats, as it were with a drum stick."[75]

The Wesleyans regularly took their place amongst the motley band of open air preachers in Birmingham during the 1830s and 40s. They argued against the Owenites, attending their meetings and distributing tracts against the 'rational religionists'.[76] Their local preachers were also heard attacking Roman Catholicism as idolatry, a grave tactical error in Finegan's judgement and no way to gain a hearing amongst the Irish, who formed an increasing proportion of the town centre population.[77] E. P. Thompson's view, given wider currency in Margaret Drabble's biography of Arnold Bennett, that Wesleyanism in the age of Bunting ceased to evangelise the working class and became wedded to maintaining mahogany-panelled chapels as symbols of social respectability, hardly matches the local evidence.[78] Wesleyan local preachers were active in the poorest parts of Birmingham, and in many impoverished areas of the Black Country.[79]

A. C. Pratt, in articles written for the Wolverhampton press in 1883-4, describes the career of two such preachers. William Hackett of Bilston established a Wesleyan cause at Gospel End in Sedgley, tract distribution, opening a Sunday school in a cottage and open air preaching led to the building of a chapel in 1846, for a congregation of miners and nailers. His attempts to establish Wesleyanism in rural villages beyond Wolverhampton all failed, but at Coven a Wesleyan locksmith's warehouse was eventually used for preaching.[80] The second was William Astle of Wolverhampton who visited from house to house in poorer districts, preaching on street corners and penetrating lodging houses and 'beggars kitchens'.[81] Another Black Country township where the Wesleyans held open air preaching was Wednesfield. There the curate forbade the parish clerk to ring the church bells to drown the preacher's voice. The Wesleyans, understandably, went to the parish church on Sunday mornings taking their Sunday scholars with them.[82]

The Wesleyan cause struggled for many years in Darlaston, but as early as 1819 the Primitive Methodists established themselves there, gaining strong support from a Wesleyan local preacher who joined the new movement.[83] Open air preaching was the normal method used initially by the Primitives to gain adherents, two or three preachers usually working as a team. At Brierley Hill, for example, three preachers entered the township. "According to the connexional custom, the preaching was first in the open air. Numbers flocked to hear; and some of the vilest of characters were benefited and saved by the word. Preaching was afterwards established in private houses and a society was formed."[84]

From the first the Primitives had adapted the American 'camp meeting' to English conditions, reducing its duration to a single day, limiting the time any one preacher could speak to ten minutes, breaking up a large gathering into smaller 'praying companies' and interspersing singing, prayer and exhortation in an organised fashion to encourage maximum participation.[85] Encouraging accounts of camp meetings were sent to the Primitive Methodist Magazine from Darlaston and Brierley Hill in the 1830s and 40s, but Birmingham proved much more resistant.[86] The account of a Birmingham camp meeting in August 1845 is distinctly reticent, with no hint of the attendance despite 'processing' seven streets in the morning and nine in the afternoon. In a conventional phrase, "an encouraging influence attended all the exercises" but only the evening love-feast where "twelve or fourteen souls were brought into the Kingdom of Christ" gets real approbation.[87]

The Primitives' method of attracting a congregation, set out by Hugh Bourne,[88] found an unsympathetic observer in Edwin Derrington, "Supplied the pulpit of the Rev. S. Parsons, Brierley Hill, preached three times and held a prayer meeting in the evening after the service. The congregations were thin during the day. The Primitive Methodists are a very stirring people and they manage, in that part of the country, to keep the attention of the people to themselves by constant excitement and this is mistaken for religion. I heard them in their chapel before I had left my room at half past six-o-clock, Sabbath morning, singing and praying. After breakfast they marched their children through the streets and so brought the people together and so managed to keep a crowded place during the day". The previous month he had "supplied the pulpit at Brierley Hill . . . The congregations were but small during the day, being much affected by the Primitive Methodists who held their camp meeting in that place. These singular people commenced their perambulations as early as between seven and eight-o-clock in the morning. So they continued during the day, walking in ranks and singing through the streets some part of the day carrying a banner with a motto and the age of the society upon it. These things disturb the peace and break in upon the sanctity of the Sabbath."[89]

Obstructing the highway rather than disturbing the sanctity of the Sabbath caused offence in Birmingham. "On Sunday last a number of Ranters were passing along Moor Street. When they came to the top of Freeman Street they suddenly stopped, fell on their knees and commenced praying. A considerable crowd assembled which rendered it necessary for the police to request they would depart and they immediately did so."[90]

The Primitives failed to make any impact on Birmingham comparable with their success in the Black Country. There they used another technique, called within Primitive Methodism a 'Salvation Meeting' but drawing on the American idea of Protracted Meetings described in Charles Grandison Finney's Lectures on Revivals of Religion, published in Britain in 1837. Throughout 1839 they were serialised in the Primitive Methodist Magazine with editorial comment. The magazine also gave a detailed account of a 'protracted meeting' from Barnard Castle and a brief description of Salvation Meetings, described as "bringing the camp meeting system more fully into use", the advantage being that they could be held indoors in winter[91]. These concentrated all the resources of the travelling and local preachers in a sustained fashion on one place for a limited period of time, rather than diffusing them throughout a circuit. On the first occasion in the Dudley circuit twelve preachers were planned for one chapel. The resulting product is best illustrated in this report from the Dudley circuit in 1840.

"Sunday February 23, 1840, was the day appointed for the Brierley Hill Salvation Meeting. The platform was erected as for a missionary meeting. We went and processioned from ten-o-clock till eleven. We had preaching by two ten-minutes men. Then a mighty prayer meeting. We met again at half past one and processioned till half past two. Then commenced speaking on the platform, two sermons, each ten minutes long. We then divided into four companies, two in the gallery and two below, for about fifteen or twenty minutes. – We platformed it again, and had two ten minute sermons, – Then divided again. – All was great and grand. – At night we held a Lovefeast . . . At about eight o'clock the praying companies took their stations in the gallery and below. Seventeen professed to find liberty in the gallery, and fifteen below. This was on the Sunday.

Monday night we held a meeting to gather them in, and four more got converted; and it was . . . carried to have another Salvation Meeting on Tuesday night, in place of the regular preaching. When the time came we platformed it again and thirty-seven more got converted. Wednesday night prayer meeting; thirty more professed to obtain pardon. Thursday night class meeting (Mr Southall's) It could not be led. Twenty more stepped into liberty. Friday night Mr Fisher's class could not be led. Above twenty more rejoiced in the Lord. Halleluia This was such a week as was never known in this country before."[92]

This method of evangelism was soon extended to other parts of the Black Country. Eric Hopkins, in his study of the strength of non-conformity, particularly Methodism, in Lye in the first half of the nineteenth century attributes it to the close knit nailing communities but does not explain why it took root in the first place. Preaching a message "of a simple fundamentalist nature" is as far as he goes.[93] The fact that some local preachers from Lye Waste came to the Brierley Hill salvation meetings "to see, and render assistance; and they went home determined to have a revival there also" helps provide an explanation.[94] In the sort of close knit community described by Hopkins, where nailing went on in domestic workshops at a pace dictated by the nailer, taking time off for a salvation meeting was relatively easy, especially if processions through the streets beforehand had aroused interest and curiosity. Given the sort of planning and enthusiasm indicated by the reports from Dudley it is easy to understand how the Primitives could effectively take over a small industrialised village for a week at a time and put immense pressure on the people to accept their message.

The sheer scale of Birmingham and Wolverhampton seems to have discouraged the Primitives from any such attempts. A smaller sized place did not always guarantee success. Willenhall lay little over a mile from Primitive Methodism's Black Country headquarters, and was as tight knit a community as Lye Waste, but it proved singularly impervious to emotional evangelism. Again and again from 1824 the Darlaston circuit planned camp meetings and, from 1840, salvation meetings at Willenhall. They all failed. The Primitive cause in Willenhall only became secure in 1847 when a dissident Wesleyan group calling themselves the Teetotal Church was accepted "upon the rules of our conference and upon no other conditions".[95]

The technique of mass evangelism by carefully orchestrated campaigns conducted by a professional evangelist had been pioneered by several American preachers. It was Finney, however, who brought it into the urban from the rural and small town context of up-state New York and publicised his methods in his Lectures on Revivals of Religion, giving the impression that human effort, rightly directed, would bring results previously ascribed entirely to Divine intervention.[96] In Birmingham John Angell James had long taken an interest in American revivals.[97] This did not mean that James adopted all of the 'measures' put forward by Finney but, in 1839 under the influence of a visiting American, Patton, James introduced a 'protracted meeting' into the programme of Carrs Lane, with "blessed results" of which he gives no further details.[98]

When Finney eventually toured Britain in 1849-51, he was fifty-seven years old and limited by his sponsors to revival meetings at Houghton, in Huntingdonshire, Worcester and Moorfields Tabernacle, London. The itinerary did, however, include Birmingham as one of those who invited Finney was C. H. Roe, pastor of Heneage Street Baptist chapel. Before inviting Finney to Birmingham Roe needed to ensure James' support as any hostile comment from him could be disastrous. After some hesitation James agreed. Finney concentrated on Heneage Street, where seventy-five new members were added, and Ebenezer Chapel, Steelhouse Lane. Writing later that year James commented, "I suppose you know we have had a visit from your Mr. Finney. He was three months in this town, where he excited some considerable attention, but did not succeed to the extent of his expectations. Most of our ministers stood aloof from him. This I could not bring myself to do. He preached five or six times for me and sometimes with great power." Altogether the visit was a disappointment with little permanent result.[99]

More success was claimed for another visiting revivalist, the Methodist James Caughey, an Irish-American authorised by the Troy Conference to visit Britain in 1841. He was warmly welcomed by Irish Wesleyans and promoted some startling revivals in well established chapels without having any equivalent impact outside them. From 1842 ad hoc arrangements enabled him to conduct successful revivals in Liverpool, Leeds, Hull, Sheffield, Huddersfield and York, all centres of Wesleyan strength, causing dissension amongst the leadership about his methods and demand to occupy pulpits to the exclusion of the appointed preachers.[100] In December 1845 he came to Birmingham, staying until May 1846 and followed by grateful resolutions from circuit quarterly meetings, claiming over 300 new members in both East and West Wesleyan circuits as a result of his preaching.[101]

Caughey used a technique, made familiar by Finney but regarded with suspicion in British Wesleyanism, of calling those whom he urged to make a decision about their souls to come forward to the communion rail. This, together with preaching apparently addressed to specific individuals, followed by a prayer meeting in the chapel, put public pressure on potential converts in a fashion hitherto unknown in Wesleyan circles. To Benjamin Gregory, Caughey "united in the same person the revivalist and the pretender. He brought to decision hundreds of hesitating, halting hearers by an urgency and fervour well befitting his message; he shocked and repelled others by preternatural pretensions to which he had no claim . . . which were sure to bring the work of an evangelist into grievous disrepute."[102] This judgement was echoed in press reports of the Birmingham campaign which, despite its impact on Wesleyan membership, did not have the wider social effects reported of revival campaigns in some American cities.[103]

Evangelistic campaigns, by enthusiastic local preachers or visiting American professionals, aimed at raising the emotional temperature through mass meetings. A different approach attempted to influence individuals through domestic visiting by paid lay agents, a strategy derived initially, like that of district visiting, from Scotland. The Town Mission established in Glasgow in 1826 by David Nasmith was the inspiration for the London City Mission, initially under Nasmith's direction, of 1835.[104] The Mission was given wide publicity in the religious press, followed by the establishment of other interdenominational and denominational Town Missions.[105] The Birmingham Town Mission and the Carrs Lane Town Mission were both inaugurated in 1837, followed by the Wesleyans in 1839 and the Unitarians in 1840. Other places in the conurbation held back until Wolverhampton established a Town Mission in 1855. Hence the evidence for this particular form of evangelism comes entirely from Birmingham, but has the advantage of being more detailed than any comparable contemporary source material. A second Unitarian Mission was begun in 1844 and Scripture Readers were employed by J. C. Miller of St Martin's from at least 1849.[106] Alongside them went the efforts of the Roman Catholic religious orders, which were active in both Birmingham and the Black Country. Anglican suspicion of lay agency was condemned in 1842 by Garbett, rural dean of Birmingham, "The church is leaving lay agency to Wesleyans, Papists and other sects; and it is not possible in overgrown parishes to stand against them. My lay agent is invaluable."[107]

The aims of nearly all the Town Missionaries were identical, reading and expounding the Bible, distributing tracts, encouraging attendance at church or chapel, engaging in 'religious conversation' and urging 'those who are living in neglect of religion to observe the Sabbath'.[108] The Wesleyan missionary was instructed to visit adherents of the town chapels, persuading them to become members and attend class meetings.[109] The Unitarians, following the ideals of Joseph Tuckerman of Boston, Massachusetts,[110] added to, "Religion preached and spoken of, unsectarianly" a concern to help the poor help themselves, providing adult evening classes and libraries.[111] In this they had been anticipated, to some extent, by the Wesleyans whose Cherry Street Tract Society had adult schools on Sunday afternoons in people's houses from at least 1827.[112]

The Wesleyan missionaries, 'Brother Bakewell' in the West and 'Brother Tunnicliffe' in the East Circuit, were bound to cover a wider area than those of the other missions. There were four town centre chapels in the West circuit and three in the East in 1839.[113] Both men would, inevitably, visit areas already penetrated by other missions, which concentrated on the poorest parts of the town. These were extensive, running from Legge Street and Gosta Green in the north and sweeping south-east in a broad semi-circle to include Dale End, Bordesley Street and Digbeth, finishing up around Hurst Street to the south of St Martin's church. The Unitarians were based in Hurst Street in the south and Lawrence Street to the north, other groups also had preaching rooms in the area, Carrs Lane at Allison Street and Palmer Street, the Town Mission and the Wesleyans in rooms hired at various times.

Those town missionaries with no contacts to follow up began systematic door to door visitation of their district. This pattern was soon abandoned firstly, because it raised expectations of financial relief amongst the poor which the missionary could not meet and, secondly, because he usually received more discouragement than attention to his message. The method was never entirely abandoned and, in certain lodging houses, the regular turnover of residents meant that a rebuff one week might be followed by a welcome the next.[114] Visiting only the homes of the poor meant that the missionaries met largely the women, the sick and the old rather than working men. Several times Thomas Finegan visited homes in heavy rain hoping to find the men indoors but, even then, he was disappointed.[115]

To meet men required visits to public houses and workshops which did not always welcome solitary evangelicals, though several such visits are recorded. Unfortunately the missionary who did so most regularly was insensitive and self-opinionated, recording only what he himself said, not the response he received. Nevertheless even he was regularly surprised by the positive attitude of the men he encountered.[116] Open air preaching is recorded by a number of missionaries usually in competition with others.[117] Like the Wesleyans some missionaries concentrated their visits on 'hearers' who had attended their preaching rooms.[118] The challenge of poverty faced every missionary and clearly affected their pattern of work. A few were led increasingly into social work by their response to destitution, particularly Finegan.[119] Others withdrew from the constant pressure of human misery into becoming ministers of a small congregation. This course was successfully pursued by some Carrs Lane men, notably Edwin Derrington.[120]

Once responsive contacts had been made 'cottage meetings' of the type familiar in rural areas could sometimes be organised. This was normal with Wesleyans whose class meetings were still a source of strength at this period, but was not limited to them. One Carrs Lane missionary mistook a Unitarian for a Wesleyan because he held prayer meetings in his house.[121]

7.6 Mixed messages

Peter Sibree's journal from April 1838 to April 1839 illustrates the range of different messages which the working class of Birmingham were getting from the various groups competing for their support. Sibree was an ardent Temperance advocate and attended a meeting addressed by the men from Preston. He preached in the house of a Wesleyan and reported having a grateful Roman Catholic amongst his hearers, noted that Swedenborgian tracts had prejudiced people against other tracts, that the curate of Bishop Ryder's church was gathering a flock, mostly ex-Wesleyans (whom he was also attempting to recruit), that the Owenite Socialists had taken over Lawrence

Street chapel from the hyper-Calvinists, that the Southcottians had only eight believers left in Birmingham, rivalry from Wesleyans depleted attendance at his own prayer meeting and Unitarians he met were very appreciative of their denomination's work. Finally, on 8th April 1839, he visited a dying man,

> "After conversing with him in the most solemn manner on the subject of faith and repentance he said, without anything to lead to such an observation, 'Do you think the present ministers will go out?' On my wishing to evade the subject he said he had been a Reformer and really did not think a Tory could be saved and evidently comforted himself that it would fare better with him in another world because he had always voted against the abuses of government and church rates."[122]

All these competing groups shared some common features. They offered their hearers a means of salvation and hope for the future, in this life or after it or both. Each was convinced that they had the one certain remedy for all human ills, and most went on to condemn any other teachings as false. Their vocabulary and rhetorical styles were largely derived from the Bible and used in an appeal for decision and commitment. These common features masked divergences sufficient to fragment efforts at Christian evangelism and give plausibility to the argument that religion in general and Christianity in particular had a negative influence on the human spirit. The attempt to define what was meant by Christianity, and then to appropriate it for a particular organisation, lay at the heart of much which now appears to be arid and unnecessary polemic.

Historians trying to make sense of the religious situation in the 1830s and 40s have acknowledged the overlap between the different sects in both doctrines and devotional styles.[123] This overlap includes movements apparently hostile to organised religion. "27th November 1839. Made fifteen visits in New Canal Street. Came into contact with a Socialist and a Chartist. The object of the Chartists is to have the majority of the House of Commons composed of working men and that of the Socialists to destroy the Christian religion. These two parties are combined. There is a most determined spirit infused into their mind" noted Henry Clay, a Carrs Lane missionary.[124] Eileen Yeo has pointed out how, after the Bull Ring Riots and Newport rising, Owenites and Chartists supported one another, providing for the working class parallel social organisations as alternatives to the churches.[125] These included forms of worship similar to those of mainstream Protestantism. The 1839 spies' reports on Birmingham Chartist activity include Sunday evening preaching services in a meeting room in Allison Street. The spy describing the sermon on 8th December as "a complete mockery of the gospel", showed his ignorance of the opening verses of John chapter five, which were given an orthodox interpretation concluding with an evangelical appeal, "if anyone there wished to be made whole he must inform them that Jesus Christ was there then to make them whole".[126] This was much less inflammatory than Chartist sermons reported in the press but not necessarily insincere. Eileen Yeo sees Chartism as a form of radical Christianity, not limited to Chartist Churches.[127]

Watts claims that Unitarians in the early nineteenth century had lost their capacity to attract a working class following because they offered "no appeal to conscience; no instruction for the poor, . . . no consolation for the afflicted."[128] Such was not the case in Birmingham where Unitarian 'missions to the poor' were sufficiently successful to worry their rivals. Peter Sibree's discovery that the man he mistook for a Wesleyan because he held prayer meetings in his house was a Unitarian resulted in two hours of heated argument.[129] The annual reports of the New Meeting Mission to the Poor complain regularly of attempts by self-appointed guardians of Christian orthodoxy to deter those whom the missionary, John Gent Brooks, had attracted by his ministry. Brooks was a former Chartist who, although he had broken with Chartism in 1842, disagreeing with Thomas Cooper over the use of force, had not lost his sympathy with the sufferings of the workers which he had first witnessed in his native Hinckley[130]. In 1848 he published a Declaration of Faith to counter hostile misrepresentations. Its content and tone are reflected in a letter written the previous year, "You must not think that because I am a Unitarian my soul is bound up in ice. Never were my feelings towards God and Christ and heaven stronger than now. Nor must you think that I reject the doctrine of the Atonement. I feel that it is the most complete evidence of God's love and the Saviour's condescension. At times my mind sinks, for mine is a difficult employment and the opposition I meet with is very trying. The orthodox condemn us because we do not believe in three persons in one God. They have not been able to draw my people from me, but I do feel pained at their want of Christian love."[131]

Elisabeth Jay's perceptive study of Anglican Evangelicalism, as portrayed in Victorian novels, points out the theological significance of the division between Calvinists and Arminians and distinguishes essential from non-essential Evangelical doctrines.[132] In broad outline its doctrinal summary would be true not only of many Independents and Baptists but also, with a different emphasis, of the Methodists. She classes as essential belief in 'original sin', conversion, justification by faith and the authority of the Bible.

Belief in 'eternal punishment', millenarianism, special providences and assurance are non-essential, being open to dispute amongst Evangelicals whereas the first four were not.[133] Methodists would see assurance and special providences as more central doctrines than Elisabeth Jay allows. Such an analysis clarifies religious features of Victorian fiction but not the approach of each brand of evangelical to potential working class converts.

In any Evangelical scheme conversion had to be preceded by 'conviction of sin' before any sense of God's forgiveness, and justification by faith in the atoning death of Christ, could be real. The Birmingham evidence indicates that there was little doctrinal difference between the moderate Calvinism of Anglican, Independent and Baptist and the Arminian theology of the Methodists, each preaching universal salvation not one limited to the elect. Nevertheless there remained a recognisable difference in emphasis. Briefly caricatured Calvinist evangelicalism had a fearful approach and a doctrinal emphasis whereas Methodism had a generally hopeful approach and a psychological rather than a doctrinal emphasis. These differences are apparent in many sources from which the following extracts are taken.

"I had a long conversation with a family in Litchfield Street. It was the first house I entered this day Monday 24th July. 'Sir', said the woman, 'it is no use to talk to us for we be working folk and we must work of a Sunday for other people, as we are bakers and pieclate makers and until all other folk of our trade give over working on a Sunday we cannot give up our living'. 'My dear friends', said I, 'You may as well say that until all other people of your trade in Birmingham made up their minds to flee from the wrath to come you would make no attempts to escape the firy indignation of an Angry God, who enforces His command by a word which he has not employed in giving any of the other commandments, that is *Remember*, which is almost saying, should you be such a slave to sin and to hell as to violate any or all of my other commandments, *Remember* this one, That thou keep Holy the Sabbath Day, . . . I followed up these observations with others in allusion to the terrors of the Lord . . . and I was much encouraged to notice a marked degree of attention paid to all my observations."[134]

Thomas Augustine Finegan, who recorded this conversation was an Episcopalian, though, as an Irish convert from Roman Catholicism, he was hardly a typical Anglican Evangelical. As a newcomer to Birmingham he may not have been aware that payment by the factors for a week's work usually took place late on a Saturday so that many working class families had to wait till Sunday morning to buy essentials like bread. Such considerations hardly seem to have entered his mind which was intent on inducing in his hearers that 'conviction of sin' which was the necessary preliminary to conversion. The authority of the Bible is used to threaten them with God's anger at breaking the only commandment in the decalogue they were obviously disobeying if, as Evangelicals argued, the Christian Sunday had replaced the Jewish Sabbath.[135] Using Sabbatarian legalism to provoke spiritual anxiety was not limited to Anglicans. On May 10th 1846 William Jackson was "returning from Chapel after the evening service, seeing crowds of boys and girls at play in Milk Street I went to them and succeeded in calling a large number of them around me, telling them that I had something to say to them. I then, of course, endeavoured to show them the evil and danger of profaning the Sabbath and reminded them that a young girl, who had formerly been in the habit of playing in the street on the Lord's Day as they were doing now, lay dead."[136] Jackson was only one of those for whom fear of hell was an integral part of their message.[137]

In opposition to relying on mystical experience of any kind, even prayer, Calvinists emphasised belief in the substitutionary doctrine of the atonement. "Some two months ago I visited a man whose name is Henry Thomas living in Bordesley Street. I found him very ignorant but willing to receive instruction. I asked him how he expected to be saved. He said by prayer, he knew no other way. I endeavoured to point out to him the danger of building on such a rotten foundation, " wrote Joseph Tye, one of the Carrs Lane missionaries, in 1849. Although Tye attempted to explain the need for justification by faith Thomas "clung tenaciously to prayer as a means of procuring pardon". Eventually, after several more visits Thomas produced the approved doctrinal formula, "In answer to the question, Well, how do you feel? . . . I feel comfortable. What is the cause of your comfort? Looking to Jesus, I have no-one else to look to. Well, I said, what has Christ done for you?. He has shed his blood for me. The poor fellow has lost the use of his limbs, seems tolerably well in himself, has a wife and three or four children and is in the very prime of manhood." Tye concluded.[138]

Like other Carrs Lane men Tye's mentor was John Angell James whose teaching provides a rationale for this approach. Writing to an enquirer in 1838 he says, "If you search the Scriptures, you will find that joy and peace are to come into the soul of the Christian by faith. What is faith? The belief of the gospel testimony concerning the person and work of Christ. The object of faith is Christ, as He is made known in the Word, not as he is pictured in the imagination . . . It is by believing, then, that we are to be saved, comforted and edified, not by endeavouring to conceive of Him by imagination . . . Learn to distinguish between the exercise of faith and imagination."[139] By contrast appeals to the imagination, with an emphasis on direct experience of God, were what distinguished Methodist approaches even though in theological terms their doctrines were very similar.

"Birmingham, where I now am, is a mighty field of labour. I have raised two new classes, and am just commencing two others. I preach almost every night. I mean to leave few streets of the town without a warning. I set the crucified Saviour before the people. I show them Jesus, the tears, the groans, the sweat, the pillar, the scourge, the cross, the nails, the hammer, the silence, the vinegar, the gall, the prayer, the cry, the death, the spear, the grave, the broken seals, the affrighted soldiers, the rising Christ, the comforted disciples, the waiting multitude, the rushing wind, the baptism of fire, the crowd of penitents. While I thus witness the Lord makes bare His arm and many are saved."

So wrote John Collins, Wesleyan local preacher, in 1832 to his son.[140]

Even when warning of God's judgement appeals to the imagination are used to awaken hope and encourage a positive response. In 1824 the Primitive Methodist Magazine printed a model 'Camp Meeting Discourse' on the text, 'The trumpet shall sound' (1 Corinthians 15:52) in which vivid imagery depicts the end of the world and the experience of being judged is utilised to bring home the inevitability of God's judgement. "Surely, then, the main care of our lives should be to obtain peace with God, to stand with acceptance before the dread tribunal. And what is sufficient for this purpose but righteousness? God is as direct on this subject as his word can make him; everywhere blazoning the defects of all things else, and everywhere extolling the perfect obedience of our Redeemer and the righteousness that is by faith in him".[141]

'Faith' in Methodist terms was not belief in a doctrine but an intense emotional commitment. This is brought out both in the tracts and magazines for the public and the private diaries of the preachers themselves in which a lack of devotional feeling is noted as a cause for concern.[142] Hence their message had to awaken such emotions by an appeal to the imagination.

The result was criticised by Calvinists like Edwin Derrington, who deplored "how some systems and the teachers of those systems make it easy for sinners to have a comforting view of Christ. Amongst these are to be found the zealous but illiterate friends of the Wesleyan body who know little or nothing of the truth as learned from the New Testament, but they have a few regular cant phrases such as are common to their body. Never do I think anyone more effectually put the cart before the horse than they when they talk about that first which should be last. There is living at present a poor woman in my district who has long opened her house for the body of people above referred to. I have been invited to see her . . . but can do little with her as she has to unlearn her errors. 'Well Mrs Hill, said I, How do you find yourself now?' 'Oh I am very unhappy, I cannot feel my sins forgiven'. 'Feel your sins forgiven, what do you mean by that?' 'I don't know but they tell me that I must feel my sins forgiven, that I must have the spirit of God within me witnessing with my spirit that I am one of His children' 'Ah Mrs Hill, this is like looking for the chimney of the house before they have laid the foundation". Derrington went on to interrogate her on the doctrine of the atonement concluding, "such believers make very poor work of it being quite unable to give a reason for the hope they profess to have."[143]

This assurance of forgiveness, proclaimed by Methodists and criticised by Calvinists, was a strength of the Roman Catholic Church which evangelicals united to condemn. J. C. Miller's Scripture Readers seem to have had no understanding of its appeal, condemning any pious practice which did not fit their narrow view of scriptural authority[144]. Finegan knew better and, though warned by the Town Mission committee to avoid controversy, clearly relished a meeting with Catholics. After detailing a lengthy discussion with some Irish tinkers, who possessed "much shrewdness, keen intellect and argumentative faculty" he admits "I was myself astonished at the patience and attention shown on this occasion".[145] Public lectures and debates between Catholic and Protestant spokesmen regularly occurred in Birmingham and the Black Country during this period. For example, in West Bromwich anti-Maynooth meetings in the Wesleyan chapel in 1845 prompted George Bent, Spencer's successor as Roman Catholic priest, to counter them with a series of public lectures.[146] In 1850 Dalton, Owen and other Anglican Evangelicals mounted a series of anti-Papal lectures in Wolverhampton, but some Anglicans needed more than anti-Catholic rhetoric to reassure them. At the 'Papal Aggression' meeting in Sedgley a Mr Wills "made a few remarks to the effect that the Popish movement in the Church ought to have been checked some years since, but he was called to order as the meeting was not convened for the purpose of making an attack on the Church".[147] In Birmingham Anglican Scripture Readers were met with the Catholic claim that, "all your learned men are coming over to our Church; and would they do that if yours was not the wrong way?"[148]

7.7 Conclusions

The Church of England undertook a variety of initiatives in attempting to minister to the whole population but these seem to have stalled in the Black Country when compared with Birmingham. Although in terms of Anglican church building Birmingham barely provided for the same percentage of the population in 1850 as it did in 1800, in terms of active clergy and lay workers the situation steadily improved. Sustained efforts appear to have had positive results shown in the 1851 census. Only in Wolverhampton, after the abolition of the Deanery, were comparable numbers of Anglican clergy available toward the end of the 1840s, the census returns indicating a positive response.[149] The political assault on church rates in Birmingham had little long term effect on Anglican fortunes though how far political issues alienated working class people from the churches is hard to determine. In Birmingham, and to a lesser extent the Black Country, Anglican and non-Anglican clergy espoused many causes, political and social, which gave rise to the reform movements of the time, though equally urgent voices were heard opposing them.

Though open air preaching took place in both Birmingham and the Black Country, mass evangelism seems only to have been attempted by Methodists in the Black Country, and this with varying fortunes. Lack of surviving evidence from the Dudley Primitive Methodist circuit means that its overall impact cannot easily be evaluated. Professional evangelistic campaigns were limited to Birmingham where Finney and Caughey only reached adherents of the denominations sponsoring them. Of these the Wesleyans gained far more members, but the 1849 Wesleyan divisions prevented this appearing in the 1851 census.[150] Domestic visitation by the 'undenominational' Town Mission and major denominations, including the Unitarians, is a distinctive feature of Birmingham. Whether working class people welcomed it or not it was hard for them to avoid hearing a variety of religious messages.

Notes

1   G. M. Young, *Victorian England, Portrait of an Age*, Oxford 1936 (second edition 1953) p. 48.

2   G. Kitson Clark, *The Making of Victorian England*, London 1962, p. 162.

3   Original broadsheets and documents in the possession of Mr. N. W. Tildesley, Willenhall.

4   National Association Gazette cited in J. Ryan, 'Religion and Radical Politics in Birmingham 1830-1850', M Lit. thesis, Birmingham 1979, p.119.

5   One of them was John Gwyther of Chilvers Coton who features as Amos

Barton in George Eliot's *Scenes from Clerical Life*, cf. Ashton, *Eliot*, pp. 170-171, 175. He was unsuccessful in the poll. cf G. Robson, 'Between town and countryside', in Baker, *Studies*, 1979, p.413.

6   Tancred, *First Report, Midland mining*, p. 16.

7   Robson in Baker *Studies*, 1979, pp. 411-412.

8   Staffordshire Record Office, Hatherton Papers, D260/M/F/5/27/10 Letter 88.

9   W. R. Ward, *Religion and Society in England 1790-1850*, London 1972, pp. 181-192.

10 Gilbert, *Industrial England*, pp. 163-165.

11 *Birmingham Journal*, 13 and 20 September 1845.

12 Dudley Libraries and Archive Services, Coseley, original poster reproduced in G. Barnsby, *The Dudley Working Class Movement 1832-1860*, Dudley 1970, p.15. For Cook's career see G. Barnsby, 'The Working Class Movement in the Black Country', Birmingham MA thesis 1965, passim.

13 Birmingham Reference Library, Duddeston-cum-Nechells Radical Reform Society, Minutes 1839-46. *Birmingham Journal* 1842, June 4, 11, 25; *Birmingham Journal* 1843, July 22 and 29.

14 *Aris's Birmingham Gazette*, 9 May 1831; D. E. H. Mole, 'The Challenge to the Church: Birmingham 1815-65', in H. J. Dyos and M. Wolff (eds.) *The Victorian City*, London 1973, Vol. 2 p.828.

15 *Birmingham Journal* 8 December 1838.

16 Ibid. 24 April, 4, 11 September, 16 October 1841, 22 January, 26 February 1842.

17 Details of the whole episode are given in D. E. H. Mole, 'The Church of England and society in Birmingham 1830-1866", PhD Cambridge, 1961, pp. 116-198.

18 *Birmingham Journal* 30 August 1845, see also *Wolverhampton Chronicle* 6 November 1850.

19 *Birmingham Journal*, 8 June 1845.

20 Ibid. 29 December 1849."I will not presume to offer an opinion upon the merits or demerits of the contending parties in this unhappy and distracted parish but it is a melancholy and heart-sickening sight to behold those, whose object ought to be the promotion of peace and goodwill among men, employed in fomenting discord or actively engaged in the turmoils of party conflict" said the report.

21 *Wolverhampton Chronicle*, 7 October 1835.

22 *Birmingham Journal*, 30 December 1843.

23 Ward, *Religion*, p.192, Gilbert, *Industrial England*, p.164.

24 *Aris's Birmingham Gazette*, 9 February 1842, *Birmingham Journal*, 12 February 1842.

25 R. W. Dale, *Life and Letters of J Angell James*, London, 4th edition 1862, pp. 284-86.

26 J. A. Langford, *A Century of Birmingham Life*, Birmingham 1868, vol. 2, pp. 494-5, 502, 509, 559; J. A. Langford, *Modern Birmingham and its Institutions*, Birmingham 1873, Vol. 1, pp. 45, 56, Vol. 2, pp. 185 ff.

27 A. W. Dale, *Dale*, p.140. J. C. Miller, *Dying Pastors and the Undying Priest* (Birmingham 1859)

28 Gilbert, *Industrial England*, pp. 168-170.

29 *Catholic Magazine* 1834, p.311.

30 There were Chartist lecture rooms at Dudley and at Bilston, where they, "prevented tract distribution by district visitors and substituting some of their own publications". Tancred, *First Report, Midland mining*, pp. 42, 75, 80, 89.

31 J. A. Langford, *Modern Birmingham and its Institutions*, Birmingham 1873, Vol. 1, pp. 9-11.

32 *Birmingham Journal*, 1840, 1 and 29 February.

33 *Birmingham Journal*, 21 March 1840, G. Barnsby, *The Dudley Working Class Movement 1832 -1860*, Dudley 1970, pp. 5-10.

34 C. Campbell, *The Marriage Vow*, Birmingham 1840, pp. 14ff. In a derogatory footnote he pointed out that a Dissenting minister's "services, however highly esteemed, gave not one iota of independent validity to the above union! . . . the services of one of his deacons or hearers would have been as valid . . . The law sends the bridegroom to a lay surrogate called a superintendent (possibly a Socialist!)".

35 Walters, 'Anglican', chapter 3, McPhail, 'Attendance', pp. 205, 226.

36 Barrs, *Four Sermons*, p. xxiv. cf. W. H. Oliver *Prophets and Millennialists*, Oxford and Auckland 1978, chapters I to VI.

37 *VCH Staffordshire*, Vol. 3, p.114, *VCH Warwickshire*, Vol. 7, p.401. Langford, *Modern Birmingham* Vol. 1, pp. 108ff.

38 J. Wolffe, *God and Greater Britain*, London 1994, p.84. "The initial policy adopted, by the Established Churches in particular, was simply to build more churches, to provide clergy for them and hope that these increased resources and greater physical proximity to working-class dwellings would be sufficient in themselves to achieve the desired end. By 1850 the limitations of this approach were already apparent, and the religious census confirmed that, although there were local shortages of church accommodation, elsewhere pews were empty while their potential occupants stayed away. So further strategies assumed considerable importance."

39 Mole in Dyos and Wolff, *Victorian City*, pp. 823-826.

40 Barrs, *Four Sermons*, p. xxviii.

41 Tancred, *First Report, Midland mining*, p.51. Port, *Six Hundred*, pp. 160-161.

42 Tancred, *First Report, Midland mining*, p.49.

43 Port, *Six Hundred*, pp. 138-9, 164-5.

44 Tancred, *First Report, Midland mining*, pp. 37-40.

45 Ibid. p.3.

46 D. W. Bebbington, *Evangelicalism in Modern Britain*, London 1989, pp. 65, 76, 118, 313.

47 Tancred, *First Report, Midland mining*, pp. 15, 36, 39, 49, 88.

48 Sources indicated on pp. 40-41, plus Clergy Lists for 1845 and 1850. If anything the table under-represents the number of churches being served as clergy lists do not always indicate dependent chapels and some gaps undoubtedly occurred. Hence the number of Black Country churches is not as great as that represented in the 1851 census. The clergy numbers are slightly conjectural as some were not resident full time in their livings. Nevertheless the incidence of non-residence decreased steadily throughout

the period so that the 1850 figures are a much closer reflection of the real situation.

49 *VCH Staffordshire* Vol. 3, pp. 329-330.

50 In Bilston, for example, C.P.A.S. funding enabled J.B. Owen to maintain a curate and a Scripture Reader and in Wednesbury two curates were thus supported. Tancred, *First Report, Midland mining*, pp. 35, 88. A. E. Owen, *J. B. Owen*, p.353. In Birmingham a total of eighteen clergy and lay workers were supported by grants amounting to £1, 400 in 1849. *Birmingham Journal*, 10 March 1849.

51 McPhail, 'Attendance', p.236, DNB q.v.

52 Dudley Libraries; Archives and Local History Services, Coseley, Manuscript minutes of the Sedgley Benevolent Visiting Society, 15 December 1831.

53 Tancred, *First Report, Midland mining*, p.49

54 Ibid. pp. 36, 39, 88.

55 *Aris's Birmingham Gazette*, 23 November 1829. But see David Mole's article on 'The Evangelical Revival in Birmingham' Part 2, which gives details of district visiting, provident institutions and other aspects of parochial organisation in the 1830s by J. G. Breay at Christ Church and William Marsh at St. Thomas's (i.e. before the arrival of G. S. Bull) in *Bulletin of the West Midlands Branch of the Wesley Historical Society*, Vol. 2, No. 11, Birmingham, September 1975 pp. 99-104.

56 *VCH Warwickshire*, Vol. 7, p.387, Tancred, *First Report, Midland mining*, p.3.

57 *VCH Warwickshire*, Vol. 7, p.381, Tancred, *First Report, Midland mining*, p.6.

58 *VCH Warwickshire*, Vol. 7, p.394, Birmingham Reference Library, St Peter's District Visiting Society, *Report 1844*, Rules and Regulations, p.6.

59 Tancred, *First Report, Midland mining*, p.3.

60 D.B. Robinson, 'Staffordshire clergy in 1830', in *South Staffordshire Archaeological and Historical Society Transactions*, Vol. XXIV, 1984, p.97, DNB q.v.

61 R. W. Dale, *James*, pp. 179, 195.

62 J. T. Wilkinson, *Hugh Bourne 1772-1852*, London 1952, pp. 189-92.

63 G. M. Young, *Victorian*, p.14.

64 J. C. Gill, *Bull*, pp. 135, 142.

65 D. E. H. Mole, 'John Cale Miller: a Victorian Rector of Birmingham', in *Journal of Ecclesiastical History* Vol. 17, 1966, p.95

66 A. W. Dale, *Dale*, p.57 and passim.

67 A. Briggs *Victorian Cities*, London 1963, pp. 195-201, *VCH Warwickshire*, Vol. 7, pp. 437, 441, 446.

68 Ibid. p.403.

69 See the illuminating series of 24 'Pulpit Photographs', well written reports on individual preachers within the context of worship, including Dale, Dawson, O'Neill, Newman and Vince, as well as other lesser Anglican and non-Anglican preachers from the latter half of the century, produced by the Birmingham Daily News in 1871. Birmingham Reference Library, newspaper cutting collection.

70 H. D. Rack, *Reasonable Enthusiast*, London 1989, pp. 223-225, 242-245 and passim.

71 Lovegrove, *Sectarian*, passim, D. M. Thompson, 'Church extension in town

and countryside in later nineteenth century Leicestershire', in Baker, *Studies*, 1979, pp. 427-440.

72   Werner, *Primitive*, passim.

73   Ashton, *Eliot*, pp. 20, 204-205.

74   Birmingham Reference Library, Carrs Lane deposit, Vol. 64, 2 August 1840.

75   Birmingham Reference Library manuscript Journal of T. A. Finegan, 2 October 1837, cf. 6 August.

76   Birmingham Reference Library, Carrs lane deposit, Vol. 71, Journal of P. Sibree 10 October 1838.

77   Finegan, 'Journal', 19 November 1837.

78   Thompson, *Making*, pp. 431-436, M. Drabble, *Arnold Bennett*, London 1974, pp. 9-19.

79   cf. BRL, Minutes of Cherry Street West Circuit local preachers meeting, 17 September 1847.

80   A. C. Pratt, *Black Country Methodism*, London 1891, pp. 73-87. McPhail questions the veracity of Pratt's account of Gospel End on the basis of the 1831 entries in the ledger of the Sedgley Benevolent Visiting Society. To him the fact that few of the Gospel End poor are recorded there as belonging to any denomination other than the Church of England counts against their subsequent recruitment to Methodism. However, his whole comparison between the 1831 entries and the 1851 religious worship returns is based on a misunderstanding. The Visiting Society ledger only records those poor people likely to be in need of parochial relief, not the whole population of Sedgley, which was 20, 577 in 1831. Not only so but many entries indicate dual allegiances, especially to both the Church of England and Methodism, which the timing of Sunday services at Gospel End facilitated. The Wesleyans only had services in the afternoon and evening at Gospel End, enabling any who wished to attend the parish church in the morning to do so, something which was quite normal for many Wesleyans, not only in Sedgley. McPhail, 'Attendance', pp. 248-9, 253-5. Wolverhampton Archives and Local Studies, Wolverhampton Darlington Street Circuit Book, passim.

81   Ibid. pp. 98-101.

82   Pratt, *Black Country*, pp. 88-89.

83   Ibid. pp. 147-157.

84   *Primitive Methodist Magazine*, Bemersley 1839, p.69.

85   Werner, *Primitive*, pp. 147-149, H. D. Rack, *How Primitive was Primitive Methodism?*, Englesea Brook 1996 pp. 7-11, J. H. S. Kent, *Holding the Fort*, London 1978, pp. 17-27.

86   *Primitive Methodist Magazine*, 1838, p.272, 1842, p.435.

87   Ibid. 1845, p.498.

88   Ibid. 1838, pp. 417-419, cf also 1835, p.72 with specific reference to Birmingham.

89   Birmingham Reference Library, Carrs Lane deposit, Vol. 63, 18 July 1841, Vol. 64, 13 July 1841.

90   *Birmingham Journal*, 2 September 1843.

91   R. Carwardine, *Transatlantic Revivalism*, London 1978, pp. 14, 73, *Primitive Methodist Magazine*, 1839, pp. 13ff, 31-34, 357-358 and passim.

92 Ibid. 1840, p.261, cf also pp. 226-228.

93 E. Hopkins, 'Religious Dissent in Black Country Industrial Villages in the First Half of the Nineteenth Century', in *Journal of Ecclesiastical History*, Vol. 34, no. 3, July 1983, pp. 411-424, esp. p. 421.

94 *Primitive Methodist Magazine*, 1840, p.261.

95 Walsall reference Library, Darlaston Primitive Methodist Quarterly Meeting Minutes, Vols. 1-5 passim, cf Robson in Baker, *Studies*, 1979, pp. 413-414.

96 Carwardine, *Revivalism*, pp. 3-28, W. R. Cross, *The Burned Over District*, New York 1950, pp. 151-184.

97 He carried on an extensive correspondence with both William Patton of New York and William Sprague, American pastors who toured Britain in the 1820s. James endorsed Sprague's own book on revivals published in 1832, R. W. Dale, *James*, 1862 edition pp. 414-467 contain this correspondence. Carwardine, *Revivalism*, p.59.

98 Ibid. p.438, Carwardine, *Revivalism*, p.74.

99 R. W. Dale, *James*, p.449, Carwardine, *Revivalism*, pp. 134-139.

100 Gregory, *Sidelights*, pp. 344-45, 368, 390-91, 400-401, Carwardine, *Revivalism*, pp. 107-133.

101 Birmingham Reference Library, Minutes of the Cherry Street West Circuit Quarterly Meeting, 30 March and 29 June 1846, *Wesleyan Methodist Magazine*, 1847, pp. 154-56.

102 Gregory, *Sidelights*, pp. 345, 401-402, who accuses him of being the first "to introduce the unworthy trickery of decoy penitents", Carwardine, *Revivalism*, p. 120.

103 Cross, *Burned Over*, p.155, 168-9, Carwardine, *Revivalism*, p.162.

104 H. D. Rack, 'Domestic Visitation, a Chapter in Early Nineteenth Century Evangelism', in *Journal of Ecclesiastical History*, Vol. 24 no. 4, October 1973, p.360. D. M. Lewis, *Lighten Their Darkness*, Westport Connecticut 1986, pp. 49-63. This was a deliberately inter-denominational 'evangelical' organisation but it fell under episcopal suspicion despite the fact that control stayed largely in Anglican hands.

105 *Wesleyan Methodist Magazine*, 1836, pp. 54-55. 528-529. The Wesleyan Methodist Magazine reported its inaugural public meeting and printed its constitution and instructions to its agents, following it up later, however, with a plea for the formation of specifically Wesleyan district visiting societies!

106 For the Birmingham Town Mission, Langford, *Modern Birmingham*, Vol. 2, pp. 185-197 and Finegan, 'Journal'; for Carrs Lane, Birmingham Reference Library, Carrs Lane deposit, Vols. 61-75 contain the first annual report and the journals of six different missionaries covering the period 1837 to 1852; for the Wesleyans, the Quarterly Meeting minutes of both East and West Birmingham Wesleyan circuits plus the minutes of the Cherry Street Tract Society, all in Birmingham Reference Library; for the Unitarians, H. New, *Hurst Street Domestic Mission, notes on the 50th Anniversary*, Birmingham 1890 and *Memoir of J. G. Brooks*, Birmingham 1854; for the Anglicans, J. C. Miller, *Our Scripture Readers*, Birmingham 1849.

107 Tancred, *First Report, Midland mining*, p.3. For Roman Catholic Sisters of

Mercy in Birmingham and Passionists in the Midland District see J. Champ, 'Assimilation and Separation' op. cit. pp. 202-206 and 268-272.

108 Constitution of the Birmingham Town Mission quoted in Langford, *Modern Birmingham*, Vol. 2, p.186.

109 Minutes of the Cherry Street West Circuit Quarterly Meeting 18 March 1844.

110 see Rack, 'Domestic', pp. 360-361.

111 New, *Hurst Street*, p.3, Brooks, *Memoir*, pp. 30-32, 92.

112 There were seven in 1829 but by 1835 only two were still in existence, Cherry Street Wesleyan Tract Society Minutes, 7 June 1827, 2 April 1829, 20 October 1835.

113 Others were added on the growing fringes of the town during the 1840s, so that there were twelve altogether by 1851. Quarterly Meeting Minutes, Cherry Street West and Belmont Row East circuits 1839-47 passim.

114 References are to single examples which could be repeated many times, Carrs Lane deposit Vol. 73, October 1851 (Mr Rennie), Vol. 61, 1 October 1838, 7 December 1838, Vol. 62, 14 May 1838 (Edwin Derrington), Vol. 72, 25 April 1839 (Mr Clay), Finegan, 'Journal', 16 and 17 August 1837.

115 Ibid. 17 September 1837.

116 Carrs Lane deposit Vol. 68, 20 July, 20 August 1842, Vol. 70, 11 December 1846, 14 January 1847 (William Jackson).

117 Carrs Lane deposit Vol. 64, 2 August 1840, Finegan, 'Journal', 6 August 1837.

118 Carrs Lane deposit Vol. 67, 18 October 1842 (William Jackson), Brooks, *Memoir*, pp. 94, 101-102, 116.

119 Robson G, 'Failures of Success, in D. Baker (Ed.) *Religious Motivation: Studies in Church History 15*, Oxford 1978, pp. 381-391. J. A. Burdett, 'A study of the relationship between evangelical urban missionaries and the working class poor in Birmingham, Norwich and Edinburgh', M Phil. Birmingham 1994. Burdett concentrates on only two of the Birmingham missionaries, Finegan and Derrington.

120 cf. 1851 census return for Palmer Street and Carrs Lane deposit Vol. 63, 4 August 1839.

121 Carrs Lane deposit Vol. 71, 7 December 1838, cf 9 November, visit to a Wesleyan snuffer maker who holds class meetings in his house (Peter Sibree).

122 Ibid. passim.

123 cf Wolffe, *God*, pp. 20-38.

124 Birmingham Reference Library, Carrs Lane deposit, Vol. 72 (Henry Clay)

125 E. Yeo, 'Robert Owen and radical Culture' in S. Pollard and J. Salt (Eds.) *Robert Owen; Prophet of the Poor*, London 1971, pp. 95-108. See also the article in the same volume by W. H. Oliver on Owenism as a religion, parallel to Christian millenarianism, ibid. pp. 166-187. The theme is fully worked out by Oliver in *Prophets and Millennialists*, Oxford and Auckland 1978.

126 Public Record Office, Home Office papers HO 40/50. (Spelling corrected)

127 E. Yeo, 'Christianity in Chartist Struggle', in *Past and Present*, No. 91, 1981, pp. 109-139, and E. Yeo, 'Chartist religious belief and the theology of liberation', in J. Obelkevich, L. Roper, R. Samuel, (Eds.) *Disciplines of Faith*, London 1987, pp. 410-421.

128 Watts, *Dissenters*, p.90.
129 Birmingham Reference Library, Carrs Lane deposit, Vol. 71, 7 December 1838.
130 Brooks, *Memoir*, pp. 17, 77.
131 Ibid. p.48, see also pp. 34-37, 103-104, 115-116.
132 E. Jay, *The Religion of the Heart*, Oxford 1979, pp. 67-69.
133 Ibid. pp. 51-105.
134 Finegan, 'Journal', 24 July 1837.
135 Jay, *Heart*, pp. 183-87, cf. Miller, *Scripture*, p.7, visit XII, p.17, visit XXIX.
136 Birmingham Reference Library, Carrs Lane deposit Vol. 69, 10 May 1846.
137 cf Ibid. Vol. 63, 10 July 1843.
138 Birmingham Reference Library, Carrs Lane deposit, Vol. 75, undated entries 1849, also January 1851.
139 R. W. Dale, *James*, 1861 edition pp. 353-4, letter to Mr Hart. This was dropped from the 1862 and subsequent editions and therefore deserves fuller quotation. Dale questioned James' idea of faith.
140 Coley, *Collins*, p.40.
141 *Primitive Methodist Magazine*, Bemersley, 1824, pp. 73-78.
142 e.g.. *Arminian Magazine*, 1795, pp. 78-81, 'An Affectionate Address to Rational Beings', (later published as a Wesleyan Tract); *Primitive Methodist Magazine*, 1822, pp. 246-250, 'An outline for class and prayer meetings'; Ibid. 1839, Hugh Bourne's comments on Finney's Lectures on Revivals, esp. pp. 296-300, 337-341. Methodist Central Archives, John Rylands Library, Manchester, manuscript diary of Joseph Entwistle junior, Dudley circuit, 3 January 1830.
143 Birmingham Reference Library, Carrs Lane deposit, Vol. 64, 9 October 1839, also Vol. 65, 15 December 1841 (both Edwin Derrington)
144 Miller, *Scripture*, p.7, visit XIII, p.8 visits XV and XVI.
145 Finegan, 'Journal', 27 July 1837, cf 18 August, 31 August, 6 September, 27 October and passim.
146 R. H. Trainor, 'Anti-Catholicism and the priesthood in the nineteenth century Black Country', in *Staffordshire Catholic History*, Vol. 16, 1976, p.22.
147 M. W. Greenslade, 'Staffordshire 'No Popery' 1850-51' in ibid. Vol. 21 1982, pp. 27, 43.
148 Miller, *Scripture*, p.8, visit XV.
149 cf Tables 20 and 38.
150 cf Methodist Central Archives, correspondence, James Methley to Dr Beecham 3 October 1850 (Marked Private), "My appointment in this circuit is one of considerable difficulty . . . Had anything untoward taken place at Conference with reference to one individual we should have lost half the Society in this circuit. Many of our principal friends, once loyal and confiding in Conference have become lately alienated from us. Not to the extent openly to confederate with our enemies, in seeking organic changes, but in producing apathy and jealousy in our connexional proceedings . . . My great difficulty is the <u>low tone</u> of piety which like a paralysis rests upon the circuit." (underline original)

CHAPTER 8

Patterns of Response

8.1 The experience of the Town Missionaries

The evidence from the conurbation refutes Inglis' suggestion that only after the 1851 census did churchmen of all denominations recognise the alienation of the urban working class from organised religion and begin to do something about it.[1] The previous chapter indicated the range of evangelistic efforts by major churches during the 1830s and 40s, many particularly directed at poor working class communities. Unfortunately only the journals of the Town Missionaries and some of their published reports indicate the variety of responses to their labours. What they recorded from their visits depended on theological concerns and the need to justify their work to the committees employing them. The evidence, therefore, has a degree of randomness compounded by the survival of the journals of only seven missionaries, all but one employed by Carrs Lane. These are fuller and earlier than the one surviving journal from the much larger London City Mission, that of Joseph Oppenheimer from 1861 to 1862, from which Lewis derives his account of the responses of the poor to the missionaries' visits.[2]

In addition to Finegan's journal covering the whole of his time with the Birmingham Town Mission, from June 1837 to the end of May 1838, the six Carrs Lane men provide between them evidence from October 1837 to July 1852. Edwin Derrington's journals from 1837 to 1845 form the most complete sequence. The others span shorter periods some, notably that of William Jackson, becoming brief and formal after fuller opening entries. This means that the evidence, though ample compared with London, is impossible to analyse quantitatively, though indications are occasionally given of how much religious allegiance the missionaries found and how many they persuaded to attend their own preaching rooms.

Lewis trusts Oppenheimer's journal because it is in manuscript and not edited for publication.[3] The missionaries must have known, however, that extracts from their journals were used in reports for the general public. They could also use their journals as a means of dialogue with their committee, including protest at its policies. This is particularly true of Finegan whose break with the Birmingham Town Mission came when he blamed Dissenters on the committee, particularly the Baptists, of trying to take over the undenominational Sunday school and evening preaching which he had established in The Gullet, a notorious alley avoided by women and respectable men.[4] Henry Clay protested at Carrs Lane's decision to move him from Legge Street and make changes in the Allison Street preaching without his permission.[5] Sometimes the missionary appealed to denominational rivalry to gain his ends. Edwin Derrington's desire for a respectable place to preach in is re-iterated many times.[6] Such considerations were bound to influence what the missionary chose to record. Nevertheless, Lewis' main point is fair. The manuscript journals are a more reliable source than extracts published to appeal for funds or justify the missionaries' activities.

Lewis analyses Oppenheimer's visits in terms of the categories of people he encountered as well as the responses they made. Thus Roman Catholics, Jews, Sabbath breakers and prostitutes are included along with the indifferent, nominal Christians and overtly hostile. It seems best not to confuse these categories so the following account concentrates on the general nature of the responses rather than the individual respondents, though some reference to their personal experiences is inevitable. The responses are considered under five headings; commitment, short-term adherence, instrumental affiliation, indifference and rejection. Such categories would be valid for any organisation, religious or secular, actively recruiting from the wider population and not just to evangelical or liberal Protestantism. Despite their theological positions, however, the missionaries' journals throw light on a wide spectrum of religious attitudes and therefore merit further treatment.

8.2 Commitment

This term indicates simply that the person was a regular worshipping member of a religious body. In most cases these would be Christian though the small Jewish population and the Mormons' activities during the 1840s and early 50s extends the possible commitments a missionary might meet. For example, William Rennie noted that out of 740 families in the twelve streets of his district, 27 were church members, 50 professed regular attendance, 23 were Roman Catholics and nine Mormons.[7] Assuming two adults per family, perhaps an underestimate, would give a religious commitment of barely 7%. Rennie's 'church members' would be spread across the Protestant denominations and relatively few would be Independents. Another Carrs Lane man, Henry Clay, commented, "nearly all the religious people at my station are either Methodists or Baptists and do not co-operate with me . . . as to holding meetings etc."[8]

Membership of any evangelical Protestant church, except the Church of England, made considerable demands on the individual, particularly poorer and less well educated men and women. At Carrs Lane candidates for membership had a private interview with the minister who, if satisfied about their "proof of a change of heart and life", proposed their names at the next church meeting. He then nominated two church members to visit them and report their findings, including any letters from the candidates, to a subsequent church meeting. After further comment from the minister the meeting voted on whether they be 'received' or not. Dale, from his own experience, gives a lengthy account of James' practice in ensuring that new members were thoroughly examined and suitably encouraged. James himself, aware that church membership was considered a guarantee of moral probity, said, "though I have been more strict than many of my brethren, there are many, very many, whom I now wish I had rejected".[9] Once 'received' their conduct was open to scrutiny from a district visiting system and subsequent lapses were the concern of a discipline committee of four deacons and five other members of the church, a system James himself introduced.[10] It is little wonder that Edwin Derrington, after much effort, still felt unable to present some of his hearers as candidates for membership at Carrs Lane.[11]

A smaller church, with a more working class membership, was not necessarily easier to join. For example, the Four Ways General Baptist Church at Cradley Heath, Rowley Regis, was formed in 1837 with 27 members. When, in 1850, they invited James Shaw to be their minister, they had 24 members and could only offer him the seat rents plus a shilling a quarter per member and a promise to buy goods from any shop he kept, so long as they were no more expensive than could be obtained elsewhere. Nevertheless candidates for baptism were visited by two elders or nominated members before being proposed to the church meeting and had to give an account of their experience in public before baptism. They were then subject to the discipline of the church which frequently records members being visited to 'enquire into the state of religion in their souls' and request their attendance at worship and other meetings. Expulsions for drunkenness, fighting and slander as well as non-attendance, and suspension for minor offences are regularly recorded.[12]

This experience of belonging to a 'gathered church', with

stringent tests to ensure that only the converted were received into membership, underlies the contempt of the Carrs Lane men for Methodists who appeared far too lenient. As Henry Clay remarked, "There is a lamentable defect in the discipline of the Methodists with respect to the admission of members into society and expulsion from it. They precipitately admit them and rejoice over them as brands plucked from the burning and as hastily expel them when overtaken with a fault, or suffer them gradually to withdraw and then charge the delinquent with self-expulsion."[13] The basis of Methodist membership, however, differed from the Baptists and Independents. It had some financial implications. The penny a week class money amounted to about the same as the shilling a quarter promised by the Baptist membership of Four Ways Cradley Heath to their minister, but Methodist members had not the same privileges of voting in church meetings, nor were they expected, before joining a class, to have experienced conversion. A desire to seek the salvation of their souls was all that was required.

This undoubtedly meant that it was much easier to join a Methodist society than to become a member of most other churches. They were supported by a more experienced member as their class leader and subject to disciplinary rules administered by the leaders' meeting. This body, chaired by the minister, investigated allegations of drunkenness, sexual misconduct and financial dishonesty, including insolvency, which, if substantiated, could lead to exclusion from Methodist membership.[14] Hence the justice of Henry Clay's complaint at the ease with which people could enter and leave the Methodist fold but, by the same token, rather less in Richard Carwardine's claim that Wesleyans were embarrassed by the number of society members who only appear to have been converted by James Caughey.[15] The fact that 20 percent of Caughey's Sheffield converts came from the existing Wesleyan membership should not have been surprising considering the emphasis on holiness and Temperance (in fact Teetotalism) in Caughey's message.[16] Methodism did not require society members but only leaders and local preachers to testify to their own conversion, though clearly it encouraged members to seek both conversion and holiness, neither of which were necessarily easy either to obtain or to retain once acquired.

Any working class person who took religion seriously needed to defend their commitment not only against members of their family or neighbours who might denigrate it but also against missionaries trying to deflect them from their chosen denomination. This was particularly true for Roman Catholics who were subjected to a barrage of tracts,[17] but also Unitarians whom evangelicals proselytised. "Whenever a new Scripture Reader comes into the district", complained Brooks in 1850, "he seems to consider it as a matter of course that a new crusade should be entered upon against the hated Unitarians".[18] Miller, from his Scripture Readers' journals, tells of one young woman and her father, formerly 'Socinians', now worshipping at St Martin's, but gives numerous accounts of their confrontations with 'Romanists'.[19] All the missionary journals recount controversy with Roman Catholics. When meeting Irish Catholics Finegan had a clear advantage in speaking their language and giving the customary Irish greeting when entering their houses. He went a little too far in attending an Irish wake to gain hearers and was rebuked as an intruder by the Catholics.[20] Although asked, as 'the Irish parson', to pray for a dying Catholic,[21] he never claims to have detached any Irish from their Catholic commitment. Instead, "I have reason to believe that many Roman Catholics who lived in a total neglect of any religious observation on the Lord's Day and were generally to be found in the Alehouse, or grouped together playing at cards in their Lodging-houses, have abandoned their wicked practices and now attend more regularly at worship in their own Chapels on the Lord's Day."[22]

Like other missionaries Finegan tabulated weekly the number of meetings held, visits made, tracts and Bibles distributed, persons induced to attend day and Sunday schools but also, uniquely, places of worship.[23] He claimed, in ten months, to have persuaded four hundred and eleven to do so.[24] By his terms of employment and personal commitment Finegan could point potential worshippers toward any evangelical church or chapel, Anglican or nonconformist. He regularly notes 'church folks' who have lapsed from worship and tells of a former fighter who had abused his wife, whom he reconciled to the Church of England before his death. At the end of 1837 he claimed 279 adults were persuaded to attend public worship, 146 in Anglican churches, 73 with Independents and 60 with the Baptists or the Countess of Huntingdon's Connexion.[25]

Unitarians also encouraged the lapsed to return. "Those who have been brought up at the parish church I have induced to attend there again; others, who are strictly orthodox, to attend their own respective chapels, and many Catholics have been encouraged to return to the duties of their church" wrote Brooks in 1846.[26] One of his converts contrasted Brooks' approach with another missionary. "I have been visited before, but instead of doing me any good it did me real harm, for the visitor had a strong voice and a hard, unfeeling manner. He told me that if I did not believe certain things which he laid down for me I should go to hell. He seemed not to consider the distracting effect produced on my head, and the feelings of horror which thrilled my nerves as he set forth his religious views. I could not love or reverence either him or the Bible; I love to hear you talk and hope you will come again", Brooks reports.[27]

Brooks' convert's description would fit some Carrs Lane men whose insensitive approach must have deterred their contacts. "I had been informed that a father and mother who had formerly lived in Allison Street and attended the preaching room were now mourning over a departed infant, " wrote William Jackson in 1843. "I went to visit them . . . to render them spiritual benefit. I reminded the father of the painful affliction from which he had sometime before been raised up . . . I reminded both parents that former impressions and resolutions had evidently been forgotten and disregarded, but nevertheless God in his mercy had spared them and visited them with another warning . . . by taking their infant to Himself. I also faithfully reminded them that God's gracious dealings in the event of continued rebellion might be turned into manifestations of wrath." Not surprisingly he concludes, "My fidelity was received in silence by these poor wanderers from the paths of peace".[28]

Among Carrs Lane men only Derrington attempts to number the commitments he obtained. Fifteen years work in Deritend and Bordesley produced 90 members, 13 of whom attended Carrs Lane, 54 remained at Palmer Street, the rest had died, moved or been expelled.[29] In 1841 Derrington hoped to present for membership a convert who had previously persecuted his Methodist wife, but, unfortunately, the man died too soon.[30] Death bed conversions, however, were regularly reported by missionaries with the advantage that their reality was not easily denied.[31] The only other statistical evidence comes from the Wesleyans. The East Circuit Quarterly Meeting was told, in September 1843, that after nine months of missionary labours "thirteen had been induced to join the society". All other evidence is indirect. Both the East and West circuits had town missionaries from 1840 to 1844.[32] A gap in the East circuit records means that membership figures have to be taken from March 1839 rather than 1840, but when compared with March 1844 they show an overall increase in the East circuit of 144 members and 159 in the West.[33] There is no way of knowing how many of these were the work of Messrs. Tunnicliffe and Bakewell, but they must have had some effect on Wesleyan membership.

8.3 Short-term adherence

Such increases in Methodist membership were bound to include some for whom initial commitment led only to short-term adherence, a characteristic much criticised by others. As Derrington put it, "It is a strange thing . . . but I suppose that on my visits I find ten backsliders of the Wesleyan denomination to two of all the sects of the Christian Church and I know not how to account for it except it is that they take conviction for conversion. We seldom hear much of backsliders among us" he added.[34] Informed Methodists would question Derrington's explanation. Wesley's hymnbook, their most accessible source of Methodist theology, clearly distinguished through his arrangement of its contents between 'mourners convinced of sin' and 'believers rejoicing'. Each was but a stage on the road to 'full redemption'.[35] Not theological confusion but inability to sustain an emotional experience explained this particular case. Sent for to visit a sick man Derrington asked if he had ever paid attention to religion. "'Yes, sir, I believe I once knew the love of God, but I am a backslider'. 'You once knew the love of God!' 'Yes sir, I did.' 'Tell me what you mean by that expression will you.' It is a phrase Wesleyans often make use of but I cannot get them to tell me what they mean by it. I pressed the question. At last he said, 'I think I had peace'". Five years previously he had been separated from the Methodists through entering domestic service in a clergyman's family and being obliged to attend the parish church. Derrington's comment was that 'religion that is fed by excitement' was very likely to be lost in such circumstances. He was nearer the truth on another occasion, "I met several Wesleyans this afternoon, my visits appeared very acceptable. They mourned their low state of spirituality and desired conversation on religious subjects. These people depend so much upon the public and social means of grace that they are drooping quickly if they are removed beyond the reach of their class meetings."[36]

The missionaries report many reasons for neglecting Methodist class meetings. In several cases poverty meant that payment of class money could not be kept up. This had always been a problem in times of economic distress.[37] When combined with movement to Birmingham in search of work the problem was compounded. Derrington details two poor families whose moves from Sheffield and Wolverhampton respectively placed them, at least temporarily, amongst the lapsed Methodists.[38] Women married to unbelieving or persecuting husbands form another category, not of course limited to Methodists, but, unlike their male counterparts, unlikely to be able to hold class meetings in their homes.[39] The attraction of rival movements is also indicated, both Owenite Socialism and Chartism proclaimed ideals with which Methodists could identify despite the disapproval of the connexional leadership.[40]

Short-term adherence was not restricted to Methodists and could result either from the deterrent effect of negative experiences or the positive attraction of other alternatives. Brooks tells of a family who had attended his chapel but stopped when a Scripture Reader denounced Unitarians as unbelievers, declining into "habits of low gossip . . . tippling and . . . quarrels" on Sundays.[41] Miller's Scripture Readers could make no impression on another contact who went to the Mormons on Sunday mornings to hear the singing "and in the evening to the Catholic chapel to hear the music, for it is grand, and besides there is something to be seen when you go there." He promised to come to church, "but . . ., if I come, I shall only stop to hear the prayers, for they are beautiful, and as soon as they are ended I shall come out."[42] Such informed eclecticism reveals the attraction of short-term adherence undertaken as a personal spiritual quest.

8.4 Instrumental affiliation

This category includes those Lewis calls 'nominal Christians', but without its pejorative implications.[43] Frances Knight has shown that large numbers of lay people considered themselves to be members of the Church of England by virtue of their baptism and felt they had a right to its services whenever they needed them regardless of the fact that in the meantime they may have attended other places of worship or none at all.[44] Such people would have endorsed Dolly Winthrop's views on the importance of church ceremonies to legitimise rites of passage without feeling that habitual neglect of public worship in the intervals between them cast doubt on the genuineness of their Christianity.

The missionaries frequently encountered this attitude, though, as laymen, they were not involved in conducting baptisms, marriages or funerals. Both Thomas Finegan and Peter Sibree experienced sick persons rejecting their ministrations and asking for a 'church minister', meaning an Anglican clergyman, to visit them.[45] Finegan was quite ready, when requested, to assist a young woman "to give thanks for the spiritual and temporal comforts she received in sickness and childbirth, through my instrumentality" by taking her and three Roman Catholic neighbours to the Wednesday evening preaching at an Independent chapel near their court. He does not refer to this as 'churching' even though he is an Episcopalian, but it probably had this significance for Phoebe Purchase, the woman concerned.[46] Miller's Scripture Readers report several cases of people who 'profess to be members of the Church of England' without attending worship, 'except for baptism, or with a funeral or wedding' for years. One of their success stories was a woman who told them, "Till this last two or three weeks I never went into a Church but twice since I was a girl, and that was to be churched with my two children".[47] The practice of 'churching' was also part of the Wesleyan tradition, class leaders had printed 'forms of thanksgiving' which they could sign and give to any who 'may have occasion for them', but only if they were society members or regular attenders.[48]

In addition to rites of passage the Sunday school was, in the words of W. R. Ward, "the only religious institution which the nineteenth-century public in the mass had any intention of using".[49] This meant that town missionaries had no difficulty either in starting them or in gaining a positive response from the surrounding population. Much of Finegan's journal is taken up with his attempts to keep control of the Sunday school he established in The Gullet, whilst Peter Sibree tried to get Carrs Lane to take over another undenominational Sunday school in his district which was in debt. The purpose behind these manoeuvres was obvious. Whatever the educational benefit to the pupils those in control looked upon the Sunday schools as recruiting grounds for their own denomination. Derrington noted that twelve of the ninety or so church members which his fifteen years' work produced had come from the Sunday school at Palmer Street.[50] Brooks was involved not only in a Sunday school but also in evening classes four times a week for older children and adults with a broader educational aim. This 'ragged school' had an average attendance of 60 boys and 70 girls in its first eight months, and 'lectures' on a range of practical and cultural topics followed. Once three hundred had been enrolled in the Sunday school others had to be turned away as there were insufficient teachers. Few of those who attended will have done so from Unitarian principles but rather to seize an opportunity for self-improvement.[51]

A less obvious instrumental affiliation was afforded by the musical opportunities in some churches. One of Miller's Scripture Readers asked a seventy year old man how long it was since he went to church. He said, "My mother used to take me when I was a little boy". But his daughter revealed he had been a bell-ringer at an Anglican church for fifty years.[52] Derrington talked to a former Sunday scholar of Carrs Lane who, having joined the choir, left it for that of St John's, Deritend and finally King Street, the Countess of Huntingdon's chapel, after going 'about the country singing here and there'. To Derrington this was a dangerous temptation.[53] The cultural and social possibilities of such activities must have been attractive well before churches developed sporting and recreational programmes later in the century.

Most references to instrumental affiliation relate, understandably considering the missionaries' clientele, to appeals for charity. The journals cover one of the worst periods of economic hardship in the nineteenth century which, particularly during the winter of 1841-42, exposed the missionaries to harrowing scenes of destitution and starvation in their normal round of visiting. Both before, during and after the most serious distress they were involved in trying to offer help to people facing appalling suffering. This aspect of their work has been studied by J. A. Burdett. He claims that, faced with the poverty caused by cyclical unemployment, missionaries ceased to ascribe destitution to individual moral failings and advocated outdoor relief in opposition to those who, on grounds of 'political economy', forced the poor into the workhouse. Relieving poverty was also part of their strategy as poverty was seen by all missionaries as an obstacle to the reception of their message.[54]

This latter point had been made by previous historians, notably Hugh McLeod and myself, quoting the missionary journals.[55] In his treatment of Birmingham Burdett appears unaware of the method of poor relief well established since the eighteenth century which, by the 1830s and 40s, involved the town missionaries alongside a large number of others. Far from wanting to abolish outdoor relief Birmingham tried to regulate it within the provisions of the Poor Law, supplementing by co-ordinated voluntary effort its inevitable inadequacies. Finegan protested that, "he had sent fifty persons the other day to the workhouse because they were in distress and they were denied relief and turned away with disdain because they were Irish".[56] This activity, though gaining him a reputation among the Irish which impressed Burdett, was misdirected. The Poor Law Guardians were within their rights, as Finegan himself recognised.[57] The town's policy not to levy poor rates on houses valued at less then ten pounds a year meant that most of the unemployed had no claim for relief from the parish, being born beyond its boundaries and having paid no rates. This policy naturally provoked popular discontent and the occasional riot. In response, from the 1760s, collections were taken in churches during the Christmas season, subscriptions were raised and a town Relief Committee co-ordinated the provision of tickets for food, clothing and fuel. Half of these were distributed by the churches, including the Roman Catholics, the remainder were kept in the hands of the relief committee for individual applicants.[58]

Town missionaries were used to distribute tickets and to check the credentials of applicants. Derrington describes this in January 1838, when, according to Burdett, he was opposed to outdoor relief.

"This day I received notes for different comforts for the poor which ... I hastened to distribute among the families I knew to be in want. The intelligence soon flew round the neighbourhood and the people came pressing upon me so that I soon had to refuse the applicants and in some cases I gave one between two". The previous week he noted people refusing, out of pride, tickets he had for relief.[59] Another account, during the early months of 1838 is given in the journal of Henry Clay, of which Burdett seems to be unaware.[60]

The missionaries were regularly expected to give charitable donations to the poor, especially those considered 'deserving', because this was a traditional role of the Anglican parson, with whom they were linked in the popular mind.[61] Derrington notes one woman who refused him entry to her home as he had not left any money on his previous visit and another who called for him to visit her, "for we are very bad off, we cannot get food to eat, my son is out of work and my husband is very short". Derrington didn't give her anything so, during his second visit, she said, "I have been thinking I would send for the Rev. W B. Smith, I did him a good turn in voting for him, perhaps he might help me".[62] Smith had been elected chaplain of St John's Deritend earlier in 1842 and, as an Anglican parson, was thought more likely to respond to appeals for money. Derrington also took issue with those who accused a poor family of attending his chapel from mercenary motives, "I never gave this family but one shilling, and that when the wife was ill and the man had long been out of work".[63] Nevertheless affiliation to any church could bring with it the possibility of charitable support. Wesleyan class leaders regularly distributed tickets on behalf of the Relief Committee as well as their own 'poor fund' and were commended by Henry Clay.[64] Finegan's committee was quite prepared to provide bread to feed the children who attended his Sunday school in The Gullet, "a quarter loaf cut up between every four of them caused their little hearts to sing for joy. Thus I divided forty loaves between 160 and had ten loaves to spare, which I gave to the ten most necessitous of the parents". Inevitably this led him to be "beset by suppliants", an experience he shared with other missionaries.[65]

8.5 Indifference

Lewis uses this category for those who listened to the missionary's message with neither a positive response nor a hostile rejection. They usually gave a reason and were often challenged in an attempt to shake their complacency.[66] The same response is found twenty years earlier in Birmingham. Here an even wider range of attitudes is comprised within this category. Sometimes it is difficult to draw the line between indifference and rejection, particularly where no overt hostility was shown. This was often the case when missionaries attempted to visit better off residents of their districts, as Finegan found, "it may perhaps be unnecessary or indiscreet to call at respectable houses".[67] Henry Clay was less selective, "Called upon twenty families in Livery Street, some of those in better circumstances treated me with contempt."[68]

In recording negative responses few missionaries distinguished between indifference and rejection. They repeatedly note their discouragement but rarely give more detail. Henry Clay, for example, simply states of Park Street, "I have no hope of this street", though later, out of 50 families totalling 210 'souls', he lists three as believers, lumping the rest together under the heading 'unbelief'.[69] Such a crude classification does not do justice to the variety of reasons given by those who did not accept the missionary's diagnosis of their spiritual state. Poverty, in very many cases, engendered a lack of interest. "The deep poverty of some of the people of this neighbourhood is truly heartrending, "wrote Derrington in 1842, "one has almost to shut up the bowels of compassion to go among them . . . They are so entirely occupied with their present necessities that it is next to impossible to turn their thoughts from things seen and temporal".[70] Above the lowest levels of poverty were many whose indifference the missionaries ascribed to spiritual pride, usually because of a past connection with a religious organisation. William Jackson complains of "the self-complacency with which persons of Arminian sentiments, and especially among the Wesleyans, will allude to what they have been in religion, or rather what they suppose they have been", noting some who claimed to have been "very happy in the enjoyment of religion" and others like them who, although 'lapsed' from Methodism, boasted that they still kept their class tickets.[71]

Other responses indicated a reasoned detachment from any specific religious body. "Recommending Christ and salvation to an elderly female whom I found at her washtub in the court where I was visiting today," wrote William Jackson, "she very readily replied that she knew all these things and did them all, said her prayers every night regular . . . Grieved by her self-confidence and delusion I endeavoured . . . to impress eternal things upon her unawakened mind when, with the utmost indifference, she intimated that she had enough to attend to without troubling about these things and no-one had ever been to the next world and returned to tell us how matters stood there."[72] Finegan encountered a man who told him, "for my part I believe very little of what is said now – for there is so many people talking of this or the other religion that I go nowhere at all except into the fields for a country walk on the Sunday if it is fine, and if the day is bad I stop at home and read the weekly news."[73] A button-shank maker excused his non-attendance at worship to Peter Sibree on political grounds, "the clergy in the town were all Tories". But when Sibree argued on behalf of the Whig and Radical Dissenters, "his own heart, he said, was the closet in which he worshipped God and believed that that was the best place to converse with the Almighty."[74] A desire to withdraw into private life clearly lay behind these and similar responses by those the missionaries failed to convince of the importance of public worship.

8.6 Rejection

Reasons for rejecting the missionaries' message ranged from possessing an alternative religious or quasi-religious commitment to continuing a life-style in which conventional Christianity had little or no place. Between these extremes there was room for reasoned scepticism, criticising Christian dogmas and rejecting Evangelical shibboleths, particularly Sabbatarianism and churchgoing. The most strongly attached to an alternative commitment were the Roman Catholics, not all of whom listened patiently to the missionary before rejecting his message, like the Irish tinkers whom Finegan met. Less skilled controversialists could be sent away angrily, particularly Scripture Readers, one of whom condemned a Catholic's trust in the final mercy of God and the devotions in his prayer book. "His passion grew higher, and I saw that my presence only caused him to be worse, so I left him".[75] Like the Catholics, Owenites and Chartists were quite capable of standing up for their beliefs in an argument with a missionary. Sibree records several discussions with Owenite Socialists who, "seem to be filled with self-conceit and to delight in argument and hearing themselves talk", Henry Clay had similar experiences with Owenites and Chartists.[76] Not all such contacts were contentious, Derrington notes friendly Socialists and Unitarians, but his approach was more sympathetic than other Carrs Lane men.[77]

Reasoned unbelief was less frequently found in the poorest parts of Birmingham, or at least it was not as regularly noted by the missionaries. William Jackson "rather expected to find persons of sceptical sentiments" when he visited a blacksmith's workshop, "but I was agreeably disappointed, there was not an infidel among them".[78] Nevertheless they did exist. Finegan recounts two lengthy disputes with a man who called the Bible a fable and quoted Paine's

Age of Reason in support of his views.[79] Derrington records a similar conversation with a man who said, "I was a fool until lately but I have had my mind enlightened and you will be surprised when I tell you what it is that enlightened me. It was Tom Paine. I believe there is a God, but none of your nonsense for me".[80] Other references are less detailed, many simply record the fact without any indication of the reasoning behind the person's views. "Held a protracted conversation with a female of infidel principles in Milk Street", noted William Jackson adding only, "dealt faithfully with her soul".[81]

The previous month Jackson had a long conversation with a sick man who, "could not believe that God would punish sinners for ever in hell, it was said to be so cruel". Jackson's syllogistic argument was unlikely to convince someone who rejected Christian dogma on moral grounds.[82] This was no isolated instance, Sibree records his inability to convince a young woman, "that the punishment denounced on the wicked was not, as she asserted, a mere upbraiding of conscience . . . She was an intelligent young woman but unwilling to believe that sin deserved hell." Not only was hellfire rejected but also the substitutionary doctrine of the atonement, "Imputed righteousness appears to them an absurd and pernicious doctrine".[83] Such criticism was well thought out, not merely an emotional reaction to the missionary's message.

Opposition to Sabbatarianism was general, exemplified in Finegan's dialogue with the bakers in Lichfield Street. Brooks, in particular, recognised that a balance needed to be struck. He does not condemn a shoemaker who had to work on Sundays to make ends meet, instead a donation from his poor fund enabled the man to buy sufficient materials to make a living without Sunday work. Brooks argued for, "a proper observance of the Christian Sabbath. I do not mean a pharisaic but an enlightened cheerful respect paid to its claims and duties as a day of rest and mental and spiritual improvement . . . It is possible the evangelical portion of society have thrown an apparent gloom around the subject of religion, and decried too many harmless indulgences; but that is no reason why we should go to the opposite extreme and relax unduly the wholesome restraint of religion".[84] Such an attitude, had it been more widely shared, might have reduced the number of those who rejected the missionaries' message because they saw it as part of a system of social control from which more affluent classes in society were exempt.[85] Like the button-shank maker encountered by Sibree others were prepared to argue against the necessity of weekly public worship. In his case rejection was combined with anti-clericalism, a regular feature of popular responses.[86]

One of Sibree's more colourful encounters was with a dying man who, although initially moved by the missionary's appeal for repentance, decided in favour of sticking to his former ways. Sibree, a Temperance advocate, was shocked when the man offered him a drink of rum, "and more so when he turned down the bedclothes, took out a bottle of ardent spirits and applied it to his lips. He confessed drinking and swearing were his besetting sins and it was now too late to leave off these evils, 'I must take my chance for another world'". The man had also been a poacher, thief and coiner, but neither threats nor prayer altered his decision to 'take his chance' without repudiating his former life-style.[87] There is an element of bravado in some responses missionaries noted. The temptation to repay them in their own coin must have been strong for those they rebuked. "Visited again a young woman to whom I have previously referred as being in a bad state of mind, " noted Derrington, "she still says she shall go to hell and she might as well swear on the way as not".[88]

Thieves and prostitutes made up a fair proportion of the missionaries' contacts in some districts. Brooks' first report describes children, "driven out to beg or pilfer, while their parents are either at home in idleness or rioting in the unholy gains of these juveniles in crime". A later one portrays the prostitution organised around the gin-palaces adjoining his chapel which attracted those attending his evening schools.[89] Miller's Scripture Readers attempted to convince a brothel keeper, now nearly eighty, of the evil of her ways only to be told, "She did not see she had done any harm – no more than many others". Threats of damnation had no effect, "she did not see her awful condition".[90] The missionaries had a powerful motive to record any successes they had amongst such characters. Some, like Finegan, succeeded in rescuing young women forced into prostitution, returning them to their families or finding them a refuge in the Magdalen Hospital. These were acts of humanitarian concern rather than results of evangelical conversion among the women themselves.[91] Despite the occasional success most of those they met in brothels and thieves kitchens must have continued their way of life undeterred by calls for repentance.

8.7 The fluidity of denominational allegiance

One of the pervasive factors in English religion during this period is the uncertain denominational pattern. Denominational statistics and family traditions lend an air of stability to a situation which, in fact, appears to have been much more fluid. David Hempton pointed out that, in Methodism, "beyond the solid core of chapel communities there was a band of denominational gypsies of no fixed abode".[92] They included Anglicans as well as nonconformists whose choice of church or chapel depended more on its style of worship than its ecclesiology and is not unknown today.[93] Some clergy and ministers could be equally volatile. One of these changes of allegiance occurred at Gornal, where the minister of Ruiton Chapel, Theodosius Theodosius, failed to persuade all the congregation to follow him into the Church of England so, between 1815 and 1823, he succeeded in getting St James's Chapel built, in which he served as Anglican incumbent till 1848, Ruiton, with its depleted congregation, remaining Independent.[94] John Gordon, who had led the Warrenite secession in Dudley did not remain long with the Methodist New Connexion but became a Unitarian, serving as minister at Coseley Old Meeting from 1837 to 1840 before departing for Coventry.[95] Warren himself became an Anglican, having a church built for him in Manchester.[96] Notable Anglicans joined the Roman Catholic church, Spencer and Newman serving within the conurbation as Catholic priests. In Birmingham George Dawson left the Baptists and Arthur O'Neill joined them. This element of fluidity must be borne in mind when statistical tables appear to give a fixed pattern to local religious allegiances. The comprehensiveness of the 1851 census of religious worship and the fact that it was never repeated gives its findings an undue finality. Nevertheless a strong case can be made for the significance of Methodism in enabling Black Country folk to appear, in 1851, more committed to public worship than those of Birmingham.

The denominational pattern is shown in Table 39. The Black Country index of attendance is 54.5 whilst greater Birmingham only reaches 37.4. If the total Methodist index had been the same in the Black Country as it was in Birmingham then their overall indexes would have been almost identical. It appears that Methodist attendances in the Black Country could, by themselves, account for the difference between church attendance there and that in Birmingham. This is not to deny the denominational variation between individual registration districts. There were pockets of Anglican strength and Methodist weakness, particularly on the fringes of the Black Country, in Wolverhampton, Aldridge and Handsworth, whilst both were relatively weak in Walsall. Except in Walsall where the Roman Catholics were strong no other denomination except the Church of England exceeded the total Methodist index anywhere in the Black Country and in thirteen districts Methodist attendances were greater, often significantly, than those of the Church of England.

The proportion of the total Methodist attendance shared by the different Methodist connexions varied considerably between districts, as Table 39 indicates. There was often some movement between Methodist denominations. In the Dudley circuit Thomas Collins noted members returning to the Wesleyans from the New Connexion, others, such as David Bowen, the Darlaston local preacher and his family, went in the other direction, leaving the Wesleyans for the Primitives.[97] The obituaries of many Methodists published in the denominational magazines show them to have begun their Methodist associations in a different branch from the one in which they ended their days.

8.8 Conviction, conversion and the pursuit of holiness

Several plausible explanations can be offered for the success of Methodism in the Black Country compared with its relative failure in Birmingham. At the institutional level it was generally easier to find sites for chapel building in the Black Country and cheaper to purchase them, although some sites involved risks from mining subsidence, which did not concern Birmingham Methodists. This problem, of course, affected other denominations and could prove costly in the longer term. Long term thinking, however, did not often characterise Black Country Methodists anxious for premises of their own. The Wesleyans of Brierley Hill, for example, began worshipping in a room above a malthouse in 1823. Nicknamed 'Noah's Ark' it was dark, with a low ceiling and the smell of malt rising from below. In 1829 they moved to a purpose built chapel, costing £1, 200 and seating 800, with a Sunday school attached to it. But between 1876 and 1881 the trustees, with a considerable debt from such ambitious building, had to pay £377-10-0d to buy the coal underneath to prevent it being undermined.[98] Nevertheless, cheaper land and buildings were an advantage. Even the relatively expensive Brierley Hill Wesleyan chapel only cost £1.50 a seat compared with £2 a seat in the Constitution Hill chapel, Birmingham opened the previous year.[99]

This helps to explain another difference between Birmingham and Black Country Methodism. There was little alternative to Wesleyanism in Birmingham for those wishing to join the Methodists until after 1849. Compared with twelve Wesleyan societies by 1850 there were only three Primitive, all very small, three MNC, two very small, and one Wesleyan Association, in a population of 233, 841. Brierley Hill was in Kingswinford sub-district, with less than an eighth of Birmingham's population (27, 301), but here Wesleyans, Primitives and New Connexion had five chapels each. In the Stourbridge district, with 57, 350 inhabitants, the Wesleyans had ten chapels, the New Connexion and the Primitives eleven each, a total of thirty two. Compared with fourteen Anglican, five Independent, four Baptist, three Unitarian, one Quaker and one Roman Catholic place of worship the Methodists had more than all the rest put together. These societies were generally fairly small. The seven Birmingham town centre Wesleyan societies had an average membership of 461 in March 1848. In that year the whole membership of the Stourbridge Wesleyan circuit was only 617, averaging barely 62 per society, before any increases arising from the 1849 cholera epidemic.[100] Even after the cholera, which increased membership, particularly amongst the Primitives, many societies remained comparatively small. The two Primitive circuits formed in 1849, Dudley and Brierley Hill, had between them 21 chapels and 1, 694 members with 809 on trial. Many of those 'on trial', subsequently fell away so that the substantive membership averaged just over 80 per society[101]. In the Black Country not only were potential Methodists given a wider choice, the societies were, by their number, less closely under the supervision of circuit ministers and, by their size, and the area's social composition, less liable to middle class control than those of Birmingham.

Such generalisations require some qualification. Working class chapels could be established in Birmingham, as The People's Chapel shows. Less permanent were the Friendly Methodists, with a membership of 150 in 1838 and a small chapel seating 300 and costing £130.[102] A larger number of small societies simply required more leg work by circuit ministers but they were not thereby removed from superintendence. Mark Smith comments on the fact that in Methodist circuit plans the larger town centre chapels almost monopolise the ministers for their Sunday worship, so distancing them from the smaller societies. He may not realise the significance of 'planned' weeknight preaching at chapels beyond the town centre, after which the minister would 'meet the society' to enquire about their spiritual progress.[103] In 1816 a Wesleyan minister thus described the Dudley circuit, "Our circuit is laborious for we have much to walk, which is partly caused by having to return home from every place, for we never sleep from home. We have to preach 3 times every Lord's Day and we have but few rest days. Our congregations are good, not only in the town but in the country also. Dudley is a very respectable congregation, many genteel people attend preaching there. Many of our own people are respectable tradesmen and some of them are rich in the world. But, as in almost all other places, the poor make up the greatest number . . .." The situation had not changed in 1841, except that Collins sometimes had a hired gig to take him to appointments.[104]

These hypotheses assume that people found Methodism, rather than the Church of England or other denominations, more attractive in the first place. The nature of this attraction still requires explanation. Michael Watts argues that Methodists appealed to fear amongst a population characterised by illiteracy and superstition. He bases his case on 670 accounts of conversions in biographies and obituaries in denominational periodicals, 594 from the Wesleyan and Primitive Methodist magazines.[105] There are problems in deriving evidence for the 1830s and 40s from these publications. The earlier biographies are much fuller than the later ones. Expanding membership increased considerably the number considered worthy of recognition, resulting in more numerous but much briefer entries, increasingly couched in conventional pious phraseology. In the Wesleyan Magazine after about 1820 most memoirs are submitted by close relatives and from the early 1840s increasingly limited to ordained ministers. In the Primitive magazine they are sent in by travelling preachers, who only occasionally knew the person over any length of time and, after about 1840, were authorised by circuit meetings, further constraining content and style. Many are really sermons on edifying death-bed scenes rather than spiritual biographies of any worth. They form part of a recognised genre and should be interpreted as such.[106] Perhaps for this reason nearly all the conversion experiences Watts quotes belong to the late eighteenth or early nineteenth century, hardly any occurred after 1830.

According to Watts, "The most important factor which induced men and women to attend chapel, which prompted them to seek salvation, which secured their conversion . . . was fear: fear of disease, fear of death, fear of judgement, fear above all of eternal punishment in the torments of hell."[107] This statement tends to conflate several distinct activities and different types of fear. Attendance at chapel in many instances was more likely to be induced by curiosity than fear, particularly if there was a singing procession around the streets before the service. This, a regular tactic of the Primitives in the Black Country, could be a positive attraction. Open air preaching, supported by such singing companies, occasionally impressed even the hostile. Near Old Hill, in Rowley Regis, a man "who had imbibed infidel principles . . . cautioned the people against the doctrine the preacher had delivered. But after the people had dispersed . . . he thought, 'These people look happier than I am and there is something in them that I do not see in other people'."[108]

Within Methodism seeking salvation was a long term process

involving conviction of sin, conversion and the pursuit of holiness. The part played by fear and the type of fear involved varied at different stages. The end envisaged was a pure love of God, which filled the heart and inspired the actions of the believer. "Our main doctrines, which include all the rest, are three: that of repentance, of faith and of holiness. The first of these we account, as it were, the porch of religion; the next the door; the third, religion itself.", wrote John Wesley in 1746 and his followers, including the Primitives, continued this tradition throughout the first half of the nineteenth century.[109]

Fear of disease and death were particularly prevalent during cholera epidemics and drove many thousands of Black Country folk into attending churches and chapels as well as pit-head prayer meetings and similar acts of piety. For the vast majority they were a short term expedient and did not result in active commitment. Some of those added to Methodism during these periods undoubtedly fell into the category of 'backsliders recovered' rather than fresh converts.[110] For all who were converted the fear engendered by the cholera acted as a 'trigger' arousing in them a more serious concern than simply surviving the immediate threat. As such it takes its place alongside other experiences, apart from fear, which provoked people into religious anxiety and facilitated their eventual conversion. As the Wesleyan Magazine put it of Mary Baugh of West Bromwich, "That fearful pestilence, the cholera morbus, which raged so awfully in the year 1832 . . . appears to have been the *occasion* of her conversion. Having found the way it was her delight to walk therein."[111]

This use of the term 'trigger', for an experience prompting deeper reflection about the purpose of life, comes initially from Marghanita Laski's book, 'Ecstasy'. Her study of some secular and religious experiences analysed responses to a questionnaire, literary texts and first hand accounts from sources such as William James' 'Varieties of Religious Experience'. She distinguishes the triggers from what her respondents said about the ecstatic experiences themselves and adopts the term 'overbelief' from James to signify the interpretations given to ecstatic experiences.[112] Without implying any causal relationship between the triggers and the experiences themselves David Hay's more recent research confirmed the value of this idea. Half of those interviewed about their experiences of the transcendent said they were 'distressed or ill at ease' at the time, others were 'confused', 'curious' or 'searching'.[113] All these features are present in many Methodist conversion accounts, for example, Mrs. Rebecca Mosley of New Mills married at the age of 24 and was subsequently impressed by the patience of her own dying child. The Sunday after the child's death she set out for the Methodist chapel, "so greatly oppressed in mind, as scarce to know how she got to the preaching house, but before her return home the Lord manifested His love and powerful consolations, in such a measure as she had never before experienced. She knew not what to call the blessing which the Lord had bestowed on her, but was conscious that now she loved God with all her heart . . . and her neighbour as herself. In this blessed Gospel liberty she persevered till her spirit returned to God", she died at the age of 62.[114]

Whereas fear of disease or death, which usually occurs in a dangerous situation, can prove a very temporary experience fear of judgement and the torments of hell are of a different order even if, in many accounts, they accompany the first two. Sidney Dimond's study of the psychology of the Methodist revival interprets eighteenth century evidence from Wesley's journal and lives of the early Methodist preachers. The phraseology of later biographical accounts draws heavily upon the tradition they established. His conclusion is that "the emotional element in almost all the cases under review is the fear of loss to the essential self consequent upon a suddenly acquired sense of the reality and holiness of God, and of the moral law by which their lives were at once judged and condemned."[115] It is this sense of the presence of a holy God which is missing from Watts' explanation. Such an experience has normally been accompanied by fear but the fear is a creaturely awe at the majesty of God and an awareness that God's holiness reveals their complete unworthiness.[116] Conviction of sin, in these circumstances, is more than a feeling of guilt for past actions, though it may well include such feelings. A lack of love for God can be equally unsettling and lead to an earnest desire for it. This was an important part of the Wesleyan tradition and characterised the ministry of preachers like Thomas Collins.[117]

This ideal of love towards God and personal holiness is the context of Methodist appeals to fear of judgement and an eternity in hell. Methodists undoubtedly utilised the opportunities given them by cholera epidemics and, in the Black Country, mining accidents which were more frequent than epidemics and appeared equally beyond human control. This facilitated their interpretation as instances of Divine intervention, or 'special providences' as they were termed in Methodism.[118] Watts' contention that this doctrine enabled Methodists to tap into popular superstitions will be addressed in the next chapter. However, he questions its cogency in the case of a Methodist miner, a class leader rescued from an underground explosion in 1797 to die in his bed. "Why providence

had allowed the explosion to occur in the first place was not
discussed."[119] The purpose of publishing such accounts was not to
argue a case for mines' inspection but for faith in an unseen God,
who had enabled one of his servants to die an edifying death rather
than be buried obscurely underground. A similar purpose was
served when in 1804 the magazine published a letter from John
Pawson describing a 'providential' response to prayers for rain, a
situation provided for in the Book of Common Prayer.[120] For
Methodists the doctrine was an essential part of Christianity even if,
as St Paul admitted, it ultimately defied rationality.[121]

Accounts of Black Country mining disasters in the Wesleyan
Magazine are by no means consistent in their interpretation. In 1791
a penitent Bilston collier asked for an account of the tragic death of
his eldest son to be published to warn parents against cursing their
children. The boy angered his father by not going to work on time
and the father, who worked in another pit, wished the devil might
dash his brains out, "and just as he began to work above a ton
weight of coals fell upon him and broke him in pieces".[122] At the
other end of the spectrum the rescue of twelve men trapped in a pit
near Bilston in 1814 became an account of a providential
deliverance. Other cases were less clear cut. The 1811 magazine,
under the 'providence' heading, told of two pious Methodists killed
in a pit at Tipton. Both had premonitions of their fate and
commended their families to God before descending to work. The
report concluded, " doubtless to these pious individuals, 'sudden
death' brought 'sudden glory!'" Less certain was John Riles,
superintendent of the Dudley circuit, who wrote the obituary of
nineteen year old William Stanfield, also of Tipton, whose work had
supported his widowed mother and younger siblings, killed by a
fall of coals. "Such are the inscrutable ways of providence, that
while profligate and disobedient children are spared, a grief to their
parents, this pious youth who was a support to his family and an
ornament to the church, was cut off in the prime of life".[123]

This uncertainty about whether such mine disasters were acts of
a benevolent God may explain why later, Primitive Methodist,
accounts are reticent, or even silent, about any providential
interpretation. John Petty's obituary of Thomas Pearson, Sunday
school teacher at Brierley Hill, tells how he was particularly fervent
at a Wednesday evening prayer meeting, "The following day he
went to his work in the coal pit as usual, and during the dinner hour
read, and endeavoured to explain to his fellow workmen, a chapter
in the Gospels. Soon after, he went to his employment, and, without
a moment's warning, he was suddenly hurried into eternity by a fall
of coals, aged eighteen years." concluding, "His death produced a

deep and mournful impression on the minds of many young persons, and it is hoped that, in some instances, at least, these impressions will be salutary".[124]

What was remarkable to some Methodists was not the deep impression made by such accidents but the fact that familiarity with tragedy left many miners unmoved. Ministers, who had to bury the dead, were particularly concerned. In his first few months at Tipton Thomas Collins buried nine men, all killed in neighbouring pits, so he announced a Sunday evening sermon addressed to colliers. Consequently the chapel was packed and hundreds turned away. His text was Luke 13, verses 4 and 5. After expounding its historical context and the need for repentance he asked, 'what is it to perish?' His answer concluded with a vivid description of the soul's journey to hell. Here the emphasis was not so much on physical suffering in flames and darkness, which miners could easily be led to imagine, as on the hopelessness of spending eternity in the company of similar unhappy souls, "There all ruined by thee will meet thee . . . What a meeting! What reproaches! What rage! What endless strife!" The final paragraph is an appeal to "flee while ye may, to Jesus", backed up by analogies from nature to give his hearers an imaginative grasp of the concept of eternity. The fear of hell being used here is moral and spiritual. Sinners are not denounced as 'fuel for the everlasting burning', rather they are given a glimpse of an eternity spent with its consequences, "all the jollity of sin over, all rejoicing done".[125]

The reason for this approach to fear of hell was that Methodist preachers who used it had to live with any penitents they obtained. According to Samuel Coley, Collins' cousin who, as a candidate for the Wesleyan ministry, regularly helped him in the Dudley circuit, forty-two penitents responded to that particular appeal. These would be placed 'on trial' under a class leader as potential society members in the hope that their conversion would prove genuine. One of the proofs of repentance on which Methodists insisted was the restoration of anything wrongfully acquired and reconciliation with anyone injured or offended. It was the circuit minister who had the responsibility of deciding, at the quarterly renewal of class tickets, whether the new recruit was living up to the required standard. Hence it would be making a rod for their own backs if they gave hearers a false idea of the moral and spiritual implications of 'fleeing from the wrath to come'. The difficulties this gave them in close knit Black Country communities are indicated by Collins and in John Petty's account of Dudley Primitive Methodist circuit.[126]

The Methodist system of placing converts in classes to discuss their spiritual progress with more experienced members was well established in the eighteenth century and will have been familiar to many in the 1830s and 40s. This 'society' dimension of conversion needs to be recognised. Whether they found 'peace with God' at a prayer meeting or in privacy no Methodist convert was a solitary pilgrim. Conversion often affected whole families, indeed it was the aim of pastoral visiting by ministers like Collins, and the support of society membership was part of Methodism's attraction and its strength. This was recognised by a contemporary observer well aware of its cultural narrowness and the inherent dangers of its approach to conversion. "Methodism is eminently social; its idea is that of journeying Zionwards in companies, gathering as they go; husbands, wives, friends, servants, little ones, 'leaving not a hoof behind'." wrote Dora Greenwell, who went on to contrast the social consciousness of Wesley's hymns with the solitary individualism of Toplady's.[127]

This contrast distinguished the Methodist approach from that of John Angell James, whose 'Anxious Inquirer after Salvation' is also quoted by Watts as an example of fear of hell being used to promote conversions. To prove his case that "the avoidance of hell was the *raison d'etre* of Evangelical preaching" Watts puts together a selection of phrases, taken from different parts of James' book.[128] They give a completely false impression of its overall argument. Far from concentrating on fear of hell James relegates it to the sidelines and takes his inquirer through a series of other considerations which, given the seriousness of the initial quest, may inhibit its successful outcome. Thus he enjoins regular worship, confiding in a minister, knowledge of basic doctrines, repentance and faith, all of which he expounds. The most significant part of the book, and the cause of its popularity, was its practical advice on coping with a range of feelings and impressions likely to be experienced by a young disciple. James warns particularly against the very thing to which Methodism appealed, trusting such feelings and impressions.[129] Although the book refers briefly to prayer meetings it cautions strongly against "depending too much upon means . . . We must depend upon God and nothing but God, who could bless his people in the darkness of a dungeon, where the Bible could not be read, or in the solitude of a wilderness, where no gospel sermon could be heard".[130] This emphasis on self-reliant individualism, together with a very unemotional understanding of faith, gave Independency a different ethos from Methodism. Their relative successes and failures cannot be explained without some appreciation of their contrasting approaches to those they encountered.

Notes

1   K. S. Inglis, *Churches and the Working Classes in Victorian England*, London 1963, p.20.

2   Lewis, *Lighten*, pp. 131-149.

3   Ibid. p. 133.

4   Finegan, 'Journal', 3 May 1838.

5   Birmingham Reference Library, Carrs Lane deposit Volume 72, August 1840.

6   e.g. Ibid. Vol. 61, 29 July 1838. "The state of the cause is encouraging but I think much more might have been done had we better accommodation . . . Must it be (that) the success of the cause of God must be confined in the narrow bounds of our place of worship? No, for the Wesleyans have scent of what we are doing and they have entered my district and will catch the birds now the bushes are bent. I say not this from sectarian feeling but I am not willing that they should take away the materials that should build up our own cause".

7   Ibid. Vol. 73, November 1851, p.13.

8   Ibid. Vol. 72, April-May 1838, p.30.

9   R. W. Dale, *James*, (1862 edition) pp. 280-282, 211.

10 Ibid. pp. 444-445, letter to Rev. E. R. Conder, 10 February 1845.

11 Birmingham Reference Library, Carrs Lane deposit, Vol. 63, 21 September 1840. "Delivered an address to those in a state of concern about their souls, about twenty attended . . . there were some who had been in the class of enquirers as much as twelve months. I know nothing that I could bring against them in a charge of inconsistency but there is such an inaptness to receive instruction . . . that it appears like labour in vain. They are constant in their attendance on the means of grace and appear to enjoy them but they still seem unable to give a reason for the faith that is in them. I have no more reason to doubt their sincerity than I have of those already received into the church. Yet I know that they would not appear so satisfactory to those who could only judge of them by conversation with them".

12 Four Ways Baptist Church Cradley Heath, church meeting minute book, passim.

13 Birmingham Reference Library, Carrs Lane deposit, Vol. 72, 10 December 1838.

14 See, for example, Birmingham Reference Library, Cherry Street West circuit deposit, Cherry Street Wesleyan Leaders' Meeting Minutes, 10 April 1828, 23 June 1829, 9 April, 16 and 24 October 1844.

15 Carwardine, *Revivalism*, p. 125.

16 See J. H. S. Kent, 'The Wesleyan Methodists to 1849' in Davies et al, *History*, pp. 234-239.

17 See J. Wolffe, *The Protestant Crusade in Great Britain*, Oxford 1991, pp. 157-158 for Birmingham.

18 Brooks, *Memoir*, pp. 115-6, "This", he added, "does no good, even to his own party, but . . . to some of the more ignorant and mercenary amongst the poor, it does positive harm". cf. pp. 103-104, detailed instances of

Unitarians refuting critics in 1848.

19   Miller, *Scripture*, pp. 10-11 (Case I), cf. pp. 7-9 (Visits IX, XII, XV, XVI).

20   Finegan, 'Journal', 26 July, 11 October 1837.

21   Ibid. 11 November 1837.

22   Ibid. 31 December 1837.

23   This column is left blank in the Carrs Lane journals, all of them had printed record pages at the back.

24   Ibid., tables kept on concluding pages at the back of the journal.

25   Ibid. 17 December 1837, cf. 25 July, 31 December 1837, Finegan includes the King Street chapel of the Countess of Huntingdon's Connexion along with the three Baptist chapels.

26   Brooks, *Memoir*, p.95, adding, " So much, however, do my poor people esteem my ministrations, that several who had not attended anywhere on the Sabbath for years, have . . . urgently requested me to open the place for services on Wednesday nights". cf. also pp. 105, 118.

27   Ibid. p.119.

28   Birmingham Reference Library, Carrs Lane deposit, Vol. 67, 26 July 1843.

29   Ibid. Vol. 66, undated entry at the end of the volume but including statistics up to 1850.

30   Ibid. Vol. 65, 21 December 1841.

31   e.g. Finegan, 'Journal', 30, 31 October, 17 December 1837; Carrs Lane deposit Vol. 61, 14 March 1839, Vol. 65, 19 October 1841, Vol. 66, 14 August 1841, with Derrington's reservations on the last.

32   They were dispensed with on financial grounds, the West circuit took three more years to liquidate the debt.

33   Birmingham Central Library, Belmont Row East and Cherry Street West Wesleyan circuit deposits, Quarterly Meeting Minutes, passim. These statistics include the following societies, East circuit: Belmont Row, Constitution Hill (Wesley), Newtown Row; West circuit: Cherry Street, Bradford Street, Islington, Bristol Road, membership of the oldest society, Cherry Street, actually declined by 42 members during this five year period.

34   Birmingham Central Library, Carrs Lane deposit, Vol. 65, 15 December 1841.

35   J. Wesley, *A Collection of hymns for the use of the people called Methodists*, London 1779, table of contents. Subsequent editions during the nineteenth century added a supplement but kept to John Wesley's original format. My own copies, dating from 1858 and 1868, are identical.

36   Birmingham Reference Library, Carrs Lane deposit, Vol. 61, 15 August 1838.

37   Ibid. Vol. 61, 28 January 1838, Vol. 72, 2 March 1838, cf. John Rylands University Library, Manchester, Methodist Central Archives, manuscript correspondence Joseph Taylor (Senior) to Thomas Jackson, dated Birmingham, 5 May 1812, "Trade has been very bad for some time and I fear not likely to mend soon. This hurts religion sadly. Many will not come to their classes nor take their tickets because they have nothing to give."

38   Birmingham Reference Library, Carrs Lane deposit, Vol. 61, 25 April 1838.

39   Ibid. Vol. 64, 5 August 1840, Vol. 65, 21 December 1841, 24 August 1842, cf.

Vol. 66, 17 January 1842, for the case of a woman persecuted by her husband for attending Derrington's chapel.

40 Ibid. Vol. 72, 20 February 1840 (Socialist ex-Ranter), Vol. 65, 9 August 1843 (Chartist, follower of O'Neill)

41 Brooks, *Memoir*, p.116.

42 Miller, *Scripture*, p.9, visit XX.

43 Lewis, *Lighten*, p.141.

44 Knight, *Nineteenth Century*, pp. 24-36, also F. Knight, 'From Diversity to Sectarianism; the Definition of Anglican Identity in Nineteenth-Century England' in R. N. Swanson (Ed.), *Unity and Diversity in the Church, Studies in Church History Vol. 32*, Oxford 1996, pp. 377-386.

45 Finegan, 'Journal', 14 September 1837, Birmingham Reference Library, Carrs Lane deposit, Vol. 71, 15 November 1838.

46 Finegan, 'Journal', 27 September 1837. The chapel was Ebenezer, Steelhouse Lane.

47 Miller, *Scripture*, pp. 5, 6 (Visits II, III, IV, VI), p.13, (Case IX)

48 Birmingham Reference Library, Cherry Street West circuit deposit, Cherry Street Leaders' Meeting Minutes, 28 January 1812, resolution reprinted in a new minute book 1822.

49 Ward, *Religion*, p.13.

50 Finegan, 'Journal', passim, Birmingham Reference Library, Carrs Lane deposit, Vol. 71, 27 September 1838, Vol. 66, end pages, the Sunday school began in Garrison Lane then moved to Palmer Street.

51 Brooks, *Memoir*, pp. 112, 114. H. G. Wilson, 'One Hundred Years of Religious and Social Work in Birmingham' in *Transactions of the Unitarian Historical Society*, Vol. VIII, 1943-46, p.114.

52 Miller, *Scripture*, p.7, (Visit X).

53 Birmingham Reference Library, Carrs Lane deposit, Vol. 66, 12 May 1842. He had gone to a 'singing party' "one Sabbath afternoon but I soon saw that it would not do for persons professing godliness and I therefore attended no more".

54 Burdett, 'Missionaries', chapters 3, 4 and 5, especially p.119, quoting William Jackson's journal for 1842.

55 H. McLeod, *Religion and the Working Class in Nineteenth Century Britain*, London 1984, p.62, Robson in Baker, *Studies* 1978, p.390, 'The sheer struggle to carry on any sort of existence was recognised by all the missionaries as deadening the mind to higher things'. Burdett's quotation from my article stops short of this significant sentence, cf Burdett p.127, hence his claim to have produced a revision of my findings must be treated with some caution.

56 *Birmingham Journal* 17 February 1838, cf Finegan, 'Journal' 7 February 1838.

57 Finegan, 'Journal', 14 August 1837, "most of whom, if not all, have no claim on parochial relief".

58 J. A. Langford, *A Century of Birmingham Life*, Birmingham 1868, Vol. 1, pp. 119-120, Vol. 2, pp. 41, 51, 57, 323. Langford quotes verbatim from contemporary reports in Aris's Birmingham Gazette.

59 Birmingham Reference Library, Carrs Lane deposit, Vol. 61, 24 January 1838, cf. 17 January entry.

60   Ibid. Vol. 72, 22-23 January, 6 March 1838.
61   Knight, *Nineteenth Century*, pp. 131-132, discusses clerical incomes and what they were expected to cover.
62   Birmingham Reference Library, Carrs Lane deposit, Vol. 61, 1 October 1838, Vol. 65, 19 April 1842.
63   Ibid. 27 July 1838.
64   Ibid. Vol. 72, 10 August 1838. cf. Birmingham Reference Library, Cherry Street West circuit deposit, Cherry Street Leaders' Meeting Minutes, 30 January, 13 and 15 February 1838.
65   Finegan, 'Journal', 11 January, 18 February 1838, cf. references given at notes 59 and 60 above.
66   Lewis, *Lighten*, p.142-143.
67   Finegan, 'Journal', 13 September 1837.
68   Birmingham Reference Library, Carrs Lane deposit, Vol. 72, 27 July 1838.
69   Ibid. 25 April 1839, 18 June 1840.
70   Ibid. Vol. 65, 19 April 1842.
71   Ibid. Vol. 67, 31 October 1843, Vol. 68, 25 August 1843.
72   Ibid. Vol. 67, 16 November 1842.
73   Finegan, 'Journal', 8 August 1837.
74   Birmingham Reference Library, Carrs Lane deposit Vol. 71, 6 July 1838.
75   Miller, *Scripture*, p.7 (Visit IX).
76   Birmingham Reference Library, Carrs Lane deposit, Vol. 71, 10 October 1838, cf. 11 September, 17 November 1838, 28 February, 31 March, 1 April, 11 April 1839, Vol. 72, 27 November 1839.
77   Ibid. eg. Vol. 62, 2 March, 25 April 1838.
78   Ibid. Vol. 68, 26 August 1842.
79   Finegan, 'Journal', 28, 29 July 1837.
80   Birmingham Reference Library, Carrs lane deposit, Vol. 65, 22 December 1844.
81   Ibid. Vol. 67, 1 November 1844.
82   Ibid. 4 September 1844.
83   Ibid. Vol. 71, 20 September 1838.
84   Brooks, *Memoir*, pp. 123-124.
85   cf. the Chartist critique of the Town Mission in Birmingham Journal 29 June 1839 quoted extensively in my earlier article, Robson in Baker, *Studies* 1978, p. 391.
86   Birmingham Reference Library, Carrs Lane deposit, Vol. 71, 10 October, 13 November 1838, cf. Vol. 74, 27 January 1848, Churchmen and Wesleyans condemned as 'enemies of the people'.
87   Ibid. Vol. 71, 13 and 14 September 1838.
88   Ibid. Vol. 65, 11 August 1843.
89   Brooks, *Memoir*, pp. 85-86, 107-108.
90   Miller, *Scripture*, p.6 (Visit VII).
91   Finegan, 'Journal', passim The following cases are recorded, Jane Osborn, Mary Robinson, Jane Gibson, Ann Bevens, Elizabeth Martin, Elizabeth Smith, Harriet Pennell, Mary Smith, Ellen Wilmot, some of whom undoubtedly convinced Finegan of their penitence, especially when their prostitution had been a consequence of seduction and abandonment by

their employer.

92 D. Hempton, *Methodism and Politics in British Society 1750-1850*, London 1984, p.12.

93 cf. G. Robson, *Christians*, Oxford 1995, p.60 (Andrew and Abigail's denominational identities).

94 Hackwood, *Sedgley*, pp. 63, 75.

95 Ibid. p.72.

96 Ward, *Religion*, p.171.

97 Coley, *Collins*, p. 170, Pratt, *Black Country*, p.156.

98 *VCH Staffordshire* Vol. 3, p.96, J. H. Mees, *The Story of a Hundred Years, 1828-1928, Handbook of the Wesleyan Methodist Church, Stourbridge Circuit*, Stourbridge 1928, pp. 31-37, Most Wesleyan chapels in the Black Country part of the Stourbridge circuit were held on leases protecting the mining rights beneath them, cf. pp. 46 (Cradley), 67 (Mount Pleasant), 87 (Bromley), 104 (Kingswinford), only Brockmoor, p.81, which the Wesleyans purchased from the MNC, included the mines beneath, see also Tancred, *First report, Midland mining*, pp. 35, 39.

99 Seating capacity at Brierley Hill is taken from the 1851 census return, Constitution Hill, Birmingham cost £2, 000 in 1828 and seated just over 1, 000, cf. *VCH Warwickshire* Vol. 7, p. 463.

100 This was a decline on 1847, then average membership was; Birmingham 475, Stourbridge 65. The Stourbridge MNC circuit had 8 societies in 1848 and a total membership of 417, an average of 52.

101 Dudley Libraries and Archives Service, Coseley, Brierley Hill Primitive Methodist Circuit Quarterly Meeting Minutes, December 1849. In the Brierley Hill circuit only Brierley Hill (417) and Lye (161) had over 100 members, thus matching the Wesleyan and MNC pattern.

102 *VCH Warwickshire* Vol. 7, pp. 419, 438. Hennock, *Fit*, pp. 99-103, Birmingham Reference Library, Carrs Lane deposit, Vol. 72, 16 February 1838, Clay's account of the Friendly Methodists.

103 M. A. Smith, *Industrial Society*, p.210.

104 John Rylands University Library, Manchester, Methodist Central Archives, correspondence, John Walmsley to Messrs. Fenton and Owen (Sheffield laymen) 16 October 1816, cf. ibid. William France to Thomas Jackson, 6 April 1833, from Dudley writes of "the unreasonable load laid upon . . . us, especially at the time of our quarterly visitations", he has "to preach seven and sometimes eight times a week and to be employed all day on Sundays and on weeknights till past ten-o-clock", Coley, *Collins*, p.179.

105 Watts, *Dissenters*, pp. 49-80, 100-110.

106 cf H. D. Rack, 'Evangelical Endings, Death beds in Evangelical biography', *Bulletin of the John Rylands Library*, Vol. 74, no 1, Spring 1992, pp. 39-56, Jay, *Heart*, pp. 154-168

107 Watts, *Dissenters*, p.72

108 *Primitive Methodist Magazine*, Bemersley 1842, pp. 132-133. He became the first in that village, Gorsty Hill, to provide the Primitives with a base for cottage meetings. cf. the journal of John Petty, circuit minister, Dudley circuit, in Ibid. 1838, p.28, "Monday, May 1. − . . . attended to my appointment at Locks Lane, Brierley Hill. To arouse the sleepy neighbours,

and to influence them to attend the house of prayer, we began to sing in the open street, and then proceeded to the preaching house."

109 John Wesley, letter to Church quoted in H. D. Rack, *Reasonable Enthusiast*, London 1989, p.389. His chapter XI has an extended discussion of these elements in Wesley's theology. Both the Wesleyan and the Primitive Methodist magazines published correspondence and excerpts from Wesley and Fletcher of Madeley throughout this period. John Petty's list of books for his local preachers' library in the Brierley Hill Primitive circuit is headed by Wesley's sermons and Fletcher's writings and includes several other treatises on perfection and sanctification. *Primitive Methodist Magazine*, London 1850, p.298.

110 Ibid. pp. 168-172, John Petty's account of Dudley circuit before and after cholera, 1832 and 1849.

111 *Wesleyan Methodist Magazine*, London 1842, Vol. 65, p.929, my italics

112 M. Laski, *Ecstasy, A study of some Secular and Religious Experiences*, London 1961, pp. 16-17, 312-359, and W. James, *The Varieties of Religious Experience*, London 1902, pp. 504-519. Although she does not realise it the pattern of overbelief she sets out applies to conversion as a religious experience. She herself specifically rejects any religious explanations of her material, which includes accounts of their own conversion by Augustine of Hippo and John Wesley.

113 D. Hay, *Exploring Inner Space*, Harmondsworth 1982, pp. 144-145, 202.

114 *Arminian (Wesleyan) Methodist Magazine*, 1793, p.329.

115 S. Dimond, *The Psychology of the Methodist Revival*, Oxford 1926, p.201, the full discussion is on pp. 140-150, 191- 207.

116 see in particular Rudolf Otto, *The Idea of the Holy*, second edition, Oxford 1950, esp. pp. 8-50.

117 Coley, *Collins*, p.140. "As a whole I feel the circuit is low", he wrote of Durham, "A few fine old saints live very near to God. The talk of two greatly comforted me today. One of them knew Mr Wesley, and the other was converted under William Bramwell. Perfect love is what my people want. I keep continually preaching it." cf. *Arminian Magazine*, 1791, pp. 356-359, Elizabeth Lowes of Hexham, died of consumption aged 26, was initially convinced not so much of sin as of lack of love and spent seven months 'seeking the Lord' before being converted at a prayer meeting.

118 The *Primitive Methodist Magazine* had a 'Providence Department' for relating such incidents. see also W. Antcliff, *A Book of Marvels*, London (Primitive Methodist Book Room)1874, chapters VII and X.

119 Watts, *Dissenters*, p.109.

120 *(Wesleyan) Methodist Magazine*, London 1804, pp. 610-612.

121 See especially *Epistle to the Romans*, chapters 9-11, particularly 11, verses 33-36.

122 *Arminian (Wesleyan) Magazine*, London 1791, p.271.

123 *Wesleyan Methodist Magazine*, London 1811, pp. 937-938, 235, Ibid. 1814, pp. 42-45.

124 *Primitive Methodist Magazine*, London 1850, p.441.

125 Coley, *Collins*, pp. 185-187. Coley gives the complete text of all eight paragraphs of this peroration.

126 "Sunday, November 7th. – Good was done at Oldbury; but good there is much hindered by the prevalence of evil speaking. Harsh judgements, tale bearing and mischief making, grieve the Spirit," wrote Collins (Coley, *Collins*, p.178). Petty tells how, "With the removal of the cholera, many, who had been religiously affected, turned back to the world, and some unpleasantness having arisen in the societies at Dudley, Netherton and a few other places the circuit declined" from 700 in 1833 to 585 in 1835. He describes his problems with the Brierley Hill society, the largest in the circuit. In 1836 he had to expel the principal troublemaker and quell an unholy agitation. *Primitive Methodist Magazine*, London 1850, pp. 169-170.

127 D. Greenwell, *Two Friends*, London 1862, pp. 111-112.

128 Watts, *Dissenters*, p.79.

129 J. A. James, *The Anxious Inquirer after Salvation Directed and Encouraged*, London 1834, pp. 27, 65-69, 87-92, 102-111.136-137, and passim. Hence the attack on Methodism that features so regularly in the journals of Carrs Lane men like Edwin Derrington.

130 Ibid. pp. 22-23.

CHAPTER 9

Popular Religion and Religions of the People

9.1 Beliefs, customs and superstitions

Any attempt to explain the success of Methodism in the Black Country must take account of the mental characteristics of its population. In his study of Upper New York State in the first half of the nineteenth century Whitney R. Cross considered this one of the most significant factors in explaining the Burned Over District's susceptibility to revivalist religion. Despite cosmopolitan influences accompanying commercial development its people were distinguished from other Easterners by "persistent superstition and credulity".[1] Plenty evidence exists to rank Black Country folk alongside their transatlantic contemporaries in this respect, though credulity should be distinguished from superstition in describing their psychology.

Customs associated with seasons of the year, stages of life, domestic and rural occupations, similar to those in other parts of Britain, persisted. For example, May day celebrations with Maypole and Morris dancing, followed by walking into the countryside to drink rum mixed with milk, decorating pit heads and ironworks with boughs and blossoms are attested by two nineteenth century Black Country historians, G. T. Lawley and F. W. Hackwood, who published their accounts in the local press. Christmas Eve sword dances and Mumming, keeping a fire burning from New Year's Eve to the morning of New Year's Day, then speaking first to a dark-haired man were equally familiar. This last custom, believed to bring good luck, was recorded of a "very respectable Sunday school teacher" in 1842 by Isaac Clarkson, vicar of Wednesbury. It amused him but he also mentioned "curious cases before the magistrates of women being beaten by others because they are supposed to have bewitched children and others" as well as the cock fighting, bull, bear and badger baiting which, until very recently, took place at the local wakes.[2]

Clarkson's statement was part of his evidence to the Midland Mining Commission, telling us more about their beliefs than any other group. This must be borne in mind when miners are singled out as specially liable to respond to Methodist preaching. Their customs need to be set within the broader framework hinted at by Clarkson of a general belief in powers of witchcraft, ghosts, rituals, tokens and talismans to promote good luck and ward off evil. The miners of the Black Country, unlike Cornish tin or Pennine lead miners, needed no special 'luck' to discover a profitable seam, the ten yard coal outcropped too near the surface. The only 'luck' they needed was protection from accidents once they were underground.

A whole range of omens were heeded and stories told of the dreadful fate of those who ignored them. Some were described by Cartwright, vicar of Dudley, as superstitions, "They attend very much to dreams. If a dog looks down a pit, they will not work in it that day; and the same if they hear "*squeakers* ", as they call them, in the air, which may perhaps be wild geese flying over their heads, or mere fancy".[3] The Cockfighters Arms at Old Moxley, near Bilston, had a board over the tap-room chimneypiece containing a colliers' guide to signs and warnings: dreaming of a broken shoe or a fire were signs of danger, meeting a woman at sunrise on the way to work was a sure sign of death, seeing a bright light or smelling a foul smell in the mine or hearing a noise like a pack of hounds (called Gabriel's Hounds) in the air were warnings. Finally, to charm away ghosts, "Take a Bible and a key, hold both in the right hand, and say the Lord's Prayer".[4] "When an accident happens in a pit . . . the pit is not worked any more until after the funeral. Men indeed go down to give food to the horses but that is all". The miners were said to believe that the dead man's spirit roamed about until after the burial.[5]

David Clark in his study of 'folk religion' in twentieth century Staithes hazards a sociological explanation for similar beliefs in North Yorkshire, particularly the ill-luck associated with meeting a woman on the way to work. His suggestion that this reflects a gender-based division of labour whereby men left the home for fishing coble or mine whilst women remained behind may well hold good of Staithes but hardly fits the Black Country where women were prominent as workers on pit banks as well as in chain, nail and brick manufacture.[6] It was a woman, with the sun behind her, coming towards the miner which was the sight to be dreaded in the Black Country, rather than any woman at all. Whatever the origin of this belief others seem related to mining reality. Foul smells and bright lights often indicated the presence of suffocating or explosive gases,[7] whilst the death of a fellow miner could well induce a dread of returning to the spot until a decent respect had been shown to his corpse. The idea that his spirit would not rest until this was done was related to pagan and Christian traditions, including the verse from the Book of Revelation (14:13) spoken at the graveside in the Prayer Book burial service.

Whatever their origin the strength of such beliefs in the mid-nineteenth century is evident as is the adaptation of Christian symbols and rituals, like the Bible, key and Lord's Prayer, to dispel dangerous spiritual powers. What is not so clear is their significance. Do they indicate a rival to 'official religion' in the form of an alternative 'popular religion' or are they in some way inextricably bound together within a common cultural continuum comprising a range of possible beliefs and attitudes?

9.2 Syncretism

James Obelkevich's account of South Lindsey includes beliefs and superstitions which were part of the popular culture of the rural peasantry. These are analysed in terms of their Christian and pagan origins and, although not consciously conceived of in direct opposition to the official beliefs of the Christian church, are nevertheless treated as detached from it, being regarded by the clergy as "'superstition', a mass of dimly perceived beliefs that were deviant at best and heathen at worst".[8] He concludes that the villagers inhabited an imaginative universe in which "paganism was rarely christianised, but Christianity was often paganised", resulting in "syncretism – the universal religion of the peasant which combined elements from the 'higher' and the 'lower' religion without regard for logical compatibility".[9] Such an apparently all pervasive and, as David Hempton pointed out, pessimistic culture was not a closed system.[10] In Warwickshire it could not hold book-loving men like Joseph Arch and Joseph Ashby who did what many of their fellow agricultural labourers in Lincolnshire must have done, entered a wider intellectual and moral world through village Methodism.[11] Such emancipation did not detach them from rural society, rather they became leaders in the Agricultural Trade Union and in local government respectively.

Like superstition, the word 'syncretism' has become a theological term of reproach. However, the possibility of such a syncretistic popular religion providing an open-ended link with more rigourous and intellectually demanding versions of the same basic tradition must not be overlooked. Whilst accepting E. P. Thompson's warning against importing concepts from distant cultures to interpret European experience it is, nevertheless, helpful to look at parallels in a non-Christian society when studying one in which Christian beliefs were still looked upon as the norm.[12] In 'The

African Child' Camara Laye describes his upbringing in French Guinea in the 1930s and 40s. His whole family were Muslims within a society where Muslim traditions went hand in hand with African animism and witchcraft. Prayer mats and charms hung side by side in his father's hut and his mother forbade him to kill a particular snake because "it is the guiding spirit of our race". At the end of Ramadan boys spent a night alone in the forest to be initiated by facing up to the terrifying bogeyman Kondén Diara, before their Muslim initiation of circumcision. But at fifteen he was sent to live with his uncle in Conakry so he could attend the technical college. On leaving home his mother gives him a bottle, containing a liquid to sip every morning to help his brain. It was bought in the nearest Muslim holy place where marabouts write prayers from the Qur'an on small boards, "When they have written down the text they erase it by washing the board: the washing water is carefully collected and, with the addition of honey, forms the main part of the elixir."[13]

In Conakry he meets a different aspect of Islam. Uncle Mamadou, his father's younger brother, wore European clothes at work but changed into traditional Muslim dress to say his prayers as soon as he got home. "His interpretation of the Koran was scrupulously correct, he did not smoke, he did not drink, he was absolutely honest, " he had learned Arabic to study the Qur'an. "The Koran guided him in everything he did. I never saw my uncle in a temper, and I never saw him enter into a dispute with his wives; he was always calm, master of himself and infinitely patient . . . I looked upon him as a saint". Discussions with his uncle changed many of his ideas but when, after four years, he is determined to pass his final exams he still writes home, "to ask his mother to go and see the marabouts and obtain their help. Should I infer from this that I was particularly superstitious at this time? I do not think so. I simply believed that nothing could be obtained without the help of God, and if the will of God is something preordained, nevertheless our actions, though just as unforeseen, have their influence on that will."[14] Thus he is trying to make theological sense of his complex African-Islamic cultural world. Belief in dreams, in friendly and hostile spirits, Muslim rituals alongside tribal ones, using sacred scriptures for magical purposes, together with study of the original text and scrupulous fulfilment of its teachings, all were experienced within the bounds of his own family and there is no suggestion that this was exceptional.

The experiences of Camara Laye and of Black Country miners are sufficiently different to prevent direct comparisons but there are similarities in the relationship between the dominant religious tradition and the subordinate one within the two societies.

Individuals could move easily between the rituals and customs associated with each with varying degrees of belief and commitment although from either end of the continuum they may appear incompatible. This does not mean there are no tensions within popular religion, or that the syncretism is unchanging. At any one time the balance between the various strands will be different depending on peoples' perception of their significance. An interactive rather than a static model is needed to interpret the evidence. But before analysing popular religion a second aspect of Black Country character will be addressed.

9.3 Credulity

Some of the available evidence must be treated with caution. Much of it was given to the Midland Mining Commission by clergy and mineowners, some of whom were magistrates, all anxious to explain to government why so many miners had been 'misled' by Chartists in the 1842 strike. Hence the description of the Black Country miner as "a heavy, superstitious, gluttonous animal, most harmless and naturally good-hearted, without a spark of political feeling", "simple minded and good hearted", "honest and well disposed", "very rough but unsophisticated, kind-hearted and easily managed". The rural dean of Birmingham made a further point, "My own impression is, that the miners are not inclined to violence, or excitable; the nailers, on the other hand, are a much rougher set."[15] The evidence, nevertheless, is impressively unanimous and unlikely to be the product of collusion. Philip James of Wednesbury Oak Works, describing the course of the strike and defending the butties, said, "The colliers easily believed the promises of high wages &c., made by the Chartist lecturers. They are honest-minded, unsuspicious men, whose reasoning powers have not been brought out and cultivated, and therefore disposed to take anything stated to them on trust".[16]

Alongside this evidence are the sayings and stories reflecting the 'simple minded' character of the local people, the many 'Aynoch and Ayli' jokes and some poking fun at particular places. Among these was the "proverbial ignorance" of Darlaston folk which the Children's Employment Commissioner thought "by no means misrepresented".[17] Stories are recorded of their failure to recognise a gold guinea dropped accidentally in the market place so a Bilston man could tell them it was a red-hot shilling, saving them the trouble of waiting for it to cool down by giving them a shilling of his own in exchange, and their ludicrous efforts to identify a gold watch similarly found.[18]

Cross ascribes some of the Burned Over District's credulity to the character of its education. By his account Upper New York State took great advantage of the American system of common schools which boys and, particularly, girls attended regularly from the ages of five to fifteen or sixteen. Their curriculum excluded religious education but it ensured literacy and numeracy producing "Men and women who were by no means learned, yet able to read their Bibles from childhood, " and who, in Cross's view, "definitely made the best subjects for religious excitement."[19] The contrast with the education available to children in Birmingham and the Black Country at this time could hardly be greater. In Birmingham in 1840 less than half the children aged between five and fifteen were attending day or Sunday schools and their average attendance was less than four years in either. Even though the statistical basis of this calculation was rather conjectural the details given in the report left no doubt about the seriousness of the situation.[20] Even in 1867 one of Her Majesty's Inspectors reckoned that 50% of Birmingham children aged between three and twelve were in schools of some sort, 10% were at work and the remaining 40% were "growing up in ignorance and idleness".[21] The Black Country was no better. Henry Moseley, in his final report as H.M.I. for the Midland District's National (Church of England) Schools, stated in 1846, "the average age of the children who attend our elementary schools is steadily sinking. We may be educating more, but they are, I believe, younger children and stay with us less time." Despite its current prosperity he singled out the South Staffordshire mining district for, "in no schools that I have visited has it been found necessary to fix the fees of admission lower; nowhere are they (i.e. teachers) worse paid, nor anywhere is the school more irregularly attended."[22]

Curriculum as well as attendance contrasted greatly with Upper New York. In both day and Sunday schools the teaching of reading was heavily dependent on religious texts, especially the New Testament and Psalms, along with catechisms, particularly in Anglican day and Sunday schools. Other curricular areas suffered neglect. Moseley instances one opulent Black Country proprietor who withdrew his £1 subscription to a National school, "because *writing* had, against his judgement, been added to the subjects of instruction."[23] This should have given young people a sound knowledge of Christian beliefs and their Biblical basis but to those who examined them the evidence was discouraging. The reports of the Children's Employment Commission and H.M.I. are full of instances of ignorance and confusion, many quite amusing in their way, but not equalled by examples of sound knowledge. Much of the fault lay with the monitorial system, which Moseley criticises at length, and using the Bible as a source of minor punishments in day schools. This was described by James Wood, who had surveyed education in Birmingham.

"Do you think that the indiscriminate use of the Scriptures as a task book tends to give the child a disgust for it afterwards? – Nothing tends more to give them a disgust for it than the way in which it is read.

It is not used as a reward, but as a common task book? – A common task book, and so much so, that when a boy has done something wrong, some of the masters, who think they are very much in advance of their neighbours in point of moral training, compel him to learn a certain portion of the Scriptures by way of task, which only confirms the child's dislike of the Scriptures."[24]

The monitorial system of instruction left children exposed to some inadequate answers to their questions about the meaning of the words they were learning to read. The word 'God' gave particular problems, though these may have appeared greater to James Wood whose abrupt and literal manner of questioning was as likely to discourage children as that of Dickens' Thomas Gradgrind.[25]

Religious instruction was not necessarily better in Sunday schools for the same reasons. Children were often crammed into unventilated rooms, giving them a headache, or even 'taught' in the chapel during worship. Horne visited the Primitive Methodists at Lower Gornal where, "The attention of the children is fixed by means of several small canes which the teachers have in use; and the monotonous buzzing of their reading lesson does not in the least affect the preacher, whose delivery . . . is invariably of the most vehement and vociferous description."[26] Their teachers were even less likely than those in day schools to have had any training. One such candidate, Thomas Delay, aged 19, a moulder in an iron works, told James Mitchell that, "I went to Sunday school until they made me a teacher, then I left. I did not like to teach".[27] Horne gives a critical account of the principal Anglican Sunday school in Walsall by a youth of sixteen who stopped teaching, after two years, "because he was ashamed of the way in which they were carrying on instruction".[28]

Horne's investigation only incidentally involved religious knowledge. He visited day and Sunday schools to obtain depositions uninfluenced by the presence of employers and check the welfare of parish apprentices, a sizeable part of the juvenile workforce in places like Willenhall. Hence, of 320 interviewed, evidence is non-existent in 237 cases, only 62 boys and 21 girls indicated any religious knowledge, mostly in single statements like the number of apostles and some of their names. They are generally more confused than knowledgeable though some sensible answers were given. In Darlaston, renowned for ignorance, thirty-nine children were interviewed, all but seven in Anglican, Wesleyan and Primitive Methodist Sunday schools, but only five gave answers related to religion. One fifteen year old apprentice, who said he went to Sunday school and chapel, didn't know who St. Peter was but knew about Jack Sheppard, who had featured in a show at the local wake. At the Wesleyans a fifteen year old boy knew that, "Jesus Christ was the Son of God", but at the Primitives a thirteen year old didn't know who St. Paul was, had never heard of Jonah and didn't know the name of the queen. Finally at the Anglicans Moses Giles, aged seventeen, didn't know who St. Peter was; knew Jesus Christ was a carpenter's son; knew the Lord's Prayer but not the creed, whilst John Hutton, sixteen, had never heard of St. Paul, didn't know how many ounces make a pound, "He be'nt no judge o'nothin".[29]

Horne and Mitchell endorse the dominance of religious texts in the reading experience of children, which many failed to find attractive, together with their readiness to admit saying private prayers at night.[30] Accurate knowledge of Christianity was limited to a small minority, much confusion reigned elsewhere, but all knew about folk heroes like Dick Turpin and Jack Sheppard who featured not only in cheap literature but, more importantly, in fairground shows.

In contrast with Cross, who stresses the influence of journalism and literary culture on the Burned Over District, the strength of oral popular culture in the Black Country must be recognised. It continued well into the twentieth century through family and local networks. George Dunn of Quarry Bank near Brierley Hill learned hundreds of songs from his father, who died in 1932 unable to read or write, but who sang them to his children when he finished work as a puddler in the iron works. George and his father sang them in pubs on Saturday nights. His father was an expert on wild life, imitating many bird calls by whistling, a poacher, cock and dog fighter long after such sports were illegal.[31] Equally good at memorising songs were women chain makers at Cradley Heath, many of them illiterate, among them Cliff Willetts' mother on whose recommendation he began work in a chain shop at fourteen in 1911. He recalls not only their singing of Sankey hymns but also the impact of an illiterate preacher from Lye, Will Challoner, "He spoke to us about the Bible (which he couldn't read), about the grandeur of living a Christian life. He had no notes, no theme, no text, just a flow of oratory and eloquence that left us spellbound."[32] It was this oral tradition which Methodism was able to exploit.

9.4 Methodism and Popular Culture: the Black Country

To explain the rise of Evangelical Dissent in the eighteenth century and its expansion in the first half of the nineteenth Michael Watts produces two apparently conflicting hypotheses. The ground for the eighteenth century Evangelical Revival was prepared by the Church of England's educational role in teaching basic Christian doctrines and emphasising morality. He is supported by David Hempton who, after reviewing the extent of catechetical instruction concludes, "Eighteenth century revival movements in all parts of Britain relied on the christianising functions of inclusive established churches to lay the foundations of basic religious knowledge upon which they could make their more emotive appeals".[33] Revivalism in the nineteenth century, however, "found its readiest converts amongst the more backward and superstitious sections of the English and Welsh people."[34] Watts defends this apparent contradiction with numerous illustrative examples intended to prove that, "Methodism in particular both reinforced and was itself sustained by such popular superstitions." Belief in providence grafted the two together.[35]

He derives examples from Cornwall, "arguably the most superstitious county in England", from John Rule's doctoral thesis, the basis of a valuable article in which the idea of a direct link between belief in special providences and local superstitions is used to explain Methodist success, on lines suggested by E. P. Thompson. "Methodist superstition matched the indigenous superstition of the common people", and "only after a period of intermingling of Methodist and folk-beliefs" was its dominant position secure.[36] Hempton, similarly, ascribes much of the initial success of Methodist preaching in Ireland to the congruity between the beliefs of the preachers and their hearers, "The wide circulation of countless providences gave an immediate spiritual authenticity to the Methodist message in a predominantly superstitious rural culture".[37] His subsequent discussion of the pattern of Methodist growth in Ireland, however, suggests that Watts' explanation oversimplifies the English situation. Even within its own framework it fails to explore the nature of the intermingling of Methodist and folk-beliefs indicated by Rule.

Belief in special providences was not limited to Methodists and others tinged with superstition. Graduates of Oxford and Cambridge amongst the Anglican clergy held similar beliefs. One of the most vigourous critics of Cornish Methodist extravagances, R. S. Hawker, wrote to a friend in 1850 about responses to prayer, "A person threatened me with injury on a fixed day. I besought rescue. On that very day the person died. A false and treacherous clergyman came to a parish close by. I shook with dread. I asked help. It came. He entered my house five days afterwards to announce some malady unaccountable to him. He went. It grew. He resigned his cure last week. And these are two only out of forty miracles".[38] This bears comparison with the Primitive Methodist preacher's list of divine punishments of opponents quoted by Rule and referred to by Watts.[39]

Similarly, in the Black Country George Barrs, vicar of Rowley Regis, proposed rebuilding and enlarging the decayed parish church. "This, however, was opposed with great virulence by some of the more monied men in the parish . . . a fact it is that certain individuals calling themselves churchmen, with a view to make a larger church unnecessary, actually solicited the Wesleyan Methodists to build a meeting house in the parish. It is not a little remarkable that of the individuals who signalised themselves in this mischievous opposition, some have been visited with very heavy calamities, others reduced from affluence to the very verge of temporal ruin, and others have died 'not the common death of all men'. Of the few who have not yet been visited in any singular manner, nearly every one has either acknowledged his error or expressed his shame and regret".[40]

Particular rather than special providences were needed by Black Country miners, especially protection from fire and roof falls. To outside observers the hymn singing and prayer meetings they witnessed at pit heads were a rare testimony to working class piety.[41] For those taking part their significance was not so straightforward. Amongst accounts of prayers in pits are hints of their protective as well as their spiritual function. "There is a great deal of religion here. There are pits in which there are prayer-meetings every day after dinner, and all are obliged to attend, as the butties and the men will not work with any who do not", Edward Oakley of Bilston told Mitchell, adding, "In most pits there are laws against swearing when the people are in the pit; and the men that swear lose their beer".[42] Tancred was told the reason for this by Mason, butty at the Oak Farm pits, Kingswinford, "the men think there are fewer accidents than where there are no prayers, and where swearing is allowed, which is not allowed in our pit." Men who left to work elsewhere had been forced to return by their wives who, "think they are safer here". Swearing may have been banned more from fear of divine wrath than obedience to the Sermon on the

Mount, but the result was the same.

What is happening here seems to be the replacement of an older by a newer, Methodist, "superstition" if this word can be used of practices which were everyday requirements of Methodist members, whether working underground or not. Hymn-singing, Bible reading and extempore prayer were the staple of the class and weeknight prayer meetings members attended. Their introduction into the pit could have had more than one motive, even if the need for divine protection was the principal one. Mason's description of what went on matches John Petty's obituary of Thomas Pearson quoted in chapter 8. "They sing and pray and ask a blessing on what they are going to have, and they then sit down in the road and eat their dinner and drink the beer, and after dinner one reads out of the scripture and explains it and tells the others what the preacher said about it. Sometimes they get God's Spirit amongst them very much and sometimes less so".[43]

There is no suggestion here of magical rituals like the use of Bible, key and Lord's Prayer to ward off evil spirits, rather the effort is being made to instruct the miners as well as offering them the assurance of divine support. Although the miner giving the instruction may not have been very knowledgeable himself, Mason reckoned only three or four could read "any book you gave them out of forty", they were drawing on the greater expertise of the preachers they heard on Sundays and weeknights, whose learning, however rudimentary at first, was bound improve with the regime of study Methodism promoted. This was true not only of Wesleyans who were required to study John Wesley's sermons and notes on the New Testament, but of any Primitives using the sort of library set up by John Petty at Brierley Hill. We may be a long way from Jack Lawson's experience of discussing Nietzsche with a fellow Methodist at the coal face in County Durham at the turn of the present century, but his mentor's capacity to read the New Testament in Greek was implicit in the educational emphasis accompanying Methodist emotional enthusiasm.[44]

The interaction between Methodism and popular culture was not a straightforward process whereby the ignorance and superstition of the locality was matched by that of the preachers. Although such points of contact existed Methodism's capacity to provide a more coherent and rational framework for experiences like disappointment, suffering and death must have been part of its attraction. Moreover its handling of 'simple minded' folk could enable them to progress intellectually as well as spiritually. The Black Country style of self-mocking humour could be turned to good effect and fitted in with the oral nature of popular culture.

Coley tells of a Tipton collier who, struck with penitence by Collins'
preaching, went home not knowing what to do but thought if he
could only read "Lord Jesus Christ" in the New Testament he would
be saved. Try as he might his capacity to spell failed him, he could
not find Jesus on the page, but the failure of this attempt at
Bibliomancy led him to genuine prayer in which "his heart was set
free".[45] Only the collier himself could have told the story, which, if
true, must have required some humility. Even if it was apocryphal
its circulation indicates sympathy for the illiterate together with
discouragement of superstition. Pratt has two stories of a Darlaston
man who aspired to be a Wesleyan preacher but was deemed
unsuitable. In one he sought humility by praying in successively
lowlier places until, in the pigstye, he eventually "found the Lord".
In the other, thinking himself now fit to be taken up to heaven in a
cloud, he climbed an apple tree, only to hear the devil laugh at him,
"You thought the Lord couldn't raise you from the earth so you
climbed a tree, where's your faith?"[46] Amidst the fun poked at
Darlaston, their point, the danger of spiritual pride, must have been
taken for such stories to be repeated.

Rule points out that the relationship between Methodism and
popular culture was ambivalent, sympathetic to some elements, like
belief in ghosts, but hostile to others, particularly rough sports and
heavy drinking. In Cornwall the latter were often effectively
superseded by other entertainments centred on the chapels so that
Temperance parades, treats and outings linked with Sunday school
and chapel anniversaries as well as festivals like Whitsun, became
the popular culture.[47] This situation is reflected in David Clark's
study of Staithes in the present century. There Methodism had been
domesticated so that the local chapel had become a sort of family
shrine, connection with which, in the form of very irregular
attendance at Sunday school and chapel anniversaries, plus
individual rites of passage, was more important than living links
with Methodism as a contemporary fellowship of believers within
the wider Christian church, the ideal promoted in denominational
magazines since the eighteenth century.[48]

In the Black Country the position was still fluid before 1850. New
chapels were being built and societies formed, the old sports
continued both overtly and covertly, Teetotalism was not yet in the
ascendancy either within Methodism or outside, where Owenism
and Chartism still had a following. But the processions and camp
meetings of the Primitives were becoming a part of popular culture,
as was their capacity to harness the dramatic tradition of the local
Mummers. Horne reports a Sunday school presentation in Sedgley
where Justice, represented by a costumed boy, argues his case

against a Victim, another appropriately clad boy kneeling on the platform, preparing to strike him. But Mercy, a white-clad girl, intercedes and the Victim is spared. The three children then sing a hymn in which the congregation joins.[49] It may be significant that in this drama, which Horne likens to a medieval miracle play, neither God, Christ nor the devil are represented but only the theological categories familiar from Methodist tracts and hymnody. In this the Primitives form a direct contrast with the Mummers' play performed in a bar parlour in Wednesbury in 1879 where Beelzebub plays a prominent part, with other traditional characters, St. George, Hector and the Doctor.[50] The latter was very much a burlesque but the Primitives' comparative restraint shows that popular culture could be transformed, rather than simply adopted, in the intermingling of Methodist and folk beliefs.

9.5 Methodism and Popular Religion: Birmingham

Placing Black Country folk amongst the ignorant, superstitious and credulous part of the population, with whom Methodism had a natural affinity, implies that Birmingham, where Methodism was much less successful, was intellectually and spiritually superior. This was the impression of its rural dean, John Garbett, who told Tancred, "Birmingham people are far milder and more intelligent, with which character they unite great firmness and determination". To his surprise working men had written him a lengthy letter on the Corn Laws, "which, from its superiority in point of composition I took to be the production of persons of superior station".[51] His view that Birmingham men were much less excitable was shared by Methodists to whom it was not necessarily a virtue. In the earlier years of the century Wesleyan itinerants repeatedly bemoaned their lack of converts and longed for "a little bit of Yorkshire zeal".[52]

The great Wesleyan revivals of the 1790s passed Birmingham by, though there was a minor flurry which fizzled out after raising doubts amongst leading preachers about its moral foundation.[53] Only steady and sober progress was reported until James Caughey's 1846 campaign. Meanwhile the other Methodist denominations made even slower progress, or none at all. The revivals reported from the Birmingham Primitive circuit occurred in tiny villages and hamlets on the fringes of the Clent and Lickey Hills, making no impact on the town itself.[54] Yet the journals of the town missionaries reveal a popular religion as intrinsically capable as that of the Black Country of responding to a Methodist approach, which the Wesleyans undoubtedly attempted. What was the nature of this religion and how, if at all, did Methodism relate to it?

Historians of more recent periods have been able to draw on interviews with people brought up early in the present century, building up a comprehensive picture of the place of religious beliefs and observances in their every day lives. This is a particular strength of Sarah Williams' work on Southwark.[55] In interviews the significance of specific beliefs and practices can be teased out. For the earlier period such significances must be inferred from fragmentary evidence. In the case of the missionary journals it was recorded by hostile witnesses, rather than a sympathetic interviewer. They were, moreover, all men and even though their visits brought them into contact with women of all ages they were unlikely to be given details of private family rituals or charms. Hence there are many aspects of popular religion in Edwardian Southwark for which no parallels are found in early Victorian Birmingham, which does not mean they did not exist, only that they were not recorded by those who visited the homes of the poor.

Their status as laymen meant that town missionaries did not conduct baptisms, weddings or funerals, hence they provide no evidence of popular beliefs associated with these rites of passage to parallel those noted by Clark and Williams.[56] Only Finegan's willingness to assist in what appears to have been the 'churching' of Phoebe Purchase testifies to a ritual whose importance has never been in doubt.

Finegan's journal also provides evidence of another popular ritual which normally involved church services. "I had a more than ordinary meeting of the poor in The Gullet this night – there were more than 200 persons present – The rooms both down and up stairs were filled – so that I was obliged to exhort the people below and then above – It being the last Sabbath evening as well as the last night of the year 1837 was perhaps the cause of the influx."[57] He gives no further indication of what they expected of him, certainly it was not a 'Watch-night' service 'seeing-in' the New Year, though for want of such a ceremony Finegan's service in The Gullet was probably taken as a substitute. John Kent quotes the surprise of ritualist Anglican priests at St. Albans, Holborn when, in 1862, their poor parishioners got them out of bed on New Year's Eve demanding a special service in the church.[58] This was a demand Methodists had been able to turn to their advantage since John Wesley instituted Watch-night services for which Charles wrote special hymns.[59] They were a regular part of Wesleyan tradition, Joseph Entwhistle, junior, recorded conducting one at Tipton in 1829 but noted that "owing to the severity of the weather the congregation was not large".[60] Unfortunately there is no evidence of their relative popularity in Birmingham during the second quarter of the century.

Sarah Williams points out the prevalence in Southwark of 'religion by deputy', many who did not attend church or chapel still sent their children to Sunday school, maintained habits of private prayer, respected the special character of Sundays and supported the church's place in the local community by defending its ministers against "what were considered to be the threatening attacks of outsiders".[61] By this period Sunday schools were no longer needed to teach working class children to read so that their religious function must have been accepted. Their popularity cannot, therefore, be directly compared with the situation before 1870. One of the problems encountered by the Carrs Lane missionaries was precisely the opposite, using Sunday school premises for preaching services deterred those adults who were willing to come but were repelled by the dirt and disorder left by the Sunday school pupils. "A school, where a number of children have been during the day, is not a fit place for public worship. Their habits are so filthy that the place needs thoroughly cleansing before decent people can enter it. This thing has been a great hindrance to my success." wrote Derrington.[62]

Defending such ministers against the attacks of outsiders also presumes a settled situation in which the population has been able to relate to particular places of worship, perhaps over several generations. The steady expansion of Birmingham and the changing population of its central districts meant that such attitudes were not well developed in the 1830s and 40s. One aspect of 'religion by deputy' did exist, linked to the ever-present reality of disease and death. William Jackson, one of the most insensitive Carrs Lane men discovered, to his surprise, "The people in the district around the chapel, to whom in the various streets I am pretty well known, are frequently applying to me . . . to visit cases of affliction and distress . . . it shows that many who cannot be persuaded to attend regularly the house of God nevertheless regard me as their best friend".[63] He was unaware of the reason for his popularity. This the more perceptive Derrington appreciated, it was the 'passport to heaven' which their prayers were believed to provide.[64]

On another occasion Derrington went to visit a sick woman but, learning that she was in a coma, didn't go upstairs to see her. "Oh', said some of those who were in the room 'he might have come up and read a prayer over her, it might have done her some good'". Although to him this was a superstition it suggests a widespread belief in the efficacy of prayer for the sick, perhaps according to the Prayer Book formulary, although this assumes the consciousness of the sick person, as did Derrington.[65] The implication in the comment is that Derrington, as a 'servant of Jesus Christ', had a special status which would give any prayer spoken by him an influence superior to those of ordinary people. The origins of this popular belief are not immediately obvious. There was a sizeable Roman Catholic community in Birmingham which, through its priests and religious orders, attempted to minister to the, largely, Irish Catholic poor of the town centre,[66] but none of the Carrs Lane men suggests that those requesting their prayers were Catholics, which they would certainly have done were this the case. The English Catholic presence in many parts of Staffordshire, Worcestershire and Warwickshire may have given rise to a more general belief in the priestly character of 'holy men', despite the anti-clericalism pervading town and countryside. It is not mentioned by Obelkevich, Clark or Williams, yet it was well established in Birmingham in the 1830s and 40s.

Derrington took these beliefs as proof of a superstitious mentality commenting, "So strange it is but my intercourse with the people shows me what an inclination there is among them to the superstitious – almost any visionary tale, it would scarcely matter how full of contradictions it might be, so that it amounted to the wonderful it would readily be received, and the more so because of its mysterious character." His journal contains a series of attacks on this attitude, revealing a popular reliance on dreams and visionary experiences. For example, a woman regaled him with an account of hearing God's voice saying to her, 'Go and sin no more', "I asked my husband if he heard it but he said, 'No, I am too wicked to hear such things', for sure I heard it". Nothing Derrington could say would remove the impression from her mind, "neither visions, dreams nor revelations are to be depended upon . . . but I find it very difficult to deal with these favoured persons so as to disabuse their mind of what appears to me to be a delusion".[67]

Most poor people rejected the missionaries' emphasis on churchgoing and Sabbatarianism, redefining the essentials of Christianity on lines parallel to those described by Sarah Williams, placing the highest religious value on their own professed practice, particularly prayer and good works.[68] " I had this day some very interesting conversations with persons in some of the houses . . . in Dale End on the subject of religion and the necessity of attending to religious requirements", wrote Finegan in 1837, "Out of sixteen houses I met with but two who habitually went to any place of worship on the Lord's Day and yet all talked as if they were Saints – their good desires – their good hearts – their good wishes – their good intentions and even the saying of their prayers in regular form as taught in childhood seemed the foundation of their hopes."[69]

This emphasis was ethical not doctrinal, right actions not right beliefs were the way to heaven. In 1849 Joseph Tye visited a cholera victim who seemed to be recovering, "After speaking in regard to the goodness in the improvement of her health I enquired into the condition of her soul. She said she trusted in God and prayed to him, she never done anyone any injury, she never was very wicked".[70] The prevalence of this view is confirmed by all the missionaries, though only Derrington was prepared, reluctantly, to accept its validity.[71]

Suffering in this life was expiatory and some assurance of salvation hereafter. Derrington explored this belief while visiting a sick man, who had heard him preach in the open air. "I enquired what he thought of his state before God. He replied, 'I am a sinner' . . . 'And that makes you unhappy?' 'Yes but I think I am getting happier because I am suffering much here'. I laboured to show him that suffering in this world, however acute and extended, could make no atonement for his sin . . . It is a little remarkable that all have the impression that an atonement is necessary. Hence this poor fellow thought that his sufferings were the consequence of his sins and making some satisfaction for them, and in another case this afternoon trying to combat the same error".[72] God's goodness was thought more trustworthy than the reality of hellfire, which even the missionaries' hearers were prepared to question.[73] Moreover death-bed repentances were possible, and could therefore be postponed, as by "the hoary-headed sinner in Aston Road" who offered Peter Sibree a drink of rum.[74]

Whether these beliefs had any intellectual foundation is difficult to discern from the evidence which largely consists of missionaries' rebuttals of what they considered to be doctrinal errors. Some of the conversations recorded indicate thoughtful criticisms of evangelical orthodoxy but these depend on the missionary's willingness to enter into discussion rather than denunciation. Not surprisingly William Jackson was simply shocked at common ignorance of the doctrine of the atonement.[75] He also met a man who declared himself an 'infidel' and, calling Jackson a 'fanatic', "demanded evidence that the Bible was the word of God – says a large section of mankind are Mahometans and their religion was the best". This provoked Jackson into recording a lengthy rebuttal but not the 'infidel''s response.[76] Derrington's encounter with a similar attack on the Bible as a 'book of wars' produced a more reasoned argument. The man eventually confessed his own religious conviction, "Well I think the man that serves God and believes in the Lord Jesus Christ is the best man" and finally agreed that the

Bible actually tells us about Jesus.[77]

There appear to be at least five characteristics of this popular religion. Firstly, it was mystical, relying on dreams, visions and private prayer. Secondly, it was not legalistic, allowing breaches of Sabbatarian and other religious observances without feelings of guilt. Thirdly, it was hopeful, about the mercy of God and the future beyond death, especially if preceded by suffering in the present life. Fourthly, it was corporate, relying on mediators and trusting their prayers. Finally, it was ethical rather than doctrinal.

This characterisation can be questioned because the evidence is so fragmentary. There is no indication that those who believed in dreams called on ministers to pray for the dying, or that those who disbelieved in hellfire thought their suffering was expiatory. It is not possible to go behind the evidence to other contemporary sources in Birmingham to get a more rounded picture of the beliefs of working class people who were relatively detached from institutional religion. Comparison with Sarah Williams' account must be qualified by the fact that her evidence represents a later and more settled period when local loyalties to religious institutions had been built up over several generations. Early Victorian Birmingham was still establishing both its religious institutions and its social structure at a time of political and economic turbulence. Nevertheless there are sufficient parallels to suggest that the Birmingham pattern fairly represents the salient features of local popular religion at this earlier date.

Sarah Williams' findings support the case for the overall coherence of popular religion, "It was a dynamic and vibrant system of belief which retained its own autonomous existence. It drew on elements, images and ideals of church-based religion, but these were appropriated, reinterpreted and internalised in a distinctly popular manner in combination with a folk idiom . . . popular religion consisted in a general belief in God, a belief that this God was just and benevolent, a confidence that good people would be judged favourably by Him with regard to the life to come and a belief that the Bible was a special book to which children in particular should be exposed". In her view popular concepts of God were not 'remote from everyday concerns' but, in addition to the use of magical charms, rituals and mascots, "the Deity could be appealed to directly within the context of ordinary life through prayer."[78] Only the emphasis on the Bible distinguishes this picture markedly from the one given above. Considering the use of the Bible to teach reading and the resultant negative attitude towards it in the minds of many people at this earlier period the difference is understandable.

There were clearly points of contact between Wesleyan Methodism and the pattern of popular beliefs outlined above. Methodism had its Sabbatarian emphasis in common with Calvinist Evangelicalism, but in many other ways it was more in tune with popular religion.[79] The mystical element in Methodism shines through the account by Joseph Tye of his visit to a poor widow whose "husband had been a profligate and drunken man, had treated her with great cruelty, but his irregular habits had brought him to an early grave. During his affliction he was visited by the Methodist friends. A great change was visible in him, his stubborn heart became softened and, according to her own account, he behaved towards her with the tenderest affection, begged her earnestly to pardon his past cruelty and died peacefully." After this she attended chapel, began to pray and told Tye, "In prayer I felt a lightness come over me, a peacefulness and I believe God has pardoned my sins".[80]

Such Methodism was hopeful rather than fearful as Derrington disapprovingly pointed out, recording a visit to a woman who had died "with an oath upon the tongue . . . Where can there be hope in a case like this when the victim of rage and passion becomes senseless, helpless and speechless and remains in that state, or nearly so, till the time of her death? And yet some Methodists give it out among the people that there is hope just because one of them was drawn out in prayer when visiting her".[81] Wesleyanism, as Derrington and his colleagues encountered it, promoted corporate rather than individualistic piety and was psychological rather than doctrinal in its emphasis. Moreover this emphasis on personal experience of God often remained a significant element in the lives of many who subsequently left Methodism.[82] The many lapsed Methodists, mostly Wesleyans, whom the missionaries met testify to the appeal of this brand of Methodism to ordinary folk, perhaps because in many ways Wesleyan and popular religion paralleled one another. To modify E. P. Thompson's view of Wesleyanism as superstition, Wesleyanism had a rationality which used trained and disciplined feeling to test the experiences of God which its members claimed to have had.[83]

9.6 Conclusions

Because the same sort of evidence about popular religion is not available for both parts of the conurbation any conclusions are bound to be tentative. Superstition and credulity could easily be found in both Birmingham and the Black Country. Nevertheless, despite their equally poor educational record in terms of preadolescent schooling, Birmingham people appear to have benefited from better adult education facilities.[84] This may help explain the marked discrepancy between Birmingham and the Black Country in the percentage of those signing the marriage registers in 1851 (Table 26), a distinction confirmed by contemporary opinion. The use of the Bible and religious tracts in the teaching of reading in day and Sunday schools will have given people a familiarity with Christian religious vocabulary, even when it was not understood, but an ambivalent attitude towards the Bible as a book for adult study.

The many similarities between Methodist beliefs and popular religion gave Methodism an advantage in recruiting from the wider population, but its pastoral organisation, whilst offering support to new converts, meant that many had only a short term association with Methodism. In the Black Country a wider range of Methodist denominations was available and their evangelistic methods were more appropriate to the smaller local communities, whereas in Birmingham Wesleyanism, though still one of the largest non-Anglican denominations, had many more rivals in the town centre, all organised to evangelise its growing population. In the Black Country Methodism was able to exploit the impact of communal disasters such as cholera epidemics and mining accidents as 'triggers' to encourage conversions, opportunities which were not available in Birmingham. The numerous small Black Country Methodist societies afforded more scope, not only for working class leadership but also for preaching, which could tap the strong oral tradition of popular culture. Despite some opportunities for open air and cottage preaching, the larger and much less numerous Birmingham Wesleyan chapels gave little scope to less educated preachers.[85] On the other hand aspiring working class people could gain educational as well as religious opportunities from the other churches and chapels, many of which had attractive preachers as their ministers. This is clearly a factor in the denominational pattern shown in Table 39.

The pattern of popular religion revealed by the Birmingham evidence affords many parallels with that of the London area later in the century, with one or two significant differences, notably the desire for a ministers' prayers for the sick and the lower priority given to ensuring children's knowledge of the Bible. The possibility that this popular religion was not regarded as a separate system but simply a part of a larger cultural whole which comprised both 'official' and 'folk' religion remains open. The impossibility of conducting the in-depth study of individual beliefs to assess their inner coherence, in the manner of oral history interviews, means that much is left to inference from fragmentary sources. Interaction between 'official' religion and popular culture is occurring in many ways at this period, for example in the introduction of prayers into Black Country collieries as well as varying degrees of affiliation between the Birmingham poor and the churches. It is clearly at a more fluid stage of development than David Clark and Sarah Williams' descriptions. Some 'official' beliefs, such as the reality of hellfire and God's justice in inflicting it on sinners, are already being rejected, both by avowed 'infidels' and people more or less attached to the churches. Some religious leaders, such as Methodist superintendents, hesitate to ascribe disasters to 'special providences' especially if they involved obviously virtuous individuals. Where fear is still a motive for religious practice it may be fear of losing something precious in the form of a personal experience of God, rather than simply an insurance against hellfire.

Notes

1   Cross, *Burned Over*, pp. 79-82.
2   Tancred, *First Report, Midland mining*, pp.35, 39. Jon Raven's *The Folklore of Staffordshire*, London 1978, draws heavily on Lawley and Hackwood including the May Day, Christmas and New Year customs mentioned above.
3   Tancred, *First Report, Midland mining*, p.39.
4   J. Raven, *The Folklore and Songs of the Black Country Colliers*, Wolverhampton 1990, p.14, with many other similar examples, mostly taken from F. W. Hackwood, *Staffordshire Customs, Superstitions and Folklore*, Lichfield 1924, re-issued, Wakefield 1974, pp. 146-147.
5   James Mitchell, *Parliamentary Papers, House of Commons, 1842, XVII, Children's Employment Commission, Appendix to the First Report, Mines, Part 1*, p.76, Raven, *Colliers*, p.15.
6   D. Clark, *Between Pulpit and Pew, Folk Religion in a North Yorkshire fishing village*, Cambridge 1982, pp. 158-159.
7   cf. Mitchell, *First Report, Children's Employment*, pp. 4, 66, 69, for fires and 'choke damp' underground in South Staffordshire pits.
8   Obelkevich, *Rural*, pp. 261-262.
9   Ibid. pp. 305-307.
10 D. Hempton, *The Religion of the People*, London 1996, p.53.
11 cf. M. K. Ashby, *Joseph Ashby of Tysoe*, Cambridge 1961, esp. chapter VI; P. Horn, *Joseph Arch, a biography*, Kineton 1971, pp. 8, 14 and passim, *Joseph Arch, The story of my life*, 1898, passim.
12 E. P. Thompson, 'Anthropology and the discipline of historical context', in *Midland History*, Vol. 1, no. 3, Birmingham 1972, pp. 41-55.
13 C. Laye, *The African Child*, Paris 1954, English Translation, Glasgow 1959, p.115, also passim.
14 Ibid. pp. 125-126, 140.

15 Tancred, *First Report, Midland mining*, quotes the following clergy; pp. 1 (Garbett, rural dean, Birmingham), 39 (Cartwright of Dudley), 50 (Lewis of Sedgley), 63 (Harris of Brierley Hill), 88 (Fletcher of Bilston), 96 (Buckridge, chaplain of Stafford Gaol).

16 Ibid. p.50.

17 Horne, *Second Report, Children's Employment*, p. Q63.

18 J. Raven, *The Folklore of Staffordshire*, London 1978, p.147, Pratt, *Black Country*, pp. 139-140.

19 Cross, *Burned Over*, p.93, his analysis of educational opportunities occupies pages 89-109.

20 *Journal of the Statistical Society of London*, Vol. III, 1840, pp. 25-49.

21 A. W. Dale, *Dale*, p.270.

22 *Minutes of the Committee of Council on Education*, London (H.M.S.O.) 1846, pp. 150, 178.

23 Ibid. p.178.

24 *Select Committee on the Education of the Poorer Classes*, Parliamentary Papers 1838, VII, p.125.

25 Ibid. p.123, cf. C. Dickens, *Hard Times*, London 1854, chapter one.

26 Horne, *Second Report, Children's Employment*, pp. Q81-82, for stifling conditions in most Sunday schools cf. Q37 (Wolverhampton), Q57 (Willenhall), Q72 (Bilston), Q79-80 (Sedgley), Q83 (Walsall), Q86 (Wednesbury).

27 Mitchell, *First Report, Children's Employment*, p.71.

28 "None of the teachers taught upon any particular method or system, but endeavoured to make the children learn to read somehow, with an occasional help from the strap and buckle," both of them conveniently manufactured in Walsall. Horne, *Second Report, Children's Employment*, p. q 68.

29 Ibid. pp. q 43-47. and passim.

30 "Many of the children told me they always said their prayers at night, and the prayer they said was, 'Our Father'. I naturally thought they meant that they repeated the Lord's Prayer, but I soon found that few of them knew it. They only repeated the first two words" Horne, *Second Report, Children's Employment*, p. Q 19.

31 Roy Palmer, *George Dunn, The Minstrel of Quarry Bank*, Dudley 1984, passim.

32 Cliff Willetts, *When I was a boy, I, II and III*, Dudley Teachers' Centre pamphlets, 1977 and 1979, passim. The quotation comes from pamphlet III, p.16.

33 D. Hempton, 'Established churches and the rise of Religious Pluralism: A Case Study, England 1700-1914', paper read at The Decline of Christendom in Western Europe Conference, Paris 1997, p.10, Watts, *Dissenters*. pp. 46, 52, 110.

34 Watts, *Dissenters*, p.100

35 Ibid. pp. 105, 107.

36 J. Rule, 'Methodism, popular belief and village culture in Cornwall, 1800-1850' in R. D. Storch (Ed.), *Popular Culture and Custom in Nineteenth Century England*, London 1982, pp. 48-70, the quotation is from p.70, cf. E. P.

Thompson, 'Anthropology', p.54.

37 D. Hempton, *The Religion of the People*, London 1996, p.34.

38 S. Baring Gould, *The Vicar of Morwenstow, being a life of Robert Stephen Hawker, MA*, London 1876 (Ninth edition 1929), p.143. Hawker was an Oxford graduate.

39 Rule, 'Methodism', p.65, Watts, *Dissenters*, p.108.(the preacher was William Driffield)

40 Sandwell Archives and Local History Service, Smethwick Central Library, Rowley Regis parish records 9/6, Manuscript notes on the parish by George Barrs, undated but probably about 1836. Barrs was a Cambridge graduate and a protégé of Simeon.

41 cf. Tancred, *First Report, Midland mining*, p. 21, asked if there were many pits around West Bromwich in which daily prayers were said, Hughes, a Wesleyan pikeman, replied, "I fear not, pits that have praying companies in them are as few as parish churches", also Mitchell, *First Report, Children's Employment*, p.5, visit to a pit at Kingswinford, "Whilst waiting for the ascent of the skip, we heard two miners who were coming up singing a melodious hymn".

42 Mitchell, *First Report, Children's Employment*, p.66.

43 Tancred, *First Report, Midland mining*, p.67.

44 J. Lawson, *A Man's Life*, London 1932 (1944), p.70. Lawson (b.1882) is too recent to have joined Eric Hobsbawm's roll call of Methodist Labour leaders, in *Primitive Rebels*, Manchester 1959, p.138.

45 Coley, *Collins*, p.180.

46 Pratt, *Black Country*, p.152-154.

47 Rule, 'Methodism', pp.50-60.

48 Clark, *Folk Religion*, passim, especially pp. 88-89.

49 Horne, *Second Report, Children's Employment*, p. Q80. cf A. W. A. White, 'The Christian Collier' in *Transactions of the Birmingham and Warwickshire Archaeological Society*, Vol. 85, 1972, pp. 203-208 with plates. The article comments on and reprints a poster, dateable to 1843-45, with hymn-like verses describing a pious collier and an 'Address to the unconverted collier' using this sequence of justice and mercy in its appeal.

50 F. W. Hackwood, *Staffordshire Customs, Superstitions and Folklore*, Lichfield 1924, pp. 54-56.

51 Tancred, *First Report, Midland mining*, p.1.

52 Methodist Central Archives, manuscript correspondence, Joseph Entwhistle, senior, to Miss Tooth, 20 September 1823, and to George Marsden, 24 June 1824, "I cannot say much concerning Birmingham. We have had a few conversions but we want an outpouring of the Holy Spirit . . . There are many pious souls- yet Religion is not so deep or lively as in Yorkshire". cf. George Morley to Jabez Bunting, 28 October 1815.

53 Ibid. cf. John Pawson to George Marsden, 18 May 1796 "I have heard that the Lord has greatly revived and increased his work in Birmingham in the present year. It has given me much pleasure to hear the account you have several times given Dicky Reece of the Lord pouring out his spirit upon you and the people. These things considered is it not a little strange that a person of great note in Birmingham should write to his friends as follows?

(viz.) 'We have had very wild and strange proceedings here and some of the new converts have gone off with other women's husbands; others have turned whores, others thieves, and many turned back into the world . . . If there is not a stop put to it we shall be the ridicule of the serious part of the nation", and Samuel Bradburn, 30 August 1797, "I preached last night at Cherry Street and after the blessing some *godly booby* gave out a hymn and began a noisy meeting. I stopped in the vestry a while and perceived that very few of the people remained. Take no notice and they will die of themselves. They are chiefly <u>young</u> and <u>low</u> people. Our best friends disapprove of them". (underline original)

54 cf. *Primitive Methodist Magazine*, London 1850, pp. 306-308, Revival meetings at Bartley Green, Dayhouse Bank, Rubery, Quinton, Madeley Heath.

55 S. C. Williams, 'Religious Belief and Popular Culture: a study of the South London borough of Southwark, c.1880-1939' D.Phil. Oxford, 1993

56 Clark, *Folk Religion*, pp. 110-144, Williams, 'Southwark', pp. 167-173.

57 Finegan, 'Journal', 31 December 1837, for Phoebe Purchase see 27 September 1837.

58 J. H. S. Kent, 'Feelings and Festivals' in Dyos and Wolff, *Victorian City*, Vol. 2, p.866.

59 H. D. Rack, *Reasonable Enthusiast*, London 1989, p.412.

60 Methodist Central Archives, Manuscript Journal of Joseph Entwhistle, junior, 31 December 1829.

61 Williams, 'Southwark', p.231.

62 BRL, Carrs Lane deposit, Vol. 64, 29 June 1840. Typical of many other comments of the same sort.

63 Ibid. Vol. 69, 28 January 1846.

64 "I was sent for to visit a poor woman who had fallen down in the street and discharged a great quantity of blood. As I entered the room she said, 'Oh I did so want to see you'. 'And what did you want to see me for?' 'That you might send me to heaven' 'That's more than I am able to do. It doesn't lie in my power to send people to heaven.' 'Don't it?' 'No it does not. There is no going to heaven but through Jesus Christ, the Bible tells us that He is the Way, the Truth and the Life' Derrington questioned her about her doctrinal knowledge only to be told she was "no scholar". A later visit elicited no further answer, "She told me she could not talk. Thus the poor creature must be left in her ignorance and her sin with very little prospect of doing her any good. We have succeeded in removing, to a very considerable degree, the delusion of sending sinners to heaven by the administration of the Lord's Supper and have instead substituted our prayers. Not that this was intended but so it is. These poor ignorant creatures think that if they can but obtain the attendance of some servant of Jesus Christ they may safely soar to heaven on the breath of his prayer". Ibid. Vol. 62, 9 November 1838, cf. Vol.66, 27 December 1843, Vol. 72 (Clay)19 May 1838, "There is a notion that if sick people have anyone to pray with them in their last moments all will be well".

65 Ibid. Vol. 63, 15 July 1841.

66 cf. Raphael Samuel, 'The Roman Catholic Church and the Irish Poor' in S.

Gilley and R. Swift (Eds.), *The Irish in the Victorian City*, London 1985, p.273.

67 BRL Carrs Lane deposit Vol. 63, 17 November 1840.

68 Williams, 'Southwark', pp. 197-230.

69 Finegan, 'Journal', 5 December 1837.

70 BRL Carrs Lane deposit Vol. 75, 1 November 1849.

71 Ibid. Vol. 65, 14 September 1843., recording this conversation with a sick woman, "'You have lived in this world a long time, do you ever think of leaving it?' 'Yes I do sometimes,' 'And where do you think you shall go then?' 'To heaven I hope,' 'What makes you hope you shall go there?' 'Why I have never done any harm but worked hard for my living,' 'Never done any harm have you?' 'No, but worked hard for my living'. The poor creature was quite right in her own way." he admits.

72 Ibid. Vol. 61, 15 August 1838.

73 Ibid. 66, 12 May 1842. Derrington visited a former Carrs Lane scholar who asked him, "Do you think there is real fire in hell?' . . . she evidently thought it would be severe of God to subject the lost to such suffering".

74 Ibid. Vol. 71, 13-14 September 1838.

75 Ibid. Vol. 68, 21 April 1843., noting of one old man who didn't know why Jesus died a cruel death, "Here was an immortal, accountable being, who had heard of the redeemer's sufferings and death, but who had not the most distant idea that his sufferings were expiatory or that his precious soul needed an interest in them."

76 Ibid. 8 December 1843.

77 Ibid. Vol. 66, 6 October 1844.

78 Williams, 'Southwark', pp. 296, 301-302.

79 cf. BRL, Cherry Street West circuit deposit, Minutes of the Cherry Street Tract Society, 1836 which claims a number of results from visitation, "such as when the Drunkard has become sober, the indigent neglecter of the Sabbath who was accustomed to saunter about in his working dress has been taught to sanctify that Day and found decently clad in the house of God". etc.

80 BRL, Carrs Lane deposit, Vol. 75, 16 June 1849.

81 Ibid. Vol. 61, 20 April 1838.

82 Ibid. Vol. 72, 10 December 1838, Henry Clay gives a florid account of a shoemaker, a former Methodist, whose belief in God was sustained by contemplating the "works of creation" particularly the wonders of sun, moon, stars and "the variegated globe on which we live". These seemed to mediate God's presence to him even when he felt rejected by the Methodists who, "when he became reduced and left the Methodist society, took no notice of him".

83 Thompson, 'Anthropology', p.54. cf. Dimond, *Psychology*, pp. 214, 234.

84 In 1838 twenty-one out of the fifty-six Sunday schools had evening classes attached to them, with 553 of the 1, 490 scholars over 15 years old. In addition 36 day schools had evening schools, with 262 out of 563 scholars over the age of fifteen. Thus just 820 out of an 1841 population of 177, 922 for the borough attended evening schools, less than 1% of total population but over 4% of those between 15 and 20 years old. *Journal of the Statistical Society of London*, 1840, pp. 48- 49.

85 Though they were reluctant to allow them to preach for other denominations, cf. BRL Cherry Street West circuit deposit, Local Preacher's Meeting Minutes, 7 August 1832. (Brother Collins requested permission to preach for others as well as the Wesleyans, request refused, Collins leaves)

CHAPTER 10

Conclusions

This thesis has addressed two distinct but interrelated aspects of mid-nineteenth century British religion: the factors promoting or inhibiting church attendance in an industrial conurbation and the character of religious responses amongst the working class. It has shown that the original returns for the 1851 census of religious worship sustain the contrast in the published report between the general level of church attendance in Birmingham and that of the Black Country. Analysis of the sub-districts reveals considerable variation between the Black Country townships, though still at levels higher than the Birmingham area as a whole. A number of possible factors has been considered none of which, taken on its own, offers a convincing explanation of the census statistics, as important exceptions exist in every case. Only the sheer size of its population distinguishes greater Birmingham from every single Black Country township although, taken together, their 1851 population was 55% higher.[1] This must be borne in mind when other factors are considered.

Neither size nor rate of population growth appears to be decisive in determining attendance levels. Though always the largest town in the conurbation Birmingham's rate of population growth during the first half of the nineteenth century was exceeded by many Black Country townships, particularly West Bromwich and Tipton, but also Bilston, Dudley, Kingswinford, Wednesbury, Willenhall and Wolverhampton.[2] Of these only Willenhall and Wednesbury fell below 20, 000 population by 1851 and they were amongst the lowest in terms of church attendance whereas West Bromwich and Tipton were amongst the highest.[3] These findings modify Perkin's claim and Callum Brown's more guarded hypothesis, neither of whom included church accommodation in their calculations.

Provision of church accommodation is equally important for those wishing to attend. In this denominational patterns differ. Nonconformist groups tended to build only for existing congregations with some room for expansion. The Church of England maintained many ancient churches whilst providing new ones in expanding areas without necessarily ensuring that they matched a local congregation. With the exception of the still largely rural outskirts of the conurbation church building by all major denominations attempted to keep pace with rising population during this period so that few places fell badly behind their 1801 provision and eleven, including Birmingham, actually increased the proportion of their population for whom church and chapel accommodation was available.[4] There were, therefore, more opportunities for the 1851 population to attend public worship than for that of 1801. Within this generally positive picture the Anglican proportions vary considerably, depending very much on their original baseline, keeping up with population increases in some, such as Birmingham, Wolverhampton and Sedgley, but falling badly behind in others, notably Tipton, Oldbury and West Bromwich.[5] There is, understandably, a positive correlation between the rank order of accommodation and the index of attendance, supporting with qualifications Robin Gill's thesis.

It could be argued that attendance figures which included Sunday school pupils were the decisive factor differentiating the Black Country from Birmingham. Deducting them from the attendances reduces the difference between Birmingham and the Black Country by 7% overall.[6] Some places had a very high percentage of Sunday scholars but these did not necessarily account for their overall index of attendance. Both the highest and lowest indexes of attendance were in places with a large percentage of Sunday scholars, Rowley Regis and Willenhall, and others such as Sedgley and Bloxwich were similarly placed.[7]

The influence of socio-economic factors is not straightforward as the industrial pattern of the conurbation presents both contrast and similarity. The iron trade dominated the Black Country whilst in Birmingham other metal-based industries, notably brassware, guns and jewellery predominated. Some specialised industries, particularly saddlery, were shared but most were located in specific places and gave a distinctive character to them, existing alongside certain basic industries, such as mining, iron founding, glass and brick manufacture, which were spread unevenly throughout. Despite the distinctiveness and greater diversity of the Birmingham trades its industrial organisation was very similar to the Black Country. Both were characterised by small industrial units, sub-contracting and outworking in either domestic or hired workshops. Its greater diversity did, however, give Birmingham the advantage of a much broader industrial base. No single group of trades dominated employment opportunities and there was much more demand for skilled labour.[8] Nevertheless there are no clear statistical links between specific occupations and either denominational or overall attendance patterns in particular places, but this must be qualified by the lack of quantifiable occupational evidence for some smaller places exhibiting both high and low attendance.[9] This calls in question Gilbert's thesis on the relationship between industrialisation and the appeal of nonconformity.

McLeod's argument that urban attendance reflected the surrounding rural pattern is only partially sustained as the contrast between Birmingham and the Black Country remains when each is compared with its immediate rural hinterland. Black Country church attendance is generally an improvement on rural Staffordshire and Worcestershire whilst that of Birmingham is markedly lower than rural Warwickshire. Rural denominational allegiance shows strong support for the Church of England in those registration districts immediately surrounding the conurbation but very much lower nonconformist attendances than either Birmingham or the Black Country. It could be argued that Anglican strength in the two largest towns in the conurbation, Birmingham and Wolverhampton, when compared with nonconformity, reflected loyalties formed in their birthplaces by immigrants. However, another explanation is needed for the strength of Methodism, particularly in the Black Country, and that of the Independents and Baptists in Birmingham, neither of which can be paralleled in surrounding counties.[10]

Another possible cause of the contrast is the incidence of cholera epidemics which, in both 1832 and 1849, struck the Black Country particularly hard without affecting Birmingham. On both occasions they had an impact on church-going but the effects were too short-lived to have influenced the 1851 census. Nor is there any obvious connection between 1849 cholera mortality and levels of church attendance, one of the worst hit places, Willenhall, having the lowest attendance whilst much higher attendances were recorded at places with very few cholera deaths, like Halesowen and Rowley Regis.[11] The effects of both epidemics can be measured by their impact on Methodist church membership, as quarterly records enable variations to be closely related to the incidence of the disease. Taken overall Methodist membership in the Black Country clearly increased during both cholera epidemics and, although it decreased thereafter, substantial additional numbers remained. This conclusion contradicts Gilbert's claim that "the impact of the epidemic was essentially impermanent".[12] At the local level only Wesleyan statistics survive and their pattern is inconsistent. Some societies near centres of the disease increased their membership, others did not, thus modifying the claims of Leese and Watts. Moreover other circuits like those of Birmingham also increased their membership above the national norm in 1832, suggesting that the Black Country pattern was part of a broader trend. In 1849, however, large Wesleyan losses in Birmingham were not matched in the Black Country where cholera seems to have directed Wesleyan energies into evangelism and away from connexional politics.

Those factors considered so far are largely external to the religious organisations and do not provide sufficient reason for their relative success in attracting and retaining adult worshippers. Providing new Anglican churches by Parliamentary grant did not guarantee numerous attendances. Nonconformist chapel building as a consequence of schism or denominational rivalry had equally uncertain results. Anglican manpower and pastoral organisation improved across the conurbation after 1835.[13] The number of clergy increased, but the ratio of clergy to churches only really improved in Wolverhampton (after the abolition of the Deanery) and Birmingham. District visiting and the use of lay agents were also attempted but only in Birmingham were these sustained, thus supporting Mark Smith's findings. Controversy over church rates and political issues does not seem to have unduly affected Anglican fortunes. Anti-clericalism, though present, was softened by the commitment of several leading clergy to humanitarian causes. Pluralism and non residence were dramatically reduced and no obvious clerical scandals marred the Anglican image after 1835.[14]

In contrast with northern industrial towns like Leeds and Bradford, Methodism was not a dominant force in Birmingham, where it was virtually limited to the Wesleyans. In the Black Country, however, three Methodist denominations were to be found in most areas, the Wesleyans and the Primitives having the largest following. These Methodist attendances account, by themselves, for the difference between the Black Country and Birmingham in the 1851 census of religious worship.[15] This capacity of Methodism to attract a substantial working class following in the Black Country is explained by a number of factors: the ease of entry into Methodist societies when compared with Independent or Baptist church membership, the impact of intensive, emotional evangelism on small self-contained communities, the support given to new converts by the system of class meetings and the nature of the theological message which resonated with elements of popular religion. All these contrasted with the approach of Calvinist Evangelicals, whether Anglican or nonconformist, whose essentially doctrinal and individualistic emphasis met with a less positive response. Detailed examination of Methodist evangelistic styles does not support the views of Watts and E. P. Thompson that their appeal was essentially superstitious.

The interaction between 'official' and 'popular' religion is found in both Birmingham and the Black Country but, because domestic visiting by paid lay agents was limited to Birmingham during this period, their manuscript journals give a much fuller picture of the Birmingham situation than any evidence available for the rest of the conurbation. The range of responses to the approaches of Town Missionaries and the ways in which Methodism and popular culture interacted in the Black Country support the view that all those involved saw themselves as within a cultural continuum which included the whole of society, although containing clear degrees of attachment to and separation from the practices of organised religion. This seriously questions Obelkevich's claim that pagan elements predominated over Christian ones in popular religion.

At the level of belief the fragmentary nature of the sources makes any characterisation of popular religion conjectural, though some features closely resemble those revealed by oral history for the period after 1870 as described by Clark, Hempton and Sarah Williams. The common needs to which religious beliefs and practices minister mean that a wide range of elements within the Christian tradition can be used, adapted and modified by each individual. The need for protection, for moral norms, for forgiveness, for hope for the future and an overall explanatory framework for the world in which we live can be obtained within the popular oral culture of family and local community and in the structured life of a religious denomination. Where the door to literacy, and thence to intellectual and social progress, is through a day or Sunday school where the Bible is used as a textbook to teach reading, then possibilities for confusion are considerable. Those who undergo the process may be impressed by the authority accorded to the scriptures and pick up a range of religious vocabulary but reject adult study of the Bible, though its stories and imagery remain a familiar part of everyday discourse.

Both Anglicans and Methodists could benefit from the sort of popular religion indicated in this thesis. Anglicans by its links with parish churches through rites of passage and charitable assistance, particularly when re-enforced by effective pastoral visiting; Methodists by their appeals to religious experiences and both through the day and Sunday schools each was establishing during this period. Methodism, unlike other nonconformist denominations, was slow to set up entirely separate religious institutions, relying on the Church of England for many rites of passage well into the second half of the nineteenth century. This gave it the sort of flexibility which enabled it to enter 'gaps' between other religious groups. David Hempton has described how this occurred in particular parts of Ulster and the Cévennes in this period. There Methodists took advantage of a temporary breakdown of the 'pre-ascribed' communities owing allegiance to specific churches; the Church of Ireland, Roman Catholic, Presbyterian and Reformed.[16]

Unlike these situations the conurbation had no such pre-ascribed communities. Even the Roman Catholics, though clearly distinct, were on the lookout for converts from the wider society, whilst all manner of Protestants saw Catholics as fit subjects for proselytism. Hence my suggestion that a continuum best represents the situation in which ordinary people found themselves in both Birmingham and the Black Country, rather than being divided between religion and irreligion as Mann, Perkin and Inglis supposed. The more intense, better organised and more ably led efforts of all the main Christian churches to appeal to working people distinguished Birmingham from most of the Black Country giving aspiring folk there a rich choice of alternatives. Even movements such as Owenism and Chartism were not necessarily seen as conflicting with Christian allegiance and popular rejection of some Christian doctrines could be found amongst those still connected with the churches as well as self-confessed 'infidels'. Its relatively poor census showing compared with the Black Country was no reflection on the quality of its religious life.

Such a judgement leaves the initial problem addressed by this thesis unresolved. One explanation is to point out that Birmingham's church accommodation was sufficient for less than 20% of its 1801 population. This makes its 1851 figure of just over 30% a very creditable reflection on the subsequent building programme but it still left the largest town in the conurbation well behind all others by at least ten percentage points.[17] This must have affected Birmingham's position in terms of possible attendances. Its sheer size, compared with the others, had positive features for organised religion. It meant that individual denominations could all obtain an encouraging response and develop lively religious communities without any one of them being able to gain a position of dominance. Even the Church of England, by far the strongest, attracted less than half of the worshippers on census Sunday.[18] It could well be that in the sort of intellectual market place described by McDonnell as many were put off by the competing sects as were recruited by them.[19] The evidence of the Town Missionaries is significant in this respect, recording the negative results of evangelistic rivalry and of the Sabbatarian and dogmatic views of many of the evangelists. The alternative use of Sundays to walk in the countryside or stay at home and read the news was clearly prevalent in the 1830s.[20]

A more conjectural possibility is that Birmingham's census Sunday attendance was significantly depleted, when compared with the Black Country, by the abnormally low Wesleyan congregations, combined with the ineffectiveness of the Primitives and the Methodist New Connexion there. The loss of over 1, 100 members between 1847 and 1851 as a consequence of internal connexional dissension would result in a far greater loss of adherents.[21] Had Birmingham Wesleyans retained their 1847 membership and adherents then approximately two and a half thousand additional evening attendances would have been added to the Birmingham total, plus a smaller proportion in the morning, bringing it to around 95, 000. This would have raised the index for greater Birmingham to 39%, just below the lowest Black Country township, Willenhall and not far below that of Walsall.[22] There is no way of knowing how many Birmingham ex-Wesleyans stayed away from church on census Sunday or where they went if they attended so that such a suggestion is pure conjecture. It also raises further questions about the religious life of Walsall and Willenhall.

As there was only one national census of religious worship its results have, perhaps inevitably, been given undue significance.[23] These attendances took place in a dynamic not a static situation, and, as in the case of the Birmingham Wesleyans, may well have fluctuated considerably over relatively short periods, so that a single set of figures gives a far from final picture. Such a consideration eases the frustration of ending this thesis on a provisional rather than a conclusive note, especially after examining such fascinating evidence, but it is more realistic than claiming to have resolved all the problems it presented.

What it has shown is the inherent ambiguity of popular responses to different presentations of Christianity during this period. These were inevitably associated with other elements which, whilst attracting some, repelled others. Social respectability, symbolised by church attendance, could be linked with economic independence, self-improvement through Sunday schools, Temperance and Trade Union activity or identified with social control through Sabbatarianism, paternalist charity and economic exploitation. Political ideologies, appeals to patriotic, cultural and class loyalties, humanitarian concerns, family continuity, gender roles and educational facilities were all bound up with institutional religion in its various denominational forms, providing fruitful sources for scholarly insight and controversy.

As historians move from factual and statistical evidence to interpreting the experiences of individual men and women their explanations increasingly depend on their understanding of religion. It must be recognised that, in addition to the ambiguity of response resulting from the association of religious allegiance with other factors, there is also an inherent ambiguity within Christianity itself. Jesus was not a successful prophet, like Muhammed, nor did he die in old age as a revered teacher, like Gotama. His death on the cross whilst still young became central to the interpretation of his message. Discipleship meant being 'made perfect through suffering' (Hebrews 2:10) and St. Paul ensured that it could not be easily reduced to a single formula (cf. 1 Corinthians10:12). Hence both the fascination and the difficulty of interpreting popular responses to Christianity in specific historical circumstances. My own interpretation reflects a personal understanding of that message, inevitably incomplete, which anticipates several possible responses from total acceptance to outright rejection with a variety of compromises in between, often changing within the life span of each individual as well as being dependent on the available range of ecclesiastical styles.

Notes

1   Greater Birmingham; 243, 354, Black Country; 377, 680.
2   Greater Birmingham 326%, for others see Table 2.(West Bromwich 644%, Tipton 581%)
3   see Table 17.
4   see Table 19.
5   see Table 20.
6   see Table 16.
7   see Table 18.
8   see Table 8.
9   see Table 23 and related discussion.
10   see Tables 12 and 24.
11   see Table 28.
12   Gilbert, *Industrial England*, p.197
13   see Table 38.
14   i.e. after the death of Moreton of Willenhall in 1834 and before the conviction of Fletcher of Bilston for fraud in 1862, see Robson in Baker, *Studies* 1979, pp. 409-413.
15   see Tables 21 and 39.
16   D. Hempton, *The Religion of the People*, London 1996, pp. 19-20, 35-43.
17   See Table 19.
18   See Table 39.

19 See section 7.3.

20 See especially sections 7.5, 7.6, 8.5, 8.6.

21 See Table 34, the loss is the same in numerical terms as that between 1848 and 1852. Taking Sunday evening congregations as a better indication of adult attendance than mornings, which included many Sunday scholars, Wesleyan chapels in the Dudley and Wolverhampton circuits returned figures between two and three times their recorded membership whilst evening congregations in the oldest Birmingham town centre chapels only equalled their 1851 membership. See G. Robson, 'Methodists and the 1851 Census of Religious Worship in Birmingham and the Black Country, Part 2', in *Bulletin of the West Midlands Branch of the Wesley Historical Society* Vol. 2, No. 11, September 1975, p.107, which summarises these findings.

22 See Table 39, There are similarities in the denominational patterns of Birmingham and Walsall.

23 This is the chief weakness of Keith Snell's otherwise admirably balanced analysis of the census. His assumption throughout appears to be that the 1851 statistics represent a more static situation than can possibly have been the case. Snell and Ell, *Rival*, passim.

Mcphail's computer-assisted analysis of the census returns

John McPhail's doctoral thesis is largely taken up with a statistical analysis of the provision for and attendance at Sunday worship based on the 1851 census returns for the area.[1] His analysis uses a particular computer software programme, FOXPAD, into which initial data from the census returns were fed to provide two parallel databases, one for the Church of England, the other for the remainder of the religious denominations. In order to provide contrasting rural evidence to balance that from the conurbation McPhail has included the registration district of Penkridge, north of Wolverhampton, along with the others used in this thesis. He also includes the whole of the Aston registration district, not only that which was part of the borough of Birmingham. Although Penkridge was a largely rural area of Staffordshire it included the developing Cannock Chase coalfield around the town of Cannock and its adjacent villages.

The analysis itself is based on the sub-districts, some of which are further sub-divided so that they fit into one of nine different categories according to the types of settlement they are held to represent. These are, in order of population size: agricultural hamlet, agricultural village, industrial village, small industrial town, declining established town, expanding established town, large industrial town and regional centre. Only Birmingham and Wolverhampton count as regional centres, some other places, such as West Bromwich, are treated as whole settlements and count as large industrial towns, others are further sub-divided so that the Halesowen sub-district offers examples of an expanding established town (Halesowen), small industrial town (Cradley), industrial village (Hasbury), mixed village (Quinton) and agricultural village (Lapal). This enables McPhail to use statistics from a total of eighty-seven settlements spread across the typological range, making numerical comparisons mathematically feasible.

The resulting statistics largely support this thesis, namely the higher level of church attendance in the Black Country compared with both Birmingham and the surrounding rural areas.[2] However the methodology and some of the assumptions behind its use lead McPhail into some questionable assertions as well as some simple errors of fact. The decision about which registration sub-districts to further sub-divide into different types of settlement appears rather arbitrary. The Halesowen sub-division referred to above is eminently sensible but some of McPhail's classifications are less obviously in line with the facts. Not only West Bromwich but also Sedgley, Rowley Regis and Kingswinford are classified as large industrial towns, perhaps on the basis of their overall populations. McPhail later recognises that this is hardly the case with Sedgley. When, in chapter 3, he gives a case study of this parish he divides it into seven separate industrial settlements.[3] But this was just as true of Rowley Regis and Kingswinford.

Other examples could be given of instances where the category into which a sub-district is alleged to fit governs subsequent judgements of the significance of the religious pattern within it. For example, Kings Norton is included as an instance of Methodism taking root in 'an established agricultural town'.[4] In fact only the smallest of the six Methodist chapels, seating 40, was actually in Kings Norton. Two were in small villages, Beoley and Rubery, between six and seven miles away at either end of the Lickey Hills and the others were much more a part of the industrial expansion of greater Birmingham, being situated in Balsall Heath, Sparkbrook and Stirchley. The origin of the last of these is obscure but its location near the Birmingham to Worcester canal suggests that it may have been similar to its fellow Wesleyan cause in neighbouring Selly Oak, which was begun in cottage meetings led by a Wesleyan inspector of canal tolls who was appointed in 1829.[5]

McPhail uses the index of attendance pioneered by Inglis and produces such indexes for all the settlements he distinguishes. However, the attempt to have a consistent baseline for all the mathematical input into the computer programme has led him into unnecessary errors of judgement. The data from the original returns has been fed in as it stood. No allowances have been made for duplicate returns such as those of the Wesleyans at Sedgley. Sunday school scholars have been included throughout and, where no figures were given, none have been substituted. This last decision has had serious consequences in some important instances.

Having only two towns in the category of 'regional centre' has led McPhail to treat their registration sub-districts as though they were separate, self-contained settlements rather than somewhat arbitrary divisions of a larger, more complex social reality. This plus the decision about data processing leads him into misunderstanding the situation in Wolverhampton. The town was divided down the middle into East and West sub-districts. The East had almost double the population of the West, 32, 333 compared with 17, 652. Not only so but, although in the West all three Anglican churches gave at least an average attendance, in the East two of the five, including St. Peter's Collegiate Church, gave no figures at all, nor did the Catholic Apostolic Church. These omissions lead McPhail into computer-produced indexes of 64.47 for the West and only 28.8 for the East, even after including, inappropriately, those at the Sabbath services in the Jewish synagogue in the total of attendances in the East sub-district. I have substituted approximate attendances of 3, 240 in total at the two Anglican churches which gave no figures and 164, the number of communicants stated in their return, for the Catholic Apostolic Church. After excluding the Jews, for reasons which will become apparent later, the resulting index for the East is 38.48, almost ten percentage points higher than McPhail's.

The unreality of this use of statistics, however, is apparent when the position of individual denominations is considered. For example, the West sub-district contained the only Roman Catholic church, the oldest in the conurbation. If its 2, 100 attendances are only added to the total for the West and not the town as a whole, they boost the West's index considerably. Had the church been situated on the other side of the Stafford Road its total congregations would have been added to the East sub-district, from which many undoubtedly came. The consequence of such a transfer of a single important church, drawing its congregations from across the town, would have been indexes of 52.43 for the West and 44.97 for the East, a much more even, though still unbalanced, result, probably more nearly reflecting the local situation. Hence my decision to combine the data from Wolverhampton into one consolidated index, in the same fashion as West Bromwich, rather than imply that there were two very different populations on either side of a line running from north to south. Certainly the West was more middle class and the East more working class, but those who attended church did not restrict their allegiances to the district in which they lived. G. B. Thorneycroft, the first mayor of Wolverhampton, went to St. Peter's church in the morning and Darlington Street Wesleyan chapel in the evening, thus attending worship regularly in each of the town's sub-districts.[6]

The same method of processing information from the central Birmingham sub-districts leads McPhail to misunderstand the situation there. Having derived very high indexes from three sub-districts, St. Philip (84.9), St. Mary (72.3) and St. Peter (68.7) compared with low indexes for the rest he says they "illustrate the patchy nature of attendance within such a large town as Birmingham".[7] What they illustrate in fact is the arbitrary way in which sub-districts parcelled out the well established churches and chapels, giving St. Philip's and St. Peter's a far greater share of them than St. Martin's and St. Paul's and giving St. Mary's the Roman Catholic cathedral with six thousand attendances on census Sunday. Relating these attendances only to the resident population of the sub-district in which they were recorded distorts the situation. It is less of a distortion to treat them as derived from the wider population of the whole town.

Equally questionable is McPhail's method of calculating the degree to which accommodation for worship was actually used. The census returns for sittings have been used to give the percentage of the population which could be accommodated in each settlement, termed an 'index of accommodation' "By dividing the Index of Attendance by the Index of Accommodation, it is possible to determine the density of the congregation by calculating the number of attenders per sitting, based on the total attendance of morning, afternoon and evening services". This may be valid mathematically as the same base population has been used in calculating both indexes. What it does not do is address the reality of the situation in each church and chapel. McPhail claims that "although religious attendance levels were far less in Birmingham than the Black Country, Birmingham's places of worship were almost as full. For example, the Birmingham sub-district of St. Mary's had the highest density rate with 2.16".[8]

As only one of the places of worship in St. Mary's had more than two services on census Sunday this figure implies that all accommodation was full to its capacity and more. Unfortunately the calculation appears to have been based on two questionable items of data in addition to the inclusion of Sunday scholars throughout. One is the duplicate return for the Bull Street Society of Friends, the other is the assumption of only single morning and evening services at St. Chad's Cathedral. The original return for St. Chad's gives a figure of 560 for the number of sittings but goes on to state that 1, 200 standing worshippers could also be accommodated. This was necessary as three masses took place on the morning of census Sunday, for which a total of 4, 300 attenders is given plus a special evening service attended by 1, 700. Certainly the places of worship in St. Mary's sub-district were well attended but the sort of statistics produced by McPhail's computer programme are not really comparable with those I have produced, by using a formula which takes account of Sunday scholars and the recorded number of services, when testing Robin Gill's hypothesis. Something like this would be necessary before McPhail's conclusions can be accepted. The initial false assumption that worshippers recorded on census

Sunday only came from the resident population of each sub-district distorts his findings for Birmingham throughout.

"Moreover those sub-districts of Birmingham with the highest attendance rates did not necessarily have the most crowded places of worship. St. Philip's (IA 84.47) had a density of 0.86 whereas St. Paul's (25.78), St. Thomas's (29.29) and St. George's (32.54) all had densities above 1.4" These calculations also fail to take account of the percentage of Sunday school scholars included in the total attendances in each sub-district. Although St. Mary's, cited as having the highest density of all, only had 9% of its total made up of Sunday scholars, in the three McPhail cites as having a density above 1.4% the percentage of Sunday scholars included in the totals is much higher, St. Paul's 27%, St. Thomas's 17% and St. George's 24%.

His findings for Birmingham are contrasted with those for Wolverhampton where "a similar pattern did not occur. Wealthier Wolverhampton West had both a higher IA (64.47) and density rate (1.78) than the poorer district of Wolverhampton East, IA 28.8 and density ratio 0.8, the lowest rate of any Black Country settlement".[9] Unfortunately the database for this calculation is questionable as the computer has been fed the total number of sittings available, 11, 303, but not the total number of attendances as three churches gave no figures at all. Adding the accommodation available in the West sub-district, 8, 308, to that of the East would produce an index of accommodation for the town of 39.2 and, using my consolidated index of attendance for Wolverhampton, a density rate of 1.16, a much more respectable figure even without the adjustment required to take account of Sunday scholars.

Two other, less important, errors have occurred. McPhail has, quite reasonably, separated Harborne from Smethwick as distinct 'settlements' within the one sub-district. In the process the resulting index of attendance for Harborne has become seriously exaggerated. In McPhail's list it ranks second only to Quinton at 92.73.[10] The 1851 population of Harborne was 2, 350 compared with 8, 379 for Smethwick. There were three churches in Harborne which sent in the following attendances: parish church 614, Independents 145, Wesleyans 160, a total of 919 resulting in an index of 39.1, not 92.73, much nearer Smethwick's index of 37.5 (McPhail's is 35.5) and my overall index for the sub-district of 37.9. How McPhail's index has been arrived at I find impossible to determine but it is clearly incorrect.

His other inaccuracy arises within his treatment of the Jews, Quakers and Mormons. These he lumps together as "less popular groups",[11] which in terms of numbers they may have been but in no other way are they comparable. The existence of small Jewish communities in Birmingham, Dudley and Wolverhampton at this date is a significant fact of social and religious history. Total attendances at three Sabbath services amounted to 317 in Birmingham, 30 in Dudley with 27 at two in Wolverhampton. They would, normally, all have been men and consisted, at each synagogue at almost all services, of the same people. The ethnic basis of Jewish identity, and their different religious beliefs and practices, means they are best given separate treatment, hence my decision not to include them in this thesis.

McPhail seems to assume that all religious groups were competing for popular support in a market situation. This may have been true of the Mormons but not of either the Jews or the Quakers. Despite his statement to the contrary, moreover, there was a Mormon congregation in Birmingham, in addition to those in Wolverhampton, Stourbridge and Womborne. In fact it was much the largest, returning a total of 1, 865 attendances on census Sunday, more than the Primitive Methodists could produce in Birmingham.

His computer software programme has helped McPhail handle the additional data from the Penkridge district, but the manual methods used in this thesis give a more sensitive interpretation of the statistics which need their appropriate context to yield meaningful results.

Notes

1   J. A. McPhail, 'Religious attendance and provision in Birmingham, the Black Country and the surrounding rural areas during the mid-nineteenth century', Ph.D. Wolverhampton 1995.
2   Ibid. p.91.
3   Ibid. pp. 230-264.
4   Ibid. p.180.
5   VCH *Warwickshire*, Vol. 7, p.462.
6   Ibid. p.29.
7   Ibid. p.93.
8   Ibid. p.105.
9   Ibid. p.106.
10 Ibid. Appendix 3.
11 Ibid. p.146

Tables

Note on the statistical methods and terms used in analysing the tabulated data

Two commonly used methods have been employed in analysing the statistical data presented in this thesis.

The most frequent is Karl Pearson's product-moment correlation co-efficient which indicates the mathematical degree to which two sets of variables are connected by a linear relationship. For example, the percentage of the 1851 population which could be accommodated in church and chapel in any registration sub-district and the Index of attendance derived from the census of religious worship for that sub-district. The result of calculations applying this formula is conventionally expressed by the letter 'r' to indicate the degree of any possible relationship. The significance of 'r' is given at two levels, 5% and 1%, indicating the mathematical likelihood that the relationship between the two variables is not due to chance. A level of significance of 1% is higher than one at 5% and means that the possibility of the relationship being due to chance or random association is exceedingly small. The number of items in the sample markedly influences the reliability of this method, hence the number of 'degrees of freedom' given alongside the percentage. The smaller the number in the sample the fewer 'degrees of freedom' and the higher the numerical result required of the calculation for 'r' to be statistically significant. (See for example, pages 73-74) This type of correlation is in such widespread use that authors commonly refer to it simply as a 'correlation' without further specification.

The other correlation uses the rank order of the items in the sample rather than their numerical values. For example, comparing the incidence of deaths from cholera in 1849 with church attendance in 1851 (Table 28). Called Spearman's rank-order correlation co-efficient it uses a different formula but gives the significance of the results in the same form as Pearson's product-moment correlation: values for 'r' at 5% and 1% levels with varying degrees of freedom. Because it is not in such general use as Pearson's product-moment correlation, Spearman's rank-order correlation is usually indicated by name when it has been employed. This practice has been maintained throughout this thesis.

It must be emphasised that these correlations are only indicators.

They point to the possibility of a cause and effect relationship between the two variables being compared but they are not proof of the existence of such a relationship. All that can be said is that numerically large correlations do not provide evidence to disprove the possibility of a relationship, which a numerically small value would. The case of Watts' correlation between the success of Nonconformity and the 'illiteracy' of those who 'signed' the marriage register with a mark is an example of an unwarranted inference being drawn from a statistical fact. The relationship between the two variables is too complex to be reduced to simple cause and effect no matter how mathematically cogent the case appears to be. See pages 103-104 and Keith Snell's argument that 'illiteracy' in 1851 is more realistically related to the incidence of child labour.

(K.D.M. Snell and P.S. Ell *Rival Jerusalems* Cambridge 2000, pp. 294-95.)

Table 1

1801 and 1851 Populations, Birmingham and the Black Country

Rank Order	Place	1801 Population	Place	1851 Population
1	Birmingham	60, 822	Birmingham	173, 951
2	Wolverhampton	12, 565	Aston	61, 281
3	Aston	11, 693	Wolverhampton	49, 985
4	Dudley	10, 107	Dudley	37, 962
5	Sedgley	9, 874	West Bromwich	36, 611
6	Walsall	8, 538	Sedgley	29, 447
7	Stourbridge	8, 199	Kingswinford	27, 301
8	Bilston	6, 914	Tipton	24, 872
9	Kingswinford	6, 464	Bilston	23, 527
10	West Bromwich	5, 687	Walsall	21, 203
11	Rowley Regis	5, 027	Stourbridge	20, 238
12	Tipton	4, 280	Willenhall	16, 789
13	Willenhall	4, 231	Wednesbury	14, 281
14	Wednesbury	4, 160	Rowley Regis	14, 249
15	Oldbury	4.055	Oldbury	12, 978
16	Darlaston	3.908	Edgbaston	11, 729
17	Halesowen	3, 833	Darlaston	10, 970
18	Kings Norton	3, 437	Harborne	10, 729
19	Handsworth	2, 719	Halesowen	9, 811
20	Edgbaston	2, 468	Kings Norton	8, 413
21	Aldridge	2, 363	Handsworth	7, 879
22	Harborne	2, 275	Bloxwich	5, 609
23	Bloxwich	1, 952	Aldridge	5, 262

Table 2

Percentage population increase, 1801-1851

Rank Order	Place	Percentage increase (ie1801=100%)
1	West Bromwich	644%
2	Tipton	581%
3	Aston	524%
4	Edgbaston	475%
5	Harborne (includes Smethwick)	472%
6	Kingswinford (incl. Brierley Hill)	422%
7	Wolverhampton	398%
8	Willenhall	397%
9	Dudley	375%
10	Wednesbury	343%
11	Bilston	340%
12	Oldbury	320%
13	Sedgley	298%
14	Handsworth	290%
15	Bloxwich	287%
16	Birmingham	286%
17	Rowley Regis	283%
18	Darlaston	281%
19	Halesowen	256%
20	Walsall	248%
21	Stourbridge	247%
22	Kings Norton	245%
23	Aldridge	223%

Table 3

Decennial population increase as a percentage, 1801-1851

(England and Wales	14%	18%	16%	14%	13%)
Place	1811	1821	1831	1841	1851
Wolverhampton	18.1	23.9	34.5	47.1	37.4
Willenhall	12.8	13.9	42.0	53.8	41.5
Bilston	39.5	24.4	20.7	39.2	16.6
Darlaston	27.5	14.0	18.8	32.9	26.5
Bloxwich	5.8	15.6	32.6	52.3	16.2
Walsall	7.5	4.9	24.4	34.0	32.0
Aldridge	13.2	2.0	11.2	54.3	12.0
Handsworth	11.3	27.5	28.1	24.1	28.4
Oldbury	15.2	18.4	17.0	52.3	49.3
West Bromwich	31.6	27.0	61.2	70.4	32.4
Wednesbury	29.1	20.4	30.4	37.8	22.8
Rowley Regis	-1.0	21.9	22.7	49.4	28.2
Tipton	96.4	37.3	29.5	26.4	31.7
Sedgley	41.1	23.4	19.7	20.6	18.6
Dudley	37.8	31.5	25.8	35.5	21.5
Halesowen	16.0	14.0	17.5	36.2	21.0
Stourbridge	16.2	17.8	23.6	26.8	15.0
Kingswinford	28.0	33.3	37.5	46.6	22.9
Harborne	14.8	28.2	26.2	57.5	61.2
Kings Norton	8.8	14.8	8.4	33.5	35.5
Edgbaston	7.3	37.8	58.1	51.3	33.1
Birmingham	15.4	21.6	29.8	24.6	25.8
Aston	22.9	33.6	67.4	42.3	34.0

Table 4

Percentage of the total 1841 population in employment and other categories

	Norm	B'ham	W'lsall	W'pton	Bilston	WBrom	Tipton	Dudley	Sedgly	Kinswf	Oldsfd
Agric.	8.2	0.5	1.6	0.1	0.2	1.2	0.3	0.8	1.0	1.0	1.0
Ming.	1.3	0.2	4.3	5.6	13.3	5.8	6.9	6.5	7.8	6.8	2.0
Bldg.	2.2	2.1	0.1	1.8	1.5	1.6	1.3	1.4	0.1	1.3	1.3
Manf.	11.3	21.9	17.1	16.6	13.1	14.2	10.3	15.8	8.5	10.9	19.3
Trans.	0.9	1.1	0.4	0.7	0.4	0.4	0.9	0.5	0.3	1.0	0.4
Deal.	2.2	2.9	2.3	2.5	1.6	1.6	1.4	2.3	2.0	1.2	3.0
Ind.S.	2.3	2.8	3.1	4.8	5.2	4.4	6.3	3.5	6.7	5.2	2.3
Prof.	1.5	1.5	0.7	0.8	0.6	0.7	0.3	0.6	0.3	0.5	0.9
Dom.S.	6.8	4.1	4.9	5.1	3.8	3.6	2.8	3.4	2.1	2.8	4.6
Indep.	2.8	2.1	1.5	1.6	0.8	0.8	0.6	1.2	0.8	1.0	1.2
Dep.	60.4	59.4	61.7	58.1	58.2	64.8	67.6	63.6	69.8	66.9	57.9

Table 5

Percentage of the 1841 population below 20 years of age dependent/employed

Place	% Dependent	% Under 20	Under 20 dependent	Women under 20 in work
Birmingham	59.4	45.8	38.1	12.3
Walsall	61.7	47.8	39.7	9.8
Wolverhampton	58.1	45.6	36.1	10.6
Bilston	58.2	48.9	37.2	13.3
West Bromwich	64.8	50.7	43.4	8.9
Tipton	67.6	51.2	44.4	7.3
Dudley	63.6	50.7	42.0	10.0
Sedgley	69.8	52.6	47.0	5.1
Kingswinford	66.9	51.1	44.4	5.5
Oldswinford	57.9	49.3	42.4	10.7

Table 6

Percentage of the population employed in Nailing, 1841

Place	% of whole population	% of employed males	% of employed females
Birmingham	0.24	0.68	0.9
Walsall	0.38	1.0	1.34
Wolverhampton	0.12	0.35	0.04
Bilston	0.005	0.01	0.08
West Bromwich	1.53	3.92	7.26
Tipton	1.44	0.97	33.18
Dudley	5.73	10.41	40.98
Sedgley	2.42	5.89	26.06
Kingswinford	1.39	4.11	6.25
Oldswinford	2.04	20.48	25.85

Table 7

Unskilled male labour as a percentage in 1841

Place	% of employed male population	% of whole population
Sedgley	24.6	6.4
Tipton	21.1	6.0
Kingswinford	16.6	4.8
Bilston	13.9	4.8
West Bromwich	13.7	4.0
Wolverhampton	11.3	3.8
Dudley	11.0	3.1
Oldswinford	9.1	2.5
Walsall	8.8	2.7
Birmingham	6.7	1.9

Table 8

Industrial pattern of Birmingham and the Black Country in 1851

Place	Main Industries						Specialisms
	Mining	Quarry	Iron Fd	Nails	Glass	Brick	
Wolverh'pton	√		√				Brass founding, locks, edge tools, cut-nails, screws, hollow ware, papier-maché, japanning
Willenhall	√						Locks & keys, currycombs
Bilston	√	√	√		√		Hollow ware, japanning
Darlaston	√		√	√		√	Nuts & bolts, gun locks
Bloxwich	√			√		√	Awl blades, bit making
Walsall	√	√	√			√	Saddlery & harness, brushes, tubes, locks, optical glass
Aldridge	√					√	
Handsworth			√				Engineering (Soho Works)
Oldbury	√		√	√			Chemicals, rolling stock
West Brom.	√		√	√		√	Hollow ware, axles, springs, soap
Wednesb'y	√		√	√	√		Tubes, axles, edge tools, heel tips
Rowley Reg.	√	√		√		√	Chains
Tipton	√		√	√		√	Heavy engineering, chains
Sedgley	√	√	√	√			
Dudley	√	√	√	√			Chains, anchors, fenders, fire irons
Halesowen	√		√	√			Edge tools, buttons
Stourbridge			√	√	√	√	Edge tools, anvils (at Lye)
Kingsw'ford	√		√	√	√	√	Edge tools, chains
Smethwick					√		Brass founding, screws, soap engineering
Birmingham & Aston					√		Brassware, guns, jewellery, pens, edge tools, japanning, wire, pins, papier-maché, saddlery, cut-nails, bedsteads, rolling stock, buttons

Table 9

Church of England organisation and accommodation 1835

Parish & dependent chapels	No. of curates	Accommodation	Population 1831	% able to be accommodated
Wolverhampton (L)				
St Peter	1	1, 560	11, 489	13.6
St John	1	1, 600	6, 000	26.6
St George**	1	2, 038	8, 000	25.5
Bilston				
St Leonard		2, 000	14, 492	23.5
St Mary**		1, 400		
Wednesfield				
St Thomas	1	300	1, 897	16.0
Willenhall				
St Giles	1	400	5, 834	6.8
Darlaston (L)	1	1, 310	6, 667	19.6
Walsall (L)				
St Matthew	1	2, 400	15, 066	28.5
St Paul		800		
Bloxwich		1, 100		
Aldridge (L)	1	300	857	29.0
Great Barr		200	859	
Handsworth (L)	1	1, 700	4, 000	42.5
Oldbury (W)		254	5, 000	5.0
West Bromwich (L)	1	1, 072	15, 327	16.25
Christ Church*		1, 420		
Wednesbury (L)		1, 300	8, 437	15.4
Rowley Regis (W)		2, 000	7, 438	26.9
Tipton (L)	1	1, 000	14, 951	6.7
Sedgley (L)	1	1, 309	8, 643	15.1
Coseley**		2, 000	1, 800	111.1
Gornal, St James		600	3, 124	19.2
Dudley (W) St Edmund	2	1, 350	16, 453	16.7
St Thomas		1, 400		
Netherton*		1, 500	6, 500	23.1
Halesowen (W)	1	800	9, 765	8.2
Cradley		400	1, 010	39.6
Oldswinford (W)	1	1, 400	13, 874	19.7
Stourbridge		630		
Lye		700		

Kingswinford (L)				
Holy Trinity**	1	1, 200	7, 356	29.9
St Mary		1, 000		
Brierley Hill	1	1, 200	7, 800	15.4
Harborne (L)	1	700	1, 551	45.1
Smethwick		300	2, 676	11.2
Kings Norton (W)	1	700	1, 700	41.0
Moseley		1, 500	1, 600	93.7
Edgbaston (L)		372	3, 954	9.4
Birmingham (L)				
St Martin	3	1, 800	73, 939	9.3
St Bartholemew		800		
Christ Church		1, 800		
St Mary	1	1, 458		
St Paul	1	1, 000		
St Philip	2	3, 900	11, 153	35.0
St George*		2, 000	11, 000	18.1
St Thomas*	1	2, 169	12, 000	18.1
Aston (L)				
St Peter & Paul	2	608	1, 802	33.7
Erdington*		700	2, 059	34.0
Deritend St John	1	775	14, 685	17.5
Holy Trinity*		1, 800		
Ashted St James		950	12, 698 (Duddeston)	7.5

Table 10

Proportion of clergy to population 1835

Number per clergyman	Names of parishes and districts
Less than 1, 000	Aldridge
1, 001-2, 000	Wednesfield, Cradley, Harborne, Kings Norton, Moseley, Aston
2, 001-3, 000	Wolverhampton St John, Willenhall, Smethwick, Erdington
3, 001-4, 000	Darlaston, Walsall, Handsworth, Gornal, Kingswinford ? Brierley Hill ? Oldswinford
4, 001-5, 000	Oldbury (5, 000), Sedgley, Deritend
5, 001-6, 000	Wolverhampton St Peter, West Bromwich, Dudley, Birmingham St Philip, Birmingham St Thomas (6, 000)
6, 001-7, 000	Netherton
7, 001-8, 000	Wolverhampton St George (8, 000), Bilston, Rowley Regis, Birmingham St Martin
8, 001-9, 000	Wednesbury
9, 001-10, 000	Halesowen
Over 10, 000	Tipton, Birmingham St George, Duddeston

Table 11

Patrons of benfices in Birmingham and the Black Country 1835

Laymen		*Clergy*	
The Crown	Wednesbury	*Bishop of Lichfield*	*Bloxwich*
	Rowley Regis		*Birmingham ChristChurch*
			Birmingham St Philip
Earl of Dudley	Dudley		*Ashsted St James*
	Sedgley		
	Netherton	*Dean & C. of Worcester*	*Kings Norton*
	Gornal		*Moseley*
	Kingswinford		
	" St Mary	*Dean & C. of Lichfield*	*Harborne*
Lord Foley	Oldswinford		*Tipton*
Lord Lyttleton	Halesowen	*Dean of Windsor*	*Wolverhampton St Peter*
Earl of Stamford	Wolverhampton		
	St John		*" St George*
Earl of Bradford	Walsall St Matthew		
Earl of Dartmouth	West Bromwich,		
	All Saints	*Perp. Curate of Bilston*	*Bilston St Mary*
	" Christ Church		
Sir E D Scott	Aldridge with		
	Great Barr	*Vicar of Sedgely*	*Coseley*
Sir Robert Peel	Handsworth		
W Calthorpe	Edgbaston	*Rector of Kingswinford*	*Brierley Hill*
T Hill	Lye		
J Gough	Wednesfield	*Vicar of Halesowen*	*Oldbury*
E Latimer	Birmingham St Paul	*Rector of St Martin*	*Birmingham*
		Birmingham	*St Bartholemew*
Corporation			
Governors of QM			
Grammar School	Walsall St Paul	*Vicar of Aston*	*Erdington*
Trustees			
J Thornton	Darlaston		
(not named)	Cradley		
Dorothy Parkes	Smethwick		
Sir G Peake	Aston		
"	Bordesley Holy Trinity		
St Martins	Birmingham St Martin		
Birmingham	" St Mary		
"	" St Thomas		
"	" St George		
Inhabitants	Bilston		
	Willenhall		
	Stourbridge		
	Deritend St John		

Table 12

Place of birth shown as a percentage of population in each registration district 1851

District: / Place of Birth 1851	Wolverhampton	Walsall	West Bromwich	Dudley	Stourbridge	Kings Norton	Birmingham	Aston
Warwicks.	3.01	4.78	7.26	2.0	1.91	31.08	64.88	66.99
Worcs.	3.1	1.59	15.33	29.27	48.22	26.17	5.42	5.61
Staffs.	69.35	77.42	60.9	56.69	37.46	22.55	7.15	8.46
Salop.	10.5	3.53	4.21	4.47	5.34	2.91	2.21	1.89
Herefords.	0.5	0.19	0.69	0.54	0.92	1.2	0.96	0.79
Glos.	0.7	0.45	1.01	0.83	0.57	1.97	1.98	1.93
Leics.	0.34	1.45	0.71	0.24	0.16	0.75	0.88	1.27
Derbys.	0.47	1.18	0.62	0.37	0.25	0.62	0.73	1.04
London	0.86	0.84	0.79	0.43	0.52	1.99	2.28	1.83
Lancs.	0.76	0.51	0.57	0.35	0.37	1.13	1.07	0.95
Yorks.	0.38	0.38	0.4	0.27	0.21	0.63	0.84	0.77
Ireland	4.73	4.15	2.89	1.25	1.12	0.9	4.75	1.85
Wales	1.99	0.46	0.93	0.91	0.88	1.0	0.6	0.51
Scotland	0.26	0.39	0.2	0.25	0.15	0.55	0.47	0.38
Elsewhere	3.05	2.68	3.49	2.11	1.92	6.55	5.86	5.73

Table 13

Differences in total attendance between published census tables and original returns

Registration District	Published Tables	Original Returns	Difference
Wolverhampton	46, 983	51, 971	+4, 988
Walsall	19, 835	19, 378	- 457
West Bromwich	35, 591	36, 851	+1, 260
Dudley	71, 320	68, 578	-2, 742
Stourbridge	31, 325	31, 446	+121
Kings Norton	9, 551	9, 747	+196
Birmingham	66, 763	70, 179	+3, 416
Aston (including Erdington)	21, 519	19, 530	-1, 989

Table 15

Differences between census Sunday and average attendance in Anglican churches

Registration Sub-district	Church	Difference
Sedgley	Sedgley parish church	-430
	St James, Lower Gornal	-300
Dudley	St Thomas, Dudley	-660
	St Andrew, Netherton	-347
Willenhall	St Thomas, Willenhall	-329
Darlaston	St Lawrence, Darlaston	-835
Walsall	St Matthew, Walsall	-969
West Bromwich South-West	Holy Trinity, West Bromwich	-550
West Bromwich North-East	St James, West Bromwich	-420
Wednesbury	St Bartholemew, Wednesbury	-308
Stourbridge	Trinity, Amblecote	-504

Table 16

Indexes of attendance with and without Sunday school scholars

Sub-district	Population	Index of attendance	Index without Sunday scholars
Tettenhall	5, 624	51.16	42.17
Kinfare	4, 099	54.51	35.25
Womborne	4, 134	58.77	40.54
Wolverhampton West	17, 652	68.3	56.59
Woverhampton East	32, 333	38.48	33.6
Willenhall	16, 789	40.72	27.2
Bilston	23, 527	58.69	45.79
Darlaston	10, 970	54.85	39.82
Bloxwich	5, 609	43.03	28.75
Walsall	21, 203	41.14	28.35
Aldridge	5, 262	42.15	29.76
Handsworth	7, 879	49.2	43.29
Oldbury	12, 978	47.4	28.78
West Bromwich SW	17, 885	44.23	31.16
West Bromwich NE	16, 716	69.14	54.97
Wednesbury	14, 281	51.46	37.53
Rowley Regis	14, 249	79.44	55.7
Tipton	24, 872	59.76	44.48
Sedgley	29, 447	71.92	50.94
Dudley	37, 962	55.9	44.42
Halesowen	9, 811	68.46	43.17
Stourbridge	20, 238	54.1	38.64
Kingswinford	27, 301	50.46	36.15
Kings Norton	8, 413	35.58	27.02
Edgbaston	11, 729	22.87	17.64
Harborne	10, 729	37.91	30.99

Birmingham Sub-district	Population	Index of attendance	Index without Sunday scholars
Ladywood	20, 173	31.04	27.45
St Thomas	26, 445	28.04	23.24
St Martin	21, 586	36.81	32.28
St Peter	14, 365	63.04	52.96
St Philip	11, 087	85.03	67.83
St Paul	11, 783	25.76	18.8
St Mary	19, 684	64.48	59.85
St George	35, 240	31.54	23.78
All Saints	13, 588	21.73	17.36

Aston Sub-district	Population	Index of attendance	Index without Sunday scholars
Deritend & Bordesley	23, 173	37.09	29.8
Duddeston	26, 448	26.03	20.03

Consolidated Indexes	Population	Index of attendance	Index without Sunday scholars
Wolverhampton	49, 985	47.57	41.72
West Bromwich	34, 591	56.27	42.66
Birmingham + Deritend, Duddeston, Edgbaston & Kings Norton	243, 714	37.5	30.8

Table 17

Rank order of Black Country indexes of attendance

Sub-District	Index	Index without Sunday scholars	Revised Order
Rowley Regis	79.44	55.7	1
Sedgley	71.92	50.94	2
Halesowen	68.46	43.17	7
Tipton	59.76	44.48	4
Bilston	58.69	45.79	3
West Bromwich	56.27	42.66	8
Dudley	55.9	44.42	5
Darlaston	54.85	39.82	10
Stourbridge	54.1	38.64	11
Wednesbury	51.46	37.53	12
Kingswinford	50.46	36.15	13
Handsworth	49.2	43.29	6
Wolverhampton	47.57	41.72	9
Oldbury	47.4	28.78	15
Bloxwich	43.03	28.75	16
Aldridge	42.15	29.76	14
Walsall	41.14	28.35	17
Willenhall	40.72	27.2	18

Table 18

Percentage of Sunday scholars in attendance returns

Sub-District	%S.S.	Index	Revised Index	
Halesowen	36.94	68.46	43.17	
Bloxwich	33.18	43.03	28.75	
Willenhall	31.93	40.72	27.2	
Walsall	31.1	41.14	28.35	
Rowley Regis	29.89	79.44	55.7	
Aldridge	29.42	42.15	29.76	
Sedgley	29.16	71.92	50.94	
Stourbridge	28.58	54.1	38.64	
Kingswinford	28.34	50.46	36.15	
Darlaston	27.41	54.85	39.82	
Wednesbury	27.08	51.46	37.53	
B'ham St Paul	27.0	25.76	18.8	
Tipton	25.49	59.76	44.48	
B'ham St George	24.63	31.54	23.78	
West Bromwich	24.18	56.27	42.66	(consolidated NE + SW)
Kings Norton	24.04	35.58	27.02	
Duddeston & N'ls	23.09	26.03	20.03	
Edgbaston	22.87	22.87	17.64	
Bilston	21.96	58.69	45.79	
Dudley	20.55	55.9	44.42	
B'ham St Philip	20.23	85.03	67.83	
B'ham All Saints	20.16	21.73	17.36	
Deritend & B'dsley	19.66	37.09	29.8	
Harborne	18.28	37.91	30, 99	
B'ham St Thomas	17.14	28.04	23.24	
B'ham St Peter	15.81	63.04	52.96	
B'ham St Martin	12.32	36.81	32.28	
Wolverhampton	12.29	47.57	41.72	(consolidated E + W)
Handsworth	12.13	49.2	43.29	
B'ham St Mary	9.14	64.48	59.85	

Table 19

Provision of accommodation for worship as a percentage of population
***Decennial population growth as a percentage**

Sub-district	1801	1811	%*	1821	%*	1831	%*	1841	%*	1851	%*
Tettenhall	47.8	41.7	14.5	35.1	18.9	35.2	14.3	31.8	10.5	37.9	9.4
Kinfare	60.7	61.9	-1.5	62.9	6.8	63.9	1.8	60.3	13.7	50.2	19.2
Womborne	62.8	60.9	3.1	58.0	15.7	52.5	10.4	53.3	5.8	51.1	11.3
Wolverhampton East + West	41.1	34.8	18.1	32.9	23.9	35.3	34.5	31.4	47.1	39.2	37.4
Willenhall	34.5	30.6	12.8	43.8	13.9	30.9	42.0	24.7	53.8	39.2	41.5
Bilston	48.4	34.7	39.5	27.9	24.4	27.8	20.7	31.9	39.2	36.6	16.6
Darlaston	35.8	42.1	27.5	36.9	14.0	32.6	18.8	44.3	32.9	41.8	26.5
Bloxwich	38.4	36.3	5.8	31.4	15.6	23.7	32.6	29.8	52.3	41.0	16.2
Walsall	38.9	38.5	7.5	36.7	4.9	45.5	24.4	38.6	34.0	41.0	32.0
Aldridge	39.6	35.0	13.2	34.3	2.0	30.8	11.2	32.5	54.3	37.9	12.0
Handsworth	78.7	74.8	11.3	60.0	27.5	45.8	28.1	41.8	24.1	44.6	28.4
Oldbury	13.6	26.1	15.2	26.2	18.4	24.9	17.0	31.2	34.3	43.5	49.3
West Bromwich SW + NE	55.9	46.5	31.6	36.6	27.0	25.5	61.2	21.6	70.4	39.4	32.4
Wednesbury	33.6	26.0	29.1	35.1	20.4	32.5	30.4	30.3	37.8	52.6	22.8
Rowley Regis	39.8	40.2	-1.0	37.9	21.9	44.6	22.7	45.4	49.4	55.1	28.2
Tipton	56.6	44.8	96.4	37.8	37.3	43.6	29.5	44.0	26.4	42.1	28.4
Sedgley	45.2	43.8	41.1	42.2	23.4	39.7	19.7	54.0	20.6	49.5	18.6
Dudley	41.8	33.2	37.8	42.1	31.5	49.2	25.8	44.4	35.5	44.2	21.5
Halesowen	67.0	83.4	16.0	73.2	14.0	69.7	17.5	63.7	36.2	59.8	21.0
Stourbridge	35.2	46.0	16.2	39.1	17.8	39.2	23.6	48.8	26.6	50.1	15.0
Kingswinford	45.1	38.8	28.0	34.1	33.3	46.7	37.5	41.4	46.6	46.4	22.9
Harborne	50.5	44.0	14.8	41.0	28.2	52.4	26.2	49.7	57.5	37.9	61.2
Kings Norton	58.3	58.9	8.8	59.5	14.8	54.9	8.4	47.1	33.5	37.1	35.5
Edgbaston	31.6	29.4	7.3	21.1	37.8	13.4	58.1	25.3	51.3	14.0	33.1
Birmingham	19.7	21.6	15.4	22.4	21.6	29.0	29.8	30.4	24.6	30.2	25.8
Aston (includes Erdington)	33.7	35.1	22.9	29.1	33.6	26.9	67.4	20.4	42.3	25.6	34.0

Table 20

Percentage of the population which could be accommodated by the Church of England decennially with 1851 Index of attendance, Free Church equivalents shown in Italics

Sub-district	1801	1811	1821	1831	1841	1851	Index of attendance
Wolverhampton	25.9	22.0	17.7	22.5	19.1	22.1	27.6
	2.0	*1.7*	*6.1*	*6.2*	*8.7*	*14.2*	*15.7*
Willenhall	34.5	30.6	26.9	18.9	13.2	12.9	15.6
	0	*0*	*3.3*	*2.3*	*7.4*	*12.7*	*25.1*
Bilston	14.5	10.4	8.3	19.5	14.0	13.3	18.2
	35.4	*25.4*	*20.4*	*16.9*	*14.9*	*20.6*	*34.4*
Darlaston	28.1	22.1	19.3	16.3	12.7	13.7	18.1
	7.7	*8.0*	*27.2*	*22.9*	*32.8*	*27.2*	*36.7*
Bloxwich	38.4	36.5	31.4	23.7	15.5	24.6	18.1
	0	*0*	*0*	*0*	*14.3*	*17.3*	*25.0*
Walsall	28.4	26.4	25.2	25.3	18.8	16.8	15.2
	10.5	*9.8*	*9.3*	*12.7*	*17.8*	*14.4*	*16.9*
Aldridge	39.6	35.0	34.3	30.9	30.6	27.3	28.1
	0	*0*	*0*	*0*	*3.0*	*10.7*	*14.1*
Handsworth	53.3	47.9	37.6	29.3	41.5	32.4	39.3
	21.3	*23.3*	*18.3*	*14.2*	*11.5*	*10.8*	*8.3*
Oldbury	6.3	5.4	4.6	3.9	17.3	12.9	7.8
	13.6	*26.1*	*26.2*	*24.9*	*34.3*	*31.4*	*39.6*
West Bromwich	17.2	13.1	10.3	14.1	11.9	12.8	19.2
	56.3	*42.7*	*33.7*	*23.7*	*19.1*	*18.3*	*34.7*
Wednesbury	33.6	26.1	21.6	16.6	13.8	29.2	24.3
	0	*16.2*	*13.4*	*15.9*	*16.5*	*23.4*	*27.2*
Rowley Regis	39.8	40.2	33.0	26.9	18.0	22.8	24.2
	0	*0*	*0*	*9.4*	*20.5*	*32.3*	*55.2*
Tipton	35.6	18.5	13.2	10.2	15.3	14.1	12.2
	21.0	*32.0*	*28.5*	*27.1*	*30.5*	*28.0*	*47.5*
Sedgley	13.3	9.9	12.8	18.5	22.8	20.4	16.6
	22.6	*25.0*	*22.3*	*21.6*	*27.6*	*27.3*	*52.4*
Dudley	18.0	13.1	13.2	17.5	18.2	15.0	13.3
	37.4	*28.6*	*25.6*	*29.6*	*26.9*	*29.4*	*38.5*
Halesowen	54.0	46.6	40.8	34.8	33.0	27.3	25.2
	17.7	*36.9*	*32.3*	*35.1*	*30.7*	*32.6*	*43.2*
Stourbridge	29.2	25.1	21.3	17.3	19.3	23.3	20.8
	6.0	*21.6*	*17.4*	*23.0*	*28.2*	*25.3*	*29.6*
Kingswinford	41.1	32.2	24.1	26.1	18.9	24.4	20.9
	7.1	*9.1*	*11.8*	*21.9*	*23.4*	*22.0*	*29.5*

Harborne	25.5	44.0	34.3	27.2	29.1	19.9	21.4
	0	*0*	*6.7*	*25.2*	*20.2*	*19.4*	*16.5*
Kings Norton	49.6	45.6	39.7	36.6	27.4	20.2	17.1
	8.7	*13.4*	*19.8*	*18.3*	*19.6*	*16.9*	*18.4*
Edgbaston	31.6	29.4	21.1	13.4	22.1	16.6	20.9
	0	*0*	*0*	*0*	*3.3*	*2.4*	*2.0*
Birmingham	12.8	13.6	11.2	14.3	14.6	13.0	17.5
	6.3	*6.3*	*7.5*	*14.9*	*15.0*	*16.0*	*18.7*
Deritend & Bordesley					11.9	13.6	18.3
					9.1	*10.3*	*10.8*
Duddeston & Nechells					10.0	7.6	10.0
					13.1	*11.2*	*16.0*

This Table understates the provision of Free Church places of worship up to 1831 and possibly beyond. The 1851 returns only occasionally indicate a chapel closed for worship, for example, Temple Street Independent chapel in Wolverhampton whose congregation had moved to Snow Hill, built in 1849, and the Countess of Huntingdon's chapel in Birmingham already mentioned. The rebuilding of many non-conformist chapels on the sites of earlier buildings means that the 1851 returns, whilst correctly indicating the date when the new building was opened, do not usually say when the former building was built, still less its seating capacity. There is no doubt, for example, that Methodism was established in Wednesbury before 1800, as it was the scene of anti-Methodist riots in 1743, but the returns give 1810 as the date of the oldest Wesleyan chapel still open in 1851. Hence the 'nil-return' for non-conformity in Wednesbury, as in other places, must be treated with considerable caution.

Table 21

Presence of Methodism as a factor in overall church attendance in 1851

Sub-District	Attendance	Methodists	Without Methodists	Index	Revised Index
Wolverhampton East + West	23, 781	4, 796	18, 984	47.57	37.9
Willenhall	6, 840	3, 736	3, 104	40.72	18.48
Bilston	13, 804	6, 318	7, 486	58.69	31.81
Darlaston	6, 019	3, 945	2, 074	54.85	18.9
Bloxwich	2, 414	1, 400	1, 014	43.03	18.07
Walsall	8, 726	1, 753	6, 973	41.14	32.88
Aldridge	2, 219	610	1, 609	42.15	30.57
Handsworth	3, 882	220	3, 662	49.2	46.48
Oldbury	6, 155	3, 835	2, 320	47.4	17.87
West Bromwich SW + NE	19, 463	8, 417	11, 046	56.26	31.93
Wednesbury	7, 351	3, 016	4, 335	51.46	30.35
Rowley Regis	11, 322	6, 353	4, 969	79.44	34.87
Tipton	14, 851	9, 441	5, 410	59.76	21.75
Sedgley	21, 180	10, 806	10, 374	71.92	35.23
Dudley	21, 225	10, 185	11, 040	55.9	29.08
Halesowen	6, 718	2, 589	4, 129	68.46	42.08
Stourbridge	10, 952	4, 334	6, 618	54.1	32.7
Kingswinford	13, 766	7, 264	6, 512	50.46	23.85
Harborne	4, 069	1, 033	3, 036	37.91	28.3
Birmingham	70, 179	9, 553	60, 646	40.34	34.86
Edgbaston	2, 684	234	2, 450	22.87	20.88
Kings Norton	2, 994	543	2, 451	35.58	29.13
Deritend	8, 598	883	7, 715	37.09	33.29
Duddeston	6, 889	1, 781	5, 108	26.03	19.31

Correlation co-efficients for the Birmingham area (with only five entries so statistically questionable) and the Black Country (nineteen entries so statistically valid) bear out the relative importance of Methodism as a factor. In the Birmingham area the correlation between the original and revised Indexes (ie with Methodists removed) is r = 0.951982, that is hardly any difference. In the Black Country r = 0.608835, that is a considerable difference. In Willenhall, Bilston, Darlaston, Bloxwich, Oldbury, West Bromwich, Wednesbury, Rowley Regis, Tipton, Sedgley, Dudley, Halseowen, Stourbridge and Kingswinford Methodism made over 20% difference to the Index.

Table 22

Anglican churches in the Black Country built before and after 1821

Sub-district	pre 1821	% full in 1851	post 1821	% full in 1851
Willenhall	2	31.5	3	30.1
Bilston	1	27.9	2	77.2
Walsall	1	22.1	2	16.1
Handsworth	1	58.6	2	50.9
Wednesbury	1	35.3	3	15.2
Tipton	2	46.8	2	33.8
Sedgley	2	45.7	3	18.0
Dudley	2	44.6	3	17.2
Stourbridge	2	43.0	2	22.6
Kingswinford	2	19.5	5	12.8

Table 23

Denominational and occupational pattern, Birmingham and the Black Country

Rank Order of Index	Attendance as % of 1851 population			Occupation as % of 1841 population					
	C of E	Nonconformist	Methodist	Mining	Nail	Manufacture	Labour	Trade	Domestic Service
Sedgley	16.6	52.4	36.7	7.8	2.4	8.4	6.4	2.0	2.1
Tipton	12.2	47.5	38.0	6.9	1.4	10.3	6.0	1.4	2.8
Bilston	18.2	34.4	26.8	13.3	0.005	13.0	4.8	1.6	3.8
West Brom.	19.2	34.7	24.3	5.8	1.5	14.2	4.0	1.5	3.6
Dudley	13.3	38.5	26.8	6.5	5.7	15.8	3.1	2.3	3.4
Stourbridge	20.8	29.5	21.4	2.0	2.04	19.3	2.5	3.0	4.6
Kingswinford	20.9	29.6	26.6	6.8	1.4	10.9	4.8	1.2	2.8
Wolverh'pton	27.6	17.5	9.6	5.6	0.1	16.6	3.8	2.5	5.1
Walsall+Blxwch	15.8	18.6	11.7	4.3	0.4	17.1	2.7	2.3	4.9
Birmingham	17.0	15.8	5.3	0.2	0.24	21.9	1.9	2.9	4.1

Table 24

Watts' church attendance Index for registration districts surrounding the conurbation

County	District	Church of England	Methodist	Independent and Baptist	Total Nonconformist
Salop.	Bridgnorth	32.8	2.5	2.8	5.4
	Shifnal	22.5	6.5	3.9	10.4
	Cleobury	30.3	5.9	0.1	6.0
Staffs.	Penkridge	21.2	7.1	2.8	10.5
	Lichfield	28.5	4.2	2.3	6.4
	Tamworth	28.5	3.7	3.7	7.6
Warwick	Meriden	21.2	2.2	2.7	4.9
	Solihull	32.0	0.5	2.1	2.6
	Alcester	20.3	4.8	9.7	15.7
Worcs.	Kidderminster	22.8	9.7	3.3	15.3
	Bromsgrove	26.6	10.2	4.8	15.0
	Droitwich	25.9	2.2	1.1	4.8

Table 25

Educational provision 1851, Black Country and Birmingham registration districts

District:	Wolverhampton	Walsall	West Bromwich	Dudley	Stourbridge	Kings Norton	Birmingham	Aston
Pop. below 20	55,989	22,574	34,880	52,131	28,751	17,079	94,964	35,812
Day School nos.	8,978	4,650	6,450	9,962	7,507	3,266	18,063	5,853
Private school %	27.0	41.3	30.4	38.7	37.3	42.1	39.0	43.6
Endowed etc.%	4.6	5.1	0.8	10.1	6.7	9.9	10.7	2.8
Denom. day nos.	6,101	2,462	4,432	4,841	4,203	1,152	7,924	3,097
%pop. below 20	10.9	10.9	12.7	9.3	14.6	6.7	8.4	8.6
Denom.% C of E	68.6	66.4	55.5	71.0	86.6	77.2	60.8	70.2
Nonconf + British	15.4	22.4	43.8	26.4	11.5	22.8	22.7	20.3
Sunday Schools Total numbers:	13,072	5,495	11,012	19,262	9,679	3,163	17,092	5,483
%pop. below 20	23.3	24.2	31.6	36.9	33.7	18.5	18.0	15.3
Denom. % C of E	36.9	36.3	33.0	21.0	39.4	45.7	40.8	41.9
Nonconformist	57.3	59.8	66.05	77.8	58.9	52.5	55.6	58.1

Table 27

Cholera mortality 1849 and church attendance 1851

District	Cholera deaths	1851 population	mortality	Index of attendance
Wolverhampton	1365	104, 158	1.31%	49.89
Walsall	186	43, 044	0.43%	45.02
West Bromwich	250	69, 729	0.36%	52.85
Dudley	412	106, 530	0.37%	64.37
Stourbridge	314	57, 350	0.55%	54.83
Kings Norton	7	30, 871	0.02%	31.37
Birmingham	29	173, 951	0.02%	40.34
Aston	6	66, 852	0.01%	32.18

Table 28

Incidence of cholera in 1849 compared with church attendance in 1851

Sub-district	Deaths	%Mortality	Rank Order	Index	Rank Order
Wolverhampton	464	1.27	4	47.57	13
Willenhall	281*	2.36	2	40.72	18
Bilston	612	3.03	1	58.69	5
Darlaston	44	0.5	10	54.85	8
Bloxwich	1	0.02	17	43.03	15
Walsall	138	0.85	6	41.14	17
Aldridge	3	0.06	16	42.15	16
Handsworth	1	0.01	18	49.2	12
Oldbury	16	0.18	12	47.4	14
West Bromwich	21	0.08	14	56.26	6
Wednesbury	212	1.82	3	51.46	9
Rowley Regis	14	0.12	13	79.44	1
Tipton	112	0.59	8	59.76	4
Sedgley	202	0.81	7	71.92	2
Dudley	84	0.26	11	55.9	7
Halesowen	7	0.08	15	68.46	3
Stourbridge	95	0.53	9	54.1	10
Kingswinford	212	0.95	5	50.46	11
Harborne	0	0.0	19	37.91	19

Table 29

1832 Cholera Mortality according to Girdlestone and Creighton

Place	Girdlestone	Creighton
Bilston	750	693
Tipton	404	281
Sedgley	290	231
Dudley	277	77
Wolverhampton	193	193
Wednesbury	95	78
Kingswinford	87	83
Walsall	85	77
Darlaston	68	57
West Bromwich	62	59
Willenhall	8	
Oldbury	37	
Birmingham	21	

Table 30

Cholera mortality in 1832 compared with 1851 Index of Attendance

Place	Cholera deaths	Mortality	Rank order	Index	Rank order
Bilston	742	5.12%	1	58.69	4
Tipton	350	2.34%	2	59.76	3
Sedgley	290	1.41%	3	71.92	2
Dudley	277	1.2%	4	55.9	6
Wednesbury	78	0.92%	5	51.46	9
Darlaston	57	0.84%	6	54.85	7
Wolverhampton	193	0.78%	7	47.57	11
Rowley Regis	55	0.73%	8	79.44	1
Walsall	77	0.64%	9	41.14	13
Oldbury	37	0.57%	10	47.4	12
Kingswinford	83	0.54%	11	50.46	10
Stourbridge	47	0.41%	12	54.1	8
West Bromwich	59	0.38%	13	56.26	5
Willenhall	8	0.1%	14	40.72	14

Table 31

Percentage rise and fall of Methodist circuit membership 1832-35

Circuit	1831	1832	1833	1834	1835
a) Wesleyan					
West Bromwich	242=100%	296+22%	438+80%	405+67%	466+92%
Wednesbury	1530=100%	1525-1%	2832+85%	2626+71%	2540+66%
Wolverhampton	625=100%	660+5%	1007+61%	1002+60%	1010+61%
Dudley	1750=100%	1790+2%	2550+45%	2164+23%	600-66%
Stourbridge	780=100%	728-7%	822+5%	830+6%	1013+29%
Aggregate					
Wesleyan	4147=100%	4999+20%	7649+84%	7027+69%	5629+13%
b) Primitive					
Darlaston	1283=100%	1181-8%	1200-7%	1076-17%	1120-13%
Dudley			700=100%	617-12%	585-17%
Aggregate					
Primitive	1283=100%	1181-8%	1900+48%	1693+31%	1705+32%
c) MNC					
Dudley		224=100%	500+123%	320+42%	335+49%
Aggregate					
Methodist	5430=100%	6404+18%	10, 049+85%	9040+66.5%	7669+41%

Table 32

Percentage rise and fall of Methodist circuit membership 1848-52

Circuit	1848	1849	1850	1851	1852
a) Wesleyan					
West Bromwich	707=100%	783+10%	750+6%	662-7%	637-10%
Wednesbury	2272=100%	2577+13%	2900+27%	2401+5%	2064-10%
Wolverhampton	1322=100%	1412+6%	1640+24%	1519+14%	1329+.05%
Dudley	1588=100%	1757+10%	2062+29%	1748+10%	1651+4%
Stourbridge	617=100%	603-3%	793+28%	714+15%	650+5%
Walsall	796=100%	774-3%	884+11%	774-3%	694-13%
Aggregate					
Wesleyan	7302=100%	7906+8%	9029+23%	7818+7%	7025-4%
b) Primitive					
Darlaston	1490=100%	1900+27%	1617+8%	1617+8%	1548+3%
West Bromwich			1100=100%	1021-8%	1000-10%
Dudley	1320=100%	1620+22%	1150-13%	1160-13%	1012-10%
Brierley Hill			1230=100%	1049-15%	930-25%
Aggregate					
Primitive	2810=100%	3520+25%	5097+81%	4847+72%	4490+59%
c) MNC					
Dudley	1348=100%	1418+5%	2118+57%	1793+33%	1618+20%
Stourbridge	404=100%	410+.01%	600+48%	430+6%	390-4%
Wolverhampton	180=100%	210+16%	303+68%	296+64%	226+25%
Aggregate MNC	1932 " "	2038+5%	3021+56%	2519+30%	2234+15%
Aggregate					
Methodist	12, 044 " "	13, 464+12%	17, 167+42%	15, 164 +26%	13, 749+14%

Table 33

Percentage rise and fall of Methodist membership 1832-35

Connexion	1831	1832	1833	1834	1835
a) Wesleyan					
Black Country	4147=100%	4999+20%	7649+84%	7027+69%	5629+13%
Birmingham	1940=100%	1919-10%	1993+3%	2190+13%	2388+23%
England		+3%	+12%	+17%	+16%
b) Primitive					
Black Country	1283=100%	1181-8%	1900+48%	1693+31%	1705+32%
Birmingham	300=100%	440+46%	550+83%	567+89%	667+122%
England		+11%	+30%	+39%	+52%
c) MNC					
Black Country		224=100%	500+123%	320+42%	335+49%
Birmingham	164=100%	186+13%	206+25%	247+50%	267+63%
England		+3.5%	+21%	+26%	+46%
Aggregate Methodist					
Black Country	5430=100%	6404+18%	10, 049+85%	9040+66.5%	7669+41%
Birmingham	2404=100%	2545+6%	2749+14%	3004+25%	3322+38%
England		+4%	+14%	+20%	+22%

Table 34

Percentage rise and fall of Methodist membership 1848-52

Connexion	1848	1849	1850	1851	1852
a) Wesleyan					
Black Country	7302=100%	7906+8%	9029+23%	7818+7%	7025+4%
Birmingham	3625=100%	3601-1%	3364-7%	2633-27%	2490-31%
England		+2.5%	+5%	-12%	-19%
b) Primitive					
Black Country	2810=100%	3520+25%	5097+81%	4847+72%	4490+59%
Birmingham	500=100%	600+20%	330-34%	359-28%	388-23%
England		+7%	+17%	+21%	+22%
c) MNC					
Black Country	1932=100%	2038+5%	3021+56%	2519+30%	2234+15%
Birmingham	247=100%	254+3%	256+3%	282+14%	271+10%
England		+4%	+13%	+9%	+6%
<u>Aggregate Methodist</u>					
Black Country	12, 044=100%	13, 464+12%	17, 167+42%	15, 164+26%	13, 749+14%
Birmingham	4, 372=100%	4, 455+2%	3, 950-10%	3, 274-25%	3, 149-28%
England		+3.5%	+8%	-3.5%	-8%

Table 35

Dudley Wesleyan circuit membership 1832-34

Society	June'32	Dec.'32	Sept.'33	Dec.'33	Dec.'34	%gain
Dudley	539	728	619	610	516	-4.3
Tipton	357	450	405	406	370	+3.6
Oldbury	175	249	254	260	246	+40.6
Dudley Port	65	129	80	78	72	+10.8
Bloomfield	58	126	115	110	90	+55.2
Darby Hand	132	278	185	175	141	+6.8
Woodside	69	123	120	122	80	+15.9
Netherton	93	136	115	95	92	-1.1
Dudley Wood	49	85	70	75	66	+34.7
Commonside	41	61	63	58	50	+21.9
Coseley	59	98	78	75	58	-1.7
Gornal	56	93	100	88	91	+62.5
Gornal Wood	45	63	64	61	50	+11.1
Rowley	19	26	25	24	19	no change
Old Hill	21	28	25	23	24	+14.3
Tividale	11	30	23	24	20	+81.8

Table 36

Dudley Wesleyan circuit membership 1849-51

Society	Mar.'49	Sep.'49	Dec.'49	Mar.'50	Mar.'51	%gain
Dudley	408	426	447	462	365	-10.5
Tipton	446	420	451	460	381	-14.6
Oldbury	142	135	137	142	109	-23.2
Bloomfield	147	157	146	150	135	-8.2
Dudley Port	45	40	49	53	45	no change
Darby Hand	90	87	82	101	108	+20.0
Dudley Wood	76	68	72	88	79	+3.9
Woodside	55	82	89	106	94	+70.9
Gornal	53	53	58	65	54	+1.8
Gornal Wood	68	94	129	110	101	+48.5
Coseley	45	55	61	102	65	+44.4
Mamble Sq.	73	64	86	108	86	+17.8
Pensnett	61	55	68	72	48	-21.3
Tividale	23	24	27	27	21	-8.7
Churchbridge	20	18	17	17	12	-40.0
Hill Top	5	5	4	4	5	no change

Table 37

Wolverhampton Wesleyan circuit membership 1849-51

Society	Mar.'49	Sep.'49	Dec.'49	Mar.'50	Mar.'51	%Gain
Wolverhampton	461	459	468	463	475	+3.0
Bilston	359	390	487	470	349	-2.8
Ettingshall	166	164	204	230	173	+4.2
Can Lane	130	139	141	126	102	-21.5
Wednesfield	30	44	40	48	52	+73.3
Tettenhall Wd	16	15	18	26	18	+12.7
Coven	26	23	24	25	27	+3.8
Lanesfield	31	60	78	84	77	+148.4
Gospel End	25	35	33	26	20	-13.0
Ladymoor	23	31	42	38	30	+30.4
Blakenall	46	40	59	63	43	-6.5
Sedgley	17	15	19	19	22	+29.4
Monmore Grn	30	44	59	72	53	+76.6
Wednsf'd Hth	46	38	32	59	48	+4.3
Codsall	6	6	7	7	7	+16.6
Willenhall*	197	no entry	226	no entry	206	+4.6

* part of the Walsall circuit

Table 38

Numbers of Anglican churches and clergy, including additional curates, 1835-50

District	'35 Churches	Clergy	'45 Churches	Clergy	'50 Churches	Clergy	'51 Index	
Wolverhampton	3	5	6	9	8	17	27.6	
Willenhall + W'fld.	2	3	2	2	5	4	15.6	
Bilston	2	2	2	2	3	5	18.2	
Darlaston	1	2	1	2	2	2	18.1	
Bloxwich + Pelsall	2	2	2	3	2	4	18.1	
Walsall	2	3	2	3	3	5	15.2	
Aldridge	3	3	4	4	4	4	28.1	
Handsworth	1	2	3	3	3	6	39.3	
Oldbury	1	1	1	2	2	3	7.8	
West Bromwich	2	3	4	4	4	6	19.2	
Wednesbury	1	1	3	5	4	5	24.3	
Rowley Regis	1	1	1	1	2	4	24.2	
Tipton	1	2	2	3	3	3	12.2	
Sedgley	3	4	5	5	5	6	16.6	
Dudley	3	5	5	5	5	7	13.9	
Halesowen	2	3	3	5	3	4	25.3	
Stourbridge	3	4	4	4	4	6	20.9	
Kingswinford	3	5	3	6	6	8	20.9	
Harborne	2	3	3	6	3	6	21.4	
Kings Norton	4	2	4	4	4	5	17.1	
Edgbaston	2	2	4	7	4	5	20.9	
Birmingham	8	16	12	21	15	28	17.6	
Deritend	2	3	2	3	3	5	18.4	
Duddeston	1	1	2	3	2	3	10.0	
Total Black Country	38	54	56	74	71	105	19.6	34.9
Total Birmingham	17	24	24	38	28	46	17.0	20.3

Table 39

Denominational Indexes of attendance 1851

District	C of E	WM	MNC	PM	Total. Mdst.	Ind.	Bapt.	Other	RC
Wolverhampton	27.6	7.1	0.8	1.7	9.6	4.0	1.3	2.6	4.2
Willenhall	15.6	16.5	1.1	4.6	22.2	-	2.9	-	-
Bilston	18.2	14.8	2.8	9.4	26.8	2.7	3.5	1.3	6.1
Darlaston	18.1	17.2	-	18.7	36.0	0.8	-	-	-
Bloxwich	18.1	15.4	-	9.5	25.0	-	-	-	-
Aldridge	28.1	4.6	0.5*	6.5	11.6	2.4	-	-	-
Walsall	15.2	7.6	-	0.6	8.3	3.3	5.3	-	9.1
Handsworth	39.3	2.8	-	-	2.8	5.5	-	-	1.7
Oldbury	7.8	8.1	8.1	13.3	29.5	5.4	2.5	2.2	-
West Bromwich	19.2	14.0	1.6	8.7	24.3	7.2	2.4	0.7	2.3
Wednesbury	24.3	14.3	3.9	2.9	21.1	2.6	3.4	-	-
Rowley Regis	24.2	2.6	12.0	29.9	44.6	-	10.6	-	-
Tipton	12.2	21.8	6.2	9.8	38.0	5.1	2.8	1.6	-
Sedgley	16.6	22.5	8.5	5.8	36.7	4.0	10.0	1.8	2.8
Dudley	13.9	9.0	10.8	6.7	26.8	3.4	5.2	3.1	3.5
Halesowen	25.3	6.9	4.8	14.6	26.4	9.4	3.8	3.6	-
Stourbridge	20.9	6.6	9.6	5.1	21.4	4.7	1.3	2.1	3.7
Kingswinford	20.9	9.4	7.4	9.8	26.6	2.1	0.7	0.2	-
Harborne	21.4	8.7	-	0.9	9.6	5.6	1.0	0.2	-
Total Black Country	19.6	11.6	4.7	7.5	23.8	3.8	3.4	1.4	2.5
Kings Norton	17.1	3.1	0.8	2.8	6.5	-	7.7	4.1	-
Edgbaston	20.9	-	1.0*	0.9	1.9	-	-	-	-
Birmingham	17.6	3.6	0.7*	0.5	5.5	4.3	3.9	4.9	4.0
Deritend & Bordesley	18.4	3.8	-	-	3.8	3.0	3.2	0.8	7.9
Duddeston & Nechells	10.0	4.8	1.1*	0.8	6.7	0.8	8.4	-	-
Total Birmingham area	17.0	3.5	1.2*	0.6	5.3	3.5	4.2	3.7	3.6

Notes: 'Others' includes Unitarians, Quakers, Countess of Huntingdon's Connexion, Mormons, Brethren, Catholic Apostolic Church and other smaller groups.

* indicates a smaller Methodist body, Independent Methodists at Aldridge, Wesleyan Methodist Association in Edgbaston, WMA +MNC in Birmingham. Wesleyan Reformers in Birmingham and Duddeston.

These have been added to the Total Methodist column.

Bibliography

Primary Sources

Manuscript

BIRMINGHAM ROMAN CATHOLIC ARCHDIOCESE, OSCOTT COLLEGE ARCHIVES
Autobiographical recollections of James Plunkett

BIRMINGHAM REFERENCE LIBRARY
Carrs Lane deposit; Vols. 61-75, Journals of Carrs Lane Town Missionaries
Methodist Central Hall deposit:
> Cherry Street Wesleyan Church, Leaders Meeting and Tract Society minutes
> Cherry Street West Wesleyan Circuit, Quarterly and Local Preachers' Meeting minutes
> Belmont Row East Wesleyan Circuit, Quarterly Meeting minutes

Duddeston-cum-Nechells Radical Reform Society minutes
Thomas Augustine Finegan, Birmingham Town Mission, manuscript journal
Town Book of St. Martins and St. Philips

DUDLEY ARCHIVES AND LOCAL HISTORY SERVICES, COSELEY
Brierley Hill Primitive Methodist Circuit, Quarterly and Local Preachers' Meeting minutes
Dudley Wesleyan Methodist Circuit Book
Sedgley Benevolent Visiting Society ledger

FOUR WAYS BAPTIST CHURCH, CRADLEY HEATH
Church Meeting minute book

MANCHESTER JOHN RYLANDS UNIVERSITY LIBRARY
Methodist Central Archives, journals and correspondence of Wesleyan itinerant preachers et.al.

OFFICE FOR NATIONAL STATISTICS, LONDON
Registrar's Notes

ORDER OF PASSIONISTS, ST. JOSEPH'S HOUSE. HIGHGATE, LONDON
Father Ignatius Spencer, journal and private papers

PUBLIC RECORD OFFICE, KEW
Home Office Papers, HO 40/50, Spies reports on Birmingham Chartism
HO 129, Original returns for 1851 census of religious worship

SANDWELL ARCHIVES AND LOCAL HISTORY SERVICES, SMETHWICK
Rowley Regis parish records

STAFFORDSHIRE RECORD OFFICE, STAFFORD
Hatherton papers

WALSALL REFERENCE LIBRARY
Darlaston Primitive Methodist Circuit, Quarterly Meeting minutes and
   membership rolls

WILLENHALL METHODIST CHURCH
Register of collections

WOLVERHAMPTON ARCHIVES AND LOCAL STUDIES CENTRE
Darlington Street Methodist Church deposit; Wolverhampton Wesleyan
   Circuit Book
Lloyd Clerical Meeting, minutes
William Dalton, manuscript sermons

Printed (place of publication is London unless otherwise stated)

OFFICIAL PUBLICATIONS
Clergy Lists
G. Graham, *Registrar General's Report on the mortality of cholera in England,*
   1848-49 (HMSO, 1852)
Minutes of the Committee of Council on Education (HMSO, 1846)
Parliamentry Debates, Vol. CXXV, House of Lords (HMSO, 1854)
Parliamentary Papers, HMSO, 1835, XXII, First Report of the Ecclesiastical
   Commission
   – *1838, VI, Select Committee on the Education of the Poorer Classes*
   – *1842, XVII, First Report of the Children's Employment Commission, Appendix,*
   Mines (J. Mitchell)
   – *1843, XIII, Second Report of the Children's Employment Commission*
   (R.H. Horne)
   – *1843, XIV, Second Report of the Children's Employment Commission*
   (R.D. Grainger)
   – *1843, XXIII, First Report of the Midland Mining Commission* (T. Tancred)
   – *1844, XXVII, Occupational Abstract, 1841 Census*
   – *1850, XXIII, Second Report of the Midland Mining Commission*
   (S. Tremenheere)
   – *1852-3, LXXXV, Population Tables, 1851 Census*
   – *1852-3, XC, Education Tables, 1851 Census*
   – *1853, LXXXIX, Report on the Census of Religious Worship, 1851* (H. Mann)
   – *1854, XXXV, Report of the Cholera Inquiry Commissioners,*
   Newcastle upon Tyne

NEWSPAPERS (Place of publication in title)
Aris's Birmingham Gazette
Birmingham Daily News
Birmingham Journal
Wolverhampton Chronicle

PERIODICALS
Arminian Magazine
Catholic Magazine (Birmingham and London)
Congregational Magazine
Primitive Methodist Magazine (Bemersley and London)

Wesleyan Methodist Magazine

OTHER WORKS

Anon. *Some Papers giving an account of the Rise and Progress of Methodism in Wednesbury in Staffordshire and other parishes adjacent* (J. Roberts, 1744)

Anon. *Voluntaryism in England and Wales; or the Census of 1851* (Liberation Society, 1854)

W. Antcliff *A Book of Marvels* (Primitive Methodist Bookroom, 1874)

J. Arch *The Story of my Life* (1898) re-issue *Autobiography of Joseph Arch* (McGibbon & Kee, 1966)

A.M. Banks (Ed.) *The Diary of Julius Hardy, Button-maker of Birmingham* (privately printed, 1973)

S. Baring Gould *The Vicar of Morwenstow, being a life of Robert Stephen Hawker, M.A.* (Methuen, 1876, 9th edn, 1929)

D. Barr *Climbing the Ladder* (Robert Culley, 1910)

F.W.G. Barrs *Four Sermons by the late Rev. George Barrs* (Hall & English, Birmingham, 2nd. edn, 1879)

J.G. Brooks *Memoir of J.G. Brooks* (W. Grew & Son, Birmingham, 1854)

C. Campbell *The Marriage Vow* (Nisbet & Co, 1840)

S. Coley *Life of Thomas Collins* (Hamilton Adams, 1868)

A.W.W. Dale *Life of R.W. Dale of Birmingham* (Hodder & Stoughton, 1898)

R.W. Dale *Life and Letters of J. Angell James* (James Nisbet, 1861, 4th edition 1862)

C. Dickens *Hard Times* (Household Words, Bradbury & Evans, 1854)

B. Disraeli *Sybil or The Two Nations* (Henry Colburn, 1845, David Bryce, revised edition, 1853, standard edition, Longman, 1870)

G. Eliot *Scenes of Clerical Life* (William Blackwood, 1857)

G. Eliot *Adam Bede* (Blackwood, 1859)

G. Eliot *Silas Marner* (Blackwood, 1861)

G. Eliot *Felix Holt* (Blackwood, 1866)

G. Eliot *Middlemarch* (Blackwood, 1871-72)

C. Girdlestone *Seven Sermons preached during the prevalence of the Cholera in the parish of Sedgley, with a narrative of that visitation* (Gilbert & Rivington, 1833)

D. Greenwell *Two Friends* (Gibbings, 1862)

B. Gregory *Sidelights on the Conflicts of Methodism 1827-1852* (Cassell, 1898)

F.W. Hackwood *Sedgley Researches* (Dudley, Dudley Herald, 1898)

F.W. Hackwood *Staffordshire Customs, Superstitions and Folklore* (Lichfield, Mercury Press, 1924, reprint Wakefield, Scholar Press, 1974)

J.A. James *The Anxious Inquirer after Salvation Directed and Encouraged* (Religious Tract Society, 1834)

J.A. James *History of Carrs Lane Church* in *Autobiography* (Hamilton Adams, 1864)

J.A. Langford *A Century of Birmingham Life* (Birmingham, E. C. Osborne, 1868)

J.A. Langford *Modern Birmingham and its Institutions* (Birmingham, E. C. Osborne, 1873)

J. Lawson *A Man's Life* (Hodder & Stoughton, 1932)

C. Laye *The African Child* (Paris, Librairie Plon, 1954, Eng. Trans, Glasgow, Collins, 1959)

W. Leigh *An authentic narrative of the awful visitation of Bilston by Cholera; August- September 1832* (Wolverhampton, William Parke, 1833)

H. Mann 'On the Statistical Position of Religious Bodies in England and Wales', in *Journal of the Statistical Society of London*, Vol. XVIII (1855)

J.H. Mees *The Story of a Hundred Years 1828-1928, Handbook of the Wesleyan Methodist Church, Stourbridge Circuit* (Stourbridge, Mark & Moody, 1928)

J.C. Miller *Dying Pastors and the Undying Priest* (Birmingham, William Willey, 1859)

J.C. Miller *Our Scripture Readers* (Birmingham, privately published, 1849)

H. New *Hurst Street Domestic Mission, Notes on the 50th Anniversary* (Birmingham, publisher not named, 1890)

E. Nightingale (Ed.) *A Bible Woman's Story, Autobiography of Mrs.A.Collier of Birmingham* (T.Woolmer, 2nd edn, 1885)

A.E. Owen *Lectures and Sermons by J.B.Owen, with a memoir* (Wm Mackintosh, 1873)

J.B. Owen 'Sketches and incidents of the cholera at Bilston in 1849' in A.E. Owen *Lectures and Sermons by J. B. Owen, with a memoir* (Wm Mackintosh, 1873)

J.B. Owen *The Wolverhampton Almanac and stranger's guide to South Staffordshire* (Wolverhampton, T. Simpson, 1855)

R. Palmer *George Dunn, The Minstrel of Quarry Bank* (Dudley, Dudley Council, 1984)

A.C. Pratt *Black Country Methodism* (Charles Kelly, 1891)

M. Ransome *The State of the Bishopric of Worcester 1782-1810* (Bishop Hurd's visitations) Worcestershire Historical Society, New Series VI (Worcester, Worcs Historical Society, 1968)

D. Robinson (Ed.) *Visitations of the Archdeaconry of Stafford 1829-1841* (Archdeacon Hodgson's visitations) *Collections for a History of Staffordshire*, 4th series No. 10 (Stafford, Staffordshire Record Society, 1980)

St. Peter's District Visiting Society *Report 1844* (Birmingham, Brierley, 1844)

J. Saville (Ed.) *The Life of Thomas Cooper written by Himself* (Hodder & Stoughton, 1872, Leicester, Leicester University Press, 1971)

W. Stokes *History of the Midland Association of Baptist Churches* (Birmingham, J.W. Showell, 1855)

F. Thompson *Lark Rise to Candleford* (Oxford, Oxford University Press, 1939 & 1945)

S. Timmins *Birmingham and the Midland Hardware District* (Robert Hardwicke, 1865)

J. Wesley *A Collection of Hymns for the use of the people called Methodists* (Wesleyan Conference Office, 1779)

C. Willetts *When I was a Boy, I, II and III* (Dudley, Dudley Teachers' Centre, 1977-79)

J. Wood 'Report on Education in Birmingham' in *Journal of the Statistical Society of London* Vol. III (1840)

Secondary Sources

Published works

G.C. Allen *The Industrial Development of Birmingham and the Black Country* (Allen & Unwin, 1929)

W.A. Armstong 'The use of information about occupations', in E.A. Wrigley (Ed.) *Nineteenth Century Society* (Cambridge, Cambridge University Press, 1972) pp. 191-310.

M.K. Ashby *Joseph Ashby of Tysoe* (Cambridge, Cambridge University Press, 1961)

R. Ashton *George Eliot: a life* (Hamish Hamilton, 1996)

G. Barnsby *The Dudley Working Class Movement 1832-1860* (Dudley, Dudley Public Libraries. 1970)

D.W. Bebbington *Evangelicalism in Modern Britain* (Routledge, 1989)

G.F.A. Best *Shaftesbury* (Batsford, 1964)

J. Bossy *The English Catholic Community 1570-1850* (Darton Longman & Todd, 1975)

F. Boulard *Introduction to Religious Sociology* (Darton Longman & Todd, 1960)

A. Briggs *Victorian Cities* (Odhams, 1963)

C. Brown 'Did urbanisation secularise Britain?' in *Urban History Yearbook* (1988) pp. 1-14.

C. Brown 'The mechanism of religious growth in urban societies' in H.D. McLeod (Ed.) *European Religion in the Age of the Great Cities 1830-1930* (Routledge, 1995) pp. 239-62.

S. Bruce *Religion and Modernisation* (Oxford, Oxford University Press, 1992)

R. Carwardine *Transatlantic Revivalism* (Greenwood Press, 1978)

J.V.L. Casserley *The Retreat from Christianity in the Modern World* (Longman, 1952)

O. Chadwick *The Victorian Church: Part 1* (3rd Edition, A. & C. Black, 1971)

J. Champ 'Priesthood and Politics in the nineteenth century, the turbulent career of Thomas McDonnell' in *Recusant History 18* (1987) pp. 289-302.

J. Champ 'The demographic impact of Irish immigration on Birmingham Catholicism 1800- 1850' in W.J. Shiels and D. Wood (Eds.) *Studies in Church History Vol.25* (Oxford, Blackwell, 1988) pp. 233-42.

D. Clark *Between Pulpit and Pew; Folk Religion in a North Yorkshire Fishing Village* (Cambridge, Cambridge University Press, 1982)

G. Kitson Clark *The Making of Victorian England* (Methuen, 1962)

P. Collinson *The Religion of Protestants* (Oxford, Oxford University Press, 1982)

J. Cox *The English Churches in a Secular Society: Lambeth 1870-1939* (Oxford & New York, Oxford University Press, 1982)

C. Creighton *A History of Epidemic Diseases in Great Britain* (Cambridge, Cambridge University Press, 1864, London, Cass, 1965)

W.R. Cross *The Burned Over District* (New York, Cornell University Press, 1950)

R. Currie, A. Gilbert and L. Horsley *Churches and Churchgoers* (Oxford, Oxford University Press, 1977)

L. Davidoff and C. Hall *Family Fortunes* (Hutchinson, 1987)

E.T. Davies *Religion in the Industrial Revolution in South Wales* (Cardiff, University of Wales Press, 1965)

S. Dimond *The Psychology of the Methodist Revival* (Oxford, Oxford University Press, 1926)

P.J. Doyle 'The General Election of 1841, the representation of South Staffordshire', in *South Staffordshire Archaeological and Historical Society Transactions Vol.XII*(Stafford, Staffordshire Record Society, 1971) pp. 57-61.

M. Drabble *Arnold Bennett* (Weidenfeld & Nicolson, 1974)

R.J. Evans *Death in Hamburg, Politics and Society in the Cholera Years 1830-1910* (Oxford, Oxford University Press, 1987)

C.D. Field 'Non-recurrent Christian Data', in *Reviews of United Kingdom Statistical Sources, Vol.XX, Religion* (Royal Statistical Society & ESRC, Pergamon, 1987) pp. 189-504.

J.D. Gay *The Geography of Religion in England* (Duckworth, 1971)

C. Geertz 'Religion as a cultural system', in M. Banton (Ed.) *Anthropological Approaches to the Study of Religion* (Tavistock Press, 1966) pp. 1-46.

A.D. Gilbert *Religion and Society in Industrial England* (Longman, 1976)

C. Gill *The History of Birmingham Vol.1* (Oxford, Oxford University Press, 1952)

J.C. Gill *Parson Bull of Bierley* (SPCK, 1963)

R. Gill *The Myth of the Empty Church* (SPCK, 1993)

S.J.D. Green *Religion in the Age of Decline 1870-1920* (Cambridge, Cambridge University Press, 1996)

M.W. Greenslade 'Staffordshire "No-Popery" 1850-51', in *Staffordshire Catholic History Vol.21* (Stafford, 1982) pp.1-43.

A. Haig *The Victorian Clergy* (Croom Helm, 1984)

D. Hay *Exploring Inner Space* (Harmondsworth, Penguin, 1982)

D. Hempton 'Established Churches and the rise of Religious Pluralism: A Case Study, England 1700-1914' paper read at the Decline of Christendom in Western Europe Conference, Paris April 1997, unpublished.

D. Hempton *Methodism and politics in British Society 1750-1850* (Hutchinson, 1984)

D. Hempton *Religion and Political Culture in Britain and Ireland* (Cambridge, Cambridge University Press, 1996)

D. Hempton *The Religion of the People* (Routledge, 1996)

E.P. Hennock *Fit and Proper Persons* (Arnold, 1973)

J. Hick *An Interpretation of Religion* (Macmillan, 1989)

E. Hobsbawm *Labouring Men* (Weidenfeld & Nicolson, 1964)

E. Hobsbawm *Primitive Rebels* (Manchester, Manchester University Press, 1959)

E. Hopkins 'Religious Dissent in Black Country Industrial Villages in the First Half of the Nineteenth Century', in *Journal of Ecclesiastical History Vol.34* (Cambridge, 1983) pp.411-24.

P. Horn *Joseph Arch: a biography* (Kineton, Roundwood Press, 1971)

K.S. Inglis *Churches and the Working Classes in Victorian England* (Routledge & Kegan Paul, 1963)

K.S. Inglis 'Patterns of Religious Worship in 1851', in *Journal of Ecclesiastical History Vol.XI* (Cambridge, 1960) pp. 74-86.

W. James *The Varieties of Religious Experience* (Longmans, 1902)

E. Jay *The Religion of the Heart* (Oxford, Oxford University Press, 1979)

J.H.S. Kent 'Feelings and Festivals', in H.J. Dyos and M. Wolff (Eds.) *The Victorian City Vol.2* (Routledge & Kegan Paul, 1973) pp. 855-71.

J.H.S. Kent *Holding the Fort* (Epworth, 1978)

J.H.S. Kent 'The Wesleyan Methodists to 1849', in R.E. Davies, A.R. George and E.G. Rupp (Eds.) *A History of the Methodist Church in Great Britain Vol.2* (Epworth, 1978) pp.213-75.

F. Knight *The Nineteenth-Century Church and English society* (Cambridge, Cambridge University Press, 1995)

F. Knight 'From Diversity to Sectarianism; the Definition of Anglican Identity in Nineteenth Century England', in R.N. Swanson (Ed.) *Studies in Church History Vol.32* (Oxford, Blackwell, 1996) pp. 377-86.

K. Knott 'Other Major Religious Traditions', in T. Thomas (Ed.) *The British, Their Religious Beliefs and Practices 1800-1986* (Routledge, 1988) pp.133-57.

T. Koditschek *Class Formation and Industrial Society, Bradford 1750-1850* (Cambridge, Cambridge University Press, 1990)

M. Laski *Ecstasy, a study of some secular and religious experiences* (Cresset Press, 1961)

E.G. Léonard *Le Protestant Francais* (Paris, Presses Universitaires de France, 1955)

D.M. Lewis *Lighten Their Darkness* (Westport, Connecticut, Greenwood Press, 1986)

Lichfield Joint Record Office *Cumulative Handlist Part 1* (Stafford, Staffordshire County Council, 1960)

D. Lovegrove *Established Church, Sectarian People* (Cambridge, Cambridge University Press, 1988)

N. McCord *British History 1815-1906* (Oxford, Oxford University Press, 1991)

A.A. MacLaren *Religion and Social Class: The Disruption Years in Aberdeen* (Routledge, 1974)

H.D. McLeod *Class and Religion in the Late Victorian City* (Croom Helm, 1974)

H.D. McLeod 'Class Community and Region', in M. Hill (Ed.) *A Sociological Yearbook of Religion in Britiain, 6* (SCM Press, 1973) pp. 29-72.

H.D. McLeod (Ed.) *European Religion in the Age of the Great Cities* (Routledge, 1995)

H.D. McLeod 'Religion', in J. Langton and K.J. Morris (Eds.) *Atlas of Industrialising Britain 1740-1914* (Methuen, 1986) pp. 212-17.

H.D. McLeod *Religion and the Working Class in Nineteenth-Century Britain* (Macmillan, 1984)

H.D. McLeod *Religion and Society in England 1850-1914* (Macmillan, 1996)

G.P. Mander and N.W. Tildesley *History of Wolverhampton* (Wolverhampton, Wolverhampton County Borough Corporation, 1960)

D.E.H. Mole 'The Challenge to the Church', in H.J. Dyos and M. Wolff (Eds.) *The Victorian City Vol.2* (Routledge & Kegan Paul, 1973) pp. 815-36.

D.E.H. Mole 'John Cale Miller, a Victorian Rector of Birmingham', in *Journal of Ecclesiastical History Vol.17* (Cambridge, 1966) pp. 95-103.

D.E.H. Mole 'The Evangelical Revival in Birmingham', in *Bulletin of the West Midlands Branch of the Wesley Historical Society Vol.2, nos.10 and 11* (Birmingham, 1975) pp. 89-94, 99-106.

R. Moore *Pitmen, Preachers and Politics* (Cambridge, Cambridge University Press, 1974)

R.J. Morris *Cholera 1832* (Croom Helm, 1976)

J. Morris 'Church and People thirty-three years on', in *Theology Vol.94* (1991) pp. 92-101.

D.J. Moss *Thomas Attwood* (Montreal, McGill Queens University Press, 1990)

G.K. Nelson 'Religious groups in a changing environment', in A. Bryman (Ed.) *Religion in the Birmingham Area* (Birmingham, University of Birmingham Institute for the Study of Worship and Religious Architecture, 1976) pp. 45-60.

M.A. Noll, D.W. Bebbington and G.A. Rawlyk (Eds.) *Evangelicalism, Comparative Studies of Popular Protestantism in North America, the British Isles and Beyond 1700-1900,* (New York & Oxford, Oxford University Press, 1994)

J. Obelkevich *Religion and Rural Society: South Lindsey 1825-1875* (Oxford, Oxford University Press, 1976)

W.H. Oliver 'Owen in 1817, The Millenialist Moment', in S. Pollard and J. Salt (Eds.) *Robert Owen: Prophet of the Poor* (Macmillan, 1971) pp. 166-87.

W.H. Oliver *Prophets and Millennialists* (Oxford and Auckland, Oxford University Press, Auckland University Press, 1978)

R. Otto *The Idea of the Holy* (Oxford, Oxford University Press, 2nd. edn, 1950)

G. Parsons (Ed.) *Religion in Victorian Britain, 4 Vols.* (Manchester, Manchester University Press, 1988)

H. Perkin *The Origins of Modern English Society 1780-1880* (Routledge & Kegan Paul, 1969)

D. Philips 'The Black Country Magistracy 1835-1860', in *Midland History Vol.3* (Birmingham, 1976) pp. 161-190.

M.H. Port *Six Hundred New Churches* (SPCK, 1961)

H.D. Rack 'Domestic Visitation, a chapter in Early Nineteenth Century Evangelism', in *Journal of Ecclesiastical History Vol.24* (Cambridge, 1973) pp. 357-376.

H.D. Rack 'Evangelical Endings, Death-beds in Evangelical biography', in *Bulletin of the John Rylands Library Vol.74* (Manchester, 1992) pp. 39-56.

H.D. Rack *How Primitive was Primitive Methodism?* (Englesea Brook, Friends of Engelsea Brook, 1996)

H.D. Rack *Reasonable Enthusiast* (Epworth, 1989)

R.W. Ram 'Influences on the patterns of belief and social action among Birmingham Dissenters between 1750 and 1870', in A. Bryman (Ed.) *Religion in the Birmingham Area* (Birmingham, University of Birmingham Institute for the Study of Worship and Religious Architecture, 1976) pp. 29-44.

J. Raven *The Folklore of Staffordshire* (Batsford, 1978)

J. Raven *The Folklore and Songs of the Black Country Colliers* (Wolverhampton, Broadside Press, 1990)

G.A. Rawlyk and M.A. Noll *Amazing Grace* (Grand Rapids, Michigan, Baker Books, 1993)

E. Roberts *Working Class Barrow and Lancaster 1890-1930* (Lancaster, Centre for North- West Regional Studies, 1976)

D.B. Robinson 'Staffordshire Clergy in 1830', in *South Staffordshire Archaeological and Historical Society Transactions Vol.XXIV* (Stafford, 1984) pp. 84-98.

G. Robson 'Between Town and Countryside', in D. Baker (Ed.) *Studies in Church History Vol.16* (Oxford, Blackwell, 1979) pp. 401-414.

G. Robson *Christians* (Oxford, Heinemann, 1995)

G. Robson 'Failures of Success', in D. Baker (Ed.) *Studies in Church History Vol.15* (Oxford, Blackwell, 1978) pp. 381-91.

G. Robson 'Methodists and the 1851 Census of Religious Worship in Birmingham and the Black Country', in *Bulletin of the West Midlands Branch of the Wesley Historical Society Vol.2 nos. 10, 11* (Birmingham, 1975) pp. 94-98, 107-108.

G. Robson 'Religion for Young Humanists', in *British Journal of Religious Education Vol.14* (Christian Education Movement, 1982) pp. 132-39.

G. Robson 'Religious Education 1985-1995', in *British Journal of Religious Education Vol.19* (Christian Education Movement, 1996) pp. 13-23.

G. Robson 'Wesley Perrins Remembers', in *Bulletin of the West Midlands Branch of the Wesley Historical Society Vol.3* (Birmingham, 1979-80) pp. 26-29, 42-45, 59-65.

R.B. Rose 'The Origins of Working Class Radicalism in Birmingham', in *Journal of Labour History Vol. IV* (Canberra, 1965) pp. 6-14.

M.R. Rowlands *The West Midlands from AD 1000* (Longman, 1987)

J. Rule 'Methodism, popular belief and village culture', in R.D. Storch (Ed.) *Popular Culture and Custom in Nineteenth Century England* (Croom Helm, 1982) pp. 48-70.

R. Samuel 'The Roman Catholic Church and the Irish Poor' in S. Gilley and R. Swift (Eds.) *The Irish in the Victorian City* (Croom Helm, 1985) pp. 267-300.

B. Semmel *The Methodist Revolution* (Heinemann, 1974)

W.O. Skeat *George Stephenson: the Engineer and His Letters* (Institution of Mechanical Engineers, 1973)

D. Smith *Conflict and Compromise: Class formation in English society* (Routledge & Kegan Paul, 1982)

M.A. Smith *Religion in Industrial Society: Oldham and Saddleworth 1740-1865* (Oxford, Oxford University Press, 1994)

S.M. Smith 'Willenhall and Wodgate, Disraeli's use of the Blue Book evidence', in *Review of English Studies, New Series 13* (Oxford, 1962) pp. 368-84.

K.D.M. Snell *Church and Chapel in the North Midlands* (Leicester, Leicester University Press, 1991)

K.D.M. Snell and P.S. Ell *Rival Jerusalems* (Cambridge, Cambridge University Press, 2000)

R.A. Soloway *Prelates and People* (Routledge & Kegan Paul, 1969)

J. Summerson *Architecture in Britain 1530-1830* (Harmondsworth, Penguin, 1953)

D.M. Thompson 'Church extension in town and countryside in late nineteenth century Leicestershire', in D. Baker (Ed.) *Studies in Church History Vol.16* (Oxford, Blackwell, 1979) pp. 427-440.

D.M. Thompson 'Churches and Society in Nineteenth-century England, a rural perspective', in G.J. Cuming and D. Baker (Eds.) *Studies in Church History Vol. 8* (Cambridge, Cambridge University Press, 1972) pp. 267-76.

D.M. Thompson 'The 1851 Census, problems and possibilities', in *Victorian Studies Vol. II* (1967) pp. 87-97.

D.M. Thompson 'The Religious Census of 1851', in R. Lawton (Ed.) *The Census and Social Structure* (Cass, 1978) pp. 241-272.

E.P. Thompson 'Anthropology and the discipline of historical context' in *Midland History Vol. 1* (Birmingham, 1972) pp. 41-55.

E.P. Thompson *The Making of the English Working Class* (Gollancz, 1963)

N.W. Tildesley *History of Willenhall* (Willenhall, Willenhall Urban District Council, 1951)

N.W. Tildesley 'William Moreton of Willenhall', in *Historical Collections Staffordshire, Fourth Series No.6* (Stafford, Staffordshire Record Society, 1970) pp. 171-85.

R.H. Trainor *Black Country Elites* (Oxford, Oxford University Press, 1993)

R.H. Trainor 'Anti-Catholicism and the priesthood in nineteenth-century Staffordshire', in *Staffordshire Catholic History Vol. 16* (Stafford, 1976) pp.19-41.

C.B. Turner 'Revivalism and Welsh Society in the nineteenth century', in J. Obelkevich, L. Roper and R. Samuel (Eds.) *Disciplines of Faith* (Routledge, 1987) pp. 311-323.

Victoria County History of Staffordshire Vol. 1 (1908) *Vol. 2* (1967) *Vol. 3* (1970) *Vol. 17* (Oxford University Press for Royal Historical Society, 1976)

Victoria County History of Warwickshire Vol. 7 (Oxford University Press for Royal Historical Society, 1964)

Victoria County History of Worcestershire Vol. 3 (Oxford University Press for Royal Historical Society, 1913)

P. Virgin *The Church in an Age of Negligence* (Cambridge, J.C. Clarke, 1989)

W.R. Ward 'Church and society in the first half of the nineteenth century', in R.E. Davies, A.R. George and E.G. Rupp (Eds.) *A History of the Methodist Church in Great Britain Vol. 2* (Epworth, 1978) pp. 11-96.

W.R. Ward *Religion and Society in England 1780-1850* (Batsford, 1972)

M.R. Watts *The Dissenters Vol. II* (Oxford, Oxford University Press, 1995)

J.S. Werner *The Primitive Methodist Connexion* (Madison, University of Wisconsin Press, 1984)

A.W.A. White 'The Christian Collier', in *Transactions of the Birmingham and Warwickshire Archaeological Society Vol. 85* (1972) pp. 203-208.

E.R. Wickham *Church and People in an Industrial City* (Lutterworth, 1957)

J.T. Wilkinson *Hugh Bourne* (Epworth, 1952)

H.G. Wilson 'One hundred years of religious and social work in Birmingham', in *Transactions of the Unitarian Historical Society Vol. VIII* (1943-46) pp. 113-121.

A. Willetts *The Black Country Nailers' Riots of 1842* (Dudley, Dudley Metropolitan Borough, 1996)

M.J. Wise (Ed.) *Birmingham and its Regional Setting* (Birmingham, British Association Local Executive, 1950)

J. Wolffe *God and Greater Britain* (Routledge, 1994)

J. Wolffe *The Protestant Crusade in Britain* (Oxford, Oxford University Press,

1991)

E. Yeo 'Chartist belief and the theology of liberation', in J. Obelkevich, L. Roper and R. Samuel (Eds.) *Disciplines of Faith* (Routledge, 1987) pp. 410-421.

E. Yeo 'Christianity in Chartist struggle', in *Past and Present No. 91* (1981) pp. 111-139.

E. Yeo 'Robert Owen and Radical Culture', in S. Pollard and J. Salt (Eds.) *Robert Owen: Prophet of the Poor* (Macmillan, 1971) pp. 83-114.

S. Yeo *Religion and Voluntary Organisations in Crisis* (Croom Helm, 1976)

G.M. Young *Victorian England, Portrait of an Age* (Oxford, Oxford University Press, 1936)

U. Young *Life of Father Ignatius Spencer* (Burns Oates, 1933)

Unpublished Theses

J.G. Barnsby 'The Working Class Movement in the Black Country' M.A. Birmingham 1965

J.G. Barnsby 'Social Conditions in the Black Country in the Nineteenth Century' Ph.D. Birmingham 1969

A. Bartlett 'The Churches in Bermondsey 1880-1939' Ph.D. Birmingham 1987

J.A. Burdett 'A Study of the relationship between evangelical urban missionaries and the working class poor in Birmingham, Norwich and Edinburgh' M.Phil. Birmingham 1994

J. Champ 'Assimilation and separation; the Catholic Revival in Birmingham c.1650- 1850' Ph.D. Birmingham 1984

A.G. Cumberland 'Protestant Nonconformity in the Black Country' M.A. Birmingham 1951

A.D. Gilbert 'The growth and decline of nonconformity in England and Wales with special reference to the period before 1850' D.Phil. Oxford 1973

B. Greaves 'Methodism in Yorkshire 1740-1851' Ph.D. Liverpool 1968

R. Leese 'The impact of Methodism on Black Country society 1743-1860' Ph.D. Manchester 1972

J.A. McPhail 'Religious attendance and provision in Birmingham, the Black Country and surrounding areas during the mid-nineteenth century' Ph.D. Wolverhampton 1995

D.E.H. Mole 'The Church of England and Society in Birmingham 1830-66' Ph.D. Cambridge 1961

R.W. Ram 'The social evolution of five Dissenting communities in Birmingham 1750-1870' Ph.D. Birmingham 1979

J. Ryan 'Religion and Radical Politics in Birmingham 1830-1850' M.Litt. Birmingham 1979

V.I. Tunsiri 'Party politics in the Black Country 1832-1867' M.A. Birmingham 1964

J.D. Walters 'The impact of Anglican Evangelicalism on the religious life of Wolverhampton and its locality in the period 1830-1870' M.A. Wolverhampton Polytechnic (CNAA) 1983

S.C. Williams 'Religious belief and popular culture; a study of the south London borough of Southwark 1880-1939' D.Phil. Oxford 1993

Index

1. Index of Persons

2. Index of Places

Studies in Evangelical History and Thought

(All titles uniform with this volume)
Dates in bold are of projected publication

Andrew Atherstone
Oxford's Protestant Spy
The Controversial Career of Charles Golightly
Charles Golightly (1807–85) was a notorious Protestant polemicist. His life was dedicated to resisting the spread of ritualism and liberalism within the Church of England and the University of Oxford. For half a century he led many memorable campaigns, such as building a martyr's memorial and attempting to close a theological college. John Henry Newman, Samuel Wilberforce and Benjamin Jowett were among his adversaries. This is the first study of Golightly's controversial career.

2006 / 1-84227-364-7 / approx. 324pp

Clyde Binfield
Victorian Nonconformity in Eastern England
Studies of Victorian religion and society often concentrate on cities, suburbs, and industrialisation. This study provides a contrast. Victorian Eastern England—Essex, Suffolk, Norfolk, Cambridgeshire, and Huntingdonshire—was rural, traditional, relatively unchanging. That is nonetheless a caricature which discounts the industry in Norwich and Ipswich (as well as in Haverhill, Stowmarket and Leiston) and ignores the impact of London on Essex, of railways throughout the region, and of an ancient but changing university (Cambridge) on the county town which housed it. It also entirely ignores the political implications of such changes in a region noted for the variety of its religious Dissent since the seventeenth century. This book explores Victorian Eastern England and its Nonconformity. It brings to a wider readership a pioneering thesis which has made a major contribution to a fresh evolution of English religion and society.

2006 / 1-84227-216-0 / approx. 274pp

John Brencher
Martyn Lloyd-Jones (1899–1981) and Twentieth-Century Evangelicalism
This study critically demonstrates the significance of the life and ministry of Martyn Lloyd-Jones for post-war British evangelicalism and demonstrates that his preaching was his greatest influence on twentieth-century Christianity. The factors which shaped his view of the church are examined, as is the way his reformed evangelicalism led to a separatist ecclesiology which divided evangelicals.

2002 / 1-84227-051-6 / xvi + 268pp

Jonathan D. Burnham
A Story of Conflict
The Controversial Relationship between Benjamin Wills Newton and
John Nelson Darby
Burnham explores the controversial relationship between the two principal
leaders of the early Brethren movement. In many ways Newton and Darby were
products of their times, and this study of their relationship provides insight not
only into the dynamics of early Brethrenism, but also into the progress of
nineteenth-century English and Irish evangelicalism.
2004 / 1-84227-191-1 / xxiv + 268pp

Grayson Carter
Anglican Evangelicals
Protestant Secessions from the Via Media, c.1800–1850
This study examines, within a chronological framework, the major themes and
personalities which influenced the outbreak of a number of Evangelical clerical
and lay secessions from the Church of England and Ireland during the first half
of the nineteenth century. Though the number of secessions was relatively
small—between a hundred and two hundred of the 'Gospel' clergy abandoned
the Church during this period—their influence was considerable, especially in
highlighting in embarrassing fashion the tensions between the evangelical
conversionist imperative and the principles of a national religious establishment.
Moreover, through much of this period there remained, just beneath the surface,
the potential threat of a large Evangelical disruption similar to that which
occurred in Scotland in 1843. Consequently, these secessions provoked great
consternation within the Church and within Evangelicalism itself, they
contributed to the outbreak of millennial speculation following the
'constitutional revolution' of 1828–32, they led to the formation of several new
denominations, and they sparked off a major Church–State crisis over the legal
right of a clergyman to secede and begin a new ministry within Protestant
Dissent.
2007 / 1-84227-401-5 / xvi + 470pp

J.N. Ian Dickson
Beyond Religious Discourse
Sermons, Preaching and Evangelical Protestants in Nineteenth-Century Irish Society
Drawing extensively on primary sources, this pioneer work in modern religious history explores the training of preachers, the construction of sermons and how Irish evangelicalism and the wider movement in Great Britain and the United States shaped the preaching event. Evangelical preaching and politics, sectarianism, denominations, education, class, social reform, gender, and revival are examined to advance the argument that evangelical sermons and preaching went significantly beyond religious discourse. The result is a book for those with interests in Irish history, culture and belief, popular religion and society, evangelicalism, preaching and communication.
2005 / 1-84227-217-9 / approx. 324pp

Neil T.R. Dickson
Brethren in Scotland 1838–2000
A Social Study of an Evangelical Movement
The Brethren were remarkably pervasive throughout Scottish society. This study of the Open Brethren in Scotland places them in their social context and examines their growth, development and relationship to society.
2003 / 1-84227-113-X / xxviii + 510pp

Crawford Gribben and Timothy C.F. Stunt (eds)
Prisoners of Hope?
Aspects of Evangelical Millennialism in Britain and Ireland, 1800–1880
This volume of essays offers a comprehensive account of the impact of evangelical millennialism in nineteenth-century Britain and Ireland.
2004 / 1-84227-224-1 / xiv + 208pp

Khim Harris
Evangelicals and Education
Evangelical Anglicans and Middle-Class Education in Nineteenth-Century England
This ground breaking study investigates the history of English public schools founded by nineteenth-century Evangelicals. It documents the rise of middle-class education and Evangelical societies such as the influential Church Association, and includes a useful biographical survey of prominent Evangelicals of the period.
2004 / 1-84227-250-0 / xviii + 422pp

Mark Hopkins
Nonconformity's Romantic Generation
Evangelical and Liberal Theologies in Victorian England
A study of the theological development of key leaders of the Baptist and
Congregational denominations at their period of greatest influence, including
C.H. Spurgeon and R.W. Dale, and of the controversies in which those among
them who embraced and rejected the liberal transformation of their evangelical
heritage opposed each other.
2004 / 1-84227-150-4 / xvi + 284pp

Don Horrocks
Laws of the Spiritual Order
*Innovation and Reconstruction in the Soteriology of Thomas Erskine
of Linlathen*
Don Horrocks argues that Thomas Erskine's unique historical and theological
significance as a soteriological innovator has been neglected. This timely
reassessment reveals Erskine as a creative, radical theologian of central and
enduring importance in Scottish nineteenth-century theology, perhaps equivalent
in significance to that of S.T. Coleridge in England.
2004 / 1-84227-192-X / xx + 362pp

Kenneth S. Jeffrey
When the Lord Walked the Land
The 1858–62 Revival in the North East of Scotland
Previous studies of revivals have tended to approach religious movements from
either a broad, national or a strictly local level. This study of the multifaceted
nature of the 1859 revival as it appeared in three distinct social contexts within a
single region reveals the heterogeneous nature of simultaneous religious
movements in the same vicinity.
2002 / 1-84227-057-5 / xxiv + 304pp

John Kenneth Lander
Itinerant Temples
Tent Methodism, 1814–1832
Tent preaching began in 1814 and the Tent Methodist sect resulted from
disputes with Bristol Wesleyan Methodists in 1820. The movement spread to
parts of Gloucestershire, Wiltshire, London and Liverpool, among other places.
Its demise started in 1826 after which one leader returned to the Wesleyans and
others became ministers in the Congregational and Baptist denominations.
2003 / 1-84227-151-2 / xx + 268pp

Donald M. Lewis
Lighten Their Darkness
The Evangelical Mission to Working-Class London, 1828–1860
This is a comprehensive and compelling study of the Church and the complexities of nineteenth-century London. Challenging our understanding of the culture in working London at this time, Lewis presents a well-structured and illustrated work that contributes substantially to the study of evangelicalism and mission in nineteenth-century Britain.
2001 / 1-84227-074-5 / xviii + 372pp

Herbert McGonigle
'Sufficient Saving Grace'
John Wesley's Evangelical Arminianism
A thorough investigation of the theological roots of John Wesley's evangelical Arminianism and how these convictions were hammered out in controversies on predestination, limited atonement and the perseverance of the saints.
2001 / 1-84227-045-1 / xvi + 350pp

Lisa S. Nolland
A Victorian Feminist Christian
Josephine Butler, the Prostitutes and God
Josephine Butler was an unlikely candidate for taking up the cause of prostitutes, as she did, with a fierce and self-disregarding passion. This book explores the particular mix of perspectives and experiences that came together to envision and empower her remarkable achievements. It highlights the vital role of her spirituality and the tragic loss of her daughter.
2004 / 1-84227-225-X / xxiv + 328pp

Don J. Payne
The Theology of the Christian Life in J.I. Packer's Thought
Theological Anthropology, Theological Method, and the Doctrine of Sanctification
J.I. Packer has wielded widespread influence on evangelicalism for more than three decades. This study pursues a nuanced understanding of Packer's theology of sanctification by tracing the development of his thought, showing how he reflects a particular version of Reformed theology, and examining the unique influence of theological anthropology and theological method on this area of his theology.
2005 / 1-84227-397-3 / approx. 374pp

Ian M. Randall
Evangelical Experiences
A Study in the Spirituality of English Evangelicalism 1918–1939
This book makes a detailed historical examination of evangelical spirituality between the First and Second World Wars. It shows how patterns of devotion led to tensions and divisions. In a wide-ranging study, Anglican, Wesleyan, Reformed and Pentecostal-charismatic spiritualities are analysed.
1999 / 0-85364-919-7 / xii + 310pp

Ian M. Randall
Spirituality and Social Change
The Contribution of F.B. Meyer (1847–1929)
This is a fresh appraisal of F.B. Meyer (1847–1929), a leading Free Church minister. Having been deeply affected by holiness spirituality, Meyer became the Keswick Convention's foremost international speaker. He combined spirituality with effective evangelism and socio-political activity. This study shows Meyer's significant contribution to spiritual renewal and social change.
2003 / 1-84227-195-4 / xx + 184pp

James Robinson
Pentecostal Origins
Early Pentecostalism in Ireland in the Context of the British Isles
Harvey Cox describes Pentecostalism as 'the fascinating spiritual child of our time' that has the potential, at the global scale, to contribute to the 'reshaping of religion in the twenty-first century'. This study grounds such sentiments by examining at the local scale the origin, development and nature of Pentecostalism in Ireland in its first twenty years. Illustrative, in a paradigmatic way, of how Pentecostalism became established within one region of the British Isles, it sets the story within the wider context of formative influences emanating from America, Europe and, in particular, other parts of the British Isles. As a synoptic regional study in Pentecostal history it is the first survey of its kind.
2005 / 1-84227-329-1 / xxviii + 378pp

Geoffrey Robson
Dark Satanic Mills?
Religion and Irreligion in Birmingham and the Black Country
This book analyses and interprets the nature and extent of popular Christian belief and practice in Birmingham and the Black Country during the first half of the nineteenth century, with particular reference to the impact of cholera epidemics and evangelism on church extension programmes.
2002 / 1-84227-102-4 / xiv + 294pp

Roger Shuff
Searching for the True Church
Brethren and Evangelicals in Mid-Twentieth-Century England
Roger Shuff holds that the influence of the Brethren movement on wider
evangelical life in England in the twentieth century is often underrated. This
book records and accounts for the fact that Brethren reached the peak of their
strength at the time when evangelicalism was at it lowest ebb, immediately
before World War II. However, the movement then moved into persistent
decline as evangelicalism regained ground in the post war period.
Accompanying this downward trend has been a sharp accentuation of the
contrast between Brethren congregations who engage constructively with the
non-Brethren scene and, at the other end of the spectrum, the isolationist group
commonly referred to as 'Exclusive Brethren'.
2005 / 1-84227-254-3 / xviii+ 296pp

James H.S. Steven
Worship in the Spirit
Charismatic Worship in the Church of England
This book explores the nature and function of worship in six Church of England
churches influenced by the Charismatic Movement, focusing on congregational
singing and public prayer ministry. The theological adequacy of such ritual is
discussed in relation to pneumatological and christological understandings in
Christian worship.
2002 / 1-84227-103-2 / xvi + 238pp

Peter K. Stevenson
God in Our Nature
The Incarnational Theology of John McLeod Campbell
This radical reassessment of Campbell's thought arises from a comprehensive
study of his preaching and theology. Previous accounts have overlooked both his
sermons and his Christology. This study examines the distinctive Christology
evident in his sermons and shows that it sheds new light on Campbell's much
debated views about atonement.
2004 / 1-84227-218-7 / xxiv + 458pp

Kenneth J. Stewart
Restoring the Reformation
British Evangelicalism and the Réveil at Geneva 1816–1849

Restoring the Reformation traces British missionary initiative in post-Revolutionary Francophone Europe from the genesis of the London Missionary Society, the visits of Robert Haldane and Henry Drummond, and the founding of the Continental Society. While British Evangelicals aimed at the reviving of a foreign Protestant cause of momentous legend, they received unforeseen reciprocating emphases from the Continent which forced self-reflection on Evangelicalism's own relationship to the Reformation.

2006 / 1-84227-392-2 / approx. 190pp

Martin Wellings
Evangelicals Embattled
Responses of Evangelicals in the Church of England to Ritualism, Darwinism and Theological Liberalism 1890–1930

In the closing years of the nineteenth century and the first decades of the twentieth century Anglican Evangelicals faced a series of challenges. In responding to Anglo-Catholicism, liberal theology, Darwinism and biblical criticism, the unity and identity of the Evangelical school were severely tested.

2003 / 1-84227-049-4 / xviii + 352pp

James Whisenant
A Fragile Unity
Anti-Ritualism and the Division of Anglican Evangelicalism in the Nineteenth Century

This book deals with the ritualist controversy (approximately 1850–1900) from the perspective of its evangelical participants and considers the divisive effects it had on the party.

2003 / 1-84227-105-9 / xvi + 530pp

Haddon Willmer
Evangelicalism 1785–1835: An Essay (1962) and Reflections (2004)
Awarded the Hulsean Prize in the University of Cambridge in 1962, this interpretation of a classic period of English Evangelicalism, by a young church historian, is now supplemented by reflections on Evangelicalism from the vantage point of a retired Professor of Theology.

2006 / 1-84227-219-5 / approx. 350pp

Linda Wilson
Constrained by Zeal
Female Spirituality amongst Nonconformists 1825–1875

Constrained by Zeal investigates the neglected area of Nonconformist female spirituality. Against the background of separate spheres, it analyses the experience of women from four denominations, and argues that the churches provided a 'third sphere' in which they could find opportunities for participation.

2000 / 0-85364-972-3 / xvi + 294pp

Paternoster
9 Holdom Avenue,
Bletchley,
Milton Keynes MK1 1QR,
United Kingdom
Web: www.authenticmedia.co.uk/paternoster

July 2005